FONTS & LOGOS

FONTS

& LOGOS

Doyald Young

Font Analysis, Logotype Design, Typography, Type Comparison, and History

INTRODUCTION BY HERMANN ZAPF

DELPHI PRESS | SHERMAN OAKS, CALIFORNIA

Also by Doyald Young,
Logotypes & Letterforms,
available from the author at:
www.delphipress.com
doyald@pacbell.net

First Edition

2 3 4 5

Copyright © 1999 by Doyald Young
Designed by Doyald Young
Printed in Hong Kong

ISBN 0–9673316–09

Published by Delphi Press
13957 Valley Vista Boulevard
Sherman Oaks, California 91423

SOME DIGITAL FONTS in this
book have been supplied by Adobe
Systems, Inc., Dutch Type Library,
International Typeface Corporation,
and the Monotype Corporation.
Garrett Boge and Paul Shaw of
LetterPerfect Design supplied their
St. Peter's face Pietra. Other fonts
are from the author's library.
Permissions to reproduce metal type
faces have been granted by Harvard
University Press for Daniel Berkeley
Updike's magnum opus, *Printing
Types, Their History, Forms, and
Use, A Study in Survivals*; from
Cassell, Jaspert, Berry and Johnson's
Encyclopaedia of Type Faces and
Oak Knoll Books for Mac McGrew's
indispensable *American Metal
Typefaces of the Twentieth Century.*

David Lemon, Adobe Systems's
Type Director verified designers and
dates of release for Adobe fonts, and
Steve Matteson of Monotype Palo
Alto, offered the history of Times
New Roman Condensed.

The metal types reproduced in
this book have in some cases been
reproduced multiple times. Their
edges are textured, unlike the sharp
reproductions of digital printing.

TO HERMANN ZAPF
whose monumental achievement has
been a source of inspiration.

Contents

Without skill our alphabet can be drawn or printed or scrawled in a hurried fashion—even backward—and still be readable. It is only when words must perform a specific task that their shapes become important for the sake of legibility. Fonts that are used in books rely on stringent rules; fonts for advertising have more latitude, and those that are designed for the moment have the greatest freedom. Yet all rely on two-thousand-year-old shapes that have inherent interrelationships.

Our roman alphabet can be generally divided into five groups for the capitals and five for the lowercase. When any one of these groups changes radically, letter or word recognition is dulled. In this book I attempt to show through analysis how vital structure is. Familiar fonts, the ones that the public has sanctioned by extensive use, are employed to illustrate character and glyph structure. These include three basic groups: serif, sans serif, and script, plus common classifications, which vary from country to country, though there are two commonly used classifications: DIN16518 and British Standards 2961:1967.

I do not attempt an evaluation of good versus bad, but only to point out design features that have endured for hundreds of years for either reasons of legibility or convention. In most instances it is difficult to separate the two and each must be seriously considered.

Fonts & Logos is about many things: the fundamentals of typography; letter construction; letter relationships; type recognition; lettering (which I call drawing); fonts; type history; type categories; how to use type; classic types; how I design logos; and my opinions about typography.

Volumes can be written on most of these subjects. What I aspire to do here is introduce each subject generally and show their relationships. Excellent treatises on each subject may be found in the bibliography.

I do not address experimental typography, because that is a different subject. Its expressions are dependent on fashion, culture, and special-interest groups—which are ephemeral. What concerns me, and has concerned me during my forty years of drawing letters and using type, is clarity of form, and only secondarily type's subtexts. In the two-thousand-year history of the roman letter nothing has changed in the way we physiologically perceive letters and words.

Fonts & Logos is divided into three sections: serif, sans serif, and script. Each of these chapters is followed by a selection of my logo designs based on the same group.

I explore different letter styles in the design of a logo, and often the sketches include all three basic groups. There are many reasons for this. A client may ask to see variations of the company's existing logo style, and/or totally new directions. Professional graphic designers the world over face these requests daily. The exploratory method of using the three basic letter styles is interwoven throughout these pages.

In the logo chapters, I show one or more type styles that have some relationship to the logo, either similarity of design, boldness, proportion, or orientation. The fonts are not always exactly kin, but are shown to illustrate heritage and how a font may offer inspiration for a design, and to enrich the reader's typographic vocabulary.

There are over three hundred fonts displayed in this book to illustrate design relationships; they demonstrate that fonts share countless character-istics—proving that it has all been done before. All that a font designer can ever hope to achieve is an innovative mix of the old.

The history of type design is a melding of styles. There are a limited number of truly original designs; everything else is derivative.

To offer the reader a historical perspective, many of the types shown are metal types produced before the age of the computer and digital fonts. I have drawn these from three major sources: Daniel Berkeley Updike's magnum opus *Printing Types, Their History, Forms and Use, a Study in Survivals*; Jaspert, Berry, and Johnson's *Encyclopaedia of Typefaces,* and Mac McGrew's monumental study, *American Metal Typefaces of the Twentieth Century.* Some of these examples have been reproduced from reproductions and the quality is not equal to digital printers. Many of the large size letters are screened to indicate that they are metal fonts. The fonts are not always a complete character set; either the capitals or lowercase are displayed, and at times either the italic or roman is not shown; many lack figures and/or punctuation. There are a few instances where only one letter of a font is shown, though the Font Sampler chapter displays the standard capitals, lowercase, figures, and punctuation.

I have credited the original font designer, and the designer of a revised version where possible. Other designers are responsible for additional weights and/or proportions, and exact credits are not available; the Helvetica family is typical. Designers of digital versions are credited when the font originates with the foundry: Robert Slimbach, Adobe Garamond, is typical. Many fonts are metal, and some reproductions are lacking in quality, yet their historical reference is invaluable for this study. Font weight descriptions may vary from foundry to foundry. Some identical weights bear different descriptions, i.e. Futura. With each font, and where space allows, the original designer and foundry are listed along with the design or introduction date; I have used the latest source material for these. Reference catalogs may list both the date of design and release. I have favored the design date; some are in question. Digital libraries comprise original font designs and licensed fonts. Some of these are age-old and have been redrawn many times by different foundries. Other collections may be hurriedly drawn and ill-fitted, and the typophile should approach an inexpensive collection with caution.

No attempt has been made to present a formal history of type; there are many excellent ones. Nor is the font selection intended to be comprehensive, but to best illustrate a design feature. Availability of the fonts, or personal preference, and space considerations were determining factors. There are many other excellent and beautifully drawn fonts that can be found in type specimen books listed in the bibliography.

I have spent my career drawing letters, studying type, and teaching. Demonstration is one of the most effective ways to teach. So is explanation, and so is the act of directing the viewer's gaze to see that which is not readily apparent. *Fonts & Logos* is about these things, how to get started, and a declaration of the joy of drawing.

DOYALD YOUNG
Sherman Oaks, California

Acknowledgments

Many clients have granted me permission to reproduce their logos in this book. The book could not exist without them or the audience of students and designers who have a love of typography, and lettering.

Nancy Green, dear friend and the *ne plus ultra* editor of *Logotypes & Letterforms,* has brought order to my unruly words and generously offered invaluable counsel.

Numerous logos that appear here were done for the clients of Mari Makinami of Mari Makinami Design Resource, and Tohru Uraoka of International Design Associates/Bikohsha Inc., Tokyo. I thank them both.

Samsung Industries, Korea, created a special fund for professors at the Art Center College of Design to pursue educational subjects. I am grateful to be a recipient. Linda Norlen, Vice President, Ramone Muñoz, Foundation chair, Mikio Osaki, Advertising Chair, and my colleagues at Art Center have supported my efforts: Carla Barr, Adele Bass, Chris Carr, John Clark, Bruce Claypool, Hal Frazier, April Greiman, Leah Hoffmitz, Dan Hoy, Richard Keyes, Gloria Kondrup, Nils Lindstrom, Gary Meyer, Jayme Odgers, Tom Schorer, Vance Studley, Sueann Valentine, Petrula Vrontikis, and Roland Young. Other educators—Julie Morton, professor at California State University, Northridge; Gregg Berryman and Alan Rellaford of California State University, Chico; Archie Boston and Tor Hovind of California State University Long Beach, Maelin Levine of San Diego Mesa College, Candice Lopez of San Diego City College, Susan Merritt of California State University, San Diego, and Mary Scott (formerly of Maddocks & Co.) of Academy of Art College, San Francisco—all have been supportive. Ray Engle, designer/educator, contributed to the Typographic Suggestions section. Numerous friends deserve thanks: David Solon, designer, and friend; Robert Maile, a West Coast lettering icon; Gerard Huerta and James Montalbano, two of the East Coast's great lights of letterforms; Robert Bringhurst; Donald H. Bartels, Corporate Identity consultant to General Electric Company; Edward Hutchings, former Director of Publications at the California Institute of Technology; Steve Matteson of Monotype; Allan Haley of Resolutions, Fred Brady, and David Lemon at Adobe Systems. Thanks to Joh. Enschedé en Zonen Utrecht; Jahan de Zoete, Curator, Enschedé Museum Haarlem, Netherlands; Frank Blokland, Director, Dutch Type Library; John Kiil, Senior Designer at Landor Associates; Juan-Carlos Fernandez, designer; Rafael Perez Iragorri, President, International Diseño Grafico Conferencia, Mexico; Jerry Eckert of ABC Letter Art. Jack Robinson; Jim Gallagher, Fontographer expert, consulted on the GE Logo font and the Prudential Insurance Company's corporate font; Tim Ryan of Source Net answered technical questions. I am indebted to Gregory Ross, of Warner Bros. Records; Patrick Reagh, Monotype expert and letterpress printer; Don Pennell and Dave Meyer of The Ligature Engravers, who supplied Master Plate alphabets; Delve Withrington, www.type-books.org; and Al Zimmerman, teacher and designer. John March, Director of Corporate Identity at Prudential Insurance Company, gave permission to reprint the Prudential logotype and corporate font development. Mac McGrew, author of the indispensable *American Metal Typefaces of the Twentieth Century,* published by Oak Knoll Books, made corrections to my manuscript and permitted me to reproduce from his monumental work. Suzanne and Gerald Labiner supplied their collector's mark; Caroline Labiner Moser gave permission to reproduce Bette Midler's logo for The Children's Museum of Los Angeles. Jim Whitney, kind friend and consultant, extended unlimited solace and solved computer problems too numerous to list.

Gudrun Zapf von Hesse and Hermann Zapf, whose work appears throughout these pages, are inspirational. I thank them for reproductions of their fonts, and I am indebted beyond measure for their support.

This book has been made possible in part through the support of David L. Brown, President of Art Center College of Design, The Art Center Faculty Enrichment Program, and the late R. Moray Armstrong, friend of many years.

Logotype design is a fascinating challenge that allows a graphic designer to display imagination and creative skill. The design can reflect a company's image, and even carry an emotional appeal: impressive, powerful, or attractive, inviting, feminine, or elegant. A successful logo should be quickly and easily remembered.

There are many ways to develop a logo design. This book explains some of those possibilities. Logos may be derived from existing typefaces, so that the final design relates to an accompanying typeface; a basic tenet of corporate identity design.

Traditionally, different interpretations and design variations are shown to clients. Young designers must learn—as always in life—that compromises must be made with clients who do not always choose the designer's favorite drawing, or version of an idea.

From a logo design, an original commission can be expanded into a total corporate identity program. There are many fine examples in this book with helpful explanations to understand how ideas are developed. This book also explains how to successfully integrate the design concept of special alphabets and typefaces. The many showings of typefaces demonstrate that there are other design solutions than the use of sans serif types. The diversity is welcome and helps the designer to differentiate designs for various clients, particularly for those who manufacture the same products.

Be aware of design, observe how some logos of multinational corporations rarely change:

Ford, Coca-Cola, GE, etc. Some refine their image slightly for a more contemporary look. A perfect example of an unchanging logo design is the London Transport designed by Edward Johnston in 1916 for London's subway system. I think that the typeface that Johnston designed to complement the logo; the red outline circle crossed with a blue stripe, is not only one of the best logo designs, but is also one of the very early examples of corporate design—still in use today, and as fresh and instructive as ever.

A wide range of examples is shown in this book that include designs for hotels, their restaurants, and cocktail lounges. These must be printed on different surfaces and function both as interior and exterior signage. There are examples for American and Japanese clients that exhibit power in their practicality in their long life. This is logo design at its best by a designer with an outstanding international reputation of many years. Study the examples to open the door into this imaginative and inspiring world of logo design.

Hermann Zapf

HERMANN ZAPF
Darmstadt, Germany

With the exception of Robert Bringhurst's classification, these lists are from Precision Type's Font Reference Guide 5.0, *a type specimen catalog of over 13,000 digital fonts.*

MAXIMILIAN VOX 1954
1. Humane
2. Garalde
3. Réale
4. Didone
5. Incise
6. Linéale
7. Mécane
8. Scripte
9. Manuaire

ATYPE I 1961
1. Humane
2. Garalde
3. Réale
4. Didone
5. Incise
6. Linéale
7. Mécane
8. Scripte
9. Manuaire
10. Fractura

DIN 1964
(*Deutscher Normenausschuss*)
1.1 Roman
1.2 Baroque
1.3 Classical
1.4 Free Roman
1.5 Linear Roman
1.6 Block
1.7 Script
2.0 Blackletter
3.0 Non-Roman

BRITISH STANDARDS 1965
1. Graphic
2. Humanist
3. Garalde
4. Transitional
5. Didone
6. Lineale
7. Slab-Serif
8. Glyphic
9. Script

MONOTYPE 1970
1. Antique
2. Blackletter
3. Brush script
4. Clarendon
5. Copperplate script
6. Didones
7. Egyptian
8. Fat face
9. Garaldes
10. Geometric sans serif
11. Glyphic
12. Gothic
13. Grotesque
14. Humanist
15. Informal script
16. Inline face
17. Ionic
18. Italic
19. Latin
20. Lineale
21. Monoline
22. Modern face
23. Oldface
24. Oldstyle
25. Outline
26. Sans serif
27. Script
28. Shadow
29. Stencil letter
30. Titling
31. Transitional
32. Venetian

ALEXANDER LAWSON 1975
1. Blackletter
2. Oldstyle
   a. Venetian
   b. Aldine-French
   c. Dutch-English
3. Transitional
4. Modern
5. Square Serif
6. Sans Serif
7. Script-Cursive
8. Display-Decorative

BITSTREAM 1986
1. Oldstyle
2. Transitional
3. Modern
4. Clarendon
5. Slabserif
6. Latin
7. Freeform
8. Sanserif
9. Engravers
10. Stencil
11. Strike-On
12. Computer
13. Decorated
14. Script
15. Exotic
16. Pi
... Non-Roman

LINOTYPE 1988
1. Old Face
2. Transitional
3. Modern Face
4. Slab Serif
5. Sans Serif
6. Decorative & Display
7. Script & Brush
8. Blackletter. Broken
9. Non-Roman
10. Pi

ADOBE SYSTEMS 1991
1. Venetian
2. Garalde
3. Transitional
4. Didone
5. Slab Serif
6. Sans Serif
7. Glyphic
8. Script
9. Display
10. Blackletter
11. Symbol
12. Non-Latin

ROBERT BRINGHURST 1995
1. Early Scribal Forms
2. Early Renaissance
3. Late Renaissance
4. Renaissance Italic
5. Mannerist
6. Baroque
7. Rococo
8. Neoclassical
9. Romantic
10. Realist
11. Geometric Modernism
12. Lyrical Modernism
13. Expressionist
14. Elegaic Postmodernism
12. Geometric Postmodernism

Jeff Level, Bruce Newman, Brenda Newman, *Precision Type, Font Reference Guide* (Commack, New York: 1995), version 5.0.

There are 10 classifications of type on the opposite page, which suggests a complex problem: there are many answers, yet no one system satisfies everyone.

In 1954 Maximilian Vox introduced his classification, and Deutscher Normenausschuss published DIN 16518 in 1964; the British Standard followed in 1965, and recently, Robert Bringhurst, author of *The Elements of Typographic Style*, used his poetic gifts to create a system. To this list, I add my simplified classification at the right, which is the one that I use in this book. There are a few additional break-downs that I favor; they can be found in the text.

Classifiers face problems. The early Garamond bears some relation to Venetians; once known as Oldstyle, it is now called Garalde. Sans serifs can be divided into those of the nineteenth and twentieth centuries. The basic difference is in letter proportion: the nineteenth-century sans are generally evenly proportioned, and the geometric German sans are based on classical proportions. Scripts pose special problems, because they can be classified as connected, unconnected, formal flexible pen, broadpen, semi-formal, casual, brush letter, brush script, upright or leaning, single-weight and multiple-weight. Display, the last group, is a catch-all and was once used to describe types larger than 14 point with unique characteristics that separated them from commonly accepted text styles. They include illustrative and textured fonts.

CLASSIC ROMAN	FRIZ QUADRATA, TRAJAN *Proportions based on a square; slight contrast thick/thin; minimum serifs; based on chisel-edge writing instrument*
BLACKLETTER	Goudy Text *Flat-sided letter; narrow; calligraphic; based on Gutenberg's types (Textura)*
VENETIAN	Bembo, Centaur, Jenson *Calligraphic; diagonal stress; slight thick/thin contrast; stubby serifs; caps based on classic roman proportions*
OLDSTYLE	Caslon, Garamond, Palatino *Greater thick/thin contrast than Venetians; mostly diagonal stress; refined bracketed serifs; caps based on classic roman proportions*
TRANSITIONAL	Baskerville, Bulmer, Caledonia *More refined than Oldstyle; mostly vertical stress; finer thins; refined bracketed serifs; caps sometimes strongly weighted and evenly proportioned*
MODERN	Bodoni, Didot, Walbaum *Extreme thick/thin contrast; vertical stress; refined unbracketed serifs; evenly proportioned caps*
SANS SERIF	Futura, Univers, Optima, **Franklin** *No serifs; monotone or two weight; Futura and Optima caps reflect classic proportions; Univers and Franklin; nineteenth-century even proportions*
SQUARE SERIF	**Beton, Clarendon, Serifa** *Usually unbracketed serifs; Clarendons are bracketed; monotone or two weight; vertical stress; known also as Egyptians*
FORMAL SCRIPT	*Palace Script, Hogarth, Künstler* *High-contrast cursive forms; based on flexible pointed pen handwriting; usually connected; leaning or upright; generous caps*
BRUSH/CASUAL	**Dom Casual,** *Freestyle Script, Mistral* *Pointed or chisel brush; leaning or upright; monotone or two weight; casual alignment; letter sizes may vary*
DISPLAY	Boutique, CALYPSO, SINALOA *14-point and larger; serif and sans serif, minimal or decorative, contempory shapes, textured, or based on period typography*

Our alphabet is not just 26 caps, 26 lowercase letters, figures, and punctuation; there are many special characters, plus thousands more throughout the world's languages. These are available to computer users through option keys and expert fonts. Shown below are some commonly used ones.

The Unicode Consortium,[1] in concert with the International Standards Organization (ISO), is defining standards for a wide variety of applications, to allow for common usage of data across computer platforms, industries, and languages. While the space here is too limited to convey the magnitude of the effort, the following definitions have been extracted from its work.

1. A **character** conveys distinctions in meaning or sounds.

A character is a concept, not the shape or appearance of an image on paper or video screen. For example, to represent the unit of information meaning "one," ISO/IEC 10646–1 encodes a large number of characters that could represent this basic "unit" (opposite).

´ acute	â circumflex a	ð eth, Icelandic	« left angle quote, guillemet
Á acute A	Ê circumflex E	Đ eth, Icelandic	{ left curly brace
á acute a	ê circumflex e	! exclamation mark	< less than
É acute E	Î circumflex I	ª feminine ordinal	a-z lowercase letters
é acute e	î circumflex i	fi f i ligature	¯ macron
í acute i	Ô circumflex O	fl f l ligature	º masculine ordinal
Ó acute O	ô circumflex o	ƒ florin	µ mu
ó acute o	Û circumflex U	` grave	· middle dot
Ú acute U	û circumflex u	À grave A	× multiply
ú acute u	: colon	à grave a	¬ not
Ý acute Y	† dagger	È grave E	# number
ý acute y	, comma	è grave e	Ω omega
& ampersand	@ commercial at	Ì grave I	½ one-half
' apostrophe	© copyright	ì grave i	¼ one-quarter
* asterisk	° degree	Ò grave O	¶ paragraph
\ backslash (reverse solidus)	Δ delta	ò grave o	(parenthesis left
	0–9 digits	Ù grave U	) parenthesis right
¦ broken vertical bar	Æ dipthong ligature	ù grave u	% percent
A-Z capitals	æ dipthong ligature	> greater than	‰ per mil (parts per thousand)
^ caret	÷ division	horizontal tab	. period
¸ cedilla	$ dollar	- hyphen	π pi
Ç cedilla C	‡ double dagger	" inches	Π pi
ç cedilla c	… ellipsis	∞ infinity	+ plus
¢ cent	– en dash	¡ inverted exclamation	± plus or minus
ˆ circumflex	— em dash	¿ inverted question mark	
Â circumflex A	= equals		

2. A **glyph** conveys distinctions in form or appearance and is a recognizable abstract graphic symbol which is independent of any specific design, *i.e.*, the letter "A," whether it is bold, italic, Helvetica, or Times Roman.

3. A **glyph shape** is an image of a glyph, as displayed on a presentation surface. This defines the visual differences between Helvetica and Times Roman.

4. **Glyph metrics** are the set of information in a glyph representation used for defining the dimensions and positioning of the glyph shape (character spacing, kerning, etc.). Other aspects of the problem that a designer may encounter include the relationship between coded characters and glyph identifiers; they may be one-to-one, one-to-many, many-to-one, or many-to-many. Spell checking, sorting, etc. present special problems, as does presentation direction: a text stream of Arabic written from right to left could contain a Latin quote written from left to right.

1. *The Unicode Standard, Version 2.0*, *The Unicode Consortium* (Reading, Massachusetts: Addison-Wesley Developers Press, 1991–96).

' prime	Þ thorn, Icelandic
? question mark	¾ three-fourths
" quotation mark, closing	~ tilde
	ã tilde a
" quotation mark, opening	Ã tilde A
	Ñ tilde N
® registered trademark	ñ tilde n
» right angle quote, guillemet	Õ tilde O
	õ tilde o
} right curly brace	¨ umlaut
] right square bracket	Ä umlaut A
Å ring A	ä umlaut a
å ring a	Ë umlaut E
§ section	ë umlaut e
; semi-colon	Ï umlaut I
Ø slashed O	ï umlaut i
ø slashed o	Ö umlaut O
ß German eszett (sz)	ö umlaut o
– soft hyphen	Ü umlaut u
/ solidus (slash), space	ü umlaut u
	Ÿ umlaut Y
[square bracket left	ÿ umlaut y
£ sterling	_ underscore
√ square root	| vertical bar (caesura)
superscript one	¥ yen
superscript two	

Consider for a moment the case with the unit of information meaning "one." ISO not only encodes a large number of characters that conceivably "represent" this "unit of information," but also encodes a number of "characters" that represent a particular form associated with this meaning. The characters that may be said to "represent" the "unit of information" designated by "one" are (at least):

0031	Digit One	"**1**"
00B9	Superscript One	"¹"
0661	Arabic-Indic Digit One	" ١ "
06F1	Extended Arabic-Indic Digit One	" ١ "
0967	Devanagari Digit One	" १ "
09E7	Bengali Digit One	"১"
09f4	Bengali Currency Numerator One	" ৴ "
0A67	Gurmukhi Digit One	"੧ "
0AE7	Gujarati Digit One	"૧ "
0b67	Oriya Digit One	"୧ "
0BE7	Tamil Digit One	"௧ "
0c67	Telugu Digit One	"౧ "
0CE7	Kannada Digit One	"೧ "
0d67	Malayalam Digit One	"൧ "
0E51	Thai Digit One	"๑ "
0ed1	Lao Digit One	"໑ "
2081	Subscript One	"₁"
215f	Fraction Numerator One	"⅟"
2160	Roman Numeral One	"Ⅰ"
2170	Small Roman Numeral One	"ⅰ"
2460	Circled Digit One	"①"
2474	Parenthesized Digit One	"⑴"
2488	Digit One Full Stop	"⒈"
2776	Dingbat Negative Circled Digit One	"❶"
2780	Dingbat Circled Sans-Serif Digit One	"➀"
278a	Dingbat Negative Circled Sans-Serif Digit One	"➊"
3021	Hangzhou Numeral One	" 〡 "
3192	Ideographic Annotation One Mark	" ㆒ "
3220	Parenthesized Ideograph One	"㈠"
3280	Circled Ideograph One	"㊀"
4E00	Cjk Unified Ideograph-4E00	"一"
58f9	Cjk Unified Ideograph-58f9	"壹"
FF11	Fullwidth Digit One	"１"

The example shown above is excerpted from the ISO/IEC 10646–1, and demonstrates the complexity of one aspect of the font problem; assigning a numeric code to a character. There are 23 additional characters not shown. (From Unicode Standard, Version 2.0.)

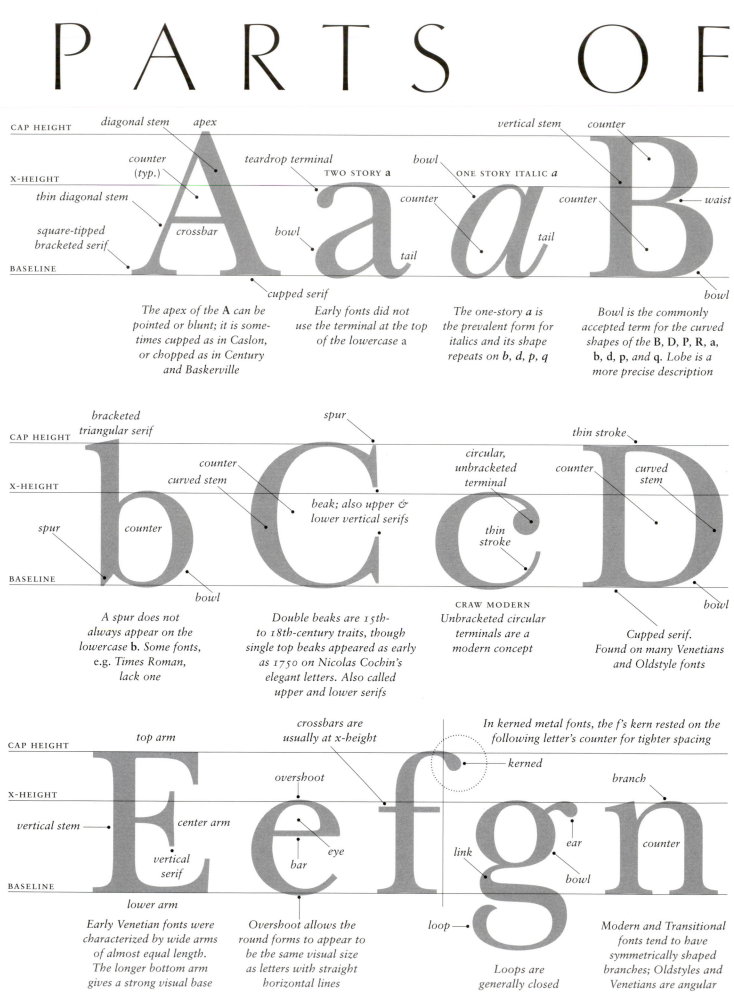

CAP HEIGHT — *diagonal stem* — *apex* — *vertical stem* — *counter*

counter (typ.) — *teardrop terminal* — *bowl*

X-HEIGHT — TWO STORY **a** — ONE STORY ITALIC *a* — *counter* — *waist*

thin diagonal stem — *counter* — *counter*

square-tipped bracketed serif — *crossbar* — *bowl* — *tail* — *tail*

BASELINE

cupped serif — *tail* — *bowl*

The apex of the **A** can be pointed or blunt; it is sometimes cupped as in *Caslon*, or chopped as in *Century* and *Baskerville*

Early fonts did not use the terminal at the top of the lowercase a

The one-story *a* is the prevalent form for italics and its shape repeats on **b, d, p, q**

Bowl is the commonly accepted term for the curved shapes of the **B, D, P, R, a, b, d, p,** and **q**. *Lobe* is a more precise description

---

bracketed triangular serif — *spur* — *thin stroke*

CAP HEIGHT

counter — *circular, unbracketed terminal* — *counter* — *curved stem*

curved stem

X-HEIGHT — *beak; also upper & lower vertical serifs*

spur — *counter* — *thin stroke*

BASELINE

bowl — CRAW MODERN — *bowl*

A spur does not always appear on the lowercase **b**. Some fonts, e.g. *Times Roman*, lack one

Double beaks are 15th- to 18th-century traits, though single top beaks appeared as early as 1750 on Nicolas Cochin's elegant letters. Also called upper and lower serifs

Unbracketed circular terminals are a modern concept

Cupped serif. Found on many Venetians and Oldstyle fonts

---

top arm — *crossbars are usually at x-height* — In kerned metal fonts, the f's kern rested on the following letter's counter for tighter spacing

CAP HEIGHT

overshoot — *kerned* — *branch*

X-HEIGHT

vertical stem — *center arm* — *eye* — *ear* — *counter*

link

vertical serif — *bar* — *bowl*

BASELINE — *loop*

lower arm

Early Venetian fonts were characterized by wide arms of almost equal length. The longer bottom arm gives a strong visual base

Overshoot allows the round forms to appear to be the same visual size as letters with straight horizontal lines

Loops are generally closed

Modern and Transitional fonts tend to have symmetrically shaped branches; Oldstyles and Venetians are angular

A LETTER

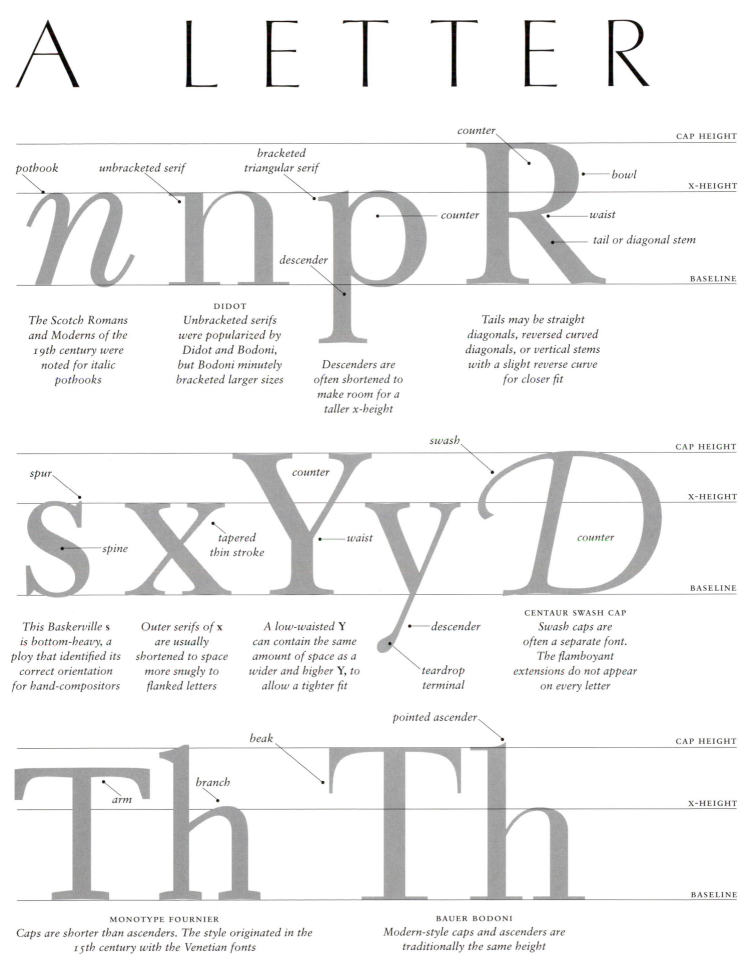

CAP HEIGHT

counter

pothook   *unbracketed serif*   *bracketed triangular serif*   *bowl*

X-HEIGHT

counter   *waist*

tail or diagonal stem

descender

BASELINE

DIDOT

The Scotch Romans and Moderns of the 19th century were noted for italic pothooks

Unbracketed serifs were popularized by Didot and Bodoni, but Bodoni minutely bracketed larger sizes

Descenders are often shortened to make room for a taller x-height

Tails may be straight diagonals, reversed curved diagonals, or vertical stems with a slight reverse curve for closer fit

---

swash   CAP HEIGHT

spur   *counter*

X-HEIGHT

spine   *tapered thin stroke*   *waist*   *counter*

BASELINE

spine

CENTAUR SWASH CAP

descender

This Baskerville s is bottom-heavy, a ploy that identified its correct orientation for hand-compositors

Outer serifs of **x** are usually shortened to space more snugly to flanked letters

A low-waisted **Y** can contain the same amount of space as a wider and higher **Y**, to allow a tighter fit

teardrop terminal

Swash caps are often a separate font. The flamboyant extensions do not appear on every letter

---

pointed ascender

beak   CAP HEIGHT

branch

arm   X-HEIGHT

BASELINE

MONOTYPE FOURNIER

Caps are shorter than ascenders. The style originated in the 15th century with the Venetian fonts

BAUER BODONI

Modern-style caps and ascenders are traditionally the same height

NOTE—Depending on the source, usage may vary from the terms given here, which are the ones used in this book. The examples are set in ITC Baskerville, except where noted.

Display figure: Fino. Text: 24/48 ITC New Baskerville

1

The Logotype. In this form the name stands alone without support from any visual device, and the name is therefore emphasized. The design relies solely on a distinctive drawing of the letterforms, each considered a constituent, to communicate positive values.

DON BARTELS

SMITH + BARTELS

Consultants in Corporate and Brand Identity

ART
CENTER COLLEGE
OF DESIGN

CAFE
CORDIALE

Cutex

audio plaza

CHECKERS

DANDELION

Blue Ribbon
400

5inco

JOHN DEERE

■

These logotypes have been chosen to
show as wide a variety of styles as
possible. All are hand-lettered; some
adhere to traditional shapes, while
others are more adventuresome in their
design. There are ultraconservative
styles for insurance companies, and
fanciful logos for rock stars. The reductions show the importance of legibility
at small sizes because a logo must be
used in a wide range of applications,
from small sizes on business cards to
large building signs. There is a mix of
illustrations: most of the reductions
are scanned images of reproduction
art; a few have been drawn in a font
program, while others are pencil comprehensive sketches that were part of
a client presentation, and are not the
selected design, which can be seen on
the page given below each logotype.

Each logo is discussed and compared to a variety of fonts, and some
history is offered. Preceding the logos
are chapters that analyze individual
letters and fonts and compare them to
similar font styles.

Cire Perdu

THE
Harry Connick Jr.
CHRISTMAS
SHOW

The
EAST

HOTEL
CREVETTE

elephant

Crown

Engineering & Science

FANCIES

158

Fantasy

222

Fontaine

224

Judy Garland

226

gift EXPRESS

160

Good Evening, CAPTAIN

104

THE
Grammy
Lifetime
Achievement
AWARD SHOW

230

Harmony

220

TJRM

162

JAPAN
Technicals

164

KHeCo

108

THE L

232

SLG

234

k.d. lang
INGÉNUE

166

A logotype is the name of a company, product, or service, and is an essential part of commerce—even the U.S. government has logos to identify its hundreds of agencies and departments. Logos are seen in academia and sports, in TV and the music industry; logos are everywhere.

A good logo must be equally legible in small and large sizes. Ideally the image should be strong and simple and easily reproduced on different materials.

Instead of the ambiguous word "logo," some corporate identity consultants choose to distinguish between the *corporate signature*, which includes a name and a graphic shape (sometimes called a mark), and the name by itself, the *logotype*. An accompanying graphic may be a symbol, an illustration (whether literal or abstract), an initial, or a monogram, which implies that the letters are connected or joined in some manner: IBM is a logo made up of separate initials, and GE is a monogram. Rarely is a graphic shape used by itself, except for decoration. In almost all instances, the name accompanies the mark for positive identification; some logos are designed so that the name is embedded in a symbol or mark.

All businesses benefit from having a logo as a simple means of identification, from the local handyman to multi-national conglomerates. Any product, inexpensive or costly, is enhanced by an identifying logo that is unique, not plain type, but styled in a manner that offers a degree of indiv-iduality, which can be trademarked and federally registered to prevent its being copied, an important point.

Live at the Beacon

LOBBY LOUNGE

1697 LORETO 1997

THE CITY OF LOS ANGELES MARATHON

Lumière

A logo should be appropriate and suggest quality. It should be distinctive and legible. There are several ways to achieve these goals. You can set the name surrounded with a distinctive shape; arrange it in an individual manner; change its width; make its letters bolder or more delicate; introduce refinements and adjustments to individual letters to make them unique but still legible; or hand-draw the name as I do. Some corporate identity programs require a proprietary font based on the logo for subsidiary names. But all of these approaches require a knowledge of letterforms to tailor the logo appropriately.

The overriding rule of logo design is: a strong off-beat image has a shorter life than a more discreet one; a well-designed logo should have a minimum life-span of fifteen years. There are exceptions, because some products are introduced to ride the crest of a fashion wave and are quickly changed when the fad recedes.

General, time-honored rules govern appropriateness. A font style may be identified with a product or a company logo when it is used repétitively. A product or service that is targeted for women may require a light and refined approach, either in the style of the name, its color or surrounding elements. Cosmetics logos are minimal and understated and so are products that promote refinement, precision, luxury, and the epicure. Food products frequently make use of casual scripts, which are friendly, accessible, and pleasing to the eye—not sophisticated, but drawn with a down-home touch. Opposed to this are

Magic Moments

240

Bette **MIDLER**

168

Mr. CRAFT

118

OLIVIER

170

OPTIKA

172

PERCEPTRONICS

174

PRIMER

245

products directed to men and the corporate workplace, transportation, sports and grooming products, which demand a bold, no-nonsense, assertive image. The multi-million-dollar entertainment industry has marketing rules of its own, and readily embraces the avant-garde.

The logos discussed in this book are mainstream logos, the *Fortune* 500 variety, with an admixture of a few logos for the TV and the entertainment industries, aimed at a mass audience. There are no avant-garde statements; while a few unconventional preliminary sketches are included, such logos are rarely chosen by a client. It is almost impossible to sell them to a highly visible multinational corporation.

In this book I display some of the world's most respected fonts. I diagram them, discuss their shapes and idiosyncrasies, sometimes in minute detail to show the bones of the designs that have endured for five hundred years. I analyze fonts and compare them to explain their relationships and heritage. When you use these classic fonts or styles for logos—and many famous corporations use them—exercise great care not to stray too far from their original shapes. Distorted shapes will appear bizarre when used with the native font.

I have stressed the importance of font family characteristics because more than any aspect of design, family characteristics are the genetic code that holds a font together and gives a logo its distinctive, unique image. Of course, embellishment and decoration are a necessary

Prix d'Or

244

 Prudential

(Prudential updated the Rock in 1987) 256

THE R

232

RPH

248

The Raymond Company

246

SINGAPORE
COUNTRY CLUB

120

Singapura

250

part of graphic art, and some logos are ornate and fanciful, designed to suggest an attitude or mood.

I compare some digital fonts to the original metal showing to illustrate design changes, which usually are slight; in less successful adaptations the subtleties and nuances of the original design have been lost. Computer technology has yet to reproduce the gently flared stem tips of a few metal sans serif fonts. But digital fonts can be developed in far less time than metal text fonts, which required separate drawings for each weight and proportion, and in carefully considered machine text fonts (6 to 14 points), a drawing for every point size. Computer fonts are malleable and easily modified. The revisions may be so slight that most viewers are unaware that a letter has been manipulated, but these changes can enliven a familiar font into a usable and distinctive logo.

Logo designers show multiple design directions to a client because there is no single answer for a specific logo. The client may want slight modifications of its existing logo to gently update the design without losing its all-important name recognition. Or the client or its marketing group may favor a particular direction and request designs shown in that scheme. These may not agree with the designer's ideas and intentions. What is important in a multifaceted presentation is the variety, which can point to the most appropriate, legible, and distinctive solution. Some designs may reinforce a favored direction; many designs are chosen for emotional reasons. Always submit

252

254

125

126

220

129

designs that will meet the job's requirement. Otherwise, an unknowledgeable client will perversely choose the wrong design. More often than not, clients request changes that combine one or more designs; the designer doesn't always win.

The fifty-three logos and development sketches in this book are discussed in relation to one or more fonts. One-third of the logos are script, or partial script, underscoring the importance of the style. Script is the most flexible of all approaches, because it may be drawn in the widest variety, from the purely formal and decorative to the casual, either light and stylish or bold and raging. Script signatures suggest the authentic or the custom-designed.

A successful logo is based on an understanding of letterform structure, spacing and proportion, legibility, and reproduction techniques. With each new commission, the designer must research the competition's logos, explore design directions, winnow, apply the form to stationery and even mock-up signage, evolving a typographic vocabulary to make a formal presentation.

In these pages I follow the method of my twenty-five years of teaching and forty-two years of designing logos—to point out and explain in simple, straightforward language my love affair with letters and the importance of their shapes.

Display figure: Fino. Text: 30/50 Renaissance italic,
60-point Renaissance Swash light italic initial cap

We best honor the achievements of the past when, inspired by their tutelage, we design for our own contemporary printing, alphabets suited to the industrial design of our century.

HERMANN ZAPF

Type Designer, Calligrapher, Designer, and Teacher

TEXTURA	**qa tradens dabo philistijm in manu** GOUDY TEXT qatradcao dabo philiftijm

JENSON   ABCDEFGHIJKLMNOPQRSTUVWXYZ&abcdefghijklmnopqrstuvwxyz

BEMBO   ABCDEFGHIJKLMNOPQRSTUVWXYZ&abcdefghijklmnopqrstuvwxyz

ARRIGHI   *ABCDEFGHIJKLMNOPQRSTUVWXYZ&abcdefghijklmnopqrstuvwxyz*

GRANJON   ABCDEFGHIJKLMNOPQRSTUVWXYZ&abcdefghijklmnopqrstuvwxyz

GARAMOND   ABCDEFGHIJKLMNOPQRSTUVWXYZ&abcdefghijklmnopqrstuvwxyz

PLANTIN   ABCDEFGHIJKLMNOPQRSTUVWXYZ&abcdefghijklmnopqrstuvwxyz

VAN DIJCK   ABCDEFGHIJKLMNOPQRSTUVWXYZ&abcdefghijklmnopqrstuvwxyz

JANSON   ABCDEFGHIJKLMNOPQRSTUVWXYZ&abcdefghijklmnopqrstuvwxyz

CASLON   ABCDEFGHIJKLMNOPQRSTUVWXYZ&abcdefghijklmnopqrstuvwxyz

FOURNIER   ABCDEFGHIJKLMNOPQRSTUVWXYZabcdefghijklmnopqrstuvwxyz

COCHIN   ABCDEFGHIJKLMNOPQRSTUVWXYZabcdefghijklmnopqrstuvwxyz

BASKERVILLE   ABCDEFGHIJKLMNOPQRSTUVWXYZ&abcdefghijklmnopqrstuvwxyz

DIDOT   ABCDEFGHIJKLMNOPQRSTUVWXYZ&abcdefghijklmnopqrstuvwxyz

BODONI   ABCDEFGHIJKLMNOPQRSTUVWXYZ&abcdefghijklmnopqrstuvwxyz

OXFORD   ABCDEFGHIJKLMNOPQRSTUVWXYZ& abcdefghijklmnopqrstuvwxyz

WALBAUM   ABCDEFGHIJKLMNOPQRSTUVWXYZ&abcdefghijklmnopqrstuvwxyz

EGYPTIAN   **LETTERFOUNDER** *(Two Lines English Egyptian, reduced)*

Typographers know the commercially used typefaces listed here, sometimes by a different name; they are not esoteric, and with a few exceptions are currently available from their manufacturers. Included are the three most popular text faces: Baskerville, Garamond, and Times New Roman.

Among the thousands of text faces, these have endured, not in their original form, because they have all been redrawn to take advantage of twentieth-century technologies: metal, photo, and now the computer. For those not familiar with type, these eighteen fonts (except the Textura and Egyptian) will appear to be virtually the same—yet to the educated eye each is as individual as a fingerprint.

Types can be classified in general overlapping time periods. Fifteenth-century types are known as Humanist, though Venetian is still a popular term for them—Jenson is the quintessential example. Sixteenth- and seventeenth-century types often called Oldstyles, typified by Garamond, are defined now as Garaldes. Transitional types developed in the eighteenth century; Baskerville is the model. The Didones, known also as Moderns and exemplified by Bodoni, emerged later in the century and held sway for most of the nineteenth century. Script types existed from the early beginnings of typefounding. The other type classifications, Slab Serif, Lineale, Glyphic,

and Graphic, are twentieth-century names. The earliest face shown here is Gutenberg's Textura (1455). In modern dress it can be seen as Goudy Text. A Venetian Centaur, Bruce Rogers's re-drawing of Jenson (1470), is popular, and recently Robert Slimbach has drawn his version of Jenson for Adobe Systems. A book face, Bembo (1495) has made great inroads into advertising typography. Xerox Corporation used it for many years as a corporate advertising face. This book's type, Sabon, redrawn from Garamond (1544)[1] is a font that was said to be in every printer's type case in America. Plantin (1567), a stodgy typeface, was transformed into Times New Roman, the generic roman font, by Stanley Morison and Victor Lardent for the London *Times* newspaper. Van Dijck, Granjon, Fournier, and Oxford, while not popular as display advertising faces, are used in fine book printing. Honda Motor Company adopted Caslon (1722) for its corporate advertising typeface more than thirty years ago. Cochin (1745) is based on engravings and is often used to signify fashion and elegance. William Golden added considerable luster to the CBS logotype with a hand-drawn Didot by Freeman Craw (1784). D. B. Updike of the famed Merrymount Press so favored Oxford (1796) that he used it as the typeface for his monumental work *Printing Types, their History, Forms, and Use, A Study*

in Survivals. Paul Rand specified Bodoni (1788) as the corporate advertising font for IBM. Walbaum (1810), Austria and Germany's answer to French Regency, is enjoying a revival.

Egyptian (1816) the sans serif by William Caslon IV of the Caslon Typefoundry, is a bold, optically single-weight font. For the past 175 years sans serifs have been endlessly drawn in different proportions, from extended fonts to compressed and illegible forms; in different weights and widths of roman, italic, and obliques. Adrian Frutiger has re-drawn Morris Benton's News Gothic and pro-

duced a total of 58 digital Univers fonts. ITC has issued Victor Caruso and David Berlow's Franklin Gothic, and Erik Spiekermann has drawn a sans serif and named it Metafont—and the beat goes on.

Discounting novelty faces, including "garage fonts," a cursory look at new fonts reveals strong ties to past ones.

1. Some versions are based on Jean Jannon's 1621 version. Stempel Typefoundry's version issued in 1924 was based on a 1592 specimen sheet from Egenolff-Berner foundry in Frankfurt, Germany, which had acquired some of Garamond's punches.
See Alexander Lawson, *Anatomy of a Typeface* (Boston, Massachusetts: David R. Godine, 1990), pages 134–136.

Our Typographic Heritage
(Dates are approximate)

TEXTURA—*Johann Gutenberg*		1455
JENSON—*Nicolas Jenson*		1470
BEMBO—*Francesco Griffo*		1495
ARRIGHI—*Ludovico degli Arrighi*		1523
GRANJON—*Robert Granjon*		1545
GARAMOND—*Claude Garamond*		1544
PLANTIN—*Christophe Plantin*		1567
VAN DIJCK—*Christoffel van Dijck*		1647
JANSON—*Nicolas Kis*		1660
CASLON—*William Caslon*		1722
FOURNIER—*Pierre Simon Fournier*		1736
COCHIN—*Nicolas Cochin*		1745
BASKERVILLE—*John Baskerville*		1754
DIDOT—*Firmin Didot*		1784
BODONI—*Giambattista Bodoni*		1798
OXFORD—*Richard Austin*		1796
WALBAUM—*Justus Eric Walbaum*		1810
EGYPTIAN—*William Caslon IV*		1816

A font of type is first a series of drawings that evolves through intricate permutations so that it can be reproduced in a wide range of sizes, proportions, and degrees of boldness.

The Century Schoolbook font below is a character set of 256 different letters, figures, and symbols. The system software determines which characters are typically shown. This group is for a Macintosh American keyboard. Our roman alphabet, figures, and symbols are called characters. When design is applied to their forms, they are called glyph shapes: a Century Schoolbook or Times New Roman **a** is a glyph shape. This character set is part of an enormous, single, universal character code, *The Unicode Standard* described on pages 18–19, that includes all of the major scripts, and common technical symbols of the world. Included are other character sets: Turkish, Indonesian, Kanji, Mandarin, etc. Each Unicode character has a name and a sixteen-bit encoding that

1234567890-=
qwertyuiop[]\
asdfghjkl;'
zxcvbnm,./
!@#$%^&*()_+
QWERTYUIOP{}|
ASDFGHJKL:"
ZXCVBNM<>?
¡™£¢∞§¶•ªº–≠
œ∑´®†¥¨ˆøπ""'«
åß∂ƒ©˙∆˚¬…æ
Ω≈ç√∫˜µ≤≥÷
⁄¤‹›fifl‡°·‚—±
Œ„´‰ˇÁ¨ˆØ∏""'»
ÅÍÎÏ˝ÓÔ ÒÚÆ
¸˛Ç◊ı˜Â¯˘¿

Century Schoolbook—Morris Fuller Benton, ATF, 1917–19

■
A digital, Type 1, 256-character font of Century Schoolbook and, on the opposite page, its companion italic. Additional extended, condensed, and bold fonts create a family. Some are numerous: Adobe Garamond Original is made up of sixteen, and Adrian Frutiger's Univers has an astounding fifty-eight fonts of different weights and proportions. Letters, figures, and symbols are known as characters, and special drawings of these as fonts are called glyph shapes.

can accommodate 65,535 separate characters. Century Schoolbook is distinguished by another feature: it is known as a text face, the kind you find in your newspaper or in a book. Fonts that are designed for large sizes, or that have special design characteristics are called display fonts, though many text fonts are used for display at large sizes.

The font on the opposite page is a roman font, indicating that its letters have a vertical orientation, and is based on letters of the Roman alphabet. The font below is italic, which means that it is inclined. (The style was devised in Italy in the early sixteenth century).

Most text and italic fonts are sold together, and often a bold version of each is included; the group is then called a family. A family may include a condensed version and an extended version. Univers has an abundant fifty-eight separate fonts of different weights and proportions. The special characters and symbols in these Century Schoolbook character sets are accessed by the option key or shift/option keys on a computer keyboard (*see* pages 18–19 for a list of standard characters and their names).

1234567890-=
qwertyuiop[]
asdfghjkl;'
zxcvbnm,./
!@#$%^&()_+*
QWERTYUIOP{}|
ASDFGHJKL:"
ZXCVBNM<>?
¡™£¢∞§¶•ªº–≠
œ∑´®†¥¨^øπ""«
åß∂ƒ©˙∆˚¬…æ
Ω≈ç√∫˜µ≤≥÷
/¤‹›ﬁﬂ‡°·‚—±
Œ„´‰ˇÁ˙˙ˆØ∏""»
ÅÍÎÏ˝ÓÔÒÚÆ
¸˛Ç◊ı˜Â¯˘¿

Century Schoolbook italic

The capital alphabet can be divided into five general groups: vertical stems; diagonal stems; vertical and diagonal stems combined; curved stems; and curved and vertical stems combined. The lowercase has a slightly different structure with the letters appearing in different positions, because four letters are made up of branches, which do not appear in the caps.

The different cap and lowercase shapes are merged into a font by using design elements that are common to all of the letters, *i.e.*, consistent stem thickness. Serifs appear on all of the letters except the Os. Vertical serifs and beaks occur on one-third of the cap letters, and in a two-weight roman each letter has a thin portion. Additional characteristics tie the letters together. The lateral, optical division of the **B, E, F, H, K, P, R,** and **X** relate otherwise disparate shapes. Even

EFHIJLTU
vertical stems

AVWXZ
diagonal stems

KMNY
vertical and diagonal stems combined

COQS
curved stems

BDGPR
curved and vertical stems combined

Sabon—Jan Tschichold, Stempel, 1964–67

■
The alphabet can be divided in groups of similar stems: vertical, diagonal, or curved. Disparate in shape, they are related by a similarity of thick-and-thin weights, and either horizontal or vertical serifs, constantly repeated.

the C, E, F, G, S, T, and Z may be grouped because they share beaks and vertical serifs of similar design, a trait that further promotes family resemblance. Proportions vary from alphabet to alphabet, but in each font, groups of similarly proportioned letters create a relationship too.

It is important that these relationships, attributes, or family characteristics (straight, diagonal, and curved stems; shading, the transition from thick to thin; weighted stems; hairlines; and serifs) apply throughout a font and make a consistent and predictable design.

The bowl's curved stems, a, b, d, p, and q, share a relationship with the bowl caps, though the lowercase bowls roll into the stems, instead of the right angle joins of the caps B, D, P, and R. Branches h, m, n, and u are related to the lowercase bowls because they usually join at the

same height. The a's top curve belongs to both groups: branch and bowls. Its vertical stem ends with a curved tail that relates to the wider ending tail of the t. In some fonts, *e.g.*, Bodoni, circular terminals relate the a, c, f, g, j, and r, or one quarter of the lowercase.

vertical stems

diagonal stems

vertical stems combined with branches

curved stems

curved and vertical stems combined

Sabon

SERIF LETTERS

A font's letters rest on a baseline. The main body of a lowercase letter is measured by the x-height (the only lowercase letter with horizontal serifs top and bottom; the **k** has an ascender). The size relationships of lowercase to capitals differ, and depend on the designer's intentions. Sabon has a lowercase-to-cap ratio of .63:1. Sheldon, a 7-point face designed for an octavo Bible for Oxford University Press by Jan van Krimpen in 1947, a ratio of .73:1[1] and Giambattista Bodoni's roman of 1771 shows a ratio of .54:1.[2] Today display fonts (14-point and larger) usually have a large x-height, which allows lines of type to be packed together for a strong statement. An approximate ratio for a display font is .6:1. There are a few text fonts with normal ascender height but with shortened descenders, because the top half of a line of type counts more for

38

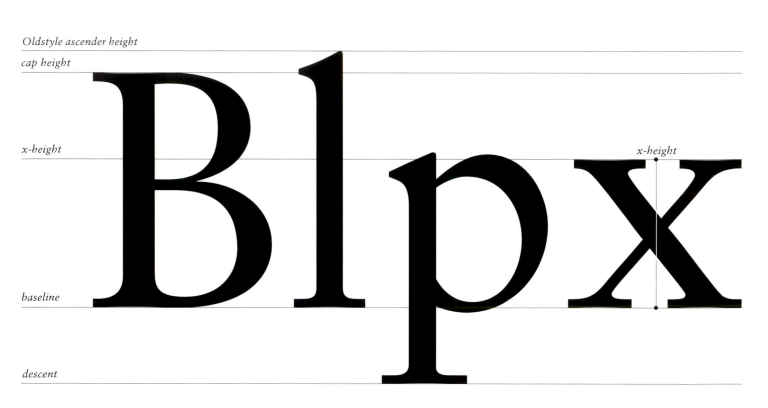

Sabon (250-point)—Jan Tschichold, Stempel, 1964–67

Sheldon (drawing)—Jan van Krimpen, Monotype, 1947

■

x-height refers to the height of the lowercase **x**. This dimension varies from font to font and is largely determined by the premise of the design. Display fonts normally have a large x-height, and text faces, a greater capital-to-lowercase ratio. Ascenders of the Oldstyles, including the Venetian fonts, are taller than the caps. Oldstyles usually have small x-heights, though Sabon, an Oldstyle (Garalde), has a generous x-height.

legibility than the lower half. This allows more lines to a page, with the added luxury of tall, legible ascenders and generous capitals. Originally, metal text faces from 6- to 12-point were designed with a small amount of space below the descender and none at the ascender top, which prevented stems from touching when two or more lines of type were set solid (without additional strips of metal called leading) to separate the lines. The ascender and descender length determine the *color* of the page: long ones will yield light color, short ones, dark color.

1. John Dreyfus, *The Work of Jan van Krimpen* (Haarlem: Joh. Enschedé en Zonen, 1952), page 48.

2. D. B. Updike, *Printing Types, Their History, Forms, and Use, A Study in Survivals* (Cambridge, Massachusetts: Harvard University Press, 1937), vol. 1, Fregie Majuscole, Parma, 1771, page 178.

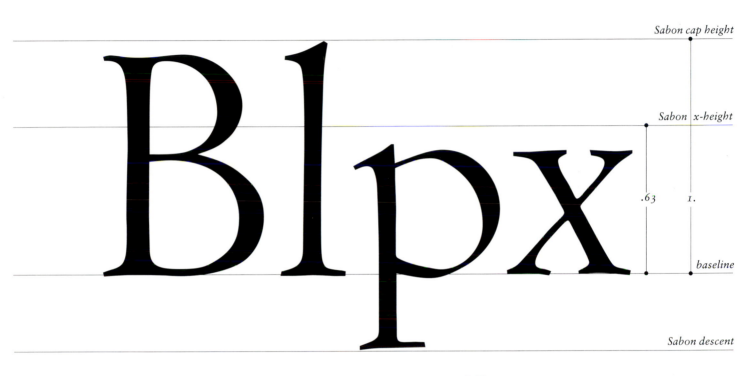

Centaur (250-point)—Bruce Rogers, Lanston Monotype & Monotype, 1929

Bauer Bodoni (105-point)—Heinrich Jost, Bauer, 1926

The 250-point Centaur has a much smaller x-height than the Sabon (opposite). Special fonts have been designed with extremely large x-heights for Bibles and phone directories to permit legibility at a very small size. The Sheldon (opposite) has the same cap height to descender length as the Bodoni above, yet Sheldon's x-height is generous at the expense of its descenders and ascenders. Metal types were cast on bodies with a small amount of space beneath the descenders to prevent them from touching the ascenders of the following line of type.

Font design relies on optical illusions. All stems, straight, curved, and diagonal, are drawn to appear optically the same thickness. A broad-pen held at an approximate 15-degree angle, will produce crescent-shaped curves that appear lighter in mass than a straight stem of constant

thickness. To compensate, the curves must be widened so that they will appear to be the same thickness as the straight stems.

The vertical stems must be equal width, and all round or curved stems should appear to match them: b, c, d, e, g, o, p, q, s, B, C, D, G, O, P, Q, R, S,

2, 3, 5, 6, 8, 9, etc. There are no set rules to accomplish this. Mortimer Leach, in his classic book *Lettering for Advertising*, drew the curves one-third wider than the straight stems, but this relationship will vary depending on the width of the letters and the thickness of the thin strokes.

40

Sabon (250-point)—Jan Tschichold, Stempel, 1964–67

ABCDEFGHIJKLMNOPQRSTUVWXYZ
abcdefghijklmnopqrstuvwxyz
1234567890

Melior—Hermann Zapf, Stempel, 1948–49

■

All straight, vertical, lowercase stems should be of equal width, and curved stems should be bolder to optically match the straight stem weight. Melior's curved stem weight is distributed more equally and requires less weight adjustment than traditional romans.

Melior, a squarish serif font designed for newspaper text by Hermann Zapf, requires less compensation because the stem is a flattened curve and holds its weight almost to the full height of the letter. Capital letters are bolder than lowercase because each capital contains more negative space, which optically erodes the stem's thickness. If constructed with the lowercase stem thickness, the caps will appear to be lighter. The slightly heavier capital weight is useful to indicate a sentence beginning. Its added weight helps distinguish a capital I from a lowercase l: Il. The capto-lowercase weight ratio and the relationship of curved weight to straight stem weight are optically determined. The stem ratios vary from font to font.

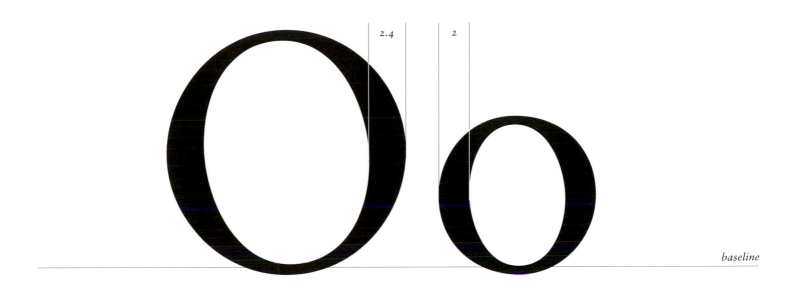

2.4   2

baseline

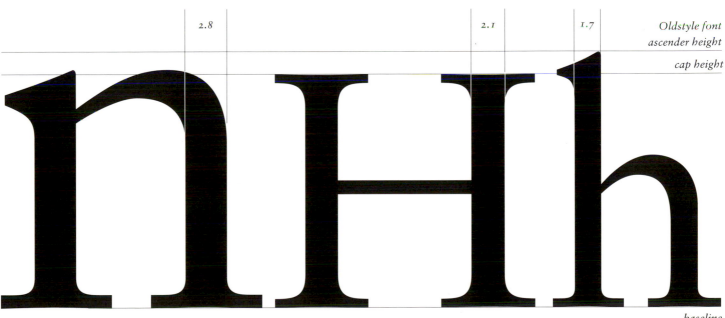

2.8   2.1   1.7   *Oldstyle font ascender height*

cap height

Sabon

baseline

■

Capitals are not enlarged lowercase. The stem weight would be too bold. The lowercase **n** *above, drawn to cap height, appears much heavier than the capital* **H**. *Capital letters are only slightly heavier than the lowercase so as to color equally and to give a slight emphasis to a sentence beginning. There should be a balance of color or mass when a word of caps is set with the lowercase.*

SERIF LETTERS

Depending on a font's boldness, the weighted diagonals may require minute thinning to match the overall weight of their vertical counterparts. Letters are read by the eye horizontally; correspondingly, a horizontal line drawn across a diagonal stroke will look physically wider than a line across a vertical stem. In lightweight text fonts no adjustment is made, but in medium weights and bolder the diagonal is thinned or tapered to avoid producing a dark letter. This is particularly important for sans serif fonts. The spine, or thick portion, of a thick-and-thin cap and lowercase **s** is a diagonal formed from a reverse curve. The thickness diminishes at x-height and at the baseline, which lessens the over-all mass, and the undulating stem must then be weighted to match the bowls and round forms.

42

kvwxyz
AKVWXYZ

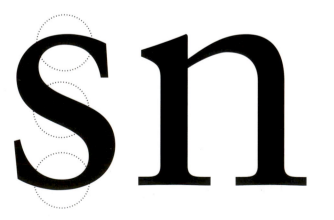

ascender height

x-height

baseline

Sabon—Jan Tschichold, Stempel, 1964–67

Left—*Because the* **s** *thins top and bottom, thickness is often added to the weighted, diagonal spine to make it appear the same thickness as the vertical stems. This* **s** *appears bolder than the vertical stem at this size.*

Opposite—*Curves and points must extend above the x-height, above the ascender height, and below the baseline so that the shapes will optically align with horizontal serifs. Font designers call this "overshoot."*

All letters, roman and italic, should appear to be the same height and to rest on the baseline. A round form or pointed letter drawn to the same height as a lowercase **x** will appear smaller because only a small portion of the curve or point touches the x-height. This point of tangency is too slight to visually align with a strong, horizontal serif. Therefore each curve or point must extend above the x-height to visually align with the horizontal serifs, and above the cap **X**, if the letter is a capital. This adjustment applies also to the teardrop or circular terminal of the lowercase **r**. For a curved form to appear to rest on the baseline, the curve must drop slightly below the line. Stems that converge to form the points of the **v**, **w**, **y**, **M**, **N**, **V**, and **W** follow the same rule. (Some text faces hold the M's point high to avoid serif congestion.) This may be determined visually by viewing the shapes from a distance or by an extreme photo reduction. Blunted points of bolder fonts require less adjustment, and the points of condensed fonts must be longer.

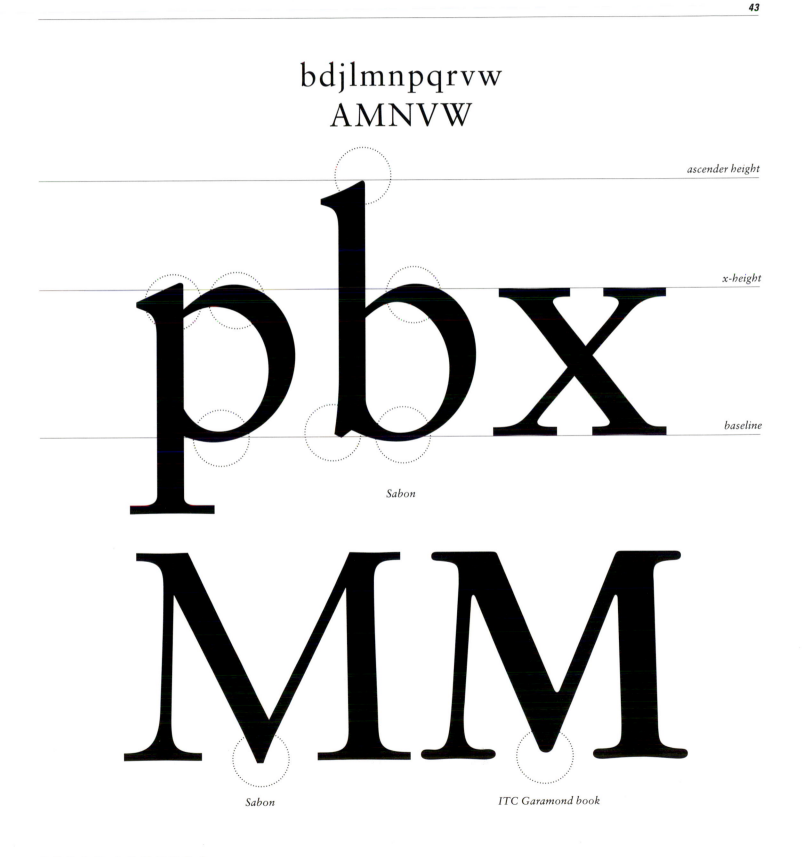

bdjlmnpqrvw
AMNVW

ascender height

x-height

baseline

Sabon

Sabon

ITC Garamond book

SERIF LETTERS

Oldstyle and Modern are the two basic serif font proportions. A third may be added, the Classic, from which the Oldstyles are derived but it pertains mainly to the capitals, whose widths have greater variety. The lowercase widths are about the same in text fonts; it is the caps that are tell-tale. Oldstyle fonts are based on the concept of a square that the Romans devised: **A, H, O, Q, N, T,** and **U** are roughly a square; **B, E, F, L, P, R,** and **S** are about one-half the square's width, and the **M** and **W** are wider than a square; simple instructions for a stone-mason chiseling letters. Modern fonts attempt a sameness of proportion—not a mathematical scheme, but one with optically equal amounts of negative space within the letters—one for the caps and one for the lowercase. The lowercase **n** and **o** best illustrate the problem. A normally proportioned **o** will fit within a

44

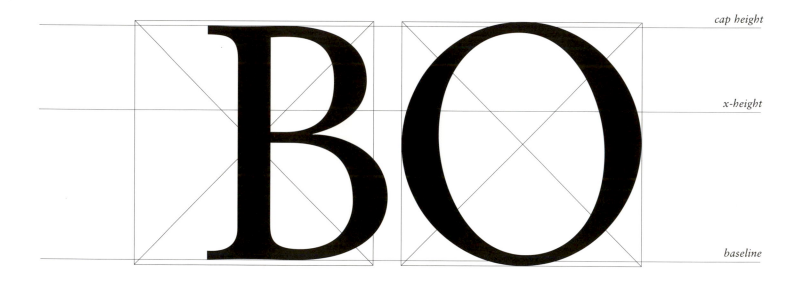

cap height

x-height

baseline

AHONQTU
BEFLPRS

Sabon—Jan Tschichold, Stempel, 1964–67

Classical and Oldstyle fonts are loosely based on a square and are therefore sometimes referred to as Quadrata. The letters **A**, **H**, **O**, **N**, **Q**, **T**, and **U** fit this scheme. **B**, **E**, **F**, **L**, **P**, **R**, and **S** are roughly one-half as wide and are divided laterally a bit above center to prevent the shapes from appearing top-heavy.

square; that is, all sides of the **o** will touch the square. If the counter of the **n** is drawn to the same width as the **o**'s counter, the additional space supplied by its corners will create a greater volume. The **n** must thus be narrowed to appear the same volume. A slightly condensed **o** may be at-

tached to a stem to produce the group **b, d, p, q.** The **c, e,** and **o** make up a group; **h, n,** and **u** are a third group. With the exception of **m** and **w,** the rest of the lowercase letters will fit with some ease into one of these groups.

The categories are general because each font has its own set of

proportions determined by the designer. Some have been based on a grid and others are intuitive. See the following pages for a discussion of Monotype's 18-unit scheme, the grand-daddy of all unit alphabets.

Serif length plays an important role in fit, but it is the relationship

of letter width, stroke weight, and letter spacing that are the most important design features of any font, Oldstyle or Modern. They are the font's lifeblood.

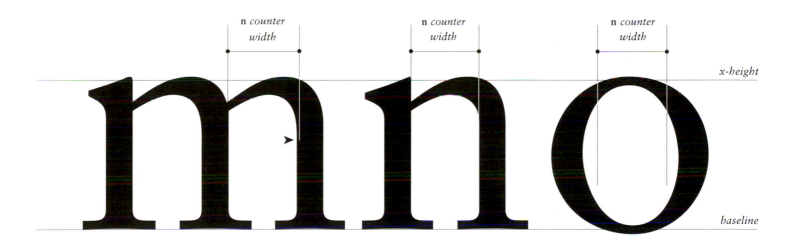

cap height

n *counter width*   n *counter width*   n *counter width*

x-height

baseline

bdpq, ceo, hnu, mw

Sabon

■
The proportions of the lowercase **o** *and* **n** *must be balanced. To appear the same volume, the counter of the* **o** *should be wider than the counter of the* **n**. *The two letters may be used to establish*

proportions for the lowercase. The counters of the **m** *are smaller than that of the* **n**; *otherwise they will appear wider.*

Round Letter Proportions

When asked about the rules of proportion, Jan van Krimpen replied, "There are none." Despite Van Krimpen's protest, type designers do use rules of proportion, some based on classical forms. The nineteenth century offered "even" proportions, and there are "fixed" or standard typewriter proportions. Monotype's 18-unit scheme fit all of a font's characters: 18 for the widest letter, and 5 units for the smallest. In place of a line of type, individual letters were cast. For one font (*below*), the following letters were assigned to a 13-unit row: M*BCE SC&w*BEFZATCLVR. The premise is that if an optically proportioned font where all letters assume equal color is desired, the **o** can be the reference letter; an **n** will be more narrow. Bowl forms are a different problem. If the counter, or interior space, of the **b, d, p,** and **q** is equal to the amount of space inside the **o**, the

46

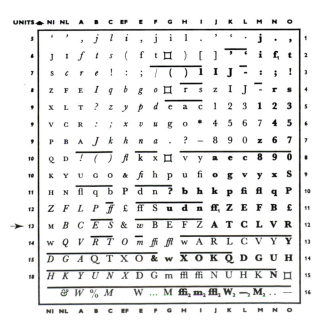

Sabon—Jan Tschichold, Stempel, 1964–67

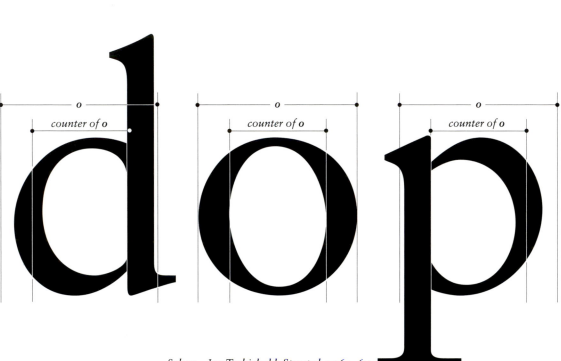

■ **Right**—*Monotype is a metal typecasting system used for over 100 years that cast indivdual letters, in contrast to Linotype's system of setting a whole line of type. This is Monotype's 16 x17 Unit-shift matrix case arrangement for Baskerville.*

■ **Above**—*Based on the width of an* **o**, *the proportion of the bowl forms* **b**, **d**, **p**, *and* **q** *are more narrow to appear the same width. The amount will vary from font to font, roman to italic, light to boldface. In condensed faces there is scant distinction, and in some flat-sided sans serifs, the proportions are equal.*

letters will not have the same color and must be reshaped. Because the e is a partially open shape, it admits more space and will appear more visually open than the o. The bar carries some authority, but more often the e should be narrowed. Its proportion relies on the thickness and placement of the bar. If the bar is high—that is, well above center—and the lower right tip placement is normal, the e will appear wider than a traditionally drawn e. A lowercase c, more open than the e, is sometimes drawn with an additional reduction in width. Some digital fonts retain their original machine unit proportions, at times to their detriment. Digital technology permits a letter of any desired proportion, widths may vary, sometimes to enhance legibility or to add a distinctive quality to otherwise pedestrian shapes. Proportions also vary within families, from light to extra-bold weights, but letter widths for a rock star's logo, a trendy boutique, or an international conglomerate are not bound by rigid rules and require different judgments.

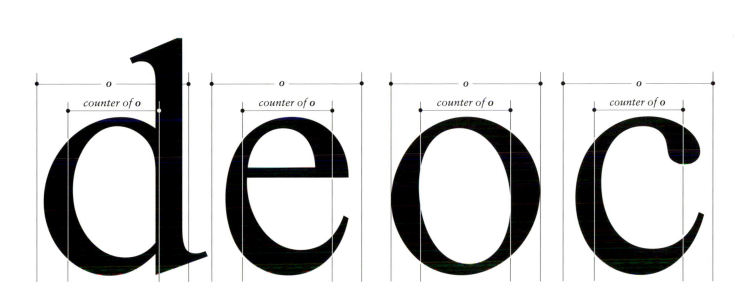

Times New Roman—Stanley Morison and Victor Lardent, Monotype, 1932

An overlapped o and l will not produce a bowl letter of even color. The distribution of weight and negative area must be refigured

Sabon

Proportions are dependent on visually admitted white space. In a traditional two-weight serif text face the letters are drawn to color equally. When a letter is too wide or too narrow, the font is said to color unevenly.

SERIF LETTERS

Generalizations often deceive, yet font serif designs were similar up to the time of Bodoni's 1818 *Tipographia Manuale.* Most were chunky and stubby with strong brackets to endure; soft metals were used in types of the day. There are four general kinds of serifs: horizontal, vertical, slanted, and triangular. In the eighteenth century, in the refined hands of Bodoni and Baskerville, serif shapes grew sleek and delicate. Bodoni's were hairlines, while Baskerville cut some of his with slim isosceles triangles. Depending on the font, vertical serifs occur on the center arms of the E and F. Serifs that are attached to the top and bottom arms of the **E**, **F**, **T**, and **Z** are called beaks; beaks also occur on the **C**, **G**, and **S** (pages 50–51). Slanted serifs are found in many text faces: Bembo, Bookman, Century Oldstyle, and Tiffany (a Modern font with references

48

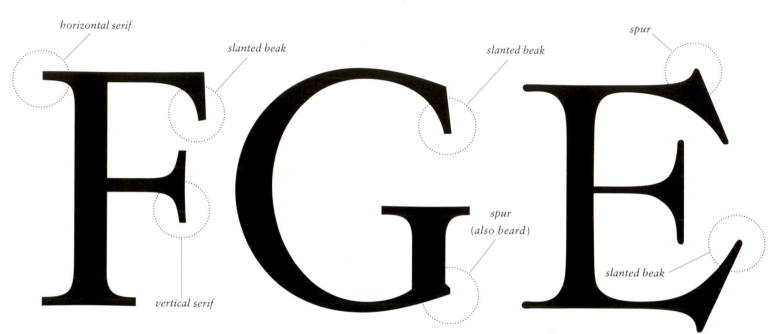

Tiffany light—Ed Benguiat, ITC, 1974

ABDEFGHIJKLMNPRTUVWXY
hklmnpqrtuvwxyz

Sabon—Jan Tschichold, Stempel, 1964–67

Original Bodoni capitals from his later period, in the Manuale Tipographia of 1818

ITC New Baskerville—G. W. Jones, 1926 (Linotype revised in 1978)

to Litho Roman and Engravers Roman, which emulates the delicate, engraved fonts of steel die engraving). The early serifed faces were drawn with lowercase ascenders that are topped by triangular serifs; **b, d, h, k,** and **l.** Descenders of the **p** and **q** were finished with a horizontal, while some Venetian types topped the **u** with triangular serifs, whose tips can be shortened only by decreasing the underside of the triangle. Triangular serifs are usually drawn with the same angle. Horizontal serifs of the Venetians and Oldstyles are often sturdy and amply bracketed, tapering to stubby, blunted points. Their widths are consistent, though some of the newer versions are elongated. Centaur's serifs are longer to fill the open space at the baseline of the **F, P,** and **r** (*below*). Lettered serifs may be varied in length to improve awkward spaces.

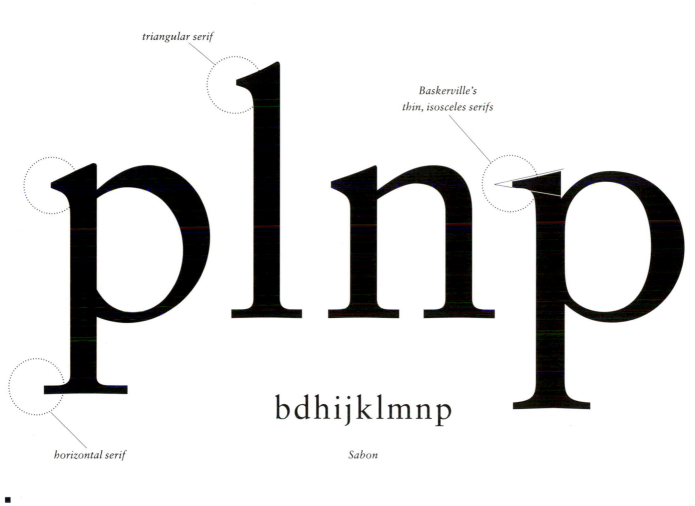

triangular serif

Baskerville's thin, isosceles serifs

horizontal serif

bdhijklmnp

Sabon

■ **Opposite top**—*Except for the* **O, C, Q,** *and* **S,** *horizontal serifs occur on all of the capitals of Oldstyle fonts. With the exception of the* **d,** *and* **u** *in some fonts, horizontal serifs occur at the baseline of lowercase vertical stems. Vertical serifs occur on the arms of the* **E** *and* **F.** **Bottom**—*Beak and vertical serif angle variations.*

■ *Triangular serifs top Oldstyle ascenders and all straight stems at x-height. On the Humanist or fifteenth-century Venetian faces, their angles are stubby. Triangular serifs became more refined in the hands of Bodoni and Baskerville.*

F. P. r. *F. P.*

Centaur—Bruce Rogers, Monotype, 1929

Robert Slimbach's Jenson with chunky, stubby triangular serifs

**Beaks, Spurs,
and Vertical Serifs**

As noted previously, beaks are small, pointed, triangular shapes attached to the thin-line endings of C, E, F, G, L, S, T, and Z. On the center arms of the E and F they are called vertical serifs. Beaks may be slanted as on most Oldstyles, or vertical, as on the Transitionals and Moderns. Monotype lumps their description under beaks, and Hermann Zapf says that in Germany they are simply called endings, or top and lower serifs. They are derived from the short calligraphic strokes designed to add mass to the airy parts of letters to produce even color in thick and thin fonts. Top and bottom beaks may have different angles: note that the Sabon E's top beak is vertical and the F's beak angular. Monotype's version are parallel with only a minute angle. Nor do the angles of the T relate to the E or S. This creates a lively quality in text type, but the disparity can be disturbing in larger sizes.

slanted beaks (Oldstyle)

vertical beak (Modern)

Adobe Sabon

Bauer Bodoni

arm

vertical serif

vertical serif

arm

Monotype Sabon

Adobe Sabon

Adobe Sabon

Beaks may be vertical or slanted, and at different angles, sometimes all in the same font. Oldstyle fonts often have rounded tips, though the digital drawings of Sabon are squared; Transitionals and Moderns are either pointed or squared off. Note that the 150 point Monotype, and 150 point Adobe Sabon types are not the same size.

Garamond indulged in poetic license and drew his cap **T** arms with different beak angles. In Transitional and Modern fonts, beaks of the **C**, **G**, and **S** are more fussy and have a small pointed spur, a remnant of the vertical stroke with its angled ends. Bruce Rogers modeled his Centaur cap

beak shape on Jenson's roman. The shape does not color as evenly as the older, simplified form, although its delicate modeling does add sparkle. The spur lends life to the forms, or "energetic repose." [1] Beaks may vary in size from letter to letter and from font to font—there are no set rules,

besides the type designer's esthetic. But congestion occurs if the **E** and **F**'s vertical serifs are too long. The **L**'s beak can be a generous height, a helpful space filler for the most troublesome letter combination of all: **LA.**

1. Robert Bringhurst, *The Elements of Typographic Style*, page 67.

spur

beak

spur, also beard　　*Centaur*

Jenson, 1470–76

spur

ITC New Baskerville

*The **T**'s beaks have different angles*

ITC Garamond light

Monotype Century Schoolbook

Top—Bruce Rogers based his Centaur on Jenson's classic 1470 font.
Center—Baskerville refined the points and Tony Stan's Garamond for ITC employs the same shapes as Sabon,

but follows Garamond with two slightly different angled serifs for the cap **T**.
Bottom—Century Schoolbook beaks are lengthy with varied angles.

SERIF LETTERS

Two design features quickly identify an Oldstyle face: triangular serifs and diagonal stress in all curved shapes. Both are evidence that the fonts evolved from writing with a flat instrument held at 15 to 30 degrees from the horizontal. The broad-pen or flat brush angle is some- what constant, and the movement of the writing instrument produces its curved shapes. The left side of a circle will be a crescent shape that has its widest area drawn below a lateral center line. A right-hand crescent is widest above the lateral center line. A straight or diagonal stem's begin- ning and ending reveal the angle at which the pen was held. Note the diagonal centerline of the cs and o, which similarly reflects the perpendicular angle of the pen.

If a pen is moved downward to the left at its beginning, and then back to the right and down with a curve, a triangular serif

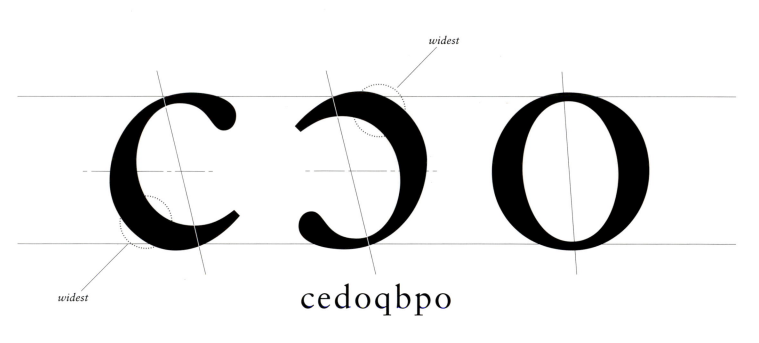

widest

widest

cedoqbpo

Sabon—Jan Tschichold, Stempel, 1964–67

The calligraphic origins of Oldstyle fonts are revealed in the curves that produce an **o** and all of the lowercase bowl shapes: **b**, **d**, **p**, and **q**. This is charac- terized by a widening below a horizon- tal centerline on a left-hand curve and above a horizontal center line center- line on a right-hand curve. But note that the counter of the **o** has a more vertical thrust than the bowl letters.

results. From these simple motions, some of the world's greatest and most enduring fonts have been drawn. Some designs cling to the original nature of the strokes, while others model them with nuance and finesse. Endless variation is possible. To this day fonts are designed making use of these centuries-old forms. The Jenson **z**, for example, clearly reveals its calligraphic origins. Held at a consistent angle that produces the other letters, the broad-pen creates a horizontally weighted stroke and a thin diagonal downstroke that is calligraphically correct, but this places the weight in an unwanted area, at the x-height and the baseline, which are normally thin-stroke areas. Sabon, a calligraphically based font, ignores the correct action of the pen and transposes the weights: thin at top and bottom with a weighted diagonal so that its center of mass corresponds to the alphabet's general distribution of weights.

Times New Roman's **Z**s are weighted on the diagonal, but revert to the thin diagonal calligraphic form for the regular and bold lowercase italic.

bdhijlmnpru

Jenson—Robert Slimbach, Adobe Systems, 1995   *Sabon*

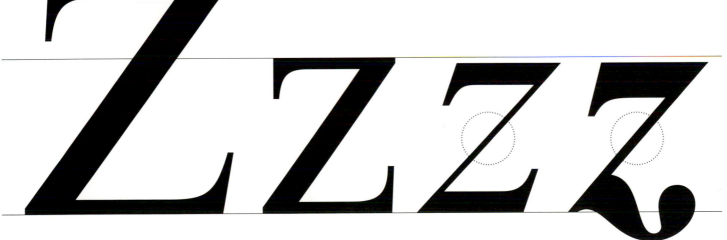

Times New Roman—Stanley Morison & Victor Lardent, Monotype, 1932   *Bold*

■

The angle of the **u**'s triangular serifs reflects Jenson's calligraphic origins. The shapes have been gently modified, but the serif's bracketed turn on the left stem is a true calligraphic stroke that reflects the pen's angle. The weights of the diagonal of the cap and lowercase roman **Z**s have been transposed, but are left in their original calligraphic placement in the lowercase italic **z**. Note that the Times New Roman bold italic **z** is drawn with a baseline swash.

S E R I F   L E T T E R S

Terminals

Terminals may be either a ball, teardrop, or a wedge shape that reveals the edge of the broad-pen. The early Venetian fonts and the Garamond show a simple wedge pen downstroke (*below, top row*). The shape appears on **c, f, j, r, y,** and, in some cases the italic *c, f, g, j, k, r, s, v, w, x,* and *y.* Later,

Caslon and Baskerville chose a teardrop and added more weight. In the nineteenth century, Bodoni drew a circular shape and bracketed it into his fine hairlines. In the 1950s Freeman Craw used a lateral ellipse for his Craw Modern. Terminals help fill the large negative areas of the letters **a, c,**

and **r.** Some designers draw a generous weighted curve at the top of the **a.** Jenson did this and Zapf added a minute downstroke to his Palatino. Eric Gill ignored the idea and left the top stroke bare on his Perpetua **a;** Richard Isbell reverted to the original pen wedge shape for his 1967 Americana.

Bembo   *Jenson*   *Centaur*   *Adobe Garamond*

Adobe Caslon   *ITC New Baskerville*   *Bauer Bodoni*   *Craw Modern bold*

Jenson—original 1470 font   *Palatino*   *Perpetua*   *Americana*

■

Ball terminals are derived from calligraphic return strokes and their shapes may reflect pen strokes, be modeled, and with refinement become elegant

*teardrop shapes. The modern versions dispense with history and are based on Bodoni's circular shapes. The Sabon **g**'s ear is a modeled calligraphic stroke, and*

Many Modern faces employ a similar teardrop shape on the top right side of the bowl on the lowercase **g**. In this position it is called an *ear* and usually points toward the next letter; the repose of some is horizontal. Times New Roman and Sabon adhere to the straight bar; Baskerville has a slim teardrop. Terminal shapes vary: often they are weighted to match the stem and curved stems. Note the calligraphic branch of the Sabon *r*. There is no rule for the use of a specific shape, but a choice may reference a historical period and suggest that type design is a process of melding.

Sabon   *Sabon*   *Sabon*

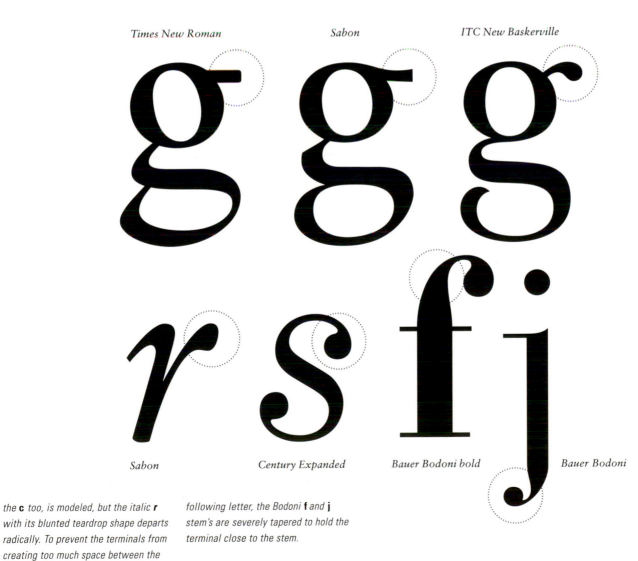

Times New Roman   *Sabon*   *ITC New Baskerville*

Sabon   *Century Expanded*   *Bauer Bodoni bold*   *Bauer Bodoni*

the **c** too, is modeled, but the italic **r** with its blunted teardrop shape departs radically. To prevent the terminals from creating too much space between the following letter, the Bodoni **f** and **j** stem's are severely tapered to hold the terminal close to the stem.

SERIF LETTERS

"Kern" is from the French *carne* and means projecting angle, or nib of a quill pen. It also means kernel, which the teardrop shape resembles. The word is found in several languages; it is used now as a verb meaning to move closer. The *Oxford English Dictionary* in previous printing terms defines kern as "a part of a metal type projecting beyond the body or shank, as the curled head of f and tail of j, as formerly made, and parts of some italic letters." Originally, hand-set metal type fs were designed with a gracefully curved terminal that projected from the right-hand edge of the type's face and counter. To fit some letters together comfortably, typographers cut portions of the metal sort away with a mortising machine—a painstaking and costly process. Computer programs allow letters to be kerned, meaning that one letter or character may invade the space of another. In the original

56

f kerned into the i space, or character cell   *fi ligature*

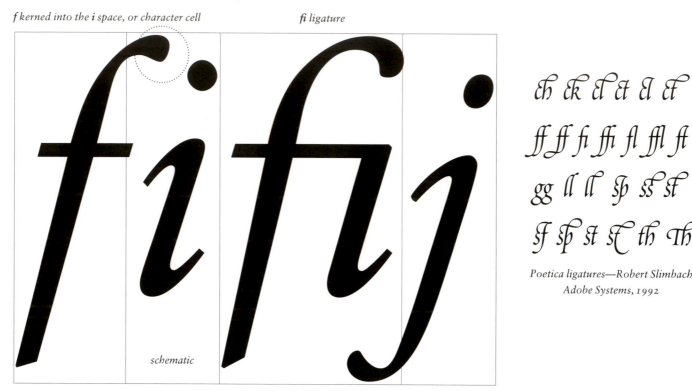

schematic

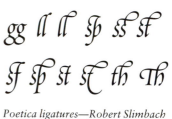

*Poetica ligatures—Robert Slimbach
Adobe Systems, 1992*

Sabon—Jan Tschichold, Stempel, 1964–67   *Garamond*

Sabon   *Adobe Garamond—Robert Slimbach,
Adobe Systems, 1989*

definition, only a few letters have projecting parts; the computer kerning is but tighter spacing between specific pairs.

Special ligatures (from Latin *ligatus*, to tie, bind; sometimes called tied letters) were available to avoid the troublesome combinations: **ff, fi, fl, ffi**, and **ffl**.

Poetica has abundant ligatures (*opposite*). Ligatures are often needed in tightly spaced hand-lettered logotypes to close up an unwanted space: **ty, rt, vy**, etc. The disadvantage is that often the join becomes a bull's-eye that is worse than the misspacing. Kerning programs permit

the user to kern an entire font—often too tightly. **FA, TA, AW, WA, VA, YA, Fo, To, Wo, Yo**, and other combinations are enhanced by kerning.

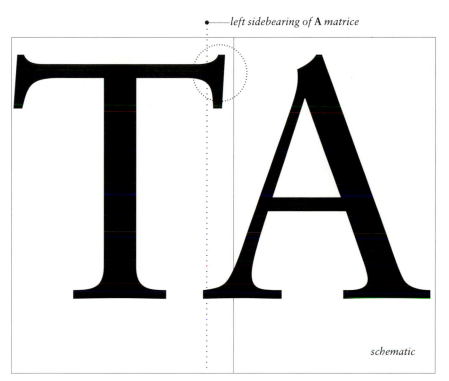

*left sidebearing of **A** matrice*

schematic

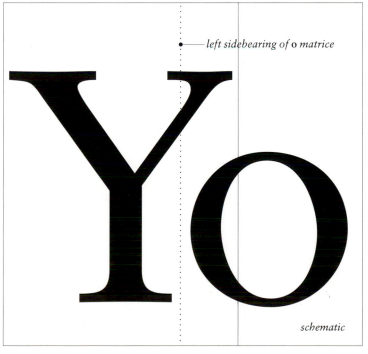

*left sidebearing of **o** matrice*

schematic

Sabon

Metal font designers extended the terminal of the **f**, a protuberance from the right-hand edge of a metal sort called a "kern," to let it rest on top of the counter of the following letter for tighter spacing. Computer kerning programs now allow individual letters to invade a following letter's matrix.

Ligatures were also designed to alleviate troublesome spacing combinations: **ff, fi, fl, ffi**, and **ffl**. Poetica has abundant ligatures, but Gutenberg designed the first ones to occupy less space in a long line so that the text could be justified without excessive word spacing. Some were designed to improve the appearance of awkward combinations. Updike lists: **as, is, us, ct, fr, ll, sp, st, tt**, as typical, but the more familiar ones are: **fi, ffi, ffl, ct**, and **st**.

S E R I F L E T T E R S

The ogee curve is a beautiful shape and it abounds in nature. William Hogarth, an eighteenth-century painter, engraver, and chronicler of the passing parade, called the ogee curve "Line of Beauty," which served as the basis of his series of prints "The Analysis of Beauty." [1] (*See* page 235.)

The Romans recognized the ogee's sensuous grace and devised architectural moldings of reverse curves to hide construction imperfections, creating graceful bands of light and shadow that in essence "broke the light." Type designers have found the ogee indispensable,

and the shape appears in different degrees of tautness in roman, italic, and script forms.

The weighted, diagonal curve of the **s** is called a spine. If the **S** is drawn as a symmetrical shape, the top curve will appear larger than the bottom one. In normal text fonts, therefore, the spine is

58

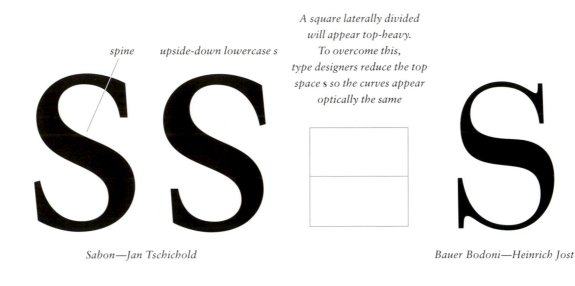

spine   upside-down lowercase s

*A square laterally divided will appear top-heavy. To overcome this, type designers reduce the top space **s** so the curves appear optically the same*

Sabon—Jan Tschichold

Bauer Bodoni—Heinrich Jost

ITC Modern No. 216 medium—Ed Benguiat   *Century Expanded—Morris Fuller Benton*

ITC New Baskerville—George W. Jones

■
Ss and **g**s are drawn with ogee-shaped reverse curves. The main portion of the spine may be constantly weighted like the Sabon **S** shown here, or the curve may taper in both directions from the

widest point. The ogee curve was widely used on the Modern italics of the nineteenth century and made its way into Benton's Century Expanded.

drawn a bit above center so that the bottom of the S is slightly larger than the top. This is apparent when the S is upside-down.

The S spine is sometimes drawn as a shape that rapidly diminishes its weight top and bottom, at 10 and 4 o'clock— the Bauer Bodoni is an example.

Fonts are commonly drawn with the spine as a constant weighted form with more weight around the left top side, and bottom right side so that it will color evenly— the S of Sabon follows this scheme (*opposite*). The g's link and loop usually are drawn with the ogee curve, and the curve is

a distinguishing characteristic of the nineteenth-century Modern italics *h, i, k, m, n, u, v, w, y,* and *z*. Century expanded is a descendant.

1. Ronald Paulson, *Hogarth's Graphic Works* (London: The Print Room, 1989).

ITC New Baskerville—George W. Jones, Linotype, 1926

ITC New Baskerville

■

These Baskerville italic letters are from a later period on which Tschichold based his Sabon forms, and show a different concept in the distribution of weight along the reverse axis of the curve. The forms are more taut, and the

top and bottom swelling strokes of the z are voluptuous. Baskerville follows the calligraphic form for the italic z and the constant weighted diagonal for the roman z.

SERIF LETTERS

Type historians call the round shapes of the letters shown below *bowls*, but I prefer that name for the **o** portion of the lowercase **g**, and like the word *lobe* instead. Though *Webster's Third New International Dictionary of the English Language Unabridged* and the *Oxford English Diction-*

ary define a lobe as a rounded projection, they deign not a single letterform reference.

Bowls occur in our uppercase alphabet on the letters **B, D, P, R**, and in the lowercase on the **a, b, d, p,** and **q**. The bowls of the **B** are required to accomplish two tasks: first their volume must

optically relate to similar forms, and a balance of the two shapes must be considered. If both bowls are drawn the same size, the top one will appear wider and taller than the lower one, and the letter will appear top heavy. To achieve optical balance, the lower bowl must

60

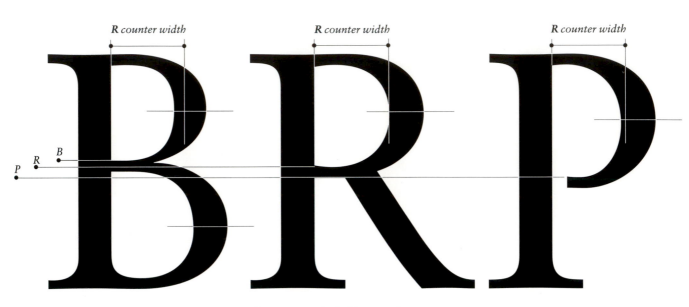

Sabon—Jan Tschichold, Stempel, 1964–67

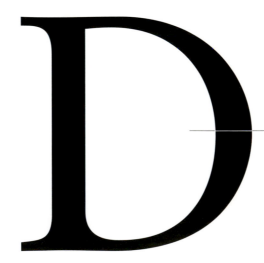

Sabon's bowls are widest at mid-point, opposed to Palatino and Trajan's off-center weight distribution

Sabon

■

Though related, the bowls of the **B**, **R**, and **P** have different widths and heights to balance the vertical space of the total letter. These dimensions vary from font to font. The calligraphic structure of the bowls is more evident in Palatino and Trajan; Sabon distributes their weight or thickness symmetrically.

extend to the right-hand edge of the top shape. Where the two bowls converge, the horizontal thin stroke must be drawn slightly above the horizontal centerline so as to appear centered.

In many cases the bowl of the **R** joins at a lower point on the vertical stem than the **B** to help fill the open space at bottom, while the **P** joins even lower for the same reason—though its width is narrowed to match the **R**'s volume (the Trajan is an exception). Oldstyle forms favor a **P** with a bowl that does not connect to the stem at the bottom. The design feature varies. The major weight distribution of the bowls is placed above center, and references their calligraphic origins. Palatino does this, but Sabon chooses a centered placement with the widest portion of the lobes dead center on the symmetrically curved **B**, **D**, **P**, and **R**. Carol Twombly's Trajan, more classical in spirit than Sabon or Palatino, follows the original weight distribution but draws the bowl of the **R** more deeply than the **P** to faithfully recall its heritage.

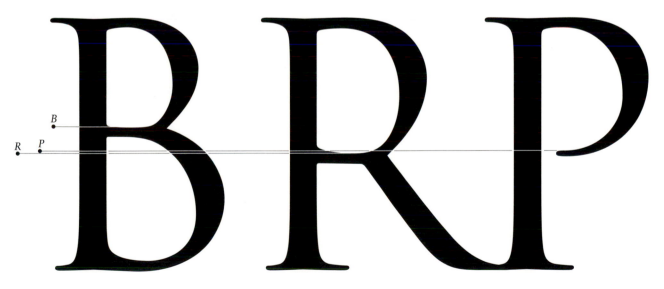

Palatino—Hermann Zapf, Stempel, 1948

Trajan—Carol Twombly, Adobe Systems, 1989

Lowercase bowls optically relate in volume—the **b**, **d**, **p**, **q** are invariably drawn equal width, because the **b** and **p** are the same shape, though inverted; flopped they create the **d** and **q**, though their horizontal and triangular serifs are switched. Eric Gill laterally flopped Perpetua's **b** to form the **d**, which he then inverted to create the **q**. In maverick fashion, he drew a differently shaped **p**, which appears to be a wrong font character. As a group, bowls are designed to optically color the same as the branch forms, *h*, *m*, *n*, and *u*. The **a** is an anomaly; its bowl is drawn with a much different shape than the quartet, yet it too must color equally. In some Oldstyles it is a rather narrow shape, but in Sabon it is more generous with an overall width that matches the **o**. Often the **a**'s bowl departs at half the height of the vertical stem, and depending on the

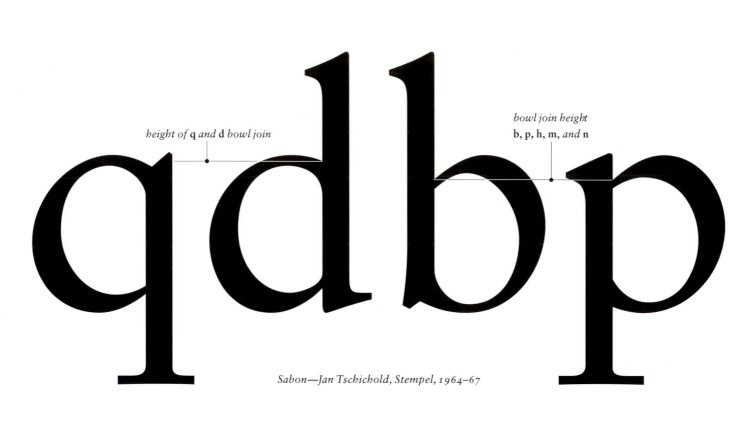

height of **q** *and* **d** *bowl join*

bowl join height
b, p, h, m, *and* **n**

Sabon—Jan Tschichold, Stempel, 1964–67

Perpetua—Eric Gill, Monotype, 1925–30

■
*With the exception of the **a**, all bowls contain the same amount of negative area or counters but have different orientations. In Oldstyles the join is deeper on the **b** and **p** but higher on the **d** and **q**. The bowl of the **a** usually departs at half the x-height with the same angle as the initial vertical calligraphic stroke, 15 to 30 degrees from the horizontal. The departing stroke is invariably thin where it joins at the lower position on the stem near the baseline. Perpetua has a different bowl scheme and draws the **p** differently.*

weight of the top teardrop kern, its width will vary. These bowl shapes are derived from the angle of the writing instrument that produced them. The Venetians and Oldstyle faces reflect this calligraphic structure, that is, they are drawn with a flat or chisel instrument held roughly at 15 to 30 degrees from the horizontal, which produces the widest part of a left-hand curve below lateral center and above center on a right-hand curve. Their joining height to the vertical stems is consistent and depends on whether the bowl is a left- or right-hand curve. Type designers are rarely content to use the direct results of a broad-pen, and often alter their shapes to achieve a preconceived distribution of weight or letter mass.

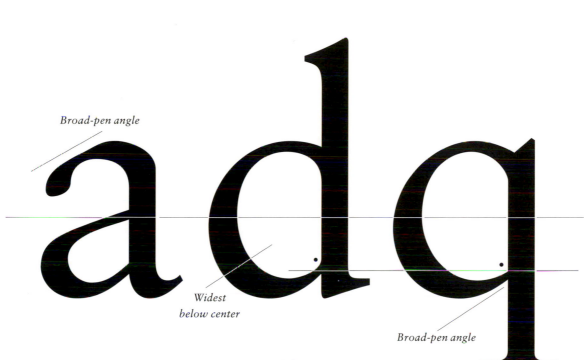

Broad-pen angle

Widest below center

Broad-pen angle

Sabon

Design idiosyncrasies abound in type design. Compare the lower join position of the **d** with the lower join of the **q** and its more flattened curve.

SERIF LETTERS

I have chosen to show a few letters at a large size to enable the reader to more clearly realize their shapes and to see the design subtleties that are necessary to make a good letter (**A**, **X**, **g**, **&**). Of great concern in the design of letters is the distribution and division of negative areas. Optical illusions also play a great part in the design of a successful letter.

In Oldstyle fonts the **A**'s shape is distinctive, usually drawn with three weights: a bold right-hand stem; a thin left-hand diagonal; and a bar of an intermediate weight. All three strokes are based on the angle at which a pen is held: 15 to 30 degrees from the horizontal.

The Romans were practical. They devised a scheme from which the alphabet could be simply constructed by stone cutters. The basic unit is the square, or *quadrato*, from the Latin word that means "square." One-third of

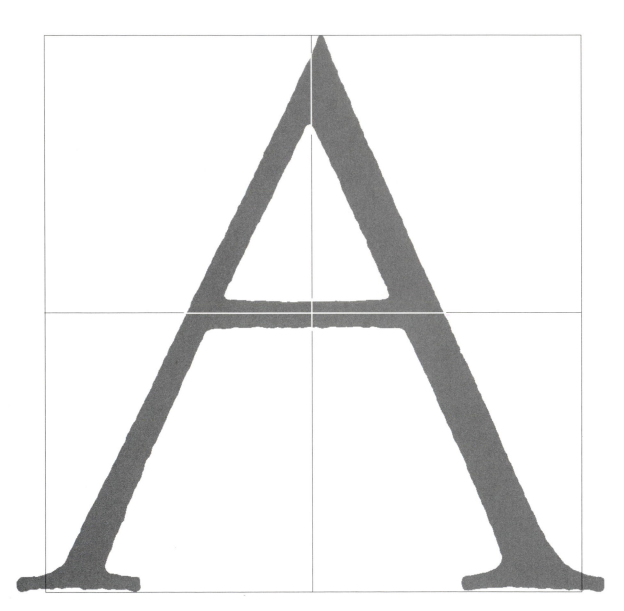

Michelangelo Titling (greatly enlarged)—Hermann Zapf, Stempel, 1949–50

Palatino

the capital alphabet is made up of triangles, an important group. The **A**'s construction is loosely based on a square divided vertically and horizontally. A triangle is constructed within the square that touches the lower corners and the point hits dead center at the top; a crossbar connects the diagonals at half the square's height.

A classicist, Hermann Zapf touched the horizontal centerline with the top of the crossbar of his Palatino. But an equal lateral division does not look equally divided, so designers of Transitional and Modern fonts lowered the bar to optically divide the space in half. Trajan, a classical letterform, drops the crossbar slightly. Angles of the Sabon **A** are mirror images; Palatino's right-hand stem is more steep than the left side, an idiosyncratic impulse based on written forms and the designer's judgment. Contemporary sans serifs, which borrow heavily from forms of the nineteenth century, employ an optically equal division of the space. Paul Renner chose a placement slightly below center for his classically proportioned Futura, which still gives the illusion of an optical center division.

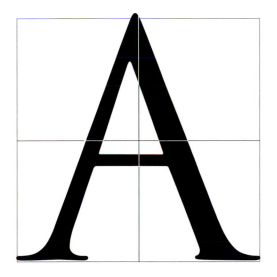

Sabon—Jan Tschichold, Stempel, 1964–67

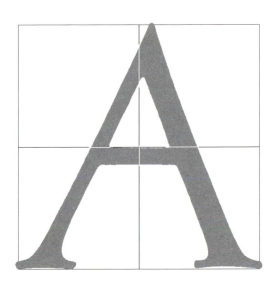

Palatino—Hermann Zapf, Stempel, 1948
(enlarged)

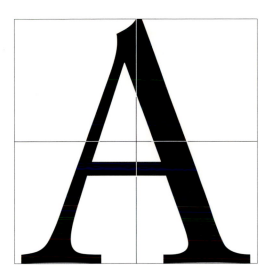

Trajan—Carol Twombly, Adobe Systems, 1989

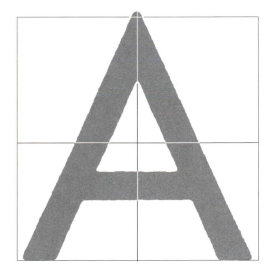

Futura medium—Paul Renner, Bauer, 1927–30
(enlarged)

■

*The Greeks and Romans loosely based their first letter on a square divided vertically and laterally—a modified inverted symbol of an oxen. Many Oldstyle fonts follow this general construction. Sabon places the crossbar of the **A** a bit below mathematical center, but still not optically center. Palatino raises the crossbar so that its top edge is tangent to the center of the square, a more classical division of space. Its sister titling face (a capitals-only font that fills the type matrix), Michelangelo, raises the crossbar even more (opposite).*

X is troublesome to draw. Like other capitals that beg a lateral division, **A**, **B**, **E**, **F**, **K**, **P**, **R**, **S**, and **Y**, it too must be adjusted to fool the eye. Drawn as a symmetrical shape, the top triangle will appear larger and wider than the bottom triangle. To compensate, the bottom triangle is drawn minutely wider so as to have the same optical width and volume. If divided in half, the point of crossing will also appear below center and make the **X** undesirably top-heavy. As an optical effect bends a half-submerged stick, so does perception fool the eye when a diagonal crosses a diagonal. A thin stroke appears to shift as it crosses a weighted diagonal; to compensate, the right-hand, thin stroke may be shifted minutely downward as in Sabon and Baskerville (*opposite*). The thins may be a slightly weighted tapering stem to make the letter color more evenly. Bold fonts

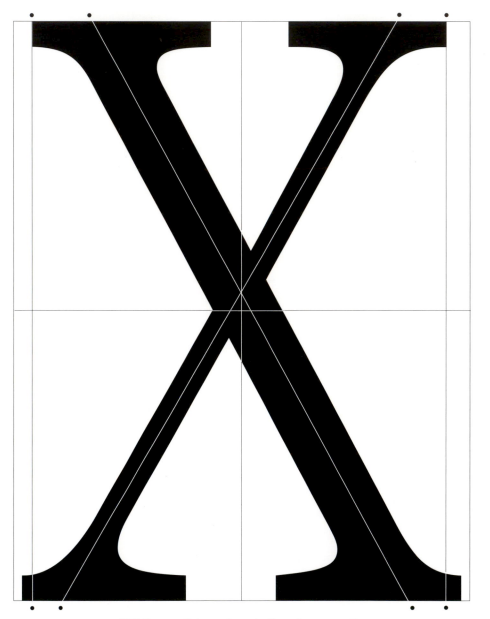

ITC Century light condensed—Tony Stan, 1975–80

require more adjustment, and bold sans serifs, extreme compensation (*see* page 139).

The roman lowercase x follows the same rules, as does the italic. All of the shapes, roman or italic, must have a centerline that divides the negative space of each triangle, or the x will appear tilted. Because its basic shape admits much negative area, it is difficult to space within flanking letters, and in large hand-lettered sizes its serifs are often shortened, more on the outside of the letter than in the interior or counter space.

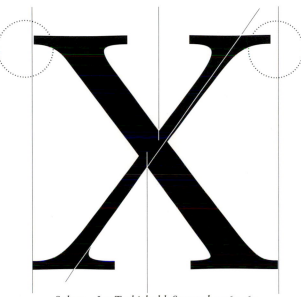

Sabon—Jan Tschichold, Stempel, 1964–67

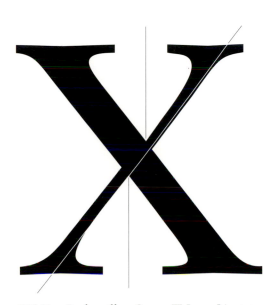

ITC New Baskerville—George W. Jones, Linotype, 1926

Sabon

■

To appear balanced, an **x** must cross above mathematical center, so that the bottom triangle will be larger, even in the italic form. In two-weight serif romans the top right thin stroke can be shifted downward so as to appear a continuous line, a nuance not offered in the Sabon lowercase italic **x**.

SERIF LETTERS

In many text fonts the g's ear is drawn entirely with curves. In the Oldstyles and Venetians, it is usually horizontal, or oblique straight lines. With the exception of the Arrighi italic that accompanies Centaur, the ear is attached to the bowl in an upper right-hand position. Sabon has a rather evenly-weighted stroke that flares at its tip. The natural diagonal ending is chopped vertically. Transitional and Modern fonts opt for a slender teardrop that from font to font slides up and down the top right-side of the bowl from 1 to 2 o'clock. Both Baskerville and Bauer Bodoni's ears are low and appear to visually slip. Some contemporary fonts position the ear in a sprightly upright position at the apex of the bowl. This position has been favored by hand-letterers because spacing can then be tighter. In a text setting this position makes the ear appear to

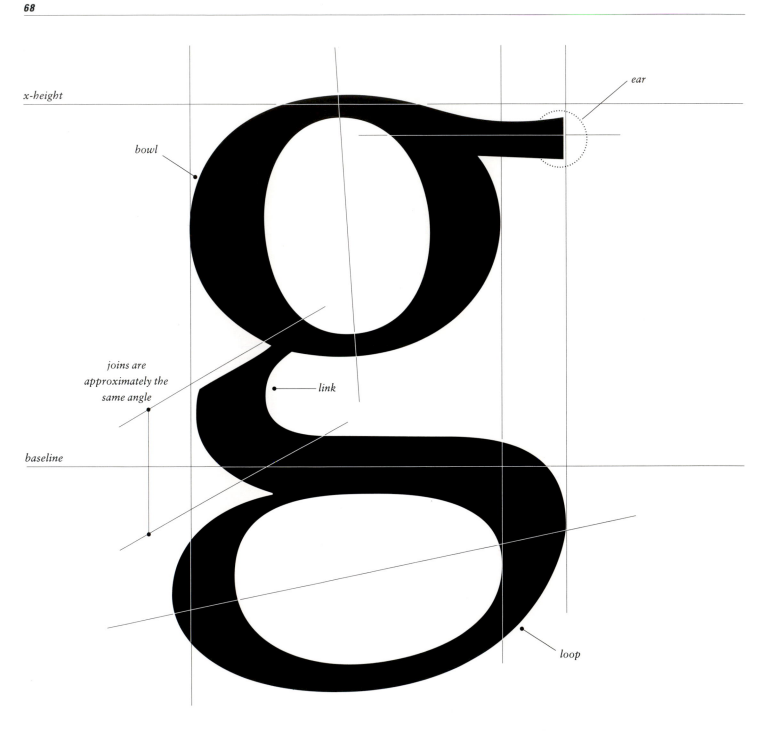

Sabon—Jan Tschichold, Stempel, 1964–67

wave—an annoying distraction. The bowl is not a reduced lowercase **o,** because that would make the letter color more darkly than the other letters. Instead, the shape is made wider to let in more air, to match the color of the **n/o** proportional scheme. The relative height of the bowl is a challenge. The greater its x-height, the more space must be borrowed from the enclosed loop. Fonts with short descenders make the *g*'s loop appear mashed. The tail almost aligns with the ear, and the protuberant ear helps to close up the right-hand space.

If the font is Oldstyle, the bowl's counter will tilt to the left.

The angle at which the link departs from the bowl and returns to close itself is the angle at which a pen is held. The left side of the loop may extend to the left of the bowl to make a graceful shape because it is never bothered with a descender: the **q** never precedes it. Rarely is the length of the **g** descender equal to other descenders. If the bowl and loop are not carefully balanced, the **g** can become a repetitive eyesore in columns of text.

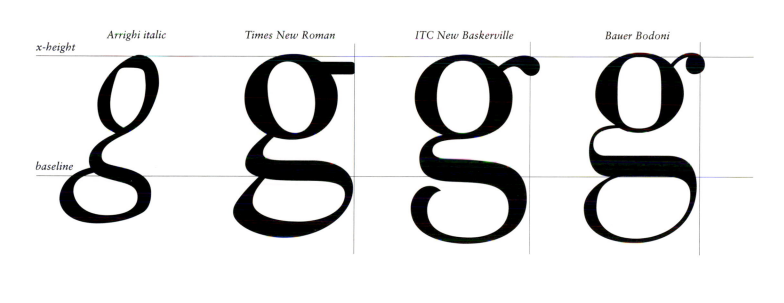

x-height · baseline

Arrighi italic · *Times New Roman* · *ITC New Baskerville* · *Bauer Bodoni*

Sabon

■ Bowls of the **g** may occupy different amounts of the x-height, which greatly influences the size of the descending tail. The straight ear is found on the Oldstyles and the teardrop/circle on the Transitional and Modern fonts. Arrighi italic, designed by Frederic Warde to accompany Bruce Rogers's Centaur, a calligraphic font, dispenses with the ear entirely.

The bowl of the **g** is seldom a reduced lowercase **o** because that would make the letter too dark. Instead, it is a wide ellipse, and in Oldstyle fonts its axis is tilted; Transitional and Modern fonts rely on vertical stress.

SERIF LETTERS

The **a** was derived over time by hurriedly writing the capital **A,** whose original, inverted shape was a Phoenician symbol for oxen. In thick-and-thin serif fonts it is usually a two-story shape with a bowl joined to the stem near half the x-height and parallel with the **e**'s crossbar. A typical text lowercase **a** is about the same width as an **n.** Because the two-story form is more complex than the single-story italic form, the letter tends to be darker than a font's branched forms: **h, m, n, u,** and the bowls: **b, d, p, q.**

The top curve, sometimes called the shoulder, through tra-dition, often relates to the **h, m,** and **n** branches, in an inverted position, to the **u** and tail of the **t.** Rarely is an **a**'s bowl merely a reduced **d** bowl, which will create a congested letter that needs to be widened if it is to match the volume of the other letters. Curves of the **a** bowl should bear

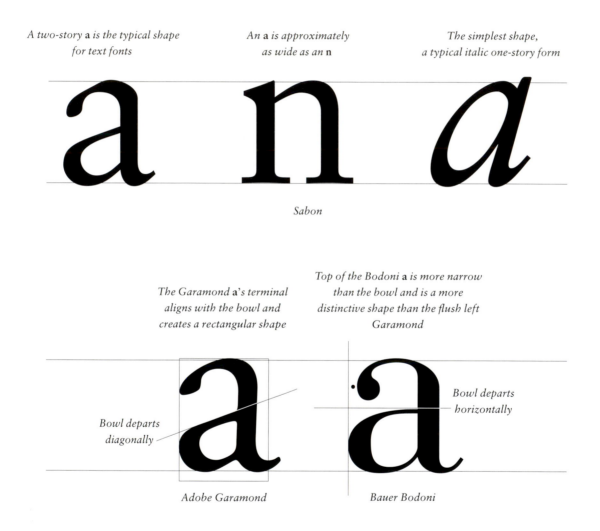

*A two-story **a** is the typical shape for text fonts*

*An **a** is approximately as wide as an **n***

The simplest shape, a typical italic one-story form

Sabon

*The Garamond **a**'s terminal aligns with the bowl and creates a rectangular shape*

*Top of the Bodoni **a** is more narrow than the bowl and is a more distinctive shape than the flush left Garamond*

Bowl departs diagonally

Bowl departs horizontally

Adobe Garamond

Bauer Bodoni

All letters are not the same point size, but have been set to the same height

■
*In many text faces the bowl of an **a** joins at half the x-height. The join near the baseline aligns with other bowls and the branch of the **u**. With rare exceptions, the two-story **a** is standard in text faces. While the one-story **a**, a simpler form, is found in most italic serif texts and some sans serif faces, it is not as distinct.*

FONTS & LOGOS

a relationship to the font's other curves whether the bowl departs horizontally, or diagonally. Where the bowl joins the vertical stem near the baseline, its point of joining should ideally line up with the font's other bowl joins; whether the vertical stem curves away as a tailed **a**, or as a footed **a**. When the top left beginning curve is a narrow shape, more air is let into the letter, and in tight settings, allows a preceding **r** to snuggle more closely: **ra**. Diotima's large bowl with its narrow, squeezed top is an example; a more distinctive shape than the rectangular shaped Garamond **a**. Terminals are used to make the letter color evenly: a circle, teardrop, or curved wedge, and these are almost always bracketed and designed to match the curve stem weight. The terminals may assume different forms, but their role is the same, to lend mass to the top leftside of the **a**.

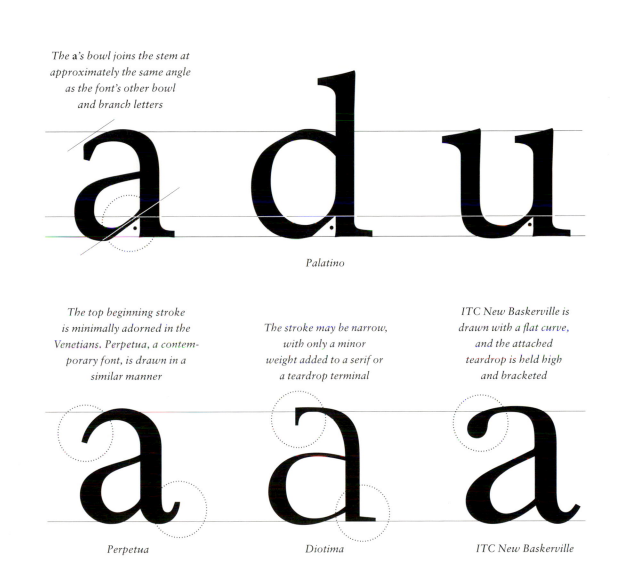

*The **a**'s bowl joins the stem at approximately the same angle as the font's other bowl and branch letters*

Palatino

The top beginning stroke is minimally adorned in the Venetians. Perpetua, a contemporary font, is drawn in a similar manner

The stroke may be narrow, with only a minor weight added to a serif or a teardrop terminal

ITC New Baskerville is drawn with a flat curve, and the attached teardrop is held high and bracketed

Perpetua

Diotima

ITC New Baskerville

The straight stem may be finished with a curved tail or be footed like Palatino or Diotima

Thin strokes breathe life into lettershapes because they create more interest than a single-weight sans serif letter. Yet thins decrease the mass of a letter and in some combinations interrupt the color of a word. This is more apparent when the type is large and combines diagonal thins, such as **KA**, **KY**, and **VA**. Even color is less problematic in the Venetians and Oldstyles because the thins are heavier, create less contrast, and appear almost monotone (Jenson, *below, top left*). The Moderns have spindly thins and unbracketed serifs, and do not color as well. Adobe Garamond, an Oldstyle, blends a generous bracketed serif well into the thin strokes to help replenish the mass. The amount of added weight varies and depends on the designer's intent. This difference is apparent in the **A** and **K**. The tapering is a welcome addition to

Jenson

Adobe Garamond—Robert Slimbach, Adobe Systems, 1989

■ To color more evenly, vertical or diagonal thin strokes of many Venetians and Oldstyle fonts have a slight addition of weight to the stroke at the juncture of a serif. Weight is then distributed in a gently tapering fashion into the stroke. Note the widened thin stroke of the **A** of both fonts as it joins the serif; it is weighted so as to give added color to the light portion of the letter. The nuance can sometimes also be found on **K**, **M**, **N**, **V**, **W**, **X**, and **Y**.

■ **Opposite**—Considered by some historians to be the first of the Moderns, Philippe Grandjean de Fouchy's *Romain du Roi* was designed for a book of medals celebrating Louis XIV's achievements. Its thin strokes are refined; there is scant bracket on the serifs. The font established the beginnings of the Modern style that culminated in Bodoni and Didot.

the diagonals, though if weighted too much, the vertical thins will produce sharp, angular stems.

Philippe Grandjean, commissioned to design an Imperial font for Louis XIV, designed 82 separate fonts for the royal printing office distinguished by spiky serifs, refined thin stems, and a horizontal x-height serif on the left side of the lowercase l, to signify a royal font.[1] Later, in attempts to design a font that would reflect the spirit of classical Greece and Rome, Bodoni and Didot independently modeled the Oldstyle fonts and refined their thin strokes. Bodoni removed the serif brackets, except in large display sizes. But Didot prefered the chilly, thin serifs even in the large sizes. The resulting letters were more minimal than classic.

1. D. B. Updike; *Printing Types, Their History, Forms and Use, A Study in Survivals,* vol. 1, page 242.

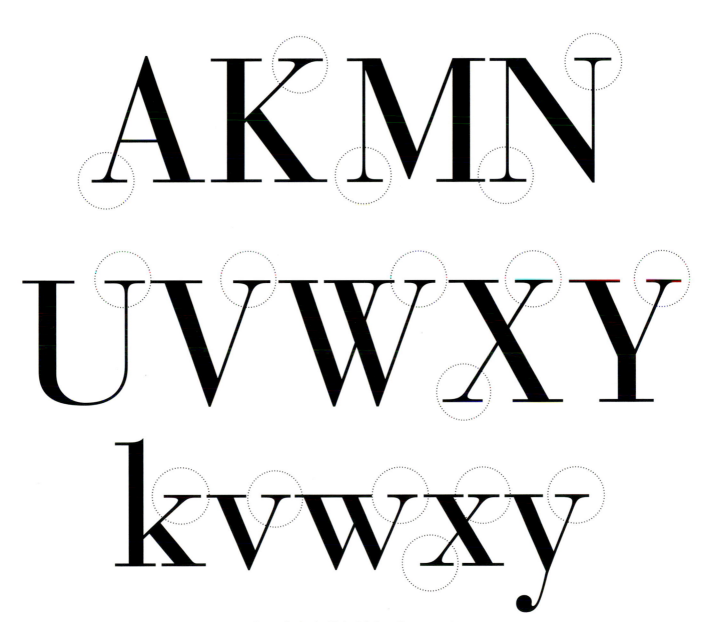

Bauer Bodoni—Heinrich Jost, Bauer, 1926

C'eſt le ſujet de cette Médaille.

Romain du Roi—Philippe Grandjean de Fouchy, Imprimerie Royale, 1702 (enlarged)
From Médailles sur les Principaux Evénements du Règne de Louis le Grand, avec des Explications Historiques. Par l'Académie Royale des Inscriptions & Médailles

SERIF LETTERS

The Romans drew the capital **E** half as wide as a square, their basic building block for the alphabet. To stabilize its shape they made the lower arm a bit longer than the top arm, and the center one a bit shorter and a tad above center. Frederic Goudy maintained that its proportion

had long been established from Egyptian pictographs, which the Greeks and Romans slavishly followed.[1]

The Sabon **E** is drawn in much the same spirit as the Trajan inscription though it is more rigid, with subtle modeling not found on the Trajan letters

whose forms are constructed with many curved lines. Generally, Venetians and Oldstyles are drawn with center arms that are long, and almost equal the length of the top and bottom arms. The Transitionals and Moderns tend to draw the center arm noticeably shorter. The **F** follows suit, but

74

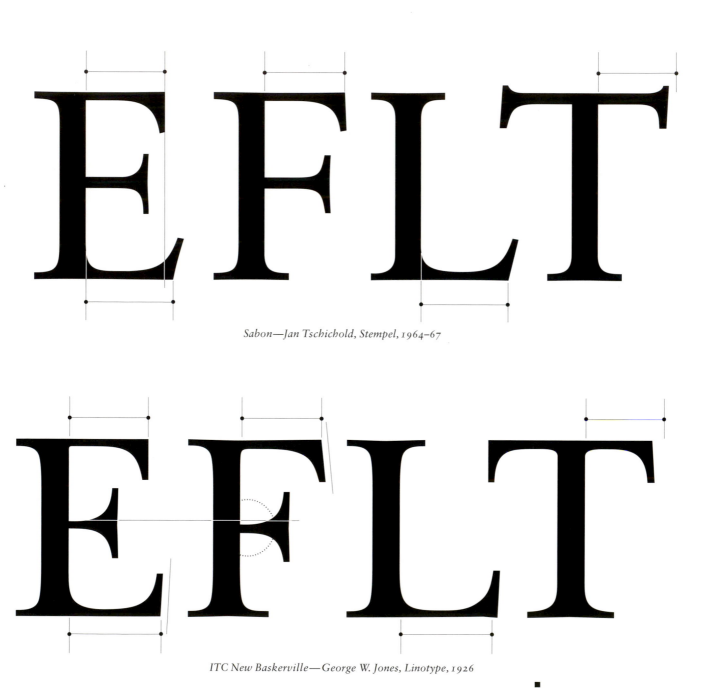

Sabon—Jan Tschichold, Stempel, 1964–67

ITC New Baskerville—George W. Jones, Linotype, 1926

■

Classical and Oldstyle proportions of the **E** *are approximately half the width of a square, and the* **F** *follows suit. The lower arm of the* **E** *is often wider than the top one to give the* **E** *a solid base. Some fonts shorten the*

since it lacks the mass of the lower arm of the **E**, the center arm of the **F** is lowered in some fonts so as to appear centered.

Compare the arm lengths of Trajan with the Oldstyle Sabon, Transitional Baskerville, and the Modern Bodoni. In Oldstyles there is often a difference in the angle of the top arm serif from the bottom arm serif—the top is steeper, and in many Bodoni versions both serifs are vertical. Hermann Zapf's Aldus, the Mergenthaler Linotype version of Palatino, dispenses with the vertical serif on both the **E** and **F** center arms, and some bold drawings of Egyptians delete the vertical serif also (*see* Serifa, Stymie, and Beton). The length of arms varies considerably from the Oldstyle to the Modern fonts.

1. Frederic Goudy, *The Capitals from the Trajan Column at Rome* (New York: Oxford University Press, 1936).

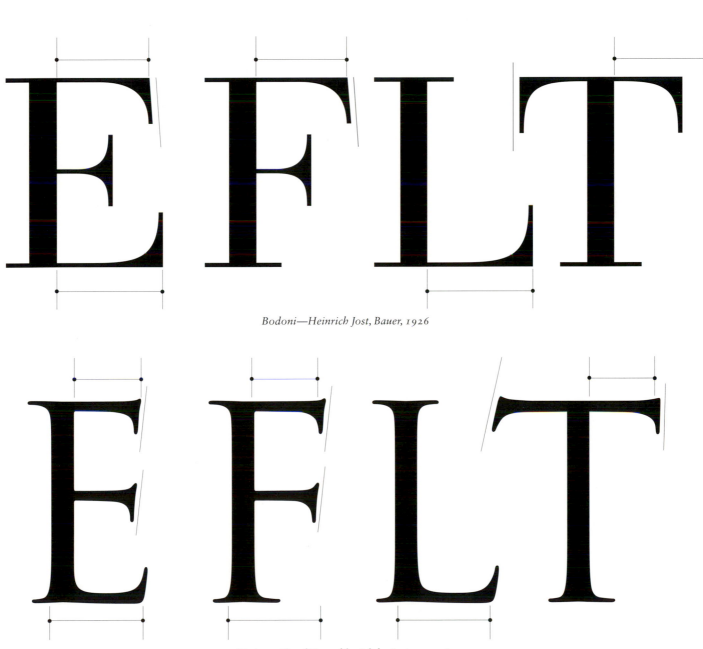

Bodoni—Heinrich Jost, Bauer, 1926

Trajan—Carol Twombly, Adobe Systems, 1989

arm of the **L** to minimize the open form. Transitional and Modern fonts draw the widths more evenly, with a shorter middle arm and often with slightly weighted vertical serifs. Note that Baskerville changes the serifs' angles, while Bodoni employs vertical serifs for the **T** and angles for the **E**. For optical centering, the Baskerville **F** lowers the center arm very slightly.

SERIF LETTERS

Calliope is the muse of epic poetry, and ampersands are the muse of alphabets when type designers compose. The structure—a ligature—is loosely based on the Latin word *et*. The italic forms, more than the upright romans, clearly reveal the shape's heritage. Some designers use a script cap **E** (Baskerville and Palatino italic), others, the lowercase **e**. Designs that pay homage to the Latin word capitalize the **T** also. Sabon has a horizontal serif as the crossbar for the capital **T**. One of the most inventive of all ampersands, Georg Trump's italic version of Trump Mediaeval, is drawn with both lowercase letters. Many contemporary fonts refuse an allusion, and end the form either with a hairline or a circular terminal, *e.g.*, Bodoni. Ampersands that are constructed with a diagonal, particularly the Oldstyles, often use an ungainly,

76

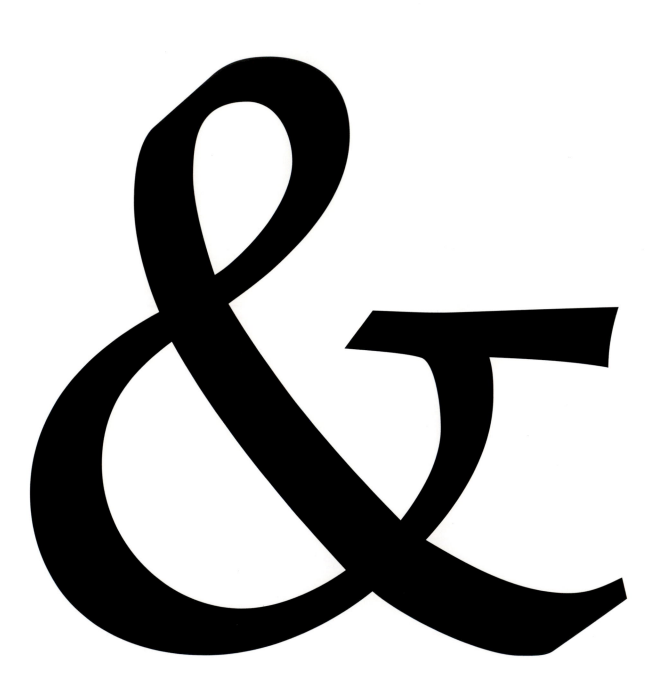

Palatino

bulging curve in the middle of the stem that keeps the counter open. The Caslon 540 italic ampersand has been a favorite with designers because of its elaborately drawn shape. Another bold example is Pistilli Roman. Zapf's Palatino italic version is a direct form, clearly defining both

the **E** and **T** in a simply drawn manner that reveals the broad-pen action. For flight of fancy, nothing measures up to Van Krimpen's Cancelleresca Bastarda, a member of the Romulus family.[1]

1. *See* Jan Tschichold, *Formenwandlungen Der Et-Zeichen* (Frankfurt am Main: Stempel Type Foundry, 1953). Tschichold's essay displays a joyful collection of 240 ampersands from the history of lettering and type.

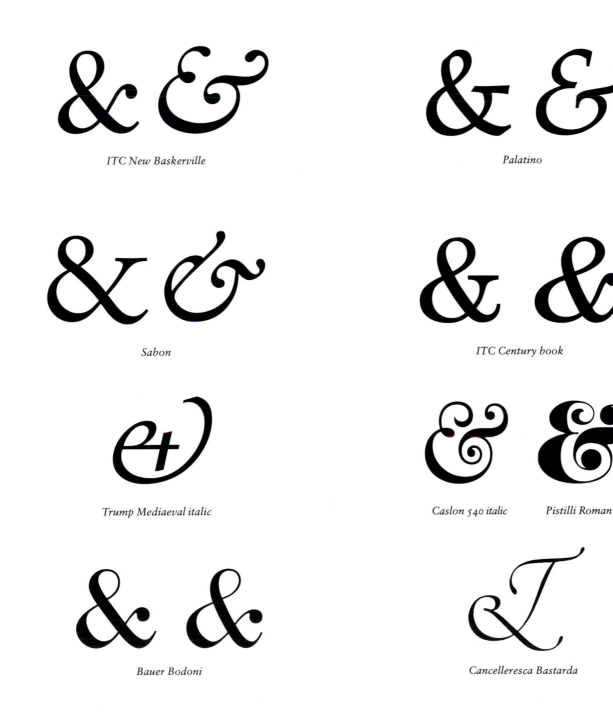

ITC *New Baskerville*

Palatino

Sabon

ITC *Century book*

Trump Mediaeval italic

Caslon 540 italic   *Pistilli Roman*

Bauer Bodoni

Cancelleresca Bastarda

■
Some ampersands reveal their descent from the Latin word **et**. *Some are drawn with a capital* **E** *in script form.*

SERIF LETTERS

Consistency is the easiest design philosophy to defend. By definition, family characteristics require consistency—the glue that holds a font together. Gut feelings are difficult to back up—articulation is needed.

Within the lowercase font, branches are one of the most important family characteristics, because they appear on one-quarter of the letters. In five instances they are at x-height, the portion of a line of type that is the most legible. The shape carries the genetic code of the alphabet's style. If the departure is a widening angular curve, it will first read as a Venetian or Oldstyle. If the branch is rounded and striving for symmetry, it belongs to the Moderns. The closer the shape relates on the various letters, the more harmonious the font will appear.

Oldstyle branches depart from stems at the same angle as

VENETIAN hmnuat

Centaur—Bruce Rogers, Monotype, 1929

In many faces, branches depart approximately where the lower angle of the triangular serif joins the stem

OLDSTYLE hmnuat

Sabon—Jan Tschichold, Stempel, 1964–67

OLDSTYLE hmnuat

Palatino—Hermann Zapf, Stempel, 1948

the basic stem: 15 to 30 degrees from the horizontal. The rule of thumb is that the join is deep enough to remain open in small sizes. The departure point is roughly the same in many faces where the lower angle of the triangular serif joins the stem; *e.g.,* Sabon, Centaur, Caslon, and

Jenson. Transitional and Modern fonts tend to depart with less angle, and in some cases the curve is symmetrical. The bowl of the **a** repeats the branch's angle, first as it departs, and then as it joins the stem near the baseline. The tail of the **a** and the **t** repeat the angle. In Sabon the

branch is thinnest at the point of departure and immediately widens as the branch begins its curve. In broad-pen styles, the branch is widest as it turns to become the vertical stem. Sabon's branches are curved except the top left of the **a**, which is a straight line. Palatino begins

with a greater angle than the serif stem, and is flat before it begins its arc. Baskerville's branch is not as angular, but Bodoni angles to prevent the triangular space from filling in at small sizes.

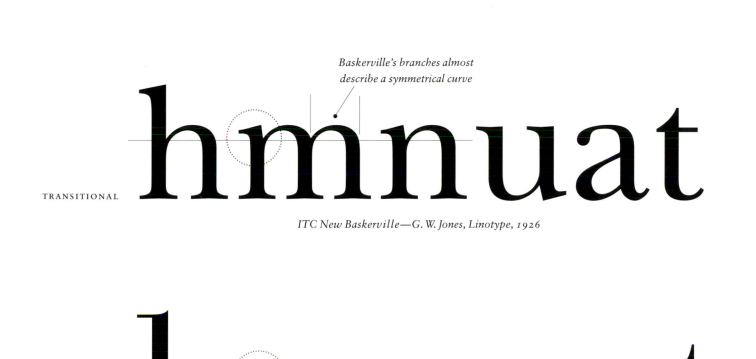

Baskerville's branches almost describe a symmetrical curve

TRANSITIONAL

ITC New Baskerville—G. W. Jones, Linotype, 1926

MODERN

Bodoni—Heinrich Jost, Bauer, 1926

■

Branches are one of the most important family characteristics of a font; their point of joining to the stems is key. Sufficient triangular space should be allowed to keep ink from being trapped there and to keep the shape visually open in small sizes.

SERIF LETTERS

Profit has propelled change throughout the ages. In 1501, Aldus Manutius, a Venetian printer, sought to increase his profits by printing smaller books at cheaper prices, volumes about which Samuel Johnson later wrote: "books that you may carry to the fire and hold readily in your hand, are the most useful after all." These were 16mo size, the standard printing sheet of the day folded to produce 16 leaves.[1] To produce the edition, a narrow typeface was needed. Updike cautiously suggested that the font's wellspring was a condensed Greek script that Manutius had developed for other modest editions.[2] Manutius hired Francesco da Bologna (Griffo), who designed a font, slightly inclined and condensed; the Aldine italic, as it is known, was copied from popular hands of the day with many ligatures. An innovative design, it was the first font to use a large

ABCDEFGHIJ KLMNOPQRS TUVWXYZ&

abcdefghijklmno pqrstuvwxyz

1234567890

1234567890

Sabon—Jan Tschichold, Stempel, 1964–67

■

Five italic fonts (above and opposite) reveal their heritage in cursive writing of the early fifteenth century, with stems produced by a sharply angled pen, which yields the greatest weight around the top and bottom turns. The departing branches and the bowls are deeply joined and give the writing an airy quality.

x-height—the cap **A** was barely higher than the dot of the **i**. The face was independent of a roman.

Most Oldstyle italics are greatly influenced by the Aldine's cursive nature. Frederic Warde based his Arrighi italic (the companion to Centaur) on similar forms designed by Ludovico Arrighi in 1522, and Bembo is based on Aldus Manutius's work.

Jan van Krimpen's faces, Lutetia, Romanée (pages 340–41), and Spectrum, are based on the fifteenth-century writings of Arrighi, Palatino, and Tagliente. Palatino is named in honor of the fifteenth-century calligrapher.

1. A sheet size roughly 16 x 24 inches.

2. D. B. Updike, *Printing Types, Their History, Forms, and Use, A Study in Survivals*, vol. 1, pages 76, 125–31.

ABCDEFGHIJKLMNOPQRSTUVWXYZ&
abcdefghijklmnopqrstuvwxyz

Palatino—Hermann Zapf, Stempel, 1948

ABCDEFGHIJKLMNOPQRSTUVWXYZ&
abcdefghijklmnopqrstuvwxyz

Spectrum—Jan van Krimpen, Enschedé, 1941–43; Monotype, 1952

ABCDEFGHIJKLMNOPQRSTUVWXYZ&
abcdefghijklmnopqrstuvwxyz

Arrighi—Frederic Warde, companion italic to Bruce Rogers's Centaur, Monotype, 1929

ABCDEFGHIJKLMNOPQRSTUVWXYZ&
abcdefghijklmnopqrstuvwxyz

Bembo—Francesco Griffo, 1495; Monotype, 1929

Palatino was first designed as a hand-set face with a narrow italic. Shown here is the text version, which was designed to occupy the same amount of space as the roman. Van Krimpen chose the slight angles of the Aldine and Arrighi italics. His forms are angular, rigid, with abrupt, finishing stroke turns at the bottom of the stems. His drawing is faithful to the action of the pen and the ascending strokes begin with the same angle. His bowl forms and branches depart deeply from the stems and introduce more white space.

The modeling is restrained. The trick with an italic is to draw it so that the letters color the same as the roman. Its angle should not be jarring in a mass of text, yet it should be clearly differentiated from the roman. Many italics depart radically from the roman, and appear not to blend. Type designers have wrestled with the task for centuries—few are successful. Compare the obliques (pages 92–93).

SERIF LETTERS

Most italic capitals are merely oblique drawings of the roman: it is the lowercase that mutates. Gone is the two-storied **a**, the rigid diagonals of the **k, v, w,** and **x**. These are replaced by the taut ogee shape: *k, v, w, x*.

In many italic fonts, the bowls lean more than the estab- lished angle of the italic, as do the formal scripts. This allows the type designer to introduce air up into the joins; this is evi- dent in Sabon. The Venetians and Oldstyle italics are narrow shapes whose weight is distrib- uted below center on the left- hand bowl curves, and above center on right-hand curves. Bowls of the Modern-style Bo- doni are wider, more rounded, and join to the straight stems much lower.

More so than the caps, the lowercase Oldstyles reveal their calligraphic heritage; turns of the lowercase are abrupt and

82

Italic bowls are often drawn with a greater angle than the staight stem, which is usually 11–17 degrees

The Sabon a counter is more narrow than the d and q and has a greater slope

Sabon

high join

Arrighi

Adobe Caslon

ITC New Baskerville

low join

Bauer Bodoni

The lowercase italic offers a more radi- cal redrawing from the roman than the capitals. Its bowls lean more than the stems and the branches are often taut ogee curves. Italics caps are frequently the same shape as the roman caps. The Oldstyles change their form more often than the Moderns.

angular; in the Centaur Arrighi, for example, the turns appear almost pointed.

In many italic fonts the straight thin diagonals of the roman have been replaced with curves. Caslon's branches bow more, but the beginning and ending stems are angled with the maximum width occurring at the bend. This feature is even more pronounced in Sabon. Tschichold bowed to Garamond's quaint drawing of the *h*, whose right-hand stem returns as if to become a lowercase *b*.

It was not until Transitional types appeared that these beginnings and endings became thin and curved. Baskerville's turns—an Oldstyle refinement—are called pot hooks. These are not consistent with the Oldstyle forms; he changed the *v* and *w*, squeezing their shapes at the top, then, to prevent holes, filled the space with a truncated, reverse curve swash. Bodoni unconventionally began his italic lowercase stems with slightly pointed, delicate, horizontal serifs that held sway for most of the nineteenth century.

Italic branches have deep joins

Sabon

Adobe Garamond

pot hook

ITC New Baskerville

Bauer Bodoni

The italic has fewer triangular strokes than the roman, i.e., strokes that angle from a diagonal center line—compare the lowercase roman **v** *with its italic counterpart* **v**. *The Transitional Baskerville is more rounded and cursive, and is similar to the connecting formal script forms.*

SERIF LETTERS

Spacing

Leading originally meant the lines of metal lead between lines of type; line spacing is now the accepted term. Word spacing is the amount between words, and letterspacing, between letters. In metal typesetting letterspaced meant a full en or word space between the letters. Space between letters is now specified in percentages.

There are only a few basic spacing rules. But there are countless decisions that must be made to properly fit a typeface for average reading conditions.

A normally proportioned font of standard weight (book weights are often light) will require slightly more space inside the letters than between individual letters, but the two should appear optically to be the same volume. This general ratio usually applies only to a few point sizes: 9, 10, and 11. At 12 points and larger, the space between the letters needs to be tighter—how much is often personal preference. Below 9-point, space between letters needs to be greater, and progressively larger as the size decreases. But something else must occur: the type must be wider and a bit

84

---

6 pt   average reading conditions — *5/0/25*

7 pt   average reading conditions — *5/0/25*

8 pt   average reading conditions — *5/0/25*

9 pt   average reading conditions — *5/0/25*

10 pt   average reading conditions — *5/0/25*

11 pt   average reading conditions — *5/0/25*

12 pt   average reading conditions — *5/0/25*

13 pt   average reading conditions — *5/0/25*

14 pt   average reading conditions — *5/0/25*

If the type is reversed from a solid color it will appear bolder and more tightly spaced than its positive counterpart, and should be letterspaced for easier reading. Small sizes of type require more line spacing. If the measure is longer than an alphabet and a half—the ideal—again more than average line spacing is required.

Spacing attributes—5 minimum, 0 desired, and 25 maximum. (PageMaker 6.5)

---

6 pt   average reading conditions — *5/4/25*

7 pt   average reading conditions — *5/3/25*

8 pt   average reading conditions — *5/2/25*

9 pt   average reading conditions — *5/0/25*

10 pt   average reading conditions — *5/-2/25*

11 pt   average reading conditions — *5/-3/25*

12 pt   average reading conditions — *5/-4/25*

13 pt   average reading conditions — *5/-5/25*

14 pt   average reading conditions — *10/-6/25*

If the type is reversed from a solid color it will appear bolder and more tightly spaced than its positive counterpart, and should be letterspaced for easier reading. Small sizes of type require more line spacing. If the measure is longer than an alphabet and a half—the ideal—again more than average line spacing is required.

Spacing attributes—5 minimum, 6 desired, and 25 maximum. (PageMaker 6.5)

Sabon—Jan Tschichold, Stempel, 1964–67

bolder if it is to make an optical match within the series, that is, a range of sizes. Distance viewing demands more open spacing. If the type is reversed from a solid color, it will appear bolder and more tightly spaced than its positive counterpart and should be gently spaced for easier reading. Small sizes of type require more line spacing. If the measure is longer than an alphabet and a half—the ideal—again more than average line spacing is required.

Word spacing is more variable—it should be greater than letterspacing for word separation. For many years, an en, or one-half of the type's point size, was standard. In hard-sell advertising text, the space was reduced to two-thirds of that, or, three-to-the-en, for unjustified text, because word spacing is variable for justified lines of text. In addition to specific letterspace values, some software programs offer five basic spacing options: very loose, loose, normal, tight, and very tight. Sans serif fonts are usually set tighter than serif fonts in text sizes, and even tighter in display sizes. As the weight or boldness increases, headlines or display text is set tighter for impact.

Sabon

■

Display type for advertising, 14-point and larger, requires tighter letterspacing than standard 9- or 10-point text type. In extra-large sizes, the space between lines invariably needs to be closer, even with negative leading. When type is reversed, slightly more letterspacing is required to overcome the effects of halation, which make the type appear bolder and more tightly spaced.

SERIF LETTERS

Small caps are a very old idea. Claude Garamond tried his hand at them in a specimen dated 1545. They are designed to set with the lowercase and usually are a bit taller than x-height. Type designers vary the height of small caps, but their form is always wider in proportion than the regular caps, to match the negative area of the lowercase. If you enlarge them to regular cap height, you will find them to be a more generous weight. Typographers are fond of small caps; they are helpful in layouts where regular-sized caps would overpower other information.

It is not always necessary to use them side by side with the lowercase. Letterspaced, their weight and proportion are graceful.

Small caps are often combined with Oldstyle figures in "expert" fonts. Oldstyle figures are used today in the same manner as small caps: for less

86

x-height

Sabon

x-height

Sabon—Jan Tschichold, Stempel, 1964–67

emphasis than modern, or aligning cap-high figures. Oldstyle figures combine unobtrusively with text matter, though most are fitted to tabulate, and they are more openly spaced than the lowercase. They are fitted within an en, which compromises their proportions. The Bodoni aligning figures below show a figure 1 with sidebearings that will create misspacings; a narrow 4; a wide 7. The 5 with an ogee crossbar has a different design concept than the 2 and 7. The horizontal strokes of the 2, 4, 5, and 7 reference calligraphy forms in which an angled writing instrument produces a heavy horizontal stroke. Metal typefoundries once offered a few hand-set fonts with normal-proportion figures to color the same as the lowercase.

(Character cells are schematic)

MODERN FIGURES

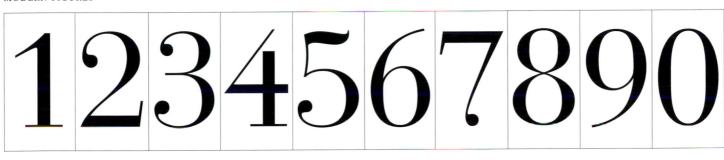

Bauer Bodoni

MODERN FIGURES

Sabon

OLDSTYLE FIGURES

Sabon

Oldstyle figures align with the lowercase, and the **3**, **4**, **5**, **7**, **9** descend and the **6** and **8** ascend. This arrangement is not consistent among Oldstyle fonts. Most fonts come with figures that are designed to tabulate, or align in columns, like the Bodoni and Sabon (middle row). To fit within the en space, their proportions must be compromised to do so (right). Sabon employs a thin single-weight line for the Oldstyle cipher or zero (a figure that dates to the tenth century). In the eighteenth century, the Industrial Revolution created a need for bookkeeping, and larger figures were designed for greater legibility.

Fashions change, and Oldstyle figures are now ubiquitous.

For the past sixty years or so, only a limited number of fonts used for book work offered the Oldstyle figures; some fonts supply Modern figures only.

1
2
3
4
5
6
7
8
9
0

SERIF LETTERS

Though not used frequently in the United States, accented capitals are used in many languages. Metal typefaces positioned the cap accents at the top edge of the metal sort, a rectangular piece of metal with a bas-relief character, and reduced the height of the cap to accommodate the accent.

This made the caps appear stingy in size, however. Full-sized accented caps were available, but required a larger mold that automatically added space between the lines, *i.e.*, a 10-point type would require a 12- or 13-point mold to accommodate the accent. Accented lowercase letters are

necessary for proper setting of languages, and these are available with most digital fonts in European and Asian languages written in the Latin alphabet. The most commonly used are those shown below. Accented caps are optional, unlike lowercase, when setting foreign words in English text.

88

line leading (schematic)

Sabon—Jan Tschichold, Stempel, 1964–67

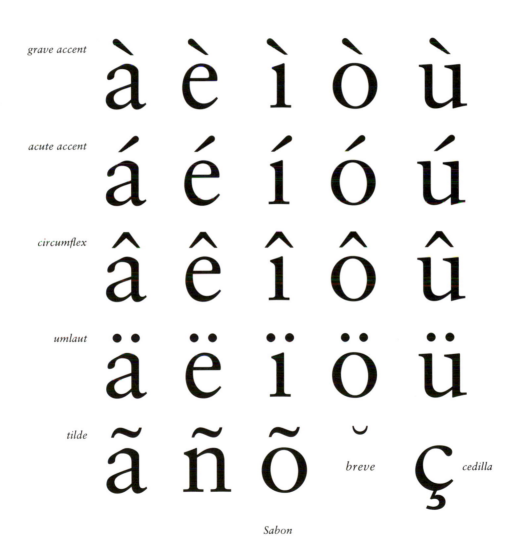

grave accent à è ì ò ù

acute accent á é í ó ú

circumflex â ê î ô û

umlaut ä ë ï ö ü

tilde ã ñ õ ˘ breve ç cedilla

Sabon

Accented letters were offered with metal fonts in the form of normal-sized caps with accents that required a special mold for casting a line, or smaller caps that fit the accent on the sort. Today's digital fonts offer some slightly smaller accented caps, but even these must be line-spaced enough to prevent descenders from overlapping the accents of a succeeding line. Commonly used accents are shown above.

SERIF LETTERS

Swash describes the extravagant, decorative extensions of letters that had their origin in the florid hands of Renaissance scribes. Swashes are usually applied to italic caps and a few italic lower-case letters, though an occasional upright font contains them. Claude Garamond was said to have devised some swash letters as a method of filling unsightly spaces between italic capital letters. Typographers caution against the excessive use of swashes.

Frederic Goudy drew some for his Garamont italic, and Frederic Warde designed an Arrighi font with a few swash caps at the same time R.H. Middleton introduced some handsome swash Garamond forms. Robert Slimbach's splendid Poetica has four sets of alternate swash capitals whose extensions of the **A** grow progressively ornate and reference forms of Arrighi, Tagliente, and Palatino, the trinity of Renaissance writing masters.

90

Garamont swash capitals—Frederic Goudy, Monotype, 1920

Arrighi swash capitals—Frederic E. Warde, Monotype, 1929
*Frederic Warde drew the preliminary Arrighi italic letters: **M, L, z, g, v, sp, Qu,** è, e, ö, û, and **ct**.*
From these, the digital version of swash caps and alternate lowercase were developed by
Patricia Saunders and Robin Nicholas at Monotype Typography Ltd., Salfords, England

Garamond swash capitals—R.H. Middleton, Ludlow, 1929

Poetica alternate swash caps I, II, III, and IIII
Robert Slimbach—Adobe Systems, 1992

Ludovico Arrighi
1522

Giovanantonio
Tagliente
1524

Giovambattista
Palatino
1545

Van Krimpen drew Cancelleresca Bastarda as a companion script for his Romulus family. Recently, Robin Nicholas and Patricia Saunders added to Warde's Arrighi swash caps in a digital version for Monotype Corporation and Adobe Systems introduced Robert Slimbach's Garamond with a generous number of swash capitals. Commonly used extensions are on the left straight stems **B, D, E, F, H, I, K, L, M, N, P, R,** and **U.** Traditionally, the left, thin diagonals of the **A** and **M** are curved and greatly extended. Swash structures vary considerably from font to font; some designers ignore swashes that others deem indispensable.

Alexander Lawson, in his *Anatomy of a Typeface*[1] relates that the first swash types were used by Ludovico Arrighi in his book, the *Coryciana*, printed in Rome in 1524, which imitated his book on calligraphy, *La Operina.*

1. Alexander Lawson, *Anatomy of a Typeface*, page 91.

A B C D E F G H I J K L M N O P Q R S T U V W X Y Z Æ Œ Ç

Cancelleresca Bastarda—Jan van Krimpen, Enschedé, 1934

Adobe Garamond swash caps—Robert Slimbach, Adobe Systems, 1989

Swash caps date from the Renaissance and beautiful as they are, without exception type critics suggest restraint in their use. They are scriptlike, and when used to form a word their ornateness invariably obscures legibility. But there are exceptions. If the word, or words, have only a few characters, or if the letters combine in a legible manner, then the practice is acceptable. The guiding principle for most typography is as always restraint. Swash letters sometimes appear in the lowercase. The Baskerville italic swash **p** derives its shape from efforts to fill the top space of a metal rectangle.

swash

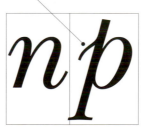

ITC New Baskerville

The Oblique

Oblique fonts are roman letters designed to lean and gracefully harmonize with their vertical roman counterpart. Slanted versions of the roman, they do not follow the traditional shapes of fifteenth-century italics. Only a few roman text faces come with an oblique version, but there are many sans serifs obliques.

Stanley Morison wrote an essay entitled "Toward the Perfect Italic" for the *Fleuron*, a typographic journal published for only a few incandescent issues. He persuaded Jan van Krimpen, the great type designer at the illustrious 300-year-old Enschedé typefoundry at Haarlem, to carry out his idea in the Romulus family, which Van Krimpen began designing in 1931. The italic was drawn as a leaning roman with no apparent change in size, proportion, weight, or fit. The idea was to pair the italic to the roman as closely as possible for ideal harmony, instead of the italic's usual change of letterform and condensed proportion. Critics of the day lauded the logic but disparaged the design.[1] Morison's idea was not new. Bookman has

A B C D E F G H I J K L M N O P Q R S T U V W X Y Z
abcdefghijklmnopqrstuvwxyz fbffffiffiflfhfifkfl 1234567890

Romulus—Jan van Krimpen, Enschedé, 1931–37

ABCDEFGHIJKLMNOPQRSTUVWXYZ&
abcdefghijklmnopqrstuvwxyz fi ff ffi fl ffl .,;:-,'?!
$1234567890 AMR Ssy   AHMR Ssy

ATF   Ludlow

Bookman—A.C. Phemister, Miller & Richard, 1860; Monotype, 1909

ABCDEFGHIJKLMNOPQRSTUVWXYZ
abcdefghijklmnopqrstuvwxyz

Augustea light—Berthold, 1905–25

ABCDEFGHIJKLMNOPQRSTUVWXYZ
abcdefghijklmnopqrstuvwxyz

Futura light—Paul Renner, Bauer, 1927–30

■

For 400 years, the angle at which the italics were drawn was predicated on the edges of the metal face on which they sat. The greater the lean, the more space was produced between letters. A slightly condensed, leaning letter allowed an adequate slope and better fit. If the slant is excessive the letter will be physically larger (not taller, but longer diagonally) and must fractionally be reduced in height so as to appear optically the same size as the roman.

Computer typesetting has escaped from these metal shackles and the leaning letters may kern, or invade the following matrix, to permit much closer letter-spacing. Now computers allow the user to produce letters of any angle—often with questionable results. The major axis or centerline is tilted, and because the process is mechanical, the ellipses appear taut and stretched (opposite). The top left side appears flat, the top right too heavy, and the opposing curves

an oblique, and Berthold's 1925 Augustea came with a quasi-oblique. Imré Reiner's Corvinus, a family of flat-sided Bodoni-like shapes, arrived in 1929, and Hermann Zapf's inimitable Optima with its companion oblique was introduced in 1958. Obliques of bookish text faces have never been popular, but display Egyptian slab serifs have enjoyed a long run, from Rudolf Weiss's Cairo (1929) to Adrian Frutiger's Serifa (1967) have been popular. These are monotone faces in their light weights, which are sometimes used for text—rarely in book form—mainly for advertising. Typographers have long accepted sans serif obliques. Helvetica and Futura, the most popular sans of the twentieth century, have obliques. Eric Gill chose a more traditional approach when he designed a few italic forms for Gill Sans: *a*, *f*, *g*, and *p*; the other letters are oblique. Sans serif obliques usually match the weight and fit of the roman, though the proportion in some is condensed.

1. John Dreyfus, *The Work of Jan van Krimpen*, pages 36–38.

A A B C D E &F G G H I J K K L M M N N O P Q R S T U V W X Y Z
abcdefghijklmnopqrstuvwwxyz

Corvinus light—Imré Reiner, Bauer, 1929–34

ABCDEFGHIJKLMNOPQRSTUVWXYZ

abcdefghijklmnopqrstuvwxyz

Optima—Herman Zapf, Stempel, 1952–55

ABCDEFGHIJKLMNOPQRSTUVWXYZ
abcdefghijklmnopqrstuvwxyz fi fl ff ffi ffl

Cairo—Rudolf Weiss, Stempel, 1929

ABCDEFGHIJKLMNOPQRSTUVWXYZ

abcdefghijklmnopqrstuvwxyz

Serifa 56—Adrian Frutiger, Bauersche Gießerei, Fundición Tipográfica Neufville S. A., 1968

of the lower half repeat the misplacement. While this is mathematically correct, the eye perceives a warped shape. Better to draw the top left and bottom right curves with more weight, shift the widest part of the left-hand curve slightly below center, and the right-hand curve slightly above center for a more relaxed shape with a deflected axis and one that is still married to a baseline.

italic   italicized roman

Bauer Bodoni—Heinrich Jost, Bauer, 1926

SERIF LETTERS

Display figure: Fino. Text: 30/54 Trajan

THE ESSENCE OF WRITING AND LETTERING IS TO MAKE LANGUAGE VISIBLE AND RETRIEVABLE . . .

FERNAND BAUDIN

Teacher and Author, *How Typography Works*

Cafe Cordiale

Sherman Oaks, California
Margaret, David, and
Peter May
Doyald Young, Designer/Artist

Owners of this upscale restaurant that features California cuisine were primarily concerned about the logo's legibility for an illuminated exterior sign. The name was also in question: **Cafe Cordiale**, **Cordiale Cafe**, or simply **Cordiale**. Different sizes and positions for **CAFE** were tried, and the approved arrangement for the sign is shown below.

Depending on the amount of room, and the scale of the logo as it appears on printed applications, **CAFE** may change size because each letter was drawn in its proper character cell in the special logo font. Size and letter-spacing can then be controlled to exactly fit each application. These are varied: menus, napkins, table and bar tent cards, guest checks, and flyers sent to customers for reminders of special occasions.

Script is often considered for restaurant logos, because the

ABCDEFGHIJKLMNOPQRSTUVWXYZ
abcdefghijklmnopqrstuvwxyz

Tiffany light—Ed Benguiat, ITC, 1974

style is associated with gourmet food: *Gourmet* magazine has a formal script masthead, and freestyle scripts can suggest a friendly atmosphere. Designs 5, 6, and 7 were seriously considered. The all-cap word poses spacing problems in all of the designs. **IAL** seems open; **LE** doesn't color well; and the tail of the **R** is troublesome. Drawing a left-hand swash on the **R** creates space in the selected design that balances the space of the **RD**. I don't know why I made the **R** taller than the other letters, except that it was easier to create a graceful bowl that was not too wide. There was concern that the overlapping **CO** would be hard to read, but the familiarity of the word and the over-scale **C** help to make it readable. The **D** references Baskerville, and the swelled pen strokes of the **C** and **R** are found on many classic italics. Tiffany-like beaks are used on the **L** and the **E**, and the blunted, bracketed serifs are long and generous.

1.
2.
3.
4.
5.
6.
7.
8.
9.
10.
11.
12.

■

A series of pencil comprehensives for an illuminated restaurant sign, which were placed in a scaled drawing of the building's fascia to test legibility and determine which logo seemed the most comfortable within the shape. The selected design was scanned, then imported into a font drawing program and the word Cordiale drawn with Bézier curves in the cap C matrix. As a Type1 font, the logo may be set with text in sizes from 4- to 650-point, and scaled even larger in drawing programs.

SERIF LOGOS

International Design Associates

Tokyo, Japan
Tohru Uraoka, President
Mari Makinami,
Executive Creative Director
Hideo Hosaka, Art Director
Doyald Young, Designer/Artist
Tokyo Hilton Hotel

Checkers is the main dining room of the Tokyo Hilton Hotel. Its logo is a modified Rivoli, which is based on Locarno (whose cursive is shaded, the roman is not). The font was designed by Rudolf Koch in 1922 and imported to the U.S. under the name Eve. Willard Sniffin redrew the font for ATF, naming it Rivoli, and used the shaded lines on both the roman and italic caps. An inline on the right side of the font's stems extends past the main body of the letter except on the round forms. Proportions of the caps are varied; they follow classical proportions with a narrow B, E, F, R, and S; the D and H are narrowed. The O and Q are circular; the U is excessively wide; the M is narrow; the V and W don't lean enough, and the Y is based on the lowercase letter. There is a quaint, provincial quality to the font. Mac McGrew describes the letters as having "a nervous

CHECKERS

CHECKERS

pen-drawn quality."[1] Its slender vertical hairlines are derived from blackletter fonts, of which Goudy Text is typical. Goudy's drawing was inspired by the Textura type of Gutenberg's 42-line bible.

Inline, gravure, or shaded fonts have been used by social printers for special invitations and announcements for many years; they are traditional. The Checkers logo is designed to suggest an embossed invitation.

For Checkers I have modified Rivoli's proportions so that each letter appears to be equal width. The S's top beak is simplified, and weight is added to the lower curve. The E's top and bottom beaks have opposing angles, and a vertical serif has been added to the middle arm.

1. Mac McGrew, *American Metal Typefaces of the Twentieth Century* (New Castle, Delaware: Oak Knoll Books, 1993), page 271.

ABCDEFGHIJJKLMNOPQRSTUVWXYZ
abcdefghijklmnopqrstuvwxyzchckflffiflLt
1234567890
ABDEGHKLMRS

Koch Cursive—Rudolf Koch, Klingspor, 1922

ABCDEFGHIJKLMNOPQRSTUVWXYZ
abcdefghijklmnopqrstuvwxyz & .,:;='"!?

Rivoli—Willard T. Sniffin, ATF, 1928

𝔄𝔅𝔆𝔇𝔈𝔉𝔊𝔥𝔦𝔍𝔎𝔏𝔐𝔑
𝔒𝔓𝔔𝔕𝔖𝔗𝔘𝔙𝔚𝔛𝔜𝔷&
fifl $1234567890 .,·:;!?æœ
abcdefghijklmnopqrstuvwxyz

Goudy Text—Frederic Goudy, Monotype, 1928

■
The Checkers logo (opposite) derives from Locarno and Rivoli, two fonts based on classical proportions that borrow the vertical hairline feature of Gutenberg's blackletter shown in the Goudy text.

SERIF LOGOS

International Design Associates

Tokyo, Japan
Tohru Uraoka, President
Mari Makinami,
Executive Creative Director
Hideo Hosaka, Art Director
Doyald Young, Designer/Artist
Dandelion Health Club

Restrained letters accompanied by extravagant caps are a design ploy found as early as the ninth century in the Book of Kells, an illuminated Celtic manuscript. The **Dandelion** logo follows this scheme, using small, conservative condensed capitals and a large matching **D** entwined with the tendril volute of the **A**. The style owes much to the natural forms of Art Nouveau. The extravagant **A** swash creates an easy-to-remember image. The small caps are faithful to Times Roman: a robust two-weight roman with thin, pointed serifs, they have an almost lapidary chiseled structure. The sharpness of the tips lends sparkle to the font and prevents the serifs from becoming heavy and important.

There are only a few popular, traditional, bold condensed roman faces based on narrow roman forms. Times Roman's bold appears more condensed than its

DANDELION

DANDELION

■
*This logo for a health club has a large cap **D** and an extravagant **A**; whose extension has its origin in the tendril shapes of Art Nouveau, a fin-de-siècle style that favored plant forms.*

normal roman. Caslon was issued in bold condensed and extra
bold condensed by ATF. Century
bold condensed, while Modern
in structure, has strong similarities to the condensed Caslon,
due partly to the inevitable loss
of subtle family characteristics
when a font is narrowed.

ITC Garamond holds its basic
design image when condensed
because the original shapes are
more distinctive than Caslon.

Dandelion   *Dandelion*

Dandelion   *Dandelion*

ABCDEFGHIJKLMNOPQRST
abcdefghijklmnopqrstuvwxyz

Times Roman bold—Stanley Morison & Victor Lardent, Monotype, 1932

ABCDEFGHIJKLMNOPQRSTUVWXYZ
abcdefghijklmnopqrstuvwxyz

Century bold condensed—Sol Hess, Monotype, 1938

abcdefghijklmnopqrstuvwxyz &!? $1234567890
ABCDEFGHIJKLMNOPQRSTUVWXYZ

Condensed Caslon—Inland & ATF, 1907

■

*Traditionally drawn fonts lose some
of their identifying characteristics
when condensed. Many condensed
fonts appear to be identical except
for weight differences. The ITC condensed Garamond is an exception;
note the highly stylized curve at the
top of the **B** that retains its identity
in the condensed version.*

**abcdefghijklmnopqrstuvwxyz
ABCDEFGHIJKLMNOPQRSTUVWXYZ
&!?1234567890**

*Times Roman bold condensed—Type Drawing Office staff,
Monotype, 1969*

ITC Garamond—Tony Stan, 1976

California Institute of Technology
Pasadena, California
Ed Hutchings, Jr.,
Director of Publications,
and Editor
Engineering & Science Magazine
Doyald Young, Designer, Artist

Caltech is one of the world's great centers of scientific learning and research. For thirty years Ed Hutchings was the editor for their official magazine, *Engineering & Science*. From time to time he liked to update the format and usually included a look at new masthead designs for the maga- zine. After a long run of Copper- plate Gothic followed by Times New Roman, one brief issue featured a sans serif that I had carefully hand-lettered and urged him to use. A disgruntled alum- nus unfavorably compared the result to a parts catalog. And that took care of that! The design illustrated below (*top*) lasted several years. I based it on Basilea, designed by Markus J. Low, and Korinna, designed at the Berthold Foundry in 1904 and later re- drawn by Ed Benguiat, Vic Caruso, and the staff of Photo Lettering, Inc. for ITC. In the regular weight, Benguiat's draw-

Engineering & Science

Hand-lettered masthead based on Korinna and Basilea

Engineering & Science

The masthead set in Korinna
Korinna—Ed Benguiat, with Vic Caruso and the staff of Photolettering, Inc., ITC, 1974

■

A previous masthead for California Institute of Technology's official publica- tion. The top version is hand-lettered.

FONTS & LOGOS

ing is almost monotone and needed some sparkle, so I thinned the horizontals to increase the contrast. *Engineering & Science* is a long name, and a generous one-line arrangement was needed, so I narrowed some of the proportions and tightened the spacing to keep the letters large. I kept the wide c and raised the e's crossbar to equal the c's volume. A symmetrical weight distribution replaced the Oldstyle calligraphic stress. The horizontal serifs were shortened and bolder triangular serifs introduced at x-height. I drew an unusual x-height ampersand to match the lowercase weight.

ABCDEFGHIJKLM
NOPQRSTUVWXYZ
abcdefghijklmn
opqrstuvwxyzftct
123456780
$¢.,;:-()""''/?!&→

Basilea—Markus J. Low's
Visual Graphic Corporation's 1965 font, redrawn
by Bob Maile in 1985 as a corporate font for
Bright and Associate's client, Sitmar Cruises

ABCDEFGHIJKLMNOPQRSTUVWXYZ
abcdefghijklmnopqrstuvwxyz

Korinna—Berthold, 1904
Ed Benguiat, Vic Caruso, and the staff of Photolettering, Inc., ITC, 1974

SERIF LOGOS

National Broadcasting Company
Burbank, California
Robert Keene,
Production Designer
Doyald Young, Designer, Artist
Captain Kangaroo, Celebratory
TV Special

I've always liked freestyle letter-forms. Their freedom is difficult to master, because first the structure of straightforward letter-shapes must be understood. Then it is fun to relax the letters, not as crude cartoon shapes of letters, but within the bounds of legibility and appropriateness.

The razor's edge is always difficult to gauge, and depends on individual preference and the job's demands.

This title for a TV special honoring Captain Kangaroo's contribution to our culture is a quasi-sans serif that leans toward the shapes of roman serifed letters. There are hints of Times Roman. The title mixes italic forms with romans—the **e**, **n**, and **v**—while the shape of the **g** is the skeletal form of Helvetica. Letters are overlapped and the **CA** forms a ligature, while the main stem of the **P** gets a swash. The thick/thin contrast is slight, and serifs are

104

formed more by a flaring of the stems than by extending a bracketed stroke from the tips.

There are some notable "bounced" fonts that, like this logo, range up and down on the baseline for an informal look. Irvin, a titling face originally designed for *The New Yorker* magazine by Rea Irvin, has a slight bounce because the round letters are a bit smaller; note the C, G, and O. Some letters tumble: the G backward, the S forward.

Emil Klumpp's Murray Hill has noticeably different size caps. The C, O, and Q are large and there is a marked difference in individual letter stem base alignment (K, M, N, U, X, and R), while the tops of the caps align. The lowercase letter alignment is more even at the baseline than at x-height; note the height of the i and u. Rudolf Koch's roughly hewn Neuland, a titling face, appears to bounce because the tips of the stems have different angles and some letters have opposing angles; note H and J.

ABCDEFGHIJKLMNOPQRSTUVWXYZ
abcdefghijklmnopqrstuvwxyz

Times Roman Bold—Stanley Morison and Victor Lardent, Monotype, 1932

ABCDEFGHIJKLMNOPQRSTUVWXYZ&
~$1234567890?!()[]¢.,"

Irvin—Rea Irvin, Monotype, 1925

ABCDEFGHIJKLMNOPQRSTUVWXYZ
abcdefghijklmnopqrstuvwxyz

Murray Hill—Emil Klumpp, ATF, 1956

ABCDEFGHIJKLMN
OPQRSTUVWXYZ

Neuland—Rudolf Koch, Klingspor, 1923

■

Few successful casual two-weight romans have been issued. There are many homemade computer fonts, but rarely do these solve the problem of casual baseline alignment. To be successful there must be alternate characters to avoid bad patterns at the baseline and x-height. Irvin, once a proprietary face, has rustic edges. Some letters subtly change size, weight, and alignment; there are even intentional misspacings to emphasize its hand-lettered quality. Neuland was cut directly into metal without preliminary drawings to achieve a brutal effect.

SERIF LOGOS

International Design Associates

Tokyo, Japan
Tohru Uraoka, President
Mari Makinami, Executive
Creative Director
Doyald Young, Designer/Artist
Hotel Crevette

The formality of this decorative font for Hotel Crevette's logo is relieved by the **R** and **V** swash letters. **Hotel** is anchored by its alignment with the **R**'s stem and contained by the **V**'s swash. Based on Bodoni Open, the letters are wider and the side shadow bolder. Beaks of the **C** and **E** are squared-off to carry the weight to the beak's tip, unlike the pointed tips of the font. I've simplified the **C** and used an upper beak only, though the lower hairline has been weighted gently at its tip for added color.

Decorative and outline letters, while suggesting special qualities, are not ideal for large exterior signs. A strong second color is usually needed to fill the letters for visual impact.

The logo is one of many hotel logotypes that I've designed for International Design Associates (the decorative elements have been designed by IDA). As a group

106

ABCDEFGHIJKLMNOPQRSTUVWXYZ&
abcdefghijklmnopqrstuvwxyzfffifflffiffl

Bodoni Open—Morris Fuller Benton, ATF, 1918

The Hotel Crevette logo is drawn in a gravure style like that of Bodoni Open, an outline letter with a heavier right-hand stroke.

the logos form a strong decorative statement created by the use of graphic marks and expansive, lightweight scripts. Many are condensed letters and eight are formal, centered arrangements, suggesting formality, quality, and luxury, natural aspirations for the hotel industry. Two of the logos are for resort hotels. Because the letters of Misty Ridge change size, and some are alternate forms (**S, T, Y, G,** and **E**), the image is less formal. Yugashima's second line of single weight script is even more casual, changing size and bouncing slightly.

TOKUSHIMA

HOTEL

HOTEL

East
21

TOKYO

Hilton
International JAPAN

HOTEL

International Design Associates

Tokyo, Japan
Tohru Uraoka, President
Mari Makinami, Executive
Creative Director
Doyald Young, Designer/Artist
Kajima Hotel Enterprises

Initials and monograms are mnemonic shortcuts to a company's name or product. There are many important ones whose letters have greater recognition than the full name: AT&T (American Telephone & Telegraph), GE (General Electric); IBM (International Business Machines); GM (General Motors), B of A (Bank of America), etc. Some are so highly recognized that the companies do not always use the full company name with the initials or monogram. For such monograms conservative letter forms are usually favored. The abbreviated naming approach has always been popular and must be considered as a vital design concept for company logos. This group of comprehensives is for Kajima Hotel Enterprises, a division of Kajima Construction Company, one of the world's largest construction firms. Kajima Hotels

1.

2.

3.

4.

are designed in traditional styles with great attention to detail and elegant furnishings. This quality is reflected in the use of conservative, traditional fonts for the comprehensives: Michelangelo, Century, Baskerville, Bodoni, Fenice, and a formal script. In two designs the **E** is used as a decorative element. In each instance it is separate from the other letters so that there may be a color change.

Some letter combinations refuse to blend easily; **KH** is an example. Only when a letter changes its shape, as in designs number 2 and 8, do the forms blend. Formal scripts or swash letters can be useful in monograms because their shapes may be manipulated to form a symmetrical design or fill unwanted space by allowing the design to evenly fill a symmetrical background.

KH 𝓔

5.

7.

KHE

6.

KHE

8.

■

Variations of Michelangelo are used in designs 1, 2, 4, and 7; number 3 is Century; number 5 is Baskerville; number 6 is Bodoni; and number 8 is Fenice.

SERIF LOGOS

The Garza Group
Pasadena, California
Agustin Garza, Executive Creative Director
Doyald Young, Designer/Artist
Loreto, Baja California Sur
Fonatur, Mexico's National Trust Fund for Tourism Development & Mexican Ministry of Tourism

Loreto, a small city in the state of Baja California Sur, sits on the twenty-sixth parallel on Baja California's east coast. Founded by the Jesuits in 1697, the first of the California missions was built there. This logo was designed to celebrate the city's three-hundredth anniversary in 1997, and to launch a tourism campaign sponsored by Fonatur, Mexico's National Trust Fund for Tourism Development and the Mexican Ministry of Tourism.

Agustin Garza, the executive creative director of the Garza Group, first suggested a design that contrasted the new with the old (1), but the design developed into a baroque Spanish Colonial logo. The cartouche-like swashes suggest seventeenth-century Spanish court hands and antique map lettering, reinforced by the **L** and **R** descenders. Garza wanted the name and dates to form a cohesive unit and be tied together.

■
Opposite—*Designs are seldom conceived full-blown; usually the germ of an idea needs a lot of work. These are first roughs, with detail gradually added. Variations must be tried, compared, and discarded. Bit by bit a design takes shape. Art directors and clients make suggestions, and gradually the design becomes cohesive. Agustin Garza wanted more baroque shapes than the the first two, so swash figures were introduced and the flourishes exaggerated. I tried to fill the space below the **L**, first with an extended arm, then, at Garza's suggestion, with two small flourishes, design 7. Pen swashes were added to the downstroke of the 7, a repeat of the topknot.*

FONTS & LOGOS

This was accomplished by crossing the figures' descenders with a double swash and curling the swash tip into the O. The 9 in 1697 was integrated with the swashes, first with a loop (design 4), then with a simple swash (design 8). Garza suggested the branched 7, (designs 7 and 8), related to the European style of crossing a 7's diagonal with a short horizontal stroke (designs 3, 5, and 6). The figure 1 of the final design is taller than usual to balance the quail-like headdress of the 7s. The figures and the name Loreto are condensed to create a vertical format that suggests a crucifix, and the elongated shape nicely fits six-foot-tall banners that flank the streets on fiesta days.

There's always a bit of luck in a logo's combination of letters. Here the ascending stem of the 6 and the descender of the 9 create a formal center.

There are traces of Goudy on the arm of the L; an open Palatino **R** bowl; suggestions of Garamond for the T's arms, and a pen-style ending of the E's middle arm repeating the tips of the swash flourish endings.

(Another design direction is shown on the following pages.)

1.

4.

7.

2.

5.

8.

3.

6.

The runner-up design contains only the city's founding date. The ogee swashes are still favored, but different type styles were explored to suggest seventeenth-century styles or provincial lettering, without the finesse of modern typefounding technology. Design 1 shows both dates in plain condensed figures, which are combined with a baroque **Loreto** to suggest both the old and the new, but Garza preferred the more elaborate designs. Design number 2 positions **1697** at top right; the T's crossbar creates an open space, overlapping and bisecting the space around its straight stem with the descender of the 9, which curls around the E's top arm. Luck also allowed the 7 to bisect the T's swash cross stroke. The forms seem to nestle naturally, but Garza thought that they were hard to read. Design 3 features small os with an underscore, a conceit that shows up as

late as the turn of the twentieth century in Germany, Austria, and Scotland in examples of the remarkable Scottish designer, Charles Rennie Mackintosh. The small, short, swelled ogee shape used as the E's center arm is identified with many Spanish and Italian designs. Sometimes used as an A's bar, it is a typographic character called a *swung dash*, the mathematical sign of similarity and in lexicography the sign of repetition. Its shape is almost identical to the tilde, but its position is mid x-height.[1]

1. Robert Bringhurst: *The Elements of Typographic Style*, page 285.

1.

4.

2.

5.

3.

6.

■

Alternate designs for the Loreto logo. Some explore various lettering styles to suggest rustic or provincial lettering, and a few bold designs were tried.

SERIF LOGOS

Stiletto

Hollywood, California
Mark Bevan
Creative Director
Doyald Young, Designer/Artist
The City of Los Angeles
Marathon
Dr. William Burke, President
Marie Patrick, Vice President

114

Dr. William Burke, president of The City of Los Angeles Marathon, requested stationery with the design of an official-appearing seal of the Marathon to present to Mayor Bill Bradley and the City Council for approval and funding. A stronger more identifiable symbol was planned for the City's Marathon for print and advertising: caps, t-shirts, jogging suits, sweat shirts, and pins. Designs of runners, palm trees, stars, wings, and sandals were studied, including a design that featured the 26-mile route, but choice for a graphic symbol was postponed. Meanwhile, the original seal, which was specifically designed for a letterhead at three-quarters-inch diameter, was used instead for the advertising logo. The design proved too weak for newspaper and billboard advertising, so the reverse-image design was made and used for a number of years.

Original ¾″ size expressly designed for engraved stationery

⅝″ size for engraved business cards

■
The official Los Angeles Marathon seal. The lettering references classic roman fonts: Forum, Friz Quadrata, Michelangelo, and Trajan.

FONTS & LOGOS

The original design was tailored to be steel-die engraved and embossed with gold metallic ink on the stationery and business cards. There are engraving restraints: large areas of solid color are best avoided because the engraving process must reproduce these as crosshatched patterns, and the results are not satisfactory. The lettering, laurel leaves, and the outline were simplified and refined for the small, five-eighths-inch size for the business cards.

The hand-lettered caps and small caps are based on classic roman letters. Goudy's Forum was one of the early fonts to aspire to the classic letter; Carol Twombly's Trajan, Ernst Friz's Friz Quadrata, and Hermann Zapf's Michelangelo (pages 328–29), are present-day versions. The lettering favors Friz Quadrata's weight and proportions, and the word-for-word line arrangement of the logo was a limitation that restricted the logotype's placement. The cap-to-small-cap ratio is modest so that the lines may be spaced more closely.

ABCDEFGHIJKLMNOPQRSTUVWXYZ&
1234567890

Forum Title—Frederic Goudy, Monotype, 1911

ABCDEFGHIJKLMNOPQRSTUVWXYZ&
1234567890

Friz Quadrata—Ernst Friz, VGC, 1965; ITC, 1974

ABCDEFGHIJKLMNOPQRSTUVWXYZ&
1234567890

Trajan—Carol Twombly, Adobe Systems, 1989

■
Forum and Trajan are titling faces, caps only, based on the classic roman letter. Each designer has a different idea of their shapes. Trajan seems to be the most authentic.

SERIF LOGOS

International Design Associates
Tokyo, Japan
Tohru Uraoka, President
Hideo Hosaka, Art Director
Doyald Young, Designer/Artist
Hotel Granvia Nihon
Okayama, Japan,
Lumière Lobby Lounge

The brothers Louis Jean and Auguste Lumière, chemists, inventors, and cinematography pioneers, developed the first motion picture machine. Coincidentally, *lumen* is the Latin word for light, and in French *lumière* means lamp. In this instance it is the name of Hotel Granvia's lobby lounge. Comprehensive design 1 is a style that was prevalent in the 1930s. The script form of the cap E found its way into fonts of the period: Allegro, Bernhard Fashion, Cancelleresca Bastarda, Caslon swash, etc. The tail of the large cap L echoes the R's tail; both are reminiscent of Baskerville. Design 2 is based on Litho light; design 3 is a softened contemporary sans. Design 4, a modified and condensed version of Radiant, attempts to mirror the Art Deco, postmodern spirit of the hotel's interior with a biform, a mix of same-

Lumière

Lumière

height caps and lowercase. Note the **u** and **m**. Design 5, the chosen design, is a condensed Times New Roman, evidenced by the heavily bracketed and pointed horizontal serifs. While the **r** is a Perpetua form, the **e**s are true italic Oldstyle, with their strong carriage of weight around the bottom curve; they resemble Garamond and Caslon. The stroke that forms the eye of the **e** is heavily weighted. Note that the interior spaces of the **m** are narrower than that of the **u**, which prevents the multiple form from admitting too much white space. The x-height is large, and the **L** is weighted more than the lowercase to color evenly. Most of the comprehensives use the grave accent in a pronounced manner, as a design element.

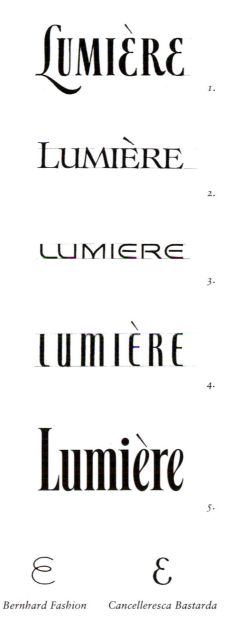

Allegro   Bernhard Fashion   Cancelleresca Bastarda   Caslon 471

*Pencil comps for Hotel Granvia's French restaurant that reference 1920s and 1930s fonts, designed to match the Art Deco interiors. Script **E**s were fashionable in the 1920s and '30s; those in the first comp are typical.*

Perpetua   Times New Roman   Adobe Garamond

SERIF LOGOS

International Design Associates
Tokyo, Japan
Tohru Uraoka, President
Hideo Hosaka, Art Director
Doyald Young, Designer, Artist
Mr. Craft, Custom Furniture

Mr. Craft is a manufacturer of special made-to-order furniture. While precision and handwork is implied in the name, the company requested that the design suggest the heritage of fine wood-working. Classic styles are appropriate. I used swash forms and ample formal script flourishes to suggest quality and uniqueness. The devices are important because they often give a word a memorable shape. Design 1 extends the classic proportions of Basilea; design 2 is a condensed and modified Friz Quadrata. Both are robust approaches. Design 3 is a simple concept with an exaggerated cap. Design 4 uses Caslon with an italic form f and an extravagant swash **M**. Classic and light, design 5 is Michelangelo graced with a traditional formal script. Design 6 is a formal script of constrasting sizes and weights. Design 7 retains the **Mr** of 6 but is paired

Mr.Craft

1.

MRCRAFT

2.

MRCRAFT

3.

4.

CRAFT

5.

6.

7.

8.

with a wide and bold Didot with bracketed teardrop kerns. Design 8 proposes equal emphasis for both words, though with four different contrasts: angle, style, weight, and case, plus a lowercase **r** redolent of its period.

The caps and lowercase letters offer a nesting place for **Mr**, a word of secondary importance. When caps are used in a tightly spaced arrangement, ligatures such as the RA are necessary for even color spacing. The italic form of the *f* is drawn in an upright orientation because it produces a descender and gives the word a more distinctive shape.

The formal *Mr*s are hand-lettered versions of script, not a font, but they pay homage to the formal scripts found in George Bickham's classic *The Universal Penman*.

ABCDEFGHIJKLMNOPQRSTUV
abcdefghijklmnopqrstuvwxyz

Basilea—Markus J. Low, VGC, 1965

ABCDEFGHIJKLMNOPQR
abcctdefghijklmnopqrsst123

Condensed Caslon—Inland, 1907; Monotype, c. 1907

ABCDEFGHIJKLMNOPQRSTUVWXYZ
abcdefghijklmnopqrstuvwxyz

Firmin Didot, 1784; Adrian Frutiger—Linotype-Hell, 1991

that you may continue in health and happiness,

Edward Dawson Script from The Universal Penman, *c. 1733*

■

The comps opposite are classic approaches; I have drawn the letters many times and they are part and parcel of my typographic vocabulary. They are styles that are adaptable to many jobs, and they continue to prove their worth. It is always interesting to compare the lettered versions against a font, because only slight variations in the design of one or two letters can create a unique image. At other times a change of proportion, weight, or spacing may be the only design approach needed to answer a job's requirements.

SERIF LOGOS

International Design Associates
Tokyo, Japan
Tohru Uraoka, President
Mari Makinami, Executive
Creative Director
Doyald Young, Designer/Artist
Singapore Country Club

Country club logotypes are traditionally conservative. Restraint seems always to have the upper hand in the choice of color and typographic elements. Graphic elements used with the name may be armorial, botanical, or decorative monogram designs. The chosen design below relates to Times Roman condensed but is even more narrow and is drawn with heavier thin strokes. Instead of the traditional pointed or cupped **A**, the peak is chopped horizontally for a better balance of mass on the right diagonal. This permits a steeper stem, which decreases the space at cap height and allows the **A**'s side-bearings to color more evenly. The **R**'s tail is curved as it departs from the waist and is reminiscent of Perpetua; the **B** is overbalanced. The capital **U** is a lowercase form that colors more evenly than the traditional heavy- and lightweight

120

SINGAPORE
COUNTRY CLUB

SINGAPORE
COUNTRY CLUB

■
The client favored the selected design direction because of the script capitals. Given appropriateness, the choice of designs is personal. I favored number 3, the most restrained design, to be used with a crest, though the other comps and the chosen design have a stronger, more memorable image.

stems. The serifed caps are relieved by two upright, descending formal script caps, which permits tight line spacing.

Design 1 is essentially the same two-weight roman but without serifs, with a softer **S** and **R**. For a less formal look it is combined with a casual script, creating an easy to remember image because the script caps, ascenders, and descenders are exaggerated, lending flair to the conservative roman caps.

Wrapping the formal script cap **C** around the **p**'s descender in design 2 creates a more cohesive unit instead of two isolated lines of two different styles. Note that the terminals are teardrops and the **e** is an italic form.

Design 3, a single-line arrangement, is useful if vertical space is limited, as on exterior signs, *porte-cocheres*, or registration-form headings. The caps here are dropped more than usual, almost centering on the lowercase x-height. For a less rigid look the **t**'s crossbar is a long reverse curve.

1.

2.

Singapore Country Club

3.

ABCDEFGHIJKLMNOPQRSTUVWXYZ
abcdefghijklmnopqrstuvwxyz
1234567890

Times New Roman condensed—Design Department, Monotype, 1969

ABCDEFGHIJKLMNOPQRSTUVWXYZ
abcdefghijklmnopqrstuvwxyz
1234567890

Perpetua—Eric Gill, Monotype, 1925–30

Landor Associates

San Francisco, California
John Kiil, Project Director
John Kiil, Designer/Artist
Doyald Young, Designer/Artist
Brown-Forman
Beverage Company
Louisville, Kentucky

One of a designer's more challenging tasks is to preserve the spirit of a brand name in a design update. Millions of dollars are spent to establish product identity, so a company approaches design modifications with great caution. Though Southern Comfort has great name recognition, its label image was weak and too tightly spaced for easy reading. John Kiil, senior designer at Landor Associates, asked to see some pencil drawings of a "close look" at the Brown-Forman Southern Comfort logo. The arced base of the two-word logotype was considered the most recognizable design feature, and the capital letters were considered an important element of its basic image. These were to be retained.

Number 1 is the original design; number 2 is a rough pencil drawing to adjust proportions. The stems were narrowed to gain

Original label logotype
(Actual size)

1.

2.

3.

more space to enhance legibility. The side shadow was weighted and the checkerboard border and cross-hatching eliminated. Number 3 has a bold side shadow without the checkerboard, and number 4 uses large S and C caps for easy reading. The letters are a mixture of Century Nova extra condensed and Caslon condensed. The C is after Century Oldstyle, and the U has double-weighted stems for better color; a thinner right-hand stem would leave a hole. Number 5 has squarish shapes to help fill space between letters. The serifs are lengthened to close the gaps at cap height, and the S and C's beaks are similar to Melior. Number 6's large caps are more adventuresome. Serifs are held to a minimum to maintain open spacing; the R's bowl is opened and its tail tip is rounded. The arms of E and F have small serifs, and the T's arms become ligatures and repeat the swash quality of the S and C return strokes. Because perspective diminishes and narrows the S, a taller cap increases legibility as the very wide logo wraps around the bottle. The logo's modified letters and adjusted spacing were accepted.

4.

5.

6.

■

Pencil comprehensives drawn in a similar manner to the original logotype (opposite, top). Proportions were modified and evened in order to space the letters more gently for greater legibility. Designs 5 and 6 ventured further in hopes of achieving greater impact and legibility on the shelfs. Large initial caps were used to increase readablity and counter the effects of perspective as the extremely long logotype wraps around the bottle.

SERIF LOGOS

Kiil then drew the elaborate, final art (number 8), retaining the logo's original decorative treatment because the client considered a plain letter too radical a change.

Number 10 (*opposite*), the original neck label, is printed in black on gold foil. The name is simplified for use at a much smaller size than the shaded, checkerboard front label. Its separated side shadow is a Victorian device, used often to suggest old-fashioned quality. Number 11 has letters perpendicular to the curve. Number 12 is a more precise, gently bolder ink version. And number 13 is John Kiil's final drawing. Designs for the bottle neck logo were looked at, but were replaced on the final packaging solution with romance copy: "The Grand Old Drink of the South."

7.

8.

9.

Top—*The original logotype (enlarged); number 8 is the final drawing by John Kiil. Number 9 is the logo as it appears on the one-fifth-gallon bottle size. Number 10 is the original bottleneck logo (enlarged); 11 a pencil drawing*

10.

11.

12.

13.

with letters re-drawn perpendicular
to the curve. Number 12 is a tighter
and slightly weighted-up ink version.
Number 13 is the final drawing by
John Kiil (enlarged).

Mari Makinami Design Resource
Tokyo, Japan
Mari Makinami, Executive
Creative Director
Doyald Young, Designer/Artist
Royal Park, Sendai Hotel
Sendai, Japan
Tiara, Sky Lounge

Tiara is based on one of the loveliest of all lightweight calligraphic fonts, Diotima, from the hand of Gudrun Zapf von Hesse. The **a** is footed and instead of a teardrop it has an angled beak. To fill the top portion of the **a**, the bowl departs high with a hairline, slopes steeply, and widens gently until it reaches the widest portion below the bowl's center. The top curve is much wider than Diotima, and the branch of the **r** has calligraphic qualities similar to H. S. De Roos's classy 1930s font Egmont and Eric Gill's Perpetua. Inverted, the shape repeats on the T's arms.

A logotype for an elegant lounge atop Royal Park Sendai Hotel, in Sendai, Japan, the treatment did not have to be assertive because it did not have to compete with other logos, except perhaps in guest room brochures or easel cards placed in the hotel's public rooms.

Tiara

Rather, the logo for an amenity can reflect the atmosphere of a particular public room. Tiara is a quintessentially formal word. This attribute can easily be suggested with a graceful script or narrow condensed letters. It wants a distinctive shape, but if cap and lowercase is the scheme, as in designs 1, 2, 3, and 6, there are no ascenders and descenders to lend it shape. This had to be supplied by the cap **T**. Designs 1, 2, and 3 have flamboyant arms fashioned into graceful ogee curves. Designs 4, 5, and 6 rely on embellishments, curved linear shaped filigree. Number 5 illustrates a crown shape with overscale letters that suggest a tiara, aided by hairline swash extensions of the cap **A**.

Tiara

1.

TIARA

4.

Tiara

2.

TIARA

5.

Tiara

3.

Tiara

6.

ABCDEFGHIJKLMNOPQRSTUVWXYZ
abcdefghijklmnopqrstuvwxyz

■

These pencil comprehensive designs suggest the regal formality of tiaras. The chosen design, opposite, is based on Gudrun Zapf von Hesse's elegant Diotima font, but in a condensed form. Terminals relate to Egmont and Perpetua.

Diotima—Gudrun Zapf von Hesse, Stempel, 1952

r r
Egmont *Perpetua*

SERIF LOGOS

Mari Makinami Design Resource
Tokyo, Japan
Mari Makinami, Executive
Creative Director
Doyald Young, Designer/Artist
Royal Park Sendai Hotel
Vincennes Main Dining Room

The castle at Vincennes dates from the twelfth century and was home to French kings, including Louis IX who administered justice beneath a favorite oak tree in the Bois de Vincennes.

In 1640 Pierre Moreau, a Parisian writing master, produced fonts that mirrored the popular script hands of the day, which he dedicated to Louis XIII.[1] Some of these scripts are stencil-like and the conceit is seen in Jan Tschichold's Saskia. Moreau's forms are a bit condensed, are not connected, and are openly spaced. An occasional italic form is included, but a voluptuous looped ascender places the style in the family of scripts. The initial cap V of the text continues to inspire designers. Zapf's Virtuosa cap *V* is designed in much the same spirit. The French not only contributed one of the world's most important faces, Garamond, but condensed romans

■
Above—A design based on Didot and Bodoni with upright italic forms.
■
Opposite—Script Vs used for inspiration in the pencil comps. Saskia references the broken letters of Moreau's seventeenth-century scripts.

and gravure types are Gallic ideas also. Royal Park Sendai's main dining room logo designs play on these ideas. Number 3, my favorite design, was bypassed for design 1, which is drawn with a script capital whose thin right stroke dots the **i** and is a mixture of a Didot-styled roman

and upright italic forms with double lowercase swash **ns**. The other designs are a combination of gravure, italic, and script, in each case graced by a swash cap or script forms.

1. D. B. Updike, *Printing Types, Their History, Forms, & Use, A Study in Survivals*, vol. 1, pages 207–8.

Vincennes

1.

VINCENNES

2.

Vincennes

3.

VINCENNES

4.

Vincennes

5.

V

Virtuosa 11—Hermann Zapf, Stempel, 1953

A D V I S
Aux persónnes de condition,
diuersement affligées.

Vous, dont la condition est chan-
gée, & qui des plus hautes pros-
peritez de la vie, vous voyez tombez
en des disgraces qui vous la font
haïr; Au lieu de vous fâcher de ces
pertes, consolez-vous-en plustost,
& les tenez pour de purs effets

Pierre Moreau Script, 1644

Eigenart voll Vornehmheit und Eleganz zutage, die sie
alles Hergebrachte und Alltägliche. Wer eindrucksvoll un

Saskia—Jan Tschichold, Schelter & Giesecke, 1932

It is a very
complicated
job to produce
something
simple.

William Golden

Design Director, CBS Television Network, late 1940s

LETTERFOUNDER

Two-lines English Egyptian—William Caslon IV, 1816

ABCDEFGHIJKLMNOPQRSTUVWXYZ
abcdefghijklmnopqrstuvwxyz

Franklin Gothic—ATF, Morris Fuller Benton, 1902

ABCDEFGHIJKLMNOPQRSTUVWXYZ
abcdefghijklmnopqrstuvwxyz

Erbar—J. Erbar, Ludwig & Mayer, 1922–30

ABCDEFGHIJKLMNOPQRSTUVWXYZ
abcdefghijklmnopqrstuvwxyz

Futura book—Paul Renner, Bauer, 1927–30

ABCDEFGHIJKLMNOPQRSTUVWXYZ
abcdefghijklmnopqrstuvwxyz

Lydian—Warren Chappell, ATF, 1939

ABCDEFGHIJKLMNOPQRSTUVWXYZ
abcdefghijklmnopqrstuvwxyz

Optima—Hermann Zapf, Stempel, 1952–55

ABCDEFGHIJKLMNOPQRSTUVWXYZ
abcdefghijklmnopqrstuvwxyz

Helvetica—Max Miedinger, Stempel, 1957

ABCDEFGHIJKLMNOPQRSTUVWXYZ
abcdefghijklmnopqrstuvwxyz

Folio extra bold—Konrad F. Bauer & Walter Baum, Bauer, 1957–62

ABCDEFGHIJKLMNOPQRSTUVWXYZ
abcdefghijklmnopqrstuvwxyz

Univers 55—Adrian Frutiger, Deberny & Peignot, 1957

ABCDEFGHIJKLMNOPQRSTUVWXYZ
abcdefghijklmnopqrstuvwxyz

Eurostile—Aldo Novarese, Nebiolo, 1962

ABCDEFGHIJKLMNOPQRSTUVWXYZ

Stop—Aldo Novarese, Nebiolo, 1970

Greek sans serif lettering, aligned vertically and horizontally.
Religious Calendar of Thorikos (detail), 440–430 B.C.
Artist unknown, Pentelic marble, H 133 cm; W 56 cm.
The J. Paul Getty Museum, Malibu, California.

133

Sans serif letters developed with written language, long before quills were beveled, slotted, and dipped in gum arabic and soot; they are the skeleton of the roman alphabet. Sans serif also refers to the so-called Gothics, and loosely includes any unconnected roman-style letter whose corners are unadorned, whether the letters are scrawled in sand or drawn with a beveled pen in the calligraphic style of Lydian.

Single-weight letters on early Greek vases indicates that the forms were produced with a blunt instrument or with grouped bristles that did not shape to a point. The Thorikos inscription (*above*) can easily pass for Futura book.

Sans-serif types showed up as early as 1780, but were known as Egyptians, a style that today describes a bold square-serif letter. This example by William Caslon IV (1816), is merely the bones of an evenly proportioned roman letter. The letter is decidedly single-weight, with no optical adjustments. It has been suggested that the style was conceived to bring more impact to posters and handbills at the dawn of commercial advertising in England. When

■

Opposite—*Caslon's original sans; Franklin Gothic, the twentieth-century workhorse; Erbar, the classically proportioned sans; Futura, Paul Renner's perennial sans; Lydian, a calligraphic sans; Hermann Zapf's Optima, a seriffless roman; a chunky Folio, with a large x-height; the ubiquitous Helvetica; Univers; Adrian Frutiger's timeless tour de force; and Stop, a fantasy by Novarese.*

more heft was demanded from letters, some elements required thinning, and by the end of the nineteenth century the thick and thin stem weight distribution of sans serif letters was fashionable.

Sans serifs are divided into single- and two-weight groups. Endless design variation is possible, though few popular fonts have strayed far from acceptable forms—Aldo Novarese's Stop is a wonderfully inventive exception. When the sans serif is regular or book weight (there are no hard and fast rules for weight distinction), the task of drawing the letter is relatively simple. It is only when the form is weighted, approaching maximum boldness, that the adjustments become critical.

Proportions greatly affect a font's over-all color, which may explain the even proportions of the early sans serifs. These are lumped into a group known as grotesques (from the Italian *grottesca*, grotto: unpolished art found in caves).

Futura and Gill Sans are classically proportioned sans and their narrow **B, E, F, P, R**, and **S** do not color as evenly as the nineteenth-century sans. Two-weight sans serifs have a better break because the negative areas are more evenly balanced: Optima, Franklin Gothic, and Peignot.

A constant battle has been waged in type design to prevent a congestion or massing of weight, more so with the sans serifs because there are fewer

thin strokes to lighten a letter shape. The troublesome areas are bowl joinings to stems and the convergence of the straight stem strokes.

Flat-sided sans serifs are often called Gothic because their narrow repetitive shapes are reminiscent of blackletter. Because there is less distinction between the individual letters, the narrow shapes are not as legible as the round-form grotesques. If not carefully spaced, the counters and the space between the letters can set up a monotonous, picket-fence pattern. Yet these condensed faces, economical in width, are vital for advertising where space is at a premium, or when an aggressive statement is demanded. The Eurostile family carries the mechanical look further with shapes that are a softened square, and there is a range from condensed to extended, from light to bold. Sans serifs find their happiest

home in advertising, particularly in signage and outdoor billboards. Seldom are books completely set in sans, though many annual reports, manuals, and instruction books choose the style. The style is invariably considered to represent the avant garde because it is malleable and its minimal shape suggests modernity.

The number of sans serifs that have found great favor in the twentieth century is small: Venus, Franklin Gothic, News Gothic, Bernhard Gothic, Futura, Folio, Helvetica, Gill Sans, Optima, Univers, and Frutiger. With the exception of Venus and Bernhard, these faces are still in wide use. Bernhard Gothic smacks of the thirties, and its generous ascenders are a bit formal for today's hard-nosed advertising. Many designs pay homage to Futura, among them Atlantis, Bernhard Gothic, Kabel, Kristal, Metro, Sans Serif, Spartan, Tempo, and Vogue.

Optical adjustments are vital if a font is to have even color, especially if the font is bold or extra bold. Even color suggests a lack of congested areas. There are three types of joins that require modification: a bowl to a stem (**a**, **b**, **d**, **g**, **p**, and **q**), a diagonal joined to a vertical stem (**N**),

or diagonal to diagonal (**M** and **W**). The first **a** in the illustration below is constructed mechanically with constant thickness and has a taller bowl to appear the same height as the straight stem. Its constant weight creates a dense area where the curves join the stem. At a large size the top and bottom

clefts of white space are barely defined; if reduced to 8- or 10-point size, all definition will be lost, the junctures will fill, and the character will be even denser. Type designers solve this by thinning the curve's horizontal thickness as it joins a stem, exercising care not to flatten the curve.

134

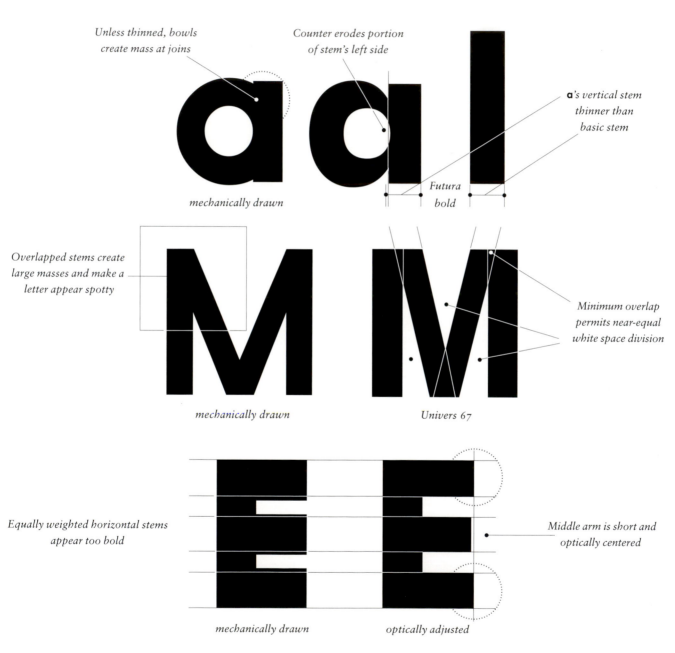

Unless thinned, bowls create mass at joins

Counter erodes portion of stem's left side

a's vertical stem thinner than basic stem

mechanically drawn

Futura bold

Overlapped stems create large masses and make a letter appear spotty

mechanically drawn

Univers 67

Minimum overlap permits near-equal white space division

Equally weighted horizontal stems appear too bold

Middle arm is short and optically centered

mechanically drawn

optically adjusted

Bold letters for use at large size may be drawn with less weight adjustment to the horizontals and diagonals than small letters, because optical adjustments that are made to accommodate the demands of 6-point type may sometimes appear exaggerated at larger display sizes. This

is important in the design of bold sans serif letters, which require thinning where a curve joins to a stem or where two diagonals meet, or a diagonal joins a vertical stem. Horizontals and diagonals should be thinned to appear the same weight as the vertical stems.

The Futura **a** shows that adjustment and tapers at the x-height and baseline. Note that the top and bottom bowl curves are thinner than the center of the vertical curve. This adjustment is made to some degree on all horizontal strokes, straight or curved.

The four mechanically drawn **M** stems are equally weighted, and appear bulky. Beside it, Univers 67 **M**'s diagonals are thinned and are not completely overlapped at the baseline. At cap height, the overlap is even less. In many bold sans, the vertical stems taper to the joining point; the inner diagonals are parallel. These adjustments are vital if the letter is to color equally with the font's simpler shapes.

The two **W**'s top stem widths shown below are equal. Inner diagonals of the top version have been thinned, the outer stems tapered, and the inner points of white space widened in efforts to make the four converging diagonals color evenly with the simpler shapes of a font. **K, R, V, X,** and **Y** diagonals require thinning also.

At a small size, the bottom **W**, whose diagonals
have not been thinned and tapered, weights up
(schematic)

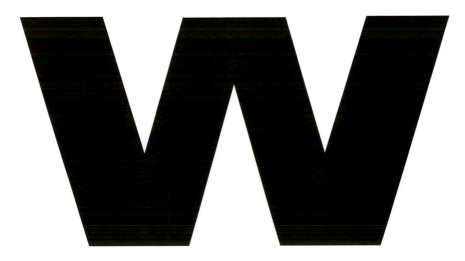

There are two basic sans serif branches: angular and symmetrical (or nearly symmetrical: in reality there is a slight angular thrust to their curves). Both are found on the evenly proportioned late nineteenth-century forms: Helvetica and Univers are symmetrical, and Franklin Gothic, angular. Futura, the classically proportioned twentieth-century German sans serif, is symmetrical. Other methods of joining have enjoyed some success, but mainly in display types. For example, Eurostile, designed by Aldo Novarese, rolls into the stem tangentially but from a horizontal branch. Handel Gothic, an evenly proportioned sans, joins both branches and bowls horizontally. Richard Juenger's Jana is horizontal too, though the branch is clipped in an angular manner at the join. But these horizontal joins reduce legibility and are best left for display sizes.

136

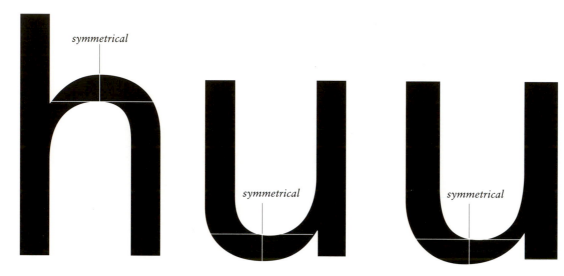

symmetrical

symmetrical

symmetrical

Helvetica—Max Miedinger, Haas, 1957   Univers 55—Adrian Frutiger, Deberny & Peignot, 1957

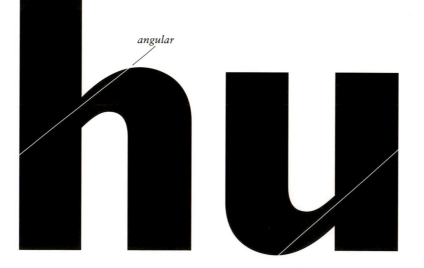

angular

Franklin Gothic—Morris Benton, ATF, 1902

The two basic branch shapes: symmetrical, based on the nineteenth-century grotesques, like Helvetica and Univers, and angular, almost parabolic in shape, typified by Franklin Gothic and News Gothic with references to calligraphic, humanist style angles.

The angular branch departure is used as a hedge against clogged joinings because the parabolic curve permits more white space at the join, and there is a bonus; its angularity introduces a lively sparkle to the font. The taut shape has more tension than the static, symmetrical Helvetica and Futura shapes. The symmetry creates trouble for type designers and letterers because the branch must be aggressively thinned to avoid congestion. Its stem may be thinned on the **m** and **n** at x-height, or at the baseline on the **u**. Sometimes the stem's tips are angled for more air. Morris Benton angled the tip of the **b** and **q** stem on his Franklin Gothic more out of respect for tradition of the broad-pen than for optical considerations (note the Sabon **b**), yet he failed to slice away the stems of the **d** and **p**, which are not mirror images on a lateral centerline.

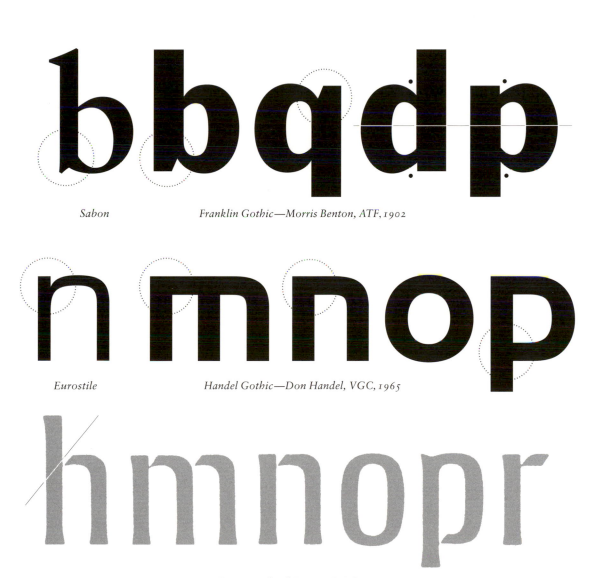

Sabon   *Franklin Gothic—Morris Benton, ATF, 1902*

Eurostile   *Handel Gothic—Don Handel, VGC, 1965*

Jana—Richard Juenger, VGC, 1966

■

Morris Benton angled the tip of the **b** *and* **q**, *more out of tradition than to open up the join area—compare the Sabon* **b**. *Note that the counters of the* **d** *and* **p** *are not the same shape as the* **b** *and* **q** *in this digital version. Eurostile and Handel Gothic have horizontal branch and bowl joins. Jana is a semistencil with a flat branch that begins with an angle.*

SANS SERIF LETTERS

Diagonals

Of all the stems that make up a sans serif alphabet, none is more critical or troublesome than the diagonals, for both the lower-case and the capitals. Depending on the weight and proportion of the font, these must be thinned or tapered to color properly. Sometimes both adjustments must be made. Seldom are the lighter versions thinned.

Vertical stems of the N and M taper from the inside. Inner diagonals of the M, N, and W don't taper but are slightly thinner than the vertical stems. Tapering, diagonal stems are found on the A, K, R, V, W, X, and Y, and are wider at their tips than the vertical stems. Yet the overall mass of the diagonal is designed to optically match the vertical stems. As a font becomes progressively bolder, the ploy becomes more obvious, decidedly so in the extra- and ultra-bold condensed versions.

138

Helvetica bold—Max Miedinger, Haas, 1957

Helvetica regular—Max Miedinger, Haas, 1957

Helvetica extra compressed—Max Miedinger, Haas, 1957

Franklin Gothic extra condensed—Morris Fuller Benton, ATF, 1906

Franklin Gothic—Morris Fuller Benton, ATF, 1902

Futura regular—Paul Renner, Bauer, 1927–30

Futura extra bold—Edwin W. Shaar and Tommy Thompson, Intertype, c. 1939–56

Morris Benton's Franklin Gothic extra condensed tapers the thin diagonal of the **K** and radically trims the thin, right-hand diagonal upstroke of the **M**. This weight reduction alone seldom prevents the stroke from massing excessively. Nor must the diagonals overlap the verticals too much or else not enough white space can be introduced into the lower portion to balance the letter. Paul Renner solved the problem differently with Futura. He angled, or splayed, the sides of the **M**, which allows an almost equal division of white space within the letter.

To produce the bold weights, the pointed joins of the light versions **A**, **N**, **V**, and **W** must be chopped horizontally, but this lessens the identifying family characteristic.

Note that white space has been forced into the center points of the **V** and **X** counters to prevent fill.

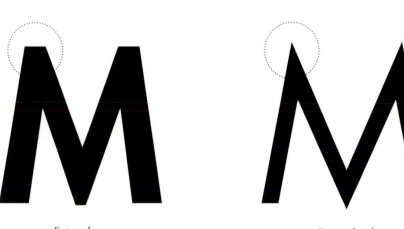

Futura heavy

Futura book

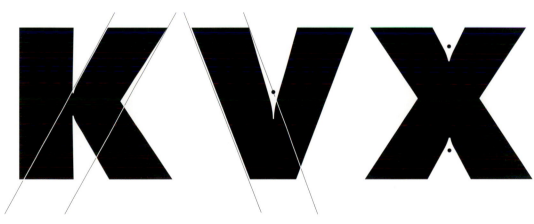

Futura extra bold

Opposite—*For even color, bold sans serif fonts have thinned diagonals, and some are tapered. To avoid massing the diagonals are not completely overlapped. Diagonals of lighter weights are seldom thinned down. Franklin Gothic, ostensibly a two-weight font, uses four distinct weights to help reduce congestion within the letter. Helvetica regular, a normally single-weight letter, is drawn with thinner inner diagonals in the extra-bold condensed version.*
Above—*Futura heavy with chopped tops loses the distinctive characteristic of the regular and book-weight pointed joinings. Futura extra bold diagonals taper, are thinner than the vertical stems and wider than the vertical stems at their tips. The **X** must be severely trimmed in width and taper to produce an enviable slim waist. This digital version forces the point of the white into the mass—a departure from Paul Renner's classic shapes.*

The **g** is often the most distinctive lowercase letter. Many sans serifs of the late nineteenth and early twentieth century favored **g**s with the traditional bowl and an enclosed loop. Typical are ATF's Franklin Gothic and Monotype's Grotesque No. 9, a design based on the 1832 Thorowgood Grotesque. The ears are treated differently: Franklin is the more traditional and Grotesque No. 9 is more sprightly. The grotesques of the late nineteenth century, which are notable for their even proportions and large x-height, introduced a bowl **g** that related to the **b**, **d**, **p**, and **q**. To gain a large x-height the descenders were shortened to favor the ascenders. With minimum space for descenders, and to avoid a mashed tail, many of these fonts reduced the size of the bowl so that its bottom curve rides slightly above the baseline.

140

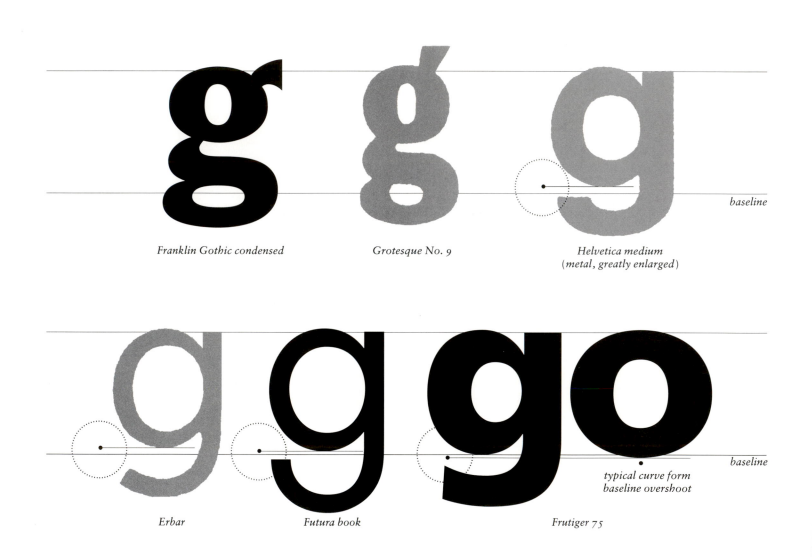

Franklin Gothic condensed

Grotesque No. 9

Helvetica medium
(metal, greatly enlarged)

baseline

Erbar

Futura book

Frutiger 75

typical curve form
baseline overshoot

baseline

Top—*Traditional nineteenth-century grotesques designed with a bowl and enclosed loops, and Helvetica with a small bowl form from the late nineteenth century to match* **b**, **d**, **p**, *and* **q**, *designed to allow for an adequate sized tail.*
Bottom—*Erbar and Futura, the first of the minimalist German sans serifs; Frutiger's quintessential sans serif for DeGaulle airport, with a canted curved-stroke ending. Note that the bowls of the* **g**s *do not descend below the baseline so that the short descending tails do not appear mashed.*

Frutiger 75, the most recent of the sans shown below, makes only a minute adjustment.

Erbar exemplified the German sans serifs of the 1920s. Rudolf Koch's Kabel came at the end of the decade, as did Futura. These were the seminal sans serifs for a host of wanna-bes: Airport, Bernhard Gothic, Metro, Spartan, Tempo, Twentieth Century, and Vogue. In 1930 Monotype issued Kabel (named to celebrate the opening of the transatlantic telephone cable). and called it Sans Serif. Monotype offered alternate **gs**, but the one shown here parallels the oddly innovative shape derived from Koch's original form: a bowl that sits atop an open circle of the same size, a nod to Morris Fuller Benton's 1914 Souvenir **g**. Herb Lubalin made the shape famous with his ITC Kabel Leggs hosiery logo.

baseline

Souvenir—Morris Fuller Benton ATF, 1914

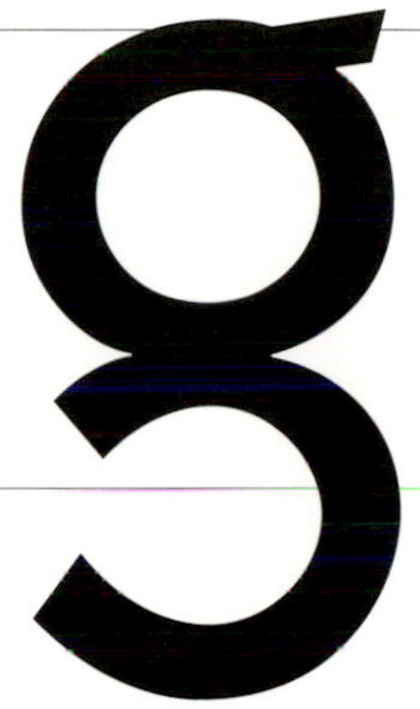

Kabel book—Rudolf Koch, Klingspor, 1927–29, Adobe 1991, Linotype-Hell AG

baseline

Sans Serif bold (Kabel)—Sol Hess, Monotype c. 1930–33

Kabel black—Rudolf Koch, Klingspor, 1927–29

■

Top—*The original metal type Souvenir (later redrawn by Ed Benguiat for ITC) that points to the shapes of the stacked circular tail of Kabel, a bizarre concept widely embraced by designers, that referenced the 1914 ATF Souvenir font.* **Bottom**—*Monotype's drawing of Kabel, one of many versions of Rudolf Koch's original font. Kabel black has a more simplified tail.*

There are only two basic ways to divide the space of a **k**: with a chevron waist or with a lower diagonal that supports the top diagonal; all others are merely variations of these two.

The early serif faces, Bembo and Garamond, have chevron waists in the manner of early Roman inscriptions.[1] Century Schoolbook and the Moderns abandoned the conceit, preferring to divide the letter with triangles and rhomboids of almost equal volume in an effort to distribute the white space more evenly. Thorowgood's 1832 Grotesque lowercase **k** is drawn in this manner; Morris Benton's Hobo, a soft, rustic face, comes with a **k** composed entirely of bowed stems. A chevron waist creates a large triangular shape that disrupts the type's color, except when the type is condensed and bold—then the chevron waist is desirable because it

142

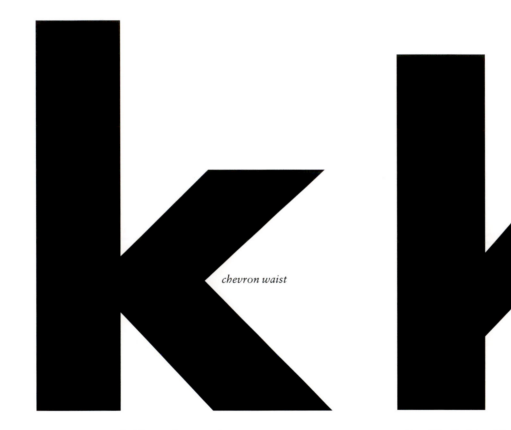

chevron waist

diagonal support

Futura bold—Paul Renner, Bauer, 1927–30

Franklin Gothic—Morris Fuller Benton, ATF, 1902

Folio bold *Folio bold condensed* *Frutiger bold* *Gill Sans bold* *Helvetica black* *Lithos* *Univers 65* *Young Sans*

■
*The two basic ways of constructing the diagonals of a **k**.*
***Bottom**—Diagonals may barely touch the vertical stem, or may be overlapped in varying amounts. My Young Sans uses the italic form with a slightly curved diagonal that joins to the waist with a radius.*

requires less width and colors more evenly. The form appears on all of the German-style sans of the 1920s: Airport, Bernhard Gothic, Futura, Metro, Spartan, Tempo, and Twentieth Century, Monotype's version of Futura. Theirs is a fitting tribute to minimalism, because the shape is the simplest way to draw a **k**. An ode to technology, Microgramma, a titling face designed in 1952 (and later Eurostile, the cap and lowercase version/s), introduced a new wrinkle to the chevron waist. To protect the rectilinear design, Novarese drew a short horizontal stroke at the **K**'s waist to attach the diagonals, and was able to promote the design device throughout the different weights and proportions. Topic's lower right stem departs from a horizontal and then curves into a vertical. Justus Walbaum, the late eighteenth-century Prussian designer, used the same connecting device. For more even color, font designers often use the diagonal support for the regular proportion and the pinched waist for the condensed versions.

1. Frederick W. Goudy, *The Capitals from the Trajan Column at Rome*, plate K.

(The illustration below is reproduced by Permission of Oxford University Press.)

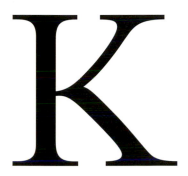

Bembo
Stanley Morison, Monotype, 1929,
Francesco Griffo, 1495

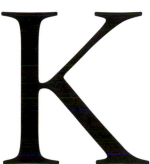

Garamond Titling
Robert Slimbach, Adobe, 1989,
Garamond, 1544

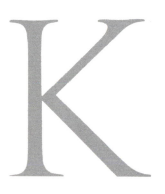

Trajan Capitals
Frederic Goudy, 1936,
after the Trajan Column, 113 A.D.

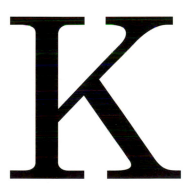

Century Schoolbook
Morris Fuller Benton, ATF, 1917–19

Grotesque No. 9
William Thorowgood—1832

Hobo—Morris Benton, ATF, 1910

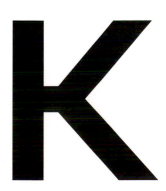

Eurostile demi-bold,
Aldo Novarese, Nebiolo, 1962

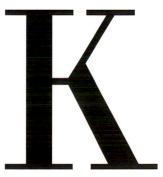

Walbaum, Berthold & Monotype, 1934,
Justus Erich Walbaum, 1810

Topic bold (Steile Futura),
Paul Renner, Bauer, 1953–1955

SANS SERIF LETTERS

Curved Stem Endings

Curved stem endings on regular-weight sans serif fonts are no problem; it is only when the bold and extra-black weights are desired that the endings become troublesome.

Single-weight sans serifs are based on the premise that an **o** is made by a chisel-edged instrument held vertically and rotated around the center axis perpendicular to the curve, producing a torus drawn with a single stroke. To make the letter **c**, a pie-shaped wedge is removed, leaving angled stroke endings perpendicular to the curve. The top flat plane may be described as a beginning stem, and the bottom plane as an ending or a terminal. When this scheme is applied to the lowercase **a**, **c**, **e**, **g**, and **s**—depending on the boldness—it is difficult to distribute the weight evenly within the letters even though the horizontal curves have been thinned. Horizontal endings are quieter and have a natural repose, since the endings are sympathetic to the type's horizontal thrust. Fonts with angular endings sparkle and are lively. Helvetica and Frutiger

144

Franklin Gothic—Morris Fuller Benton, ATF, 1902

Helvetica bold—Max Miedinger, Stempel, 1957   *Helvetica black*

angled endings

Frutiger 75—Adrian Frutiger, Stempel, 1976

vertical endings

Frutiger 95—Adrian Frutiger, Stempel, 1985

■

Sans serifs are drawn with different curved form and stem endings. Franklin Gothic uses a total of seven different ending angles; Helvetica uses only the horizontal; Frutiger has consistent,

almost vertical endings, which permits the font to be heavily weighted without visually clogging in small sizes while Futura (opposite) mixes vertical, diagonal and horizontal, and changes the

endings in the extra bold. Extra bold extended fonts are a challenge to design and color well; Frutiger 95, Twentieth Century and Information are exceptions.

fonts have round forms with opposed endings: Helvetica's endings are horizontal (**a**, **c**, **e**, and **s**) or vertical (**f** and **t**). Frutiger's are mostly vertical, while Futura uses a mix of vertical, angular, and horizontal endings. In the ultra-bold weights horizontal endings of Helvetica and Futura create small slivers of white space. Frutiger's vertical endings permit a generous amount of space to enter the letters, and thus adjust the color more evenly. Some endings cant minutely inward (note the **c** and **s**), while the 95 ultra black has vertical ends. All fonts that strive for boldness must sacrifice even weight. To accomplish the ultra weights, horizontals must be thinned, and verticals must bear the armor of weight. Note Futura extra bold's extremely thin **e** crossbar and the thin diagonal spine of the **s**.

Some bold fonts stand out: Monotype's Twentieth Century ultra-bold extended; Information extra-bold wide, a nineteenth-century squarish, thick/thin font; Helvetica black, and Frutiger 95.

cefgs

Futura regular—Paul Renner, Bauer, 1927–30

cefgs

Note that in the extra black the e's ending becomes horizontal to add mass to the letter

Futura extrabold—Edwin W. Shaar & Tommy Thompson, Intertype, c. 1939–56

acefgs

Gill Sans Display extra bold—Eric Gill, Monotype, 1927–30

ABCDEFGHIJKLMNOPQR
STUVWYXZ
abcdefghijklmnopqrstuv
wxyz 1234567890&$

Twentieth Century ultra bold extended—Sol Hess, Lanston Monotype, 1947

ABCDEFGHIJKLM
abcdefghijklmnop
1234567890

Information extra bold wide—F. K. Sallway, Klingspor, 1958

S A N S   S E R I F   L E T T E R S

An O is a deceptively simple shape. It may be a circle (1), ellipse (2), oval (3), rounded square (4), rectangle (5), or triangle (6). A circular **O**, while geometrical, does not appear to be of constant thickness; the horizontal curves seem bolder than the vertical curved sides.

If an optically single-weight letter is desired, the top and bottom curves must be thinned to appear the same as the left and right vertical curves. When the bolder versions are drawn for a family, the letter is often wider and the contrast between the horizontal and vertical

curves is increased; more weight is added to the vertical curves than to the horizontals.

Bold, squarish Os often show up in packaging, or when impact is wanted. The version of Franklin Gothic shown has pronounced squarish shoulders; even the lighter Helvetica has

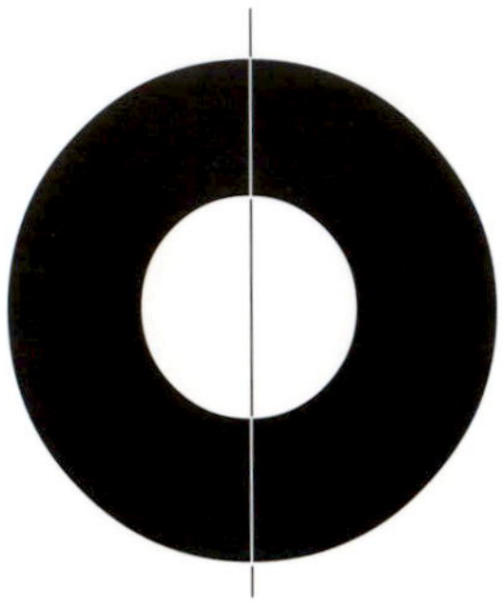

mechanically drawn

1.

Eurostile

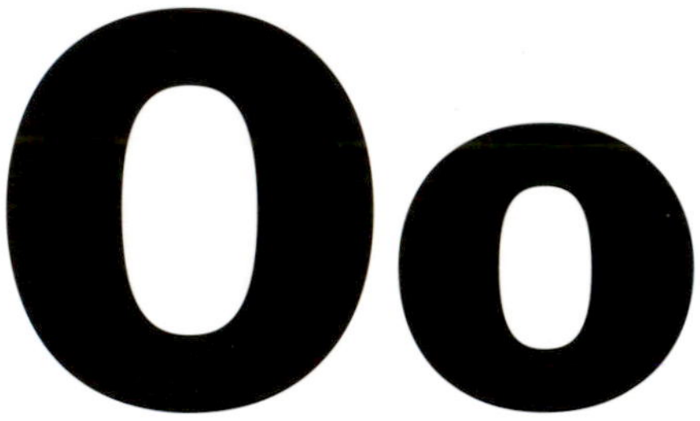

4.

Franklin Gothic

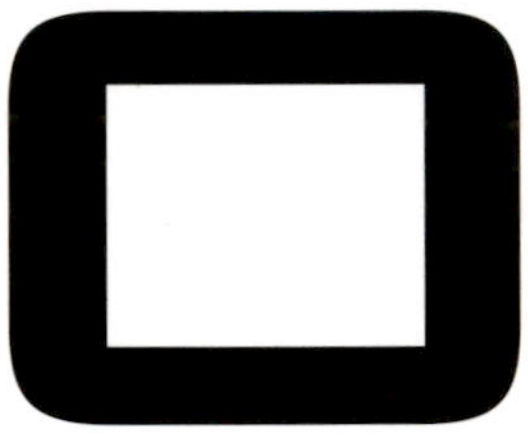

2.

Bank Gothic

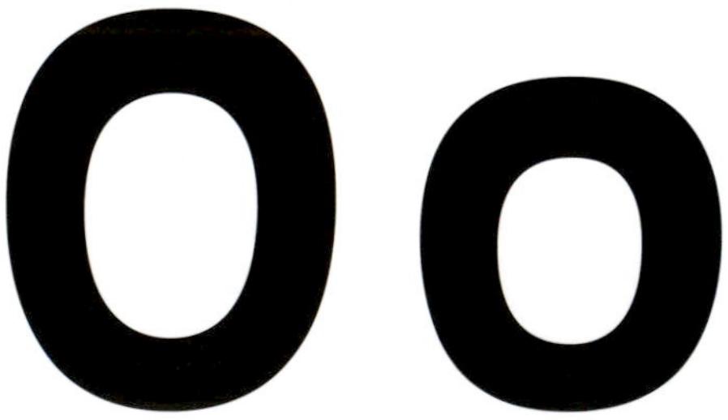

5.

Antique Olive bold

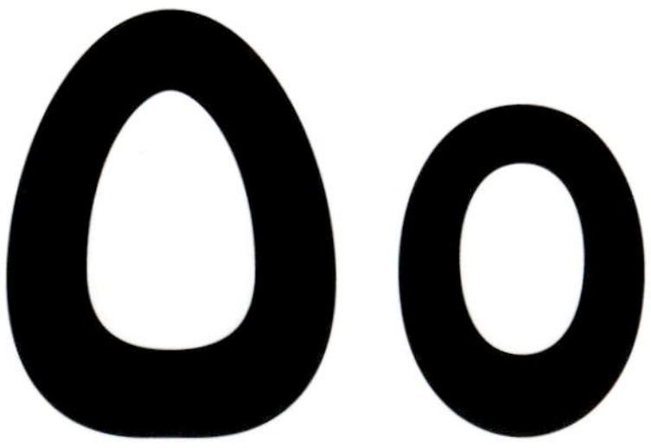

3.

Hobo

6.

No thinning has been applied to the mechanically drawn **O** and the top and bottom curves appear heavy. The **O**s are not true circles, but are slightly shorter on the vertical measure with slight

thinning top and bottom. Sans serif **O**s are often drawn with squarish shapes to help fill the space created by the loss of serifs like those shown opposite. Supposedly single-weight fonts are often a

mix of two-weight forms. Apparent, too, in these examples are the condensed qualities of the capitals when compared to their lowercase counterpart. Designers break the rules: note

that the Gill Sans cap **O** is proportionately wider than the lowercase. Gill Sans and Futura are both called light by their manufacturers, evidence that no standard of weight classification is possible.

curves that turn abruptly. Adrian Frutiger drew the O and other round forms of his Univers with more shoulders to fill the space created by the loss of serifs. Despite their light weight, Gill Sans and Futura have curves that are thinned top and bottom—rotate this book 90 degrees to see the stroke width difference. In some lightweight fonts this adjustment is not made.

Adjustments must be made to balance the capital and lowercase size relationship (*see* the serif letter, pages 38–39). If a lowercase o is enlarged to cap height, it appears to have wider proportions than the lowercase, so type designers reduce the widths of caps. Note that the proportion of the Helvetica cap O is narrower than the lowercase, and the Futura extra bold uses the same scheme. Enigmatically, Eric Gill drew a visually single-weight capital, and then a decidedly two-weight, thick-and-thin lowercase.

There is no formula to direct the type designer.

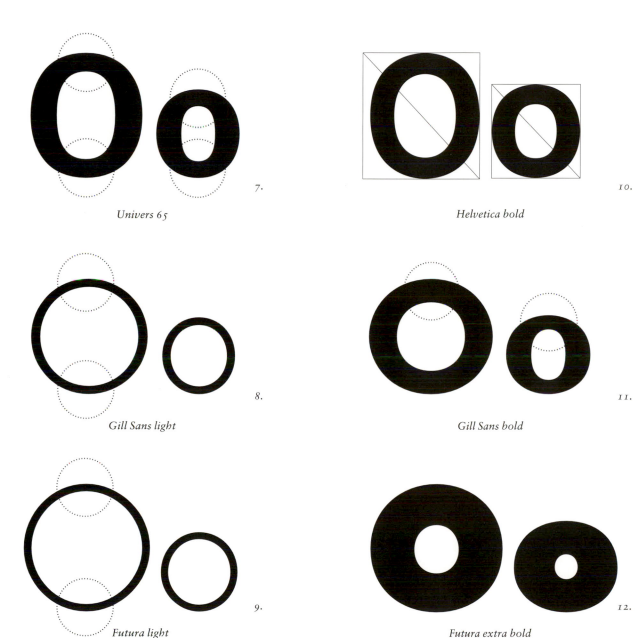

Univers 65 7.

Gill Sans light 8.

Futura light 9.

Helvetica bold 10.

Gill Sans bold 11.

Futura extra bold 12.

Many of the grotesques from the nineteenth century have capital Es and Fs with short center arms. The idea is of value because stems of different lengths create a more identifiable shape than ones of equal length. And there's a bonus—the letter may be tucked closer to a round form when snug spacing is needed. The classically proportioned sans serifs introduced by the Germans in the 1920s generally follow the proportions of the Trajan roman (*see* pages 346–47). For example, the cap E is approximately half the width of its height and drawn with horizontals of equal length; B, F, P, R, and S follow the scheme. Despite their greatest use in advertising that demands large, punchy, tightly spaced, attention-grabbing headlines, these classically proportioned types' spacing should be gently increased for ideal color spac-

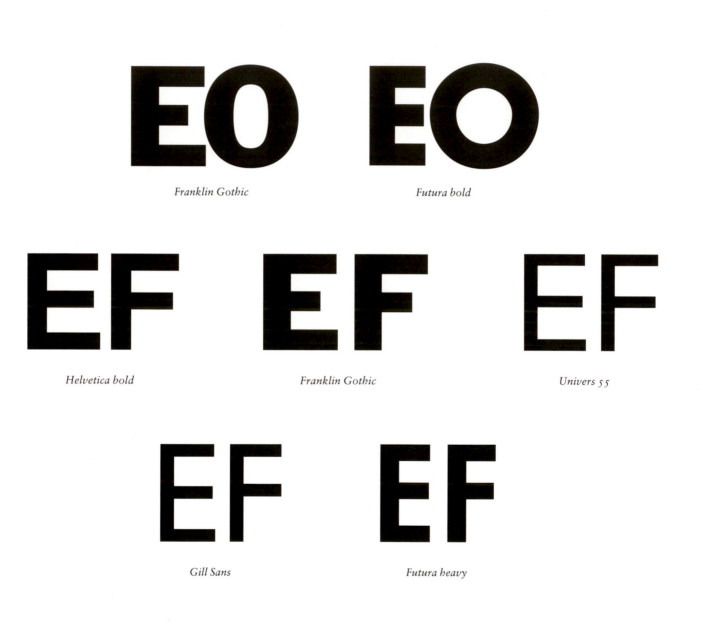

Franklin Gothic

Futura bold

Helvetica bold

Franklin Gothic

Univers 55

Gill Sans

Futura heavy

Center arms come in different lengths. Some are flush with the top and bottom arms; Franklin Gothic has a shorter arm. The short arm creates a more indentifi-able **E** and also allows for tight spacing arrangements because it easily tucks snugly against a round form.

Arms can be joined to correct a mis-spacing, particularly in large sizes or on packaging where space is at a premium. Sometimes a ligature makes for an interesting logo, providing that legibility is maintained.

ing. Narrow caps have a wimpy look when used as the first letter of a sentence, especially when the letters **B, E, F, E, S,** and **T** are followed by full-blown circular **O**s. There are pluses. Within a word, the short **E**s, **L**s, and **T**s diminish otherwise excessive spacing combinations: **LA, LT,** TY, etc. Horizontal strokes are malleable—by hand or in drawing programs, they may be lengthened, shortened, or joined to create a ligature, all in efforts to create more even color spacing. In metal hand-set composition, typesetters added a brass (one-half point), a copper (one-quarter point, or tissue paper between the characters to lessen congestion. This was done by eye, there were no rules. To decrease the space between letters the metal was painstakingly sawed away.

For conservative settings, avoid ligatures.

Univers 55

Univers 65

Univers 65

Display figure: Fino. Text: 22/56 Univers 45, 23-point initial cap

The notion that a sans serif is an impoverished type design is in no way correct, its letterforms show the essentials of a typeface. No terminal strokes or other extensions deflect the eye from the essential form, which is exceedingly sensitive and registers the smallest errors of shape.

ADRIAN FRUTIGER

Type Designer

Art Center College of Design
Pasadena, California
Bernyce Polifka, Art Director
Doyald Young, Designer/Artist
Poster Lettering

Bernyce Polifka taught graphics and color theory at Art Center for over forty years. She was also an accomplished "romantic" hard-edge painter. One of her important contributions was a study for the Metropolitan Museum of Art, showing color relationships within a group of Old Masters. Several West Coast galleries showed her work and just before her retirement Art Center College of Design hosted a retrospective show and printed a large giveaway poster with lettering based on this font, which is also used for the dust jacket of this book. The style, though bolder, is the same that I used for an invitation to her first show in the early 1960s at the Paideia Gallery on La Cienega Boulevard, Los Angeles's gallery row. The light qualities of the letters are not ideal for a poster, but Polifka was fond of the lettering and she wanted to use it. The style refer-

152

ART CENTER OF

■ *This is not Art Center's official logo, but a font based on a poster title for a retrospective exhibition of Bernyce Polifka's paintings sponsored by Art Center. (The name appears in one line on the poster but has been reformatted here to display the words as large as possible.)*

enced her painting signature, an ultra-refined, single-weight capital letter, which had become her distinctive logo.

Based on the classical proportions of the 1920s German sans serifs, some proportions are widened and others narrowed. The O is drawn with a slight diagonal centerline found in Oldstyle fonts, and the overall qualities of the style suggest an ultra-thin, elegant drawing of Zapf's Optima whose stems flare slightly at their tips. Arms of the T, F, and E angle and ending strokes of the C and S are calligraphic in shape, terminating with a slight diagonal to reveal the angle of the pen's nib. Bases of the stems are flat, and round bowls of the R, D, and G swell in thickness and reach a hairline quickly, lending brilliance and sparkle to the letter. The G has no bar on its vertical stem. The S is over-balanced and the the N is pointed. Classic roman Ps are drawn with a smaller bowl that is about half the cap height; this one is lower and wider (number 2). In the fashion of Oldstyles, the bowl is open. Note that the top departing hairline of the P and R are not horizontal lines, but curve upward gently in the manner of Optima.

COLLEGE DESIGN

1.

Fino Titling light—Doyald Young, 1998

A logo for Bernyce Polifka's first exhibition at Paideia Gallery in Los Angeles. It is based on Hermann Zapf's Optima, through much lighter in weight. The proportions are classical, i.e., the **O** is a circle, and the letters **B**, **E**, **F**, **K**, **P**, **R** and **S** are about half as wide.

POLIFKA 2.

International Design Associates
Tokyo, Japan
Tohru Uraoka, President
Mari Makinami, Executive
Creative Director
Doyald Young, Designer/Artist
Haneda Air Terminal
Tokyo, Japan

Audio Plaza is a state-of-the-art audio store in Tokyo's Haneda Airport. Its logo has traces of Handel Gothic and Folio bold condensed.

In a bustling atmosphere a logo must first be arresting, and be either big, bright, or bold, and sometimes all three. Over-sized signs tend to suggest cheapness. Bold letters seem always to be the best answer, but the trick is to restrain their size while keeping them sufficiently large for distance reading. Since the early 1950s, geometric, sans serif letterforms, often in all-lower-case and flat-sided, have been used to suggest state-of-the-art sound equipment. These designs aspire to simplicity, and fit in long narrow signs. The first of the designs (*opposite*) is similar to Futura extra bold condensed, yet the slight two-weight quality can be traced to Franklin Gothic Condensed. The cap **A** is pure

154

audio plaza

audio plaza

■

Minimal flat-sided forms designed to suggest state-of-the-art sound equipment in an airport shopping concourse.

Art Deco with a crossbar that adds legibility and interest to the word. The script contrasts with the sans serif and lessens the tough boldness of the word. Its overlapping cap **P** links the two words, and the staggered alignment "lifts" **Audio**. Design 2 has overtones of Eurostile, which was originally called Microgramma, a titling, caps only face. The typeface has been a favorite of architects and engineers. I removed the crossbars of the **A**s for a clean, minimal look. The **A**s are oblique, but relate to the roman forms because the right-hand stroke is plumb. Since there are three **A**s, their repetition creates a distinctive pattern echoed by the parallel diagonal of the **Z**. Design 3 is a condensed letter with domed **A**s; the **P**'s broken bowl echoes the breaks of the **A**'s shifted crossbars. Design 4 is a modified Folio. Design 5 resembles Optima and Radiant. Design 6 is the strongest of the group; the flat-sided sans dispenses with bowls that roll tangent into the vertical stems; instead, the horizontal joins create a simplified statement and add mass to the letter.

1.

abcdefghijklmnopqrstuvwxyz
ABCDEFGHIJKLMNOPQRSTUVWXYZ

Futura extra bold condensed—Intertype, Edwin W. Shaar & Tommy Thompson, 1939–56

ЛUDIO PLAZA

2.

ABCDEFGHIJKLMNOPQRSTUVWXYZ

Eurostile bold extended—Aldo Novarese, Nebiolo, 1962

ЛUDIO PLAZA

3.

ABCDEFGHIJKLM NOPQRSTUVWXYZ &
abcdefghijklmnopqrstuvwxyz

Phenix—Morris Fuller Benton, ATF, 1935

Audio PLAZA

4.

abcdefghijklmnopqrstuvwxyz
ABCDEFGHIJKLMNOPQRSTUVWXYZ

Folio extra bold—Konrad F. Bauer & Walter Baum, Bauer, 1957–62

AUDIO PLAZA

5.

abcdefghijklmnopqrstuvwxyz
ABCDEFGHIJKLMNOPQRSTUVWXYZ

Optima bold—Hermann Zapf, Stempel, 1952–55

audioplaza

6.

abcdefghijklmnopqrstuvwxyz
ABCDEFGHIJKLMNOPQRSTUVWXYZ

Eurostile bold condensed—Aldo Novarese, Nebiolo, 1962

Deere & Company
Tim O'Connor, Manager
Corporate Design and Graphics
Moline, Illinois
Henry Dreyfuss, Designer
Deere & Company design staff
Doyald Young, Artist

John Deere is synonymous with quality farm equipment the world over. Their tractors are legendary. For decades Henry Dreyfuss Associates have helped design John Deere farm equipment and made their green-and-yellow farm tractors one of the most recognizable vehicles in the world. Dreyfuss, one of the important founders of twentieth-century industrial design, updated and simplified their logo, a leaping deer on a yellow background outlined in green, with the name John Deere letter-spaced within the rectangle. Franklin Gothic wide typeface was the model, with its weight and proportions modified for greatest legibility. Dreyfuss preferred to design logotypes that strongly referenced existing typeforms for maximum compatibility. This version was created as an advertising logo, and it has since been modified

156

JOHN DEERE

JOHN DEERE

The John Deere signature. Reproduced courtesy Deere & Company

■
Above—*An advertising logotype for John Deere is based on Franklin Gothic wide.*

for the John Deere corporate signature shown here.

Less contrast is used for the thick / thin ratio; this is apparent on the horizontal stems of the **D**, which is heavier than the **R**'s horizontal stems. The thick/thin contrast relates more to Victor Caruso's ITC Franklin Gothic than to the original Franklin Gothic, on which it was modeled. Shoulders of the round forms were beefed up, and the tips of the horizontal strokes of the **Es** were angled slightly. To color more evenly, the center arm was lengthened. The bowl of the **R** was lowered to keep the counter open for legibility at a distance and use in small sizes. The taper of the diagonal stem was retained, but it is more restrained. For vertical stem consistency, the weight distribution of the **N** was transposed; the diagonal was thinned and the verticals were weighted.

ABCDEFGHIJKLMNOPQR STUVWXYZ abcdefghijklmnopqrstuv

Franklin Gothic wide (metal)—John L. Renshaw ATF, c. 1952

ABCDEFGHIJKLMNOPQR STUVWXYZ abcdefghijklmnopqrstuvwxyz

Franklin Gothic—Morris Fuller Benton, ATF, 1902

ABCDEFGHIJKLMNOPQR STUVWXYZ abcdefghijklmnopqrstuvwxyz

Franklin Gothic heavy—Victor Caruso, ITC, 1979

International Design Associates
Tokyo, Japan
Tohru Uraola, President
Mari Makinami, Executive
Creative Director
Doyald Young, Designer/Artist
Japan Air Ministry,
Japan Air Terminal (Haneda)

Fancies is a gift shop in the Japan Air Terminal shopping concourse. Some fancy design approaches that seemed to fit the problem were shown first, but the client preferred the simple contemporary sans serif design. Often in the development of a logo, multiple directions are explored, and the reasons for the final choice can be many: a marketing shift, client personal preference, or changes in management. (There are many answers to any given logo assignment.) The selected logo references several styles: Novarese's Stop and Glaser Stencil; a swash F based on Plaza ultra; and a C from Handel Gothic.

A stencil font has a subtext: it implies imported goods, because for many years letters were stenciled on shipping crates. Stop, the logo's major type reference, is an unconventional stencil because its breaks do not fall

FANCIES

FANCIES

■
Gift shop and wrapping services in the Haneda Airport terminal. Final art with influences of Handel Gothic, Stop, Glaser Stencil, and Letraset's Plaza.
Opposite—*Initial comprehensives for the gift boutique, all designed as decorative statements with exaggerated caps.*

in the standard breakup of letters, which traditionally favor the downstroke. Glaser Stencil breaks the pattern also. Letraset's version is a traditional example based on Clarendon. The stencil breaks in the logo are evenly spaced, a bit of luck in the logo's sequence of letters (though the **A** could have been broken). The **A**'s lack of a crossbar doesn't cause confusion because no other letter is shaped the same, and it cannot be mistaken for a V. Breaking the **C** or **S** is unnecessary, because both are simple shapes, and not every letter has to break; it is a design and not a metal stencil where the letters must be held together with small connecting strips.

The comprehensive presentations are diverse, and each design is tinged with fancy and references the spirit of a particular letter style or font: Trafton (1); Lutetia inline (2); single-weight script (3); traditional formal script (4); condensed Bodoni (5); Bernhard Tango (6); Modern No. 216 (7); and Stencil (8).

1.

2.

3.

4.

5.

6.

7.

8.

ΛBCDEFGHJKLMNOPQRSTUVWXYZ&

Stop—Aldo Novarese, Nebiolo, 1970

*Glaser Stencil—Milton Glaser,
Letraset, n.d.*

ABCDEFGHIJKLMNOPQRSTUVWXYZ&

Handel Gothic—Don Handel, VGC, 1965

ABCDEFGHIJKLMNOP
QRSTUVWXYZ&

Stencil—Letraset, 1987

Plaza—Letraset, 1975

SANS SERIF LOGOS

International Design Associates
Tokyo, Japan
Tohru Uraoka, President
Mari Makinami, Executive
Creative Director
Doyald Young, Designer/Artist
Haneda Airport,
Japan Air Ministry
Tokyo, Japan

160

Gift giving is ingrained in the Japanese culture. First-class hotels sell specially designed gift wrapping papers for the marriages, showers, and anniversaries that are held in their many elegant private banquet rooms. The shop for which this logo was designed is in an airport shopping concourse and offers expertly and quickly wrapped and mailed gifts or packages. The logotype is hard-sell, bold and heavily italicized to suggest speed, efficiency, and prompt service. The letters are a relation of the early sans serifs named Grotesques; Franklin Gothic is a descendant. The bowl-and-tailed g relates to traditional serif fonts, though the ear is greatly stylized and lies flat and lines up with the dot of the *i*. The *f* descends cursively and its angled ending almost touches the tail of the **g**. Because the word is so snugly spaced, the *f*'s crossbar has been deleted on the stem's left side but

creates a ligature with the cross-bar of the *t*. Its top ending normally parallels the main stem. Here it angles and almost touches the top of the *t*. The *t*'s tail is more curved than its Franklin model, but the ascender has a diagonal chop in the same style as Franklin. Another ligature, the *EX* in *Ex-press*, evolved from the proportion and tight spacing scheme. The style is a modified and italicized version of Bank Gothic.

The logo is an example of contrasts: a two-weight sans with a single-weight sans; a round sans with rectilinear forms; and an all-lowercase word against an all-cap word. An organized design is created by aligning *Express* with the left side of the *t*. For contrast, the word *Express* is much smaller to let the important word *gift* have first reading.

ABCDEFGHIJKLMNOPQRSTUV WXYZÆŒ& abcdefghijklmnopqrstuvwxyzæ

Grotesque No. 8—Stephenson Blake & Monotype, n.d.

abcdefghijklmnopqr stuvwxyz $1234567 ABCDEFGHIJKLMN OPQRSTUVWXYZ &

Franklin Gothic wide—John L. Renshaw, ATF, 1952

ABCDEFGHIJKLMNOPQR STUVWXYZ

Bank Gothic medium—Morris Fuller Benton, ATF, 1930–33

■

Gift Express is a wrapping / mail service shop in the Tokyo Haneda Airport terminal. The logo references Franklin Gothic wide and Grotesque No. 8, an early nineteenth-century font, and Bank Gothic. The design is a study in contrast: round versus straight; single- and two-weight; lowercase and caps; large and small.

TJRM

Tom Jacobson and
Ramone Muñoz
Los Angeles, California
Doyald Young, Designer/Artist

The owners of a multi-use building wanted a logo that would express their interests: an art gallery and an actor's rehearsal hall. Muñoz wanted to see some monogram designs that could be used on invitations for special exhibitions. The sans serif monogram was chosen and comp

number 5, the script monogram, was so well received that I was asked to create final art for it also.

Monograms suggest connected letters, and the use of swashes helps tie them together. Swash caps also help to soften the brittle qualities of sans serifs; Tempo italic caps and Goudy Sans are

typical. Tempo is more script-like; Goudy suffers from fussy **M** and **N** loops at cap height.

Several arrangements can be used in monogram design: the first letter of the last name singly, or all initials combined, in one or more styles, or the last initial may dominate.

162

ABCDEFGHIJKLMNOPQRSTUVWXYZ

Tempo light italic—R. H. Middleton, Ludlow, 1930

AABCDEFGHIJKLMMNNOPQRSTUVWXYZ&

Goudy Sans Serif light italic—Frederic Goudy, Monotype, 1931, ITC, 1986

Script monograms are a favorite, though many sans serif and serif styles are used. In their design the trick always is to find a graceful way to combine sometimes disparate shapes. Scripts offer the greatest flexibility, because extensions of the letters, either loops, swashes, or flourishes, can be stretched to fill a space and/or create an outer shape with some degree of symmetry.

Letters can be modified to join to another letter. The first design (*opposite*) is economical because the R's lower swash creates a J that joins the two sets of initials. Increasing the M's angles allows the R to join without drawing a long diagonal tail (a vertical-stemmed M would create a much longer diagonal). In all five designs, the swashes are extensions of each letter and not separate flourishes. Comp 2 is a quasi-script roman; comp 3 makes use of an extended fat Bodoni with overlapping leaning script; comp 4 is a lighter-weight condensed Bodoni, and 2, 3, and 4 use bracketed serifs. Comp 4 references Typo Upright (*see* page 179).

1.

4.

2.

5.

3.

6.

■

Monograms assume many shapes—a cartouche, or one or two lines—and may be of any font style, though script monograms are prevalent. Two styles may be combined.

SANS SERIF LOGOS

International Design Associates
Tokyo, Japan
Tohru Uraoka, President
Mari Makinami,
Executive Creative Director
Doyald Young, Designer/Artist
Japan Technicals

This logotype is tailored for a computer software firm.

One of the most important ways to create a strong logotype is to establish relationships between the letters and/or words to create order. The relationship should be apparent, not a subtle device of which only the designer is aware. Two even-length words make one of the more obvious pairings. In the example below, the words are of different length, but they are related by several means. Both are sans serif. They align flush right, and the crossbar of the **T** lines up optically with the **J**'s tail. The ascenders of the **h** and **l** invade the counters of the **A** and **N** and visually lock the two words together. Contrast is another scheme used to add interest to otherwise mundane letter combinations: a bold letter against a light-weight letter; caps contrasted to lowercase; roman (upright) opposed to italic; and script versus

■
Relationships of letters and words can be designed for harmony and to create a strong graphic image.

sans serif. These are preliminary design steps made *before* the letters are individually styled. Boldness plays an important role in guiding the viewer. A word may be a large size, but less important because of its light weight, or a word may be first reading—even though it is small—by use of an extreme bold weight. Letters may be stylized to add interest. Crossbars of **A**s may be deleted as long as the word reads easily; here, the word Japan is easily recognized. The lack of crossbars is a minimal statement that also suggests state-of-the-art, and the undotted **i** repeats the ploy. The sans serif style of **Technicals** is similar to the ultra-bold extended versions of Helvetica, Folio, and Univers, and has an extremely large x-height. Considerable thinning occurs on the horizontals to keep the counters of the **e**, **c**, **a**, and **s** from closing up. The thinning is most apparent in the **e**'s crossbar, and the thin portions of the **a**'s bowl. Note the small reverse curve bracket that connects the bowl to the vertical stem. Folio extra bold and Helvetica black use this bracket, Univers 85 does not.

ABCDEFGHIJKLMNOPQRSTUVWXYZ
abcdefghijklmnopqrstuvwxyz
ABCDEFGHIJKLMNOPQRSTUVWXYZ
abcdefghijklmnopqrstuvwxyz

Helvetica black and Helvetica light—Max Meidinger, Haas, 1957

ABCDEFGHIJKLMNOPQRSTUVWXYZ
abcdefghijklmnopqrstuvwxyz
ABCDEFGHIJKLMNOPQRSTUVWXYZ
abcdefghijklmnopqrstuvwxyz

Folio extra bold and Folio light—Konrad F. Bauer and Walter Baum, Bauer, 1957–62

ABCDEFGHIJKLMNOPQRSTUVWXYZ
abcdefghijklmnopqrstuvwxyz
ABCDEFGHIJKLMNOPQRSTUVWXYZ
abcdefghijklmnopqrstuvwxyz

Univers 85—Adrian Frutiger, Haas, 1984
Univers 45—Adrian Frutiger, Deberny & Peignot, 1957

Right—The bracketed bowl of the **a** adds more mass to the letter. Helvetica and Folio use the conceit, but Univers joins at right angles.

Helvetica black   *Folio extra bold*

Univers 85

SANS SERIF LOGOS

Warner Bros. Records
Burbank, California
Jeri Heiden, Chief Art Director
Gregory Ross, Art Director
Doyald Young,
Logotype Designer
CD logotype

Gregory Ross chose the font Lithos for a CD for **k.d. lang**, a country music/cross-over singer from Calgary, Canada (design number 1). Lithos is a titling face of capital letters designed to fill most of the font matrix height. It is relaxed and bounces slightly; there are several weights.

Ms. lang liked the font style but preferred her name set in all-lowercase letters. The exploratory designs sought a lowercase that would maintain the flavor of the titling font, while satisfying Ms. lang's preference. In design number 2, **k. d. lang** is weighted slightly, branches of the **n** are rather flat, and the bowls are drawn to match Lithos caps. Design number 3 uses softer, more rounded curved shapes, with branches and bowls that join close to the tips of the straight stems. The **a**'s bowl is exaggerated. In design number 4 **d**, **a**, and **g** and the branch of the **n** depart at the very tips of the

k.d. lang
INGÉNUE

k.d. lang
INGÉNUE

A logo for a Warner Bros. Records CD that creates a mix of caps and lower-case letters from an all-cap titling font to produce a biform.

FONTS & LOGOS

straight stems. The lowercase **g**'s bowl is is fully rounded and shortened, its stem descends slightly below the baseline.

The chosen design has a large x-height with strong diagonal-thrust bowls. The **g** is a cap with a straight stem that descends to produce a quasi cap/lowercase **g**.

Ms. Heiden missed the crisp cap **N** and this was introduced into the logo. With the addition of a cap **G** and **N**, the logotype becomes a biform, a mix of lowercase and x-height caps reinforced by the **i**, which has lost its dot. The slightly heavier periods are freely drawn square spots.

K.D. LANG
INGENUE

1.

Lithos extra light

k.d. lang
ingenue

3.

k.d. lang
ingenue

2.

k.d. lang
ingenue

.4

ABCDEFGHIJKLMNOPQRSTUVWXYZ

Lithos extra light—Carol Twombly, Adobe, 1989

SANS SERIF LOGOS

Bette Midler is an acclaimed comedienne, a serious actress and singer, but her real *shtik* is camp, defined by the *American Heritage Dictionary* as "an affected affection for the artificial, vulgar, or banal." Bette is particularly fond of the 1930s and '40s variety. This logotype was designed to face the invitation cover for a Los Angeles Children's Museum benefit.

Bette is a light, two-weight, faux pen script; it is as flamboyant as Midler's personna. The word was written hurriedly in pencil, carefully traced and adjusted, and inked with a felt pen on tracing paper. The *B*'s top beginning curve stroke is exaggerated, with a subtly curving stem that exceeds the curve's boundaries. The word's upward thrust creates a dynamic movement that is echoed by the elongated ellipses of the *B*. This upward angle repeats on the exaggerated

168

sweeping crossbar of the *t*s, and angles more steeply with the ebullient finishing stroke of the *e*, which ultimately gives the logotype its image. The weight distribution closely follows formal script, though more freely drawn, with two differently shaped *e*s.

The campy silhouette **Midler** caps are bold extended shapes, and though the font is not a great statement of legibility, this particular combination of letters is legible. The style is reminiscent of the fonts of the Parisian designer, A. M. Cassandre. His fonts Acier Noir, Bifur, Peignot,

and Touraine, designed in collaboration with the type designer/ typefounder Charles Peignot (with the exception of Peignot), are mainly illustrations of letters. Because the forms are offbeat and geometric, they are closely associated with the period in which they were designed: Pari-

sian Moderne and Art Deco. The shapes are posterish, without finesse—they appear to be tossed-off. In contrast, Roger Excoffon's Calypso is a design tour de force: his initial concept of a shaded piece of material folded to form a capital letter is brilliantly and absolutely resolved.

SOUVERAINES

Acier Noir (Black Steel)—A. M. Cassandre, Deberny & Peignot, 1936

WITCH DENAR

Bifur (Fork)—A. M. Cassandre, Deberny & Peignot, 1929

ABCDEFGHIJKLMNOPQRSTUVWXYZ
abcdefghijklmnopqrstuvwxyz
1234567890

Peignot demi—A. M. Cassandre, Deberny & Peignot, 1937

Touraine

Touraine bold—A. M. Cassandre and Charles Peignot, Deberny & Peignot, 1947

Calypso—Roger Excoffon, Olive, 1958

■

These fonts designed over a 30-year period reflect the extreme. They are not particularly legible, but seldom are they used en masse. Instead, their use denotes a period of time or attitude, as do the Cassandre-style caps of Midler's name.

SANS SERIF LOGOS

International Design Associates
Tokyo, Japan
Tohru Uraoka, President
Ken Nakata, Art Director
Doyald Young, Designer/Artist
Hotel Granvia Nihon
Japan Railways,
Okayama, Japan

Olivier is a coffee house in the Hotel Granvia, whose lobby and graphics are Art Deco style. The logo is designed in the manner of Art Deco fonts, many of which are based on geometric classical forms: circular **O**s and the group of narrow letters: **B, E, F, L, P, R, S** and **T**. The logo's smaller caps are centered on the over-scale cap **O** and hang there in a more comfortable position than at the **O**'s baseline. One of the more difficult tasks of a font or a logo designer is to balance the cap and lowercase weights. In this example the large cap **O** must color equally with the smaller caps. Note that its curved stem is minutely heavier. For greater legibility, the ascender of the **L** is taller than the cap **O**, a feature of the lowercase Peignot font.

Type design basics are evident in the point of the **V**, which descends below the baseline so that it optically aligns with the other

Olivier

Olivier

■
This design is based on the geometric sans of 1920s Germany, coupled with exaggerated Art Deco influences, and modified classical proportions.
***Opposite**—A series of comprehensives for a hotel coffee house that explored friendly scripts, bold extended shapes, and elegant inlines.*

letters. Typical of the Art Deco style, which had its heyday in the late 1920s and '30s, are the low crossbar of the **E** and the top-heavy bowl of the **R**. Expansive crossbars were popular. Bernhard Fashion employs the scheme and even applies it to the **S**. The **E**'s middle arm extends to the left of the vertical stem, which is also a design feature of Bernhard Fashion. Designs 2 and 3 are suggestive of the Art Deco period, with the highly placed arm of the **E** and high-waisted **R**, other Art Deco features. Decorative inline fonts were issued by several foundries in the '30s and the types graced many a piece of social printing. Designs 4, 5, and 6 are more traditional examples, and were included to show a variety of weights and forms that were not as mechanical as the chosen design.

OLIVIER

1.

OLIVIER

4.

OLIVIER

2.

Olivier

5.

OLIVIER

3.

Olivier

6.

abcdefghijklmnopqrstuvwxyz

Peignot light lowercase—A. M. Cassandre, Deberny & Peignot, 1937

ABCDEFGHIJKLMNOPQRSTUVWXYZ

Bernhard Fashion—Lucian Bernhard, ATF, 1929

SANS SERIF LOGOS

Paul Hinckley
Los Angeles, California
Art Director, Designer
Doyald Young, Artist
Optica, Eye Boutique
Beverly Hills, California

Rome boasts the Via Condotti; Paris, Fauborg St.-Honore; Tokyo, Amoto Sandi; and Beverly Hills, Rodeo Drive. Adjacent to Rodeo's few illustrious blocks is Camden Drive, with less bustle but still lined with elegant and fashionable shops. Paul Hinckley, space planner, designed the ex-terior and interior space as well as the logotype for this Camden Drive boutique.

Hinckley asked me to draw the finished art. Along the way we explored different proportions, weights, and letterspacing, and made some refinements to the letters. Hinckley's initial design is geometric: the O is a circle, and the bowl of the P, a portion of a circle. The C is the logo's hook, or grabber, and it is drawn in a chevron shape. The French call chevrons guillemets; they are less elegantly nicknamed "chicken" or "duck" feet. Their shape is more reminiscent of early

172

OPTICA

OPTICA

sans serif Greek forms than French types.

Optica's **A**, without a crossbar, resembles the Greek letter lambda; some of the comped **A**s are like the Greek delta, with different-length crossbar widths. Horizontal stem endings for the C and A were tested (design 13), but angled endings won out. Arms with parallel tips of the **T** in both directions were tried (designs 3 and 4) but a traditional crossbar was the final choice. The **P**'s bowl is broken (except in design 9), widened, and is less mechanical; the O while appearing monotone has thinner horizontal curves.

1. OPTI<Λ
2. OPTI<Δ
3. OPTI<Λ
4. OPTI<Λ
5. OPTI<Δ
6. OPTI<Δ
7. O P T I < Λ
8. O P T I < Λ
9. OPTI<Λ
10. OPTI<Λ
11. **OPTI<Λ**
12. OPTI<Δ
13. **OPTI<Λ**
14. **OPTI<Λ**
15. O P T I < Λ
16. **OPTI<Λ**

◼

Top—Design 1 is Paul Hinckley's logo design for an elegant Beverly Hills optical shop. I explored design variations: different cap **A**s seeking maximum legibility and style (designs 2, 5, 6, and 8). Then I tried horizontal endings on the **C** and **A** (designs 12 and 13) and opposing angles for the **T**'s crossbar (designs 10 and 11). I didn't care for the mechanical-looking **O** and the bowl of the **P** and drew them as elliptical shapes for the finished art. The exact weight is always a problem; we looked at different spacing arrangements, and settled on a much bolder weight than the original comprehensive design, with a slightly tighter spacing scheme.

French quotes   Lambda   Delta
(*guillemets*)

Ulf Helgesson, Industrial Design
Woodland Hills, California
Ulf Helgesson, Executive
Creative Director
Doyald Young, Designer/Artist
Perceptronics, Human Factors
Woodland Hills, California

A long name requires judicious spacing for maximum legibility, and the spacing may even contribute the logo's distinguishing characteristics.

Perceptronics designs and manufactures virtual reality simulators, used in combined arms tactical training, for the Department of Defense. Design number 1 is normally spaced, but lacks quick legibility. Designs 2 and 3 are letterspaced by 150 percent, which helps the word's readability. The additional space lends a cleaner and more contemporary look to the logo. Design number 3 uses a larger intitial **P**. The logo style is a blending of two fonts, Franklin Gothic and Adrian Frutiger's eponymous sans serif. The bowl of the **R** does not touch the stem—a characteristic of Eras. It is the **C** and **S** that resemble Frutiger's inimitable letterforms, which are decidedly two-weight. Some sparkle is introduced by

174

PERCEPTRONICS 1.

PERCEPTRONICS

PERCEPTRONICS 2.

PERCEPTRONICS

PERCEPTRONICS 3.

PERCEPTRONICS

PERCEPTRONICS 4.

PERCEPTRONICS

■

Different spacing arrangements for a logotype with many letters. The style is based on Franklin Gothic and Frutiger with slight influences of Futura. Version 4 was the selected design.

FONTS & LOGOS

chopping the arms and **C** and **S** endings at a discreet, barely perceptible angle. Design number 4 was chosen. Futura was one of the early sans serifs that chopped the round forms with vertical endings. Note both the capital and lowercase **C**s; the bold condensed **S** has a vertical chop. This allows the letters to fit more snugly without creating congestion. Some sans serifs use consistent curve angle endings; both Helvetica and Univers are horizontal, Franklin Gothic is angled, and Futura uses a mixture of all three.

ABCDEFGHIJKLMNOPQRSTUVWXYZ
abcdefghijklmnopqrstuvwxyz
1234567890

Franklin Gothic—Morris Fuller Benton, ATF, 1902

ABCDEFGHIJKLMNOPQRSTUVWXYZ
abcdefghijklmnopqrstuvwxyz
1234567890

Frutiger 65—Adrian Frutiger, Stempel, 1976

ABCDEFGHIJKLMNOPQRSTUVWXYZ
abcdefghijklmnopqrstuvwxyz
1234567890

Eras bold—Albert Boton & Albert Hollenstein, ITC, 1976

ABCDEFGHIJKLMNOPQRSTUVWXYZ
abcdefghijklmnopqrstuvwxyz
1234567890

Futura extra bold—Edwin W. Shaar & Tommy Thompson,
Intertype, 1939–56

ABCDEFGHIJKLMNOPQRSTUVWXYZ
abcdefghijklmnopqrstuvwxyz
1234567890

Futura bold condensed—Paul Renner, Bauer, 1930,
Mergenthaler Type Library

SANS SERIF LOGOS

But in Order to
write well, there must
be just Rules given, and
much Practice . . .

George Bickham

18th-century Writing Master, Engraver,

and Author,

The Universal Penman

Script is a general word used to describe written letters that are usually connected. Dictionaries define script as cursive (which stems from Middle Latin *cursivus*, running, coursing), and describe the writing as "flowing." Scripts do not always connect. The distinction is inexact. Formal scripts are based on flexible pen handwriting and may slope, be upright, or even slant backwards. Scripts have long been associated with social correspondence. In eighteenth- and nineteenth-century Europe it was customary for a guest's arrival to be announced with a script calling card with ample room to accommodate a brief, handwritten message. To this day, books of etiquette suggest a reserved engraved script for proper stationery. Formal scripts suggest elegance, quality, and refinement, and frequently official communication. The Constitution of the United States and the Bill of Rights were written in a small, careful formal script. Script has many uses, including

Civilité—Robert Granjon, 1557

Zapf Civilité

A B C D E F G H I J

K L M N O P Q R S T

U V W X Y Z &

$ 1 2 3 4 5 6 7 8 9 0 ¢

a b c d e f g h i j k l m

n o p qu r s t u v w x y z

(« . , - : ; ! ? ß »)

Zapf Civilité—Hermann Zapf, Paul Hayden Duensing Foundry, 1971–74

Script types may be divided into two general categories, formal and casual, either slanting or upright.

Robert Granjon's Civilité, a formal, upright script, mimicked the fashionable hands of the day. His script was florid, with strong pointed descenders and exuberant ascenders. The majority of the letters resemble upright minuscules. Civilités, as the name implies, were used primarily for official documents. While called script, the letters do not connect but are characterized by elaborate, sweeping flourishes and swashes. Hermann Zapf's Civilité, designed for the private typefoundry of Paul H. Duensing, is a more refined contemporary version.

In Italy, Arrighi fashioned the chancery hand with only a slight slope. It is

invitations and ceremonial forms (diplomas and certificates). Formal scripts are often used to advertise quality products: cosmetics, gourmet foods, wine, jewelry, and furs.

Many scripts were derived from a writing style known as chancery, developed for writing papal briefs in the fifteenth century. The connected scripts that are familiar to us today can be traced to seventeenth-century French scripts typified by that of the writing master Pierre Moreau. In eighteenth-century England the hand became more rounded and flowing. The technical problems of creating script metal type somewhat modified the shapes of the written letters and the manner in which they were connected. Many of the popular scripts of the late nineteenth century were similar to Bank Script and Palace Script, known in England as copperplates, from the engraved copper plates that were used to emboss stationery and calling cards. In the United States the term refers to Copperplate Gothic, distinguished by minute, hairline finishing serifs (*see* pages 310–11).

Ludouicus Vicentinus scribebat Romæ anno salutis **M DXXIII**

The chancery hand
Ludovico Arrighi—La Operina, Rome, 1522

Metamorphoses. 87
visible fait apres sa mort, en la personne, tant de luy-mesme, que

Script type by Pierre Moreau, 1644

ABCDEFGHIJKLMNOPQRSTUVWXYZ
abcdefghijklmnopqrstuvwxyz

Typo Upright (originally Tiffany Upright)—Morris Fuller Benton, ATF, 1905

ABCDEFGHIJKLMNOPQRSTUVWXYZ
abcdefghijklmnopqrstuvwxyz

Palace Script—Stephenson Blake and Monotype, 1923

the model for many italic fonts. Subsequent scripts, both upright and sloping, are derivative. Moreau's script, a bâtarde (a formal sloping hand), is based on papal chancery forms, which were usually sloped and reflected the haste in which they were written. Morris Benton's Typo Upright is based in part on Moreau's early upright forms. Scripts of the late eighteenth and early nineteenth centuries were drawn with a split, pointed quill or metal pen that produced a hairline on the upstroke where less pressure is applied. The weight distribution of scripts, whether upright or slanting, is usually below center on left-hand curves and above center on right-hand curves.

SCRIPT LETTERS

Formal Scripts

Royal Script, Bank Script, Typo Script, Formal Script, and Commercial Script have been America's mainstay script fonts for the greater part of the twentieth century. They are based on nineteenth-century forms known as Spencerian scripts after the American writing master Platt Rogers Spencer.[1] This group is among my favorites, despite their tight turns, which mirrored a fashionable style of handwriting of the day. Bank and Typo are typical. Note that the six fonts shown below share the same cap *A*. Commercial and Royal script are wide with wide connecting hairlines. Middleton's Formal Script does not connect. Commercial Script has been the most popular because of its strength, though Typo and Royal Script are still popular with social printers because of their lightweight elegance. Palace Script is a handsome British import, immensely popular in England. Its drawing, too, is based on nineteenth-century scripts.

Ed Benguiat's Edwardian Script has a tight fit, and Matthew Carter's Snell Round-

Royal Script—Central Type Foundry Branch, ATF, 1893

Bank Script—James West, BB&S, 1895

Typo Script—Morris Fuller Benton, ATF, 1902

Commercial Script—Morris Fuller Benton, ATF, 1906

Formal Script—R. H. Middleton, Ludlow, 1956

Palace Script—Stephenson Blake and Monotype, 1923

hand, based on the eighteenth-century writing of Charles Snell, is open. Their lowercase forms do not have the tight turns of Bank Script; Snell has a wider fit. Both are available in a variety of weights and the former has alternate characters. Künstler, a forty-year-old font is enjoying a revival.

All of the script fonts shown reference in some manner the English roundhand style of the eighteenth-century master penman, George Bickham.[2]

To this day social printers also use a special group of script templates to create what is commonly called "engraved" stationery. These are not metal foundry letters that are set by hand, or digital fonts; instead, the fonts are engraved on 19"x 3⅜" rectangular pieces of steel called Pantograph Master Plates. The letters are reproduced with a pantograph to a specified size, letter by letter, with a drill that cuts the letter into the steel die used to die-stamp, or "engrave" stationery.

1. Mac McGrew, *American Metal Typefaces of the Twentieth Century*, page 319.

2. George Bickham, *The Universal Penman* (reprint, New York: Dover Publications, 1941).

ABCDEFGHIJKLMNO
PQRSTUVWXYZ
abcdefghijklmnopqrstuvwxyz 1234567890

ITC Edwardian Script regular—Ed Benguiat, 1994

ABCDEFGHIJKLMNOPQRS
TUVWXYZ
abcdefghijklmnopqrstuvwxyz1234567890

Snell Roundhand regular—Matthew Carter, Linofilm, 1966

ABCDEFGHIJKLMNOPQ
RSTUVWXYZ
abcdefghijklmnopqrstuvwxyz 1234567890

Künstler Script medium (Künstlerschreibschrift)—Hans Bohn, Stempel, 1957

■

Opposite—*Popular formal scripts of the twentieth century, designed around 1900 and based on mid-nineteenth-century forms, descendants of the English round-hand style popularized by George Bickham in the eighteenth century.*
Above—*Fonts based on eighteenth-century English roundhands.*
Right—*Steel-die engraving scripts. These were specially designed alphabets; some are baroque, many are shaded Victorian faces. Each alphabet was engraved on a long steel plate and pantographed to size on steel dies for social printing. (Master Plate fonts courtesy The Ligature Engravers, Los Angeles, California.)*

Miss Katherine Betty Robertson
ENGLISH SCRIPT

Mrs. Carl Edward Brownstone
COLONIAL SCRIPT

Mrs. Charles Barkley Kenniston
SOCIAL SCRIPT

Miss Norma Louise Garrison
SPENCERIAN SCRIPT

Mrs. William Norton Edwards
FRANCISCAN SCRIPT

Master Plate alphabets for steel-die engraving
The Cronite Company

SCRIPT LETTERS

The most distinguishing characteristic of casual scripts is their free form. There are no exact rules for their shapes because the variations are infinite, but within a design concept, some guidelines are helpful. The fonts are bountiful and may be designed to fit many moods. The distinction between formal and casual scripts is often blurred, because some fonts mix a staid lowercase with flamboyant caps, or combine exaggerated brush caps with sedate pen forms. Salto script is an example (*opposite, bottom*).

Casual scripts may be single-weight, two-weight, upright, slanted, base-aligned or bounced, brush- or pen-inspired, and are available as type or hand-lettered styles. They may be mechanically constructed forms, which I call novelty scripts, as there are novelty romans. Some scripts are based on handwriting, but many styles are modeled shapes, intellectually drawn and impossible to even faintly duplicate by handwriting. Some are bizarre, designed for a specific product, market, or age group. These are short-lived—their usage incandescent in fash-

182

Bernhard Cursive (Madonna)—Lucian Bernhard, Bauer, 1925

Brush Script—Robert E. Smith, ATF, 1942

Trafton Script—Howard Allen Trafton, Bauer, 1933

Elite—Aldo Novarese, Nebiolo, 1968

Futura Demi-Bold Script—Edwin W. Shaar, Intertype, 1954

Grayda—Frank H. Riley, ATF, 1939

Legend—F. H. E. Schneidler, Bauer, 1937

ion periodicals or tabloid style magazines that trumpet the new. But what's cool today is pitifully *not* cool tomorrow. Some well-designed scripts survive overuse and are revived to become fashionable statements.

I have chosen these 13 fonts for their diversity and design.

With the exception of Elite, Futura demi-bold script, Ondine, Salto, and Venture, all are enjoying a revival. Type preference is personal and I confess that Brush, while popular, is not a favorite. I admire Trafton. It is beautifully drawn to impeccable, calligraphic standards. A fash-

ion-oriented face, it embodies 1930s elegance. Elite and Futura demi-bold script are good; I particularly admire Novarese's Elite caps. Freestyle Script, a joined style designed by Martin Wait, is a font of simple shapes that has enjoyed wide usage since its introduction in 1987.

No two lists of good and bad scripts are ever remotely the same, which indicates that lists are highly subjective.

The use of scripts is prevalent in all forms of advertising that promote style, fashion, recreation, toys, and food products, and mundane sale notices.

ABCDEFGHIJKLMNOPQRSTUV WXYZabcdefghijklmnopqrstuvwxyz1234567890

Murray Hill—Emil Klumpp, ATF, c. 1956

ABCDEFGHIJKLMNOPQRSTUVWXYZ **abcdefghijklmnopqrstuvwxyz1234567890**

Mistral—Roger Excoffon, Olive, 1953

ABCDEFGHIJKLMNOPQRSTUVW **abcdefghijklmnopqrst uvwxyz**

Ondine—Adrian Frutiger, Deberny & Peignot, 1954

ADCDEFGHIJKLMNOPQRSTUVWXYZ *abcdefghijklmnopqrstuvwxyz $1234567890*

Freestyle Script—Martin Wait, Letraset, 1987

The Annual Dinner of the Club

Salto—Karlgeorg Hoefer, Klingspor, 1952–53

ABCDEFGHIJKLMNOPQRSTUVWXYZ *abcdefghijklmnopqrstuvwxyz*

Venture—Hermann Zapf, Linofilm, 1960–67

■
These scripts reveal the diversity of written scripts; some are connected, others not. Their angles vary, and they suggest different moods. The uprights have a quiet repose, and as the angle or bounce increases, so does their visual impact.

SCRIPT LETTERS

Formal script is the general type classification to which English roundhand belongs. It describes script fonts based on seventeenth- and eighteenth-century styles written with pointed, flexible pens using more or less pressure to create the thick-and-thin lines. The style is notable for its round, flowing, connecting hairlines and bold downstrokes.

Only a few shapes are necessary to create the script: straight downstroke; bowl, reverse curve; straight and looped ascender and descenders. With few exceptions the letters connect with hairlines.

John Ayres, George Bickham, Joseph Champion, Willington Clark, William Leekey, George Shelly, and Charles Snell were the writing masters of the late seventeenth and early eighteenth centuries whose styles have influenced many of our present-day fonts. Their work is

184

Note: The annotations of Young Baroque are specific to the font. Other fonts may be drawn with different design concepts.

Bowl is widest below x-height center

Left-side curves at point of join and weight diminishes near the baseline

Join one-third to one-half of x-height

Swelling stroke reverses at x-height center

connecting hairline

Young Baroque—Doyald Young, ITC, 1992

Some metal types had hairline stubs to connect to the previous letter

abcdefghi

Bank Script—James West, BB&S, 1895

Formal script is composed of five shapes: straight stems, bowls, swelled strokes, looped ascenders, and descenders.

Young Baroque, an English roundhand designed as a display font, has a tight fit to match its narrow proportion.

Bank Script illustrates the problem of metal type joins; as the type became worn, the joins tended to separate.

sumptuously displayed in a large bookkeeper's writing manual of the period, George Bickham's *The Universal Penman*, flawlessly engraved by the author.

Joseph Champion Scripsit.

Above—*From* The Universal Penman, *1743*

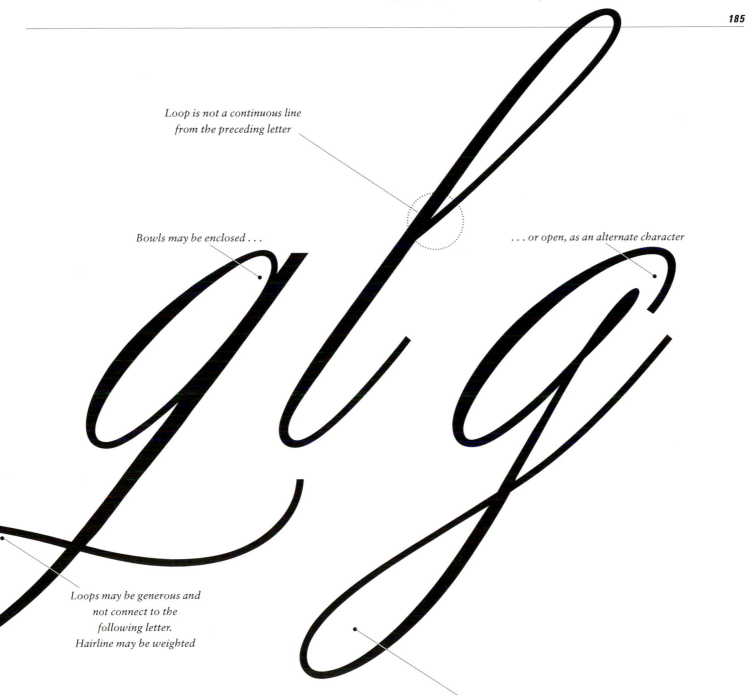

Loop is not a continuous line from the preceding letter

Bowls may be enclosed . . .

. . . or open, as an alternate character

Loops may be generous and not connect to the following letter. Hairline may be weighted

looped descender

SCRIPT LETTERS

The Basic Stem

The basic stem occurs ten or more times in most lowercase scripts, in normal and inverted positions; the *i*, *u*, and *n* are typical. It is a simple shape that decreases in width below where the preceding hairline joins. This point of join varies from font to font. The right side of the *i* has a longer straight line than the left side. Inverted, the shape forms the left side of the *n* and *m*. In hand-lettered versions, the radius of the baseline curve is drawn smaller for the tighter spacing required for straight-to-curve letterspacing than for straight-to-straight stems. Smaller radii are necessary for tightly spaced scripts and bold scripts. Traditionally, scripts carry a minimum amount of weight around the baseline curve. For consistency, the joins should align horizontally and, I think, look best and color evenly if the hairline join is tangent to the stem. This may vary from one-third to one-half the x-height. Angled joins create tension and interrupt the script's flow but may be necessary in a bold or tightly spaced line.

Script fonts based on metal designs often use the original

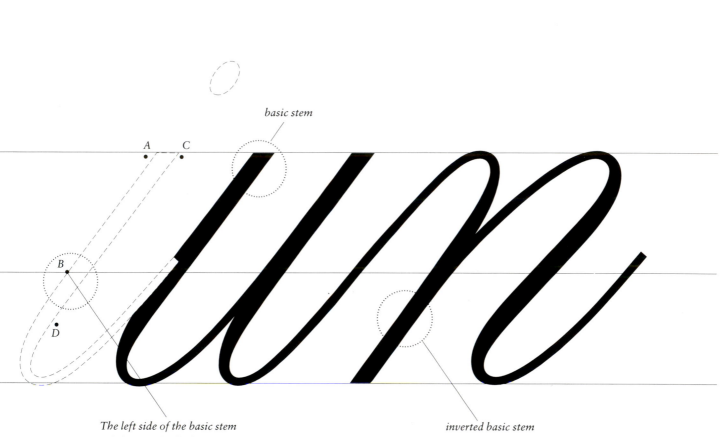

basic stem

The left side of the basic stem curves and thins gradually from point of join to bottom turn. Note that the straight line C-D is a longer dimension than A-B

inverted basic stem

Young Baroque—Doyald Young, ITC, 1992

Straight stems thin and arc below the preceding letter's connecting hairline join. The slopes of scripts vary: in some hand-lettered versions the slant may be as great as 45 degrees, though 30–35 degrees is a more comfortable angle. Some are drawn with an angle close to the standard 12- to 15-degree angle of the italics.

spacing, which depended on a letter's angle on a rectangular piece of metal type. As the angle of the type increased, so did the space between the letters, unless the letters were kerned, with the top right portion extended past the right-hand edge of the type, to rest on top of the next letter. As early as the nineteenth century, typefounders sought to overcome this by casting the letters on angle and offset bodies, and later, on wing bodies (*below left and right*).[1] All versions were troublesome: the kerns were fragile, and the angle and wing bodies required special spaces to begin and end the line. Some designers found this daunting and contented themselves with a more upright script, which can be spaced more snugly; Novarese's Juliet is one. To fill the space between the cap and the lowercase, Novarese introduced an arcing hairline that rests on the baseline and connects to the lowercase. Digital fonts are freed from these restrictions and kern extravagantly left and right.

1. Mac McGrew, *American Metal Typefaces of the Twentieth Century*, pages xiv–xv.

Methods of casting scripts and italics (schematic)

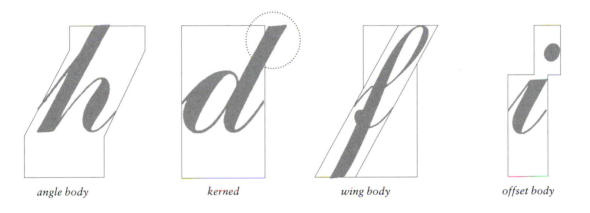

| angle body | kerned | wing body | offset body |

Commercial Script—Morris Fuller Benton, ATF, 1906

ABCDEFGHIJKL
MNOPQRSTUVW

Juliet—Aldo Novarese, Nebiolo, 1955

Hairlines to fill unwanted space

Top—*Some letter shapes have been greatly determined by the shape of the metal casting. These different methods of casting scripts and italics on metal bodies were solutions designed to overcome excessive letterspacing. Fonts for the computer may kern, that is, easily invade another character cell, to improve letterspacing.*
Bottom—*Aldo Novarese, one of the twentieth century's great type designers, filled the space between Juliet's capital and lowercase with a short hairline so that the font would color evenly.*

SCRIPT LETTERS

The Bowl

Whether a bowl belongs to a wide or narrow script, its structure is similar to the bowl of calligraphic broad-pen faces. Left-hand bowls are weighted below center, and right-hand bowls are weighted above center, demonstrated by the remarkable, flexible, pointed pen script of one of the seventeenth-century's great writing masters, Willington Clark (*below*). Pressure is exerted to produce the widening (the stroke's thickness), but an immediate lessening of the pressure produces a rather abrupt, curved transition from the weighted stem to the thin, elegant hairline. The majority of modern formal script fonts modify this shape by drawing a more gradual transition from weight to hairline. This produces an almost symmetrically shaped bowl that is blunted top and bottom, wider near the baseline than at x-height. Weight is seldom

Round Text.

Aabbcdefffghhbiÿkkklllmn oppqqrzsftttuvvnxyyyz

Oldstyle p drawn with swelled stroke instead of the traditional bowl of the a, d, p, q

Willington Clark, Round Text Script (from The Universal Penman, *1743)*

Abrupt transition from stem weight to hairline

Alternate, freestyle bowl

adgpq

Alternate bowls Young Baroque—Doyald Young, ITC, 1992

■
Top—*Eighteenth-century flexible pen calligraphy that shows the quick turns at the baseline and traditional shapes with beautiful, even color.*
Bottom—*Young Baroque's elaborate, looped ascenders and descenders* restrict its usage to only a few words for stationery, or for headings where opulence and decorative shapes are desired.

carried past a diagonal centerline of the bowl counter. In some fonts a centerline drawn through the bowl reveals a shape that leans more than the established diagonal of the stem. To let more space up into the letter, the bowl is kicked out near the baseline so that a higher join can be made—to keep the letter light and airy. The bowl appears on the *a*, *b*, *d*, *g*, *p*, and *q*; some fonts use alternate eighteenth-century forms for the *b* and *p*; a loop and an ogee curve respectively (*opposite*). In most instances the bowl is attached to stems with hairlines that join smoothly at top and bottom without a trace of a corner. These letters are of the same width, and the repetition of their shapes, plus the letters *b*, *m*, *n*, and *u*, is one of the reasons that formal scripts appear so rhythmically spaced. The same bowl shape, a bit wider, is used to form the *c* and *e*. Young Baroque has alternate bowl forms. The alternate letters *a*, *d*, and *g* are drawn more freely, overhanging the stem near the x-height.

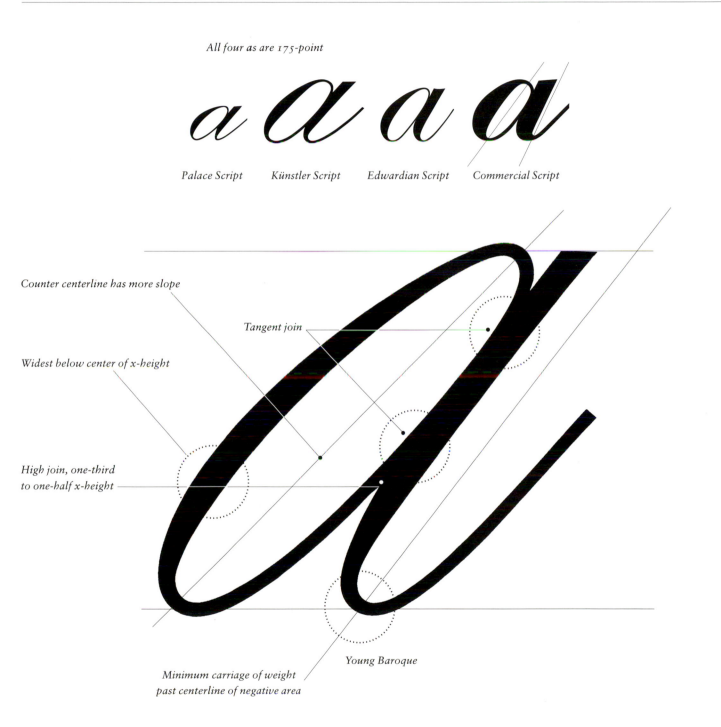

All four **as** *are 175-point*

Palace Script   *Künstler Script*   *Edwardian Script*   *Commercial Script*

Counter centerline has more slope

Tangent join

Widest below center of x-height

High join, one-third to one-half x-height

Young Baroque

Minimum carriage of weight past centerline of negative area

Top—Bowls of fonts based on traditional nineteenth-century forms have similar structures. Each joins tangent to the basic stem, and there is a minimum carriage of weight past the counter's centerline, whether the forms are condensed or drawn with different slopes.
Bottom—Analysis of the basic bowl shape, common to many script fonts.

SCRIPT LETTERS

In beginning penmanship we are taught to form our letters first with a series of continuous loops. Once comfortable with these, we tackle the more complex shapes. With continued practice, the act of writing becomes second nature, an exercise that we rarely think about.

Later, fast, scribbled college notes destroy much of the finesse that was rigidly taught.

Loops are the secret of beautiful penmanship, whether they are the plump, elliptical forms of the *O* or the smaller more narrow and elegant loops of the *l* and *e*. We are taught to form

these in a continuous line that seamlessly connects them to form a word. The loops may have different angles, *i.e.*, the ascending stem of the *l* and the descending stem of the *g* bend gradually from the rigid angle of the script. The descending loops may depart radically from

190

The simple straight stem has a tailored look. Depending on the design, both straight and looped forms may be used in a group of words

A loop is not formed by a continuous line from the preceding connecting hairline. This would change the join angle and interrupt the script's flow

Font angle

Loop angle

Loops may have different angles

Font's established diagonal

Stem begins its gradual curve away from the diagonal for a less rigid and more graceful loop

Smooth hairline join

Young Baroque—Doyald Young, ITC, 1992

Continuous loop

George Bickham—The Universal Penman (*enlarged*), 1743

Top—*The traditional straight-stemmed* **l** *(top, middle) and an exuberant looped* **l** *made possible by digital kerning.* **Bottom**—*George Bickham's use of the continuous looped* **l** *in his tour-de-force, The Universal Penman.*

the established angle of the font if these are flamboyant shapes.

George Bickham in his *Universal Penman* (*bottom, opposite*) rarely adopted the looped *l*. These are found in his pages only when an *l* begins a word, or where the preceding letter, an *o* or an *r* for instance, can comfort-ably be connected. Then Bick-ham uses a hairline join to roll into a looped *l*. Many fonts that are designed with looped *l*s make no attempt to draw them as a continuous line from the preceding letter; instead the loop is formed by a hairline upstroke attached mid-height to the right side of the stem; a continuous loop from the preceding letter would alter the angle of the up-swinging hairline and destroy the flow of the script. Continuous loops are usually found on the casual or brush scripts that mimic handwriting (*see* page 218).

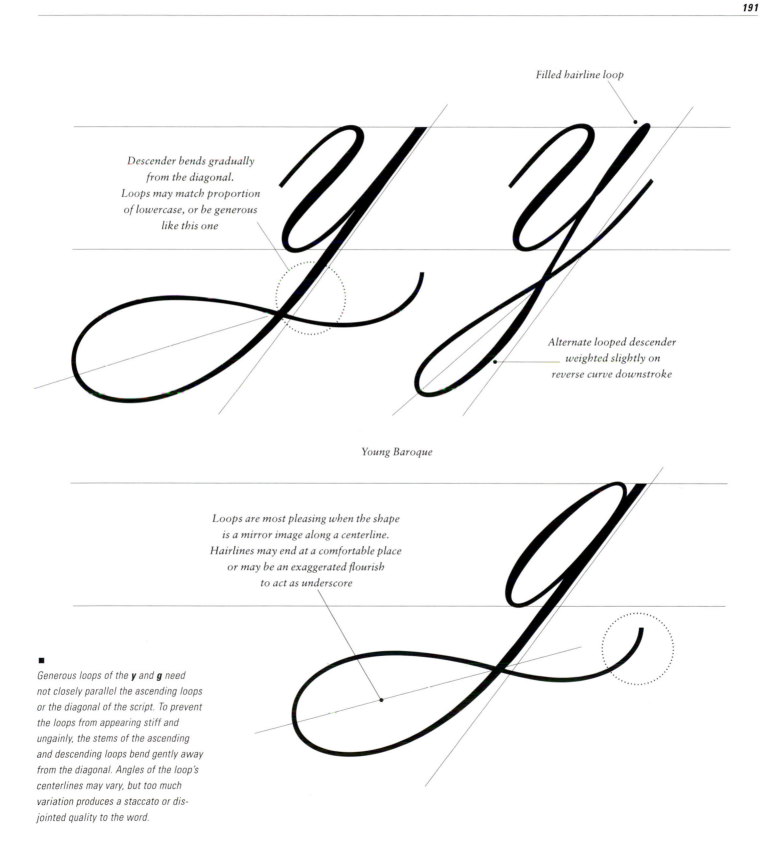

Filled hairline loop

Descender bends gradually from the diagonal. Loops may match proportion of lowercase, or be generous like this one

Alternate looped descender weighted slightly on reverse curve downstroke

Young Baroque

Loops are most pleasing when the shape is a mirror image along a centerline. Hairlines may end at a comfortable place or may be an exaggerated flourish to act as underscore

Generous loops of the **y** and **g** need not closely parallel the ascending loops or the diagonal of the script. To prevent the loops from appearing stiff and ungainly, the stems of the ascending and descending loops bend gently away from the diagonal. Angles of the loop's centerlines may vary, but too much variation produces a staccato or dis-jointed quality to the word.

SCRIPT LETTERS

Of all formal script curves, the ogee hairline is one of the most beautiful. It is used to connect letters that are drawn with hairline beginnings that in italic fonts are known as pothooks: *m, n, u, v, w, x,* and *y,* and sometimes *p* (depending on its particular shape). In script type the hairline is formed by a letter's ending as it connects to the pothook that begins the following letter. The most graceful form of the hairline is one that leans slightly more than a font's established diagonal, though in condensed scripts the ogee hairline may parallel the font's diagonal. At half the x-height the hairline reverses itself and, at x-height, rolls into the weighted downstroke. A slight swelling may be introduced to the line to even the color, though the addition of thickness should be restrained. A rule-of-thumb spacing is to make the lettered ogee hairline divide a

192

pothook

This space is approximately one-and-a-half times greater than straight-to-straight stems

Young Baroque

The additional hairline weight between the **en** that adds color is optional

Detail from a former Art Center College of Design diploma

Center—The ogee hairline is graceful when drawn with a slightly greater lean, though in tight settings it is by necessity parallel with the script's angle.

Bottom—An elegant nuance of color spacing, the ogee hairline may be swelled slightly.

space that is one-and-a-half times greater than the space of two straight-to-straight stems. This looks good in a word that is composed of open letters (*c*, *e*, *r*, and *s*). If letters of double stem weights (*a*, *d*, *g*, *h*, etc.) predominate, the space is usually tightened. This rule does not apply to fonts based on metal forms, many of which are evenly spaced, like the Künstler and Commercial Script below.

Some fonts are drawn with the left sides of the letters *m*, *n*, *p*, *r*, *u*, *v*, *w*, *y* as straight stems instead of the graceful pothook (*below, top row*). This produces a more narrow set, but the joining areas tend to clog and mass; note the *nu* of Künstler and Commercial Script. The hairline's steep angle almost parallels the weighted stem's angle, leaving only a sliver of white. Palace Script tries to avoid the problem by curving the hairline of the *i* and *u* outward, which lets air up into the triangular space. Compare angle, weight, and the shapes of the original metal Commercial Script font with the digital version and note the change of angle, hairline weight, and turns.

Smooth joins

Joining area around a straight stem appears congested in small sizes

Pencil comp

Künstler Script—Hans Bohn, Stempel, 1957

Commercial Script, digital version

Commercial Script—Morris Fuller Benton, ATF, 1906
Original foundry type (hand-set)

Palace Script—Stephenson Blake and Monotype, 1923

Top left—*When simplified forms are wanted, or when space is at a premium, hairlines may connect to the alternate forms of **n**, **m**, **v**, **u**, and **y**, drawn with straight left stems; straight stems joined by hairlines at the x-height produce clogged areas. The graceful pothook colors better. Compare the Commercial Script metal type with the digital version. Hairline weight of the metal type is more delicate and there appears to be less angle. The turns are more rounded and less pointed.*

SCRIPT LETTERS

Platt Rogers Spencer and Austin Norman Palmer wrote two of the most popular penmanship copy books of the nineteenth century. Palmer advocated a simplified style that was taught in the U.S. public schools as late as the 1930s. In the sixth grade I had to take a class in Palmer penman-

ship. I diligently practiced rows of circular pencil loops, which, we were told, would eventually produce beautiful handwriting, a trait that was thought to reflect good character.

The earlier Spencerian method was based on flexible pens; the Palmer method stressed the pen-

cil in school lessons, a less demanding instrument. Today's popular formal script types are based on the earlier flexible pen method, but many modifications are made to their structure to create a font of closely related letters. Script capitals are related by a simple swelling, ogee down-

■

The basic stem is one of the building blocks of a formal script cap font—a stroke that is usually drawn with an ogee curved shape, characterized by a beginning hairline that swells to midway where it reverses, diminishing to

a hairline with varying terminal endings or flourishes.

The cap **L** from Young Baroque shows two variations of the swelling stroke—one as a stem, the other as a diagonal finishing flourish.

stroke, the number of which, and specific letters, vary from font to font. Stephenson Blake's Palace Script shows a typical group with the ogee downstroke: *B, D, F, G, H, I, J, K, L, P, R, S,* and *T*; Young Baroque contains two less. This essential shape has a definite structure. The stroke begins with a clearly defined point (sometimes with a long hairline) that gradually widens, and then reverses its curve at its widest point to become an ogee, an elongated *s* shape. Many of Palace Script's stems end with a fat ball; *F, K,* and *T* are topped with generous horizontal ogee curves. The ogee shape is also stretched to form the *J*. Because the basic stem is repeated so many times, it is an important family characteristic. It appears in the lowercase too: *h, k, m, n, r, s, v, w, x,* and *y*, and also creates the looped descenders. Many formal script types end the down-stroke with a loop, which can be simple or complex, with a single-weight hairline, or drawn with a slight widening, which is not as wide as the main downstroke. Ed Benguiat's Edwardian Script is typical.

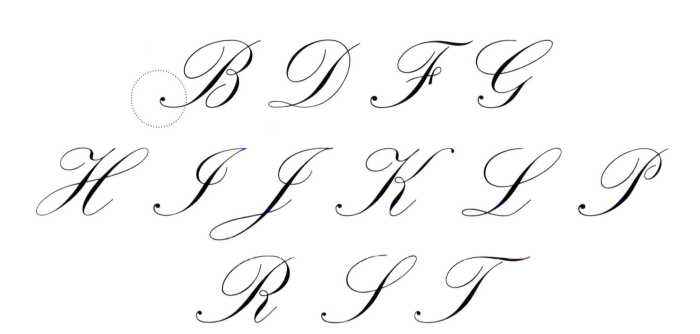

Palace Script—Stephenson Blake & Monotype, 1923

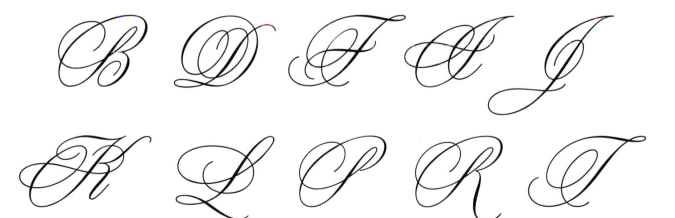

Young Baroque—Doyald Young, ITC, 1992

■

In Palace Script the swelling stroke appears thirteen times as the main stem in the cap alphabet, in Young Baroque, ten times. Stems may be finished with balls or enhanced with generous volutes as in Edwardian Script.

Edwardian Script regular—Ed Benguiat, ITC, 1994

SCRIPT LETTERS

Almost half of formal script caps are made up of curved stems: *C, G, O,* and *Q*; the right side of the *D,* and a *Q* that is reminiscent of the figure 2. The other right-hand curved forms are bowls, and appear on the *B, P,* and *R.* Smaller curved stems are stacked and joined with a loop to form the capital *E.* Some caps are drawn with left-hand loops that define the letter. Young Baroque's *B, P,* and *R* have two kinds: large, which counts, and small, which doesn't count, to define the letter—it is drawn for decoration. The larger loop has been weighted, but on other fonts, the shape may be a fine, light hairline. Whichever is chosen for a font scheme, it is best to draw them consistently on similar letters. Curved stems of the *C, G, O,* and *Q* are nothing but the basic curved stem bowls of the lowercase, enlarged and reduced in weight so that they relate to the

196

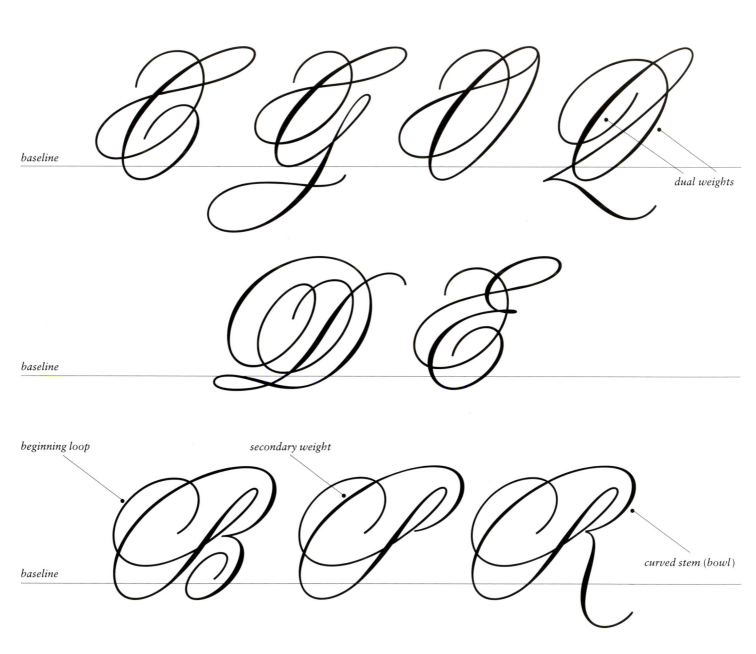

Young Baroque—Doyald Young, ITC, 1992

lowercase. Once the skeleton shape of the letter is delineated, the puffery, or elegant decoration, may be added in quantity or be restrained, depending on taste or the demands of an assignment, though ornamentation is never a substitute for basic design. Formal scripts, whose letters connect (printers call them announcement scripts), have cap and lowercase Os that are mostly drawn with dual weights: the left side carries the boldest weight and the right side is noticeably lighter.

Stephenson Blake's beautiful Palace Script uses only a delicate hairline to define the shape. The size and weight ratio of caps to lowercase vary widely, but generous caps are the usual style, which produces small x-heights, typified in England by Palace Script and in America by ATF's Royal and Typo Scripts. These are drawn with a cap-to-lowercase ratio of approximately 3:1. Designed as a display font, Young Baroque was planned to prevent the caps from overpowering its lowercase, with a cap-to-lowercase ratio of only 8:3, with each cap descending generously below the baseline.

Palace Script—Stephenson Blake & Monotype, 1923

Typo Script—Morris Fuller Benton, ATF, 1902

Royal Script—Central Typefoundry Branch, ATF, 1893

Opposite—Curved weighted stems occur on roughly one-third of the script caps. Some of these are right-hand bowls, as shown in the bottom row. A secondary weighted loop defines the shapes of these letters. The small beginning loops of this group are for decoration only, and partially establish its design style. The **O** and **Q** are traditionally dual-weighted: heavy on the left side, with a secondary weight on the right side. Palace Script (above) drops the weight entirely on the letter's right side.

SCRIPT LETTERS

Without decoration the world of design would be pitifully barren. A single-weight, mechanically constructed letter offers little to satisfy our need for opulence.

A few minimal script fonts have been designed as monotone weight with an absence of flourishes, but these have not caught the public's fancy. Formal scripts beg for flourish and embellishment. Whether the initial or ending stroke is exuberant or the capitals are encrusted with volutes, pen scripts find elegant decoration a receptive partner. I have owned a copy of *The Universal Penman* for more than forty years. The mastery, artistry, and grace of its pages continue to inspire me. It is the seminal work from which many of our most popular fonts are descended, as demonstrated by the unparalleled beauty of the examples below. They were conceived in the Baroque era,

198

Joseph Champion

Honour Love

Aurelius King Solomon

Assistance Diligence

Nature, I

Learning Mr Leonard

Of the

A random selection of beautiful caps from George Bickham's The Universal Penman. *Throughout the book, Bickham uses contrast of size as an important and vital design technique, a device that is as valid today as it was in the Baroque era.*

yet most of the caps are surprisingly spare and derive their richness from sweeping, graceful volutes and near-parabolic curves—it is their environment that is elaborate and decorative. Many of Bickham's examples are signatures filled with peregrinating hairlines—Joseph

Champion's is one of the more notable. Beginning volutes rarely parallel the angle of the letters. Their shapes are often plump ellipses, which are stressed on either the up- or the down-stroke. Note the widened stroke on the bottom loop of the cap *P*, and the flourish of the *r* in the

word ***Honor***. Commonplace titles are treated in inventive ways. The *r* of ***Mr.*** is gracefully and naturally suspended on the finishing stroke of the *M*; its placement fills the word spacing and creates a two-word unit. Letters like the cap *S*, written by apparent single-stroke motion,

divide the space with subtle shapes that swell and taper to delectable hairline endings. The cap *O* is a fluid vortex of curves with three separate weights, with minimal hairline widening beginning at the top of the letter—never mind that it is misspaced with the *f*!

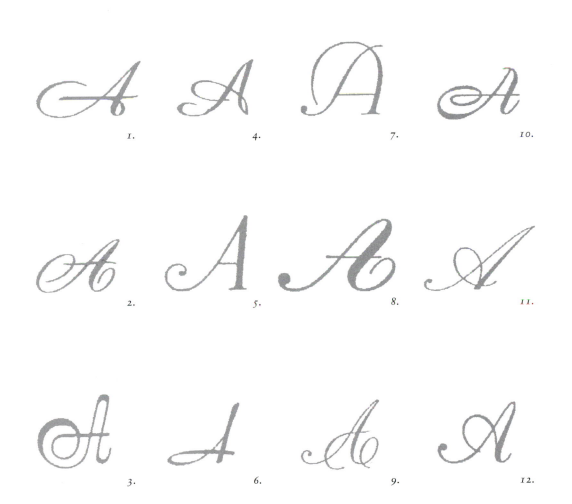

1. Adagio, 2. Diane, 3. Stradivarius, 4. Amazone, 5. Dorchester Script, 6. Trafton Script, 7. Bernhard Cursive (Madonna), 8. Künstler Script, 9. Victoriana, 10. Boulevard, 11. Palace Script, 12. Virtuosa II.

■

*Only three separate strokes are needed to construct a sans serif **A**. In scripts the shape may be drawn with one less, and in economical forms with only one stroke. The strokes used to develop the above are extravagant. In the strictest definition, all are formed by decoration —the lifeblood of delight. The trick though, once an identifying shape is chosen, is to repeat the design on the other letters with elegant variation, or draw them to echo or reference the original concept.*

SCRIPT LETTERS

I like to describe this font as a sports script. It's bold, and it's tough. If you're going to put script on the backs of baseball players, this is as minimal as script can be drawn without resorting to sans serif shapes, though the *p* and *q* can cross-dress. The style has been around for a long time. Variations of it can be seen in the Campbell's soup and Coca-Cola logos. The face is based on traditional formal script forms, narrow and snugly spaced. The difference, an important one, is the beefy thin strokes and chunky stems. The lowercase has plain shapes; there is one looped ascender, and five looped descenders. The fit is tight and based on an optical similarity of the negative space inside the letters and between the letters. Thins join low and there is considerable weight carried around the bottom turns. The thins taper gently at their joining tips in order to produce the highest join. Each capital letter has a simple swash extension based partly on the shape of a chisel pen held at an extreme angle and partly on the traditional pointed pen, which must be pressed so that the slotted point spreads to

200

Bold Condensed Script—Doyald Young, 1999

■

Above—*A beta version of a bold condensed script with heavy thins.*

■

Opposite—*An early pencil sketch to determine basic letterspacing, proportion, and joining height (85% reduction).*

produce the shape. I tried to laterally align the cap swashes; the *I* and *Z* are exceptions. Both the *Y* and *Z* are more italic than script; scripts are usually more cursive. The *S*'s descending curve drops generously below the baseline (it is used as an alternate swash in some italic alphabets).

Palatino italic served as a model for the cap *N* and *M*. The *G*, *J*, and *S* have alternates. The *I* is a troublesome shape and is often confused with the *J*. In some script fonts it is difficult to distinguish between the two.

The drawing below is an early one, the letters were drawn in random positions to better determine proportions. I considered some of the letters too narrow and some leaning too much or not enough. The *Fl* is a troublesome combination, and I overlapped the two for a better fit. The *Z* (*fourth line*) was reconsidered and the wider shape appears on the third line.

SCRIPT LETTERS

Type design is based on many optical adjustments. More than any other style, script shapes must be adjusted so that they appear to lean in the same flowing angle. This bold leaning script best illustrates the method.

For the *a*'s bowl to appear parallel to the stem, its angle must be increased. In handwriting there is a natural increase of pressure on a downward curved stroke, evidenced by the bowl's widening below lateral center. Some script fonts' interior counters lean a great deal, but here the condensed's counters appear to hug the straight stem at approximately the same angle. Both the exterior bowl's centerline and the looped turn of the stem at the baseline lean more so that a high join can be made to the following letter and a rhythmic flow held. The *o*'s counter and exterior shape repeat this scheme. Reverse curves are abundant in

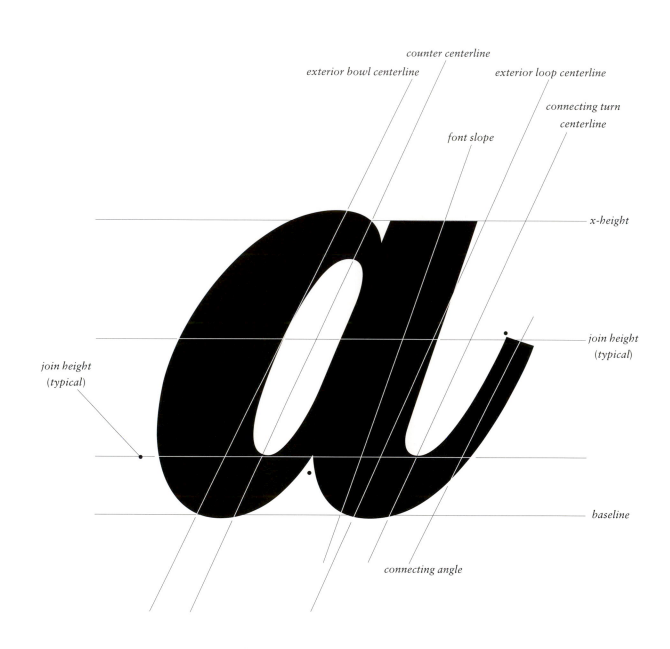

Bold Condensed Script—Doyald Young, 1999

Letters have deceiving skeletons. Centerlines of the bowl forms must lean more than the font's slope to appear parallel. Connecting turns at the baseline lean more too, so that a high join can be made to prevent massing of weight. Because this script is bold, more weight is carried proportionately around the bottom turn than a normally weighted formal script. Note that the centerline of triangular-shaped letters must parallel the font's basic diagonal.

script fonts, and also must lean more to visually match the font's slope: note the main stem of the *L* and *R*, and the *n*'s right-hand stem. If the right side of the *n* is drawn with the established angle, the area nearest the baseline will appear too wide, angular, and more upright. Center lines of the *A*, *V*, and *M* should match the font slope with equidistant sides.

I think enclosed loops look best when the counter is a long mirror-image teardrop. Despite the *s*'s right-hand reverse-curved side, the *s* is also a triangular shape and should be constructed similarly. The swash extensions of the condensed caps are narrow shapes. This is determined by an extreme slope to their visual centerline; note the swash curve of the cap *R*. Tails of the cap *K* and *R* have similar shapes to Century expanded and are true swelled strokes, widening to a maximum width at center, diminishing to the basic thickness of thin stroke. The looped, thin joining stroke that is attached to the *o*'s right side may shift up or down; there is no fixed rule.

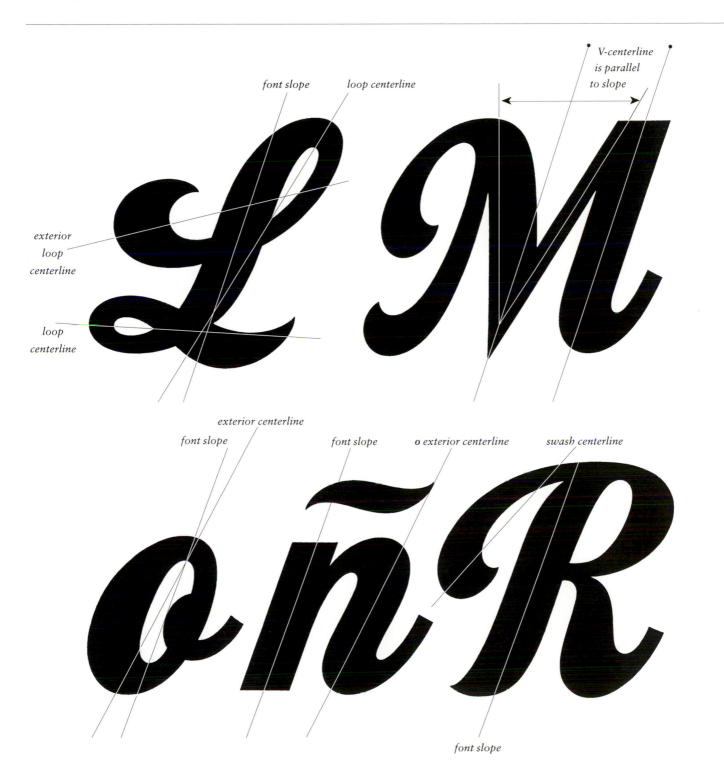

Display figure: Fino. Text: 42/60 Bold Condensed Script

*Typography today
does not so much need
Inspiration or Revival
as Investigation.*

Stanley Morison

*Historian and Typographic Consultant to the
Monotype Corporation*

Mary B. Sheridan & Associates
Los Angeles, California
Mary Sheridan,
Executive Creative Art Director
Nelson Davis, Designer
Doyald Young, Artist
The Music Center of
Los Angeles County

Whether the cause is music, opera, theater, dance, or museums, the arts rely on private money raised by dedicated volunteers. The amazing Blue Ribbon women lend their persuasive talents to ensure that the Music Center, founded by Dorothy Chandler, has ample money to present the arts. The Blue Ribbon logotype was designed to look classy, to project the implied quality of the name, necessary ingredients when hundreds of thousands, nay millions, of dollars are begged for donation. Formal script always suggests quality and an important event (a graduation, a party, a concert, an opening, affairs of state, a coronation). The forms here echo many Spencerian styles with generous swash hairline endings to the caps and to the *l* and *e*. The extension of the *R*'s ogee stem is a natural for dotting the *i* and adds richness to the logo.

206

Florid formal script combined with decorative outline figures.

The multi-segment circular design within the ribbon is the official logo of the Music Center complex and was designed by Welton Beckett & Associates, architects of the complex.

FONTS & LOGOS

Decorative type styles like those shown below may lend interest and opulence to logotypes. The Kortversaler derives its charm from its casually drawn shapes. Bodoni Open is sometimes called gravure, which suggests that it has been engraved with a burin, an engraving tool. It has graced many a formal invitation. Chevalier is typical of many nineteenth-century shaded and outline fonts that the banking industry embraced. Chic suggests 1920s and '30s Art Deco. Jan van Krimpen's Lutetia Open is a particularly beautiful inline font. The decorative Blue Ribbon figures are called *outline*. *Gravure* may be an outline letter whose right-hand side is bolder, known also as *shaded*. Some gravure fonts have a thin white line at the stem's left edge, and are called *hand-tooled*. Shaded suggests a cross-hatched letter with either an outline or a side shadow. *Inline* is a single white line that divides a stem; known also as *open*, though open may refer to an outline letter. The terminology is not consistent.

Often the 4's crossbar is a secondary weight; the one in this logo is equal to the main stems.

ABCDEFGHIJKLMNOPQRSTU VWXYZÅÄÖ

Berling Kortversaler—Albert Augspurb, Berling (n.d.)

ABCDEFGHIJKLMNOPQRSTUV WXYZ&! abcdefghijklmnopqrstuvwxyz $1234567890

Bodoni Open—Morris Fuller Benton, ATF, 1918

ABCDEFGHIJKLMNOPQR STUVWXYZ 1234567890

Chevalier—Haas (n.d.)

ENCOURAGE

Chic—Morris Fuller Benton, ATF, 1927

ABCDEFGHIJKLMN OPQRSTUVWXYZ

Lutetia Open—Jan van Krimpen, Enschedé, c. 1930

■ *Gravure, outline, open, shaded, and decorated faces are vital styles used to enrich dull and staid blocks of text. From the casual charm of Kortversaler to the formal elegance of Bodoni Open, the fiducial Chevalier, and the decorative Chic, to the classic, swallow-tail, pen-stripe Lutetia Open, these faces are only a minuscule portion of the decorated faces available. Designed by some of typography's greatest designers, they are classics and worthy of serious consideration. (See also page 181 for a discussion and showing of engraved font styles.)*

International Diseño Conferencia
Mexico, D.F.
Rafael Iragorri, President
Antonio Iragorri,
Creative Director

Guanajuato, one of Mexico's seven Colonial cities, was the site of the Fifth Annual International Diseño Conferencia, where I was a speaker. Rafael Iragorri, the president, asked all the speakers to design or illustrate a "five" for the conference. I drew a small pencil sketch first,

enlarged it to about six inches wide, and then did the final drawing with sharp F and HB pencils on Clearprint vellum. The script logo combines a figure 5 and the Spanish word for five (*cinco*) for surprise. The 5 serves as a cap; large and descending below the baseline, topped off with an ex-

travagant flourish reminiscent of fluttering, celebratory pennants. The diagonal hairline downstroke connects to the flourish with a filled loop, which rolls to form the lower round bowl portion, and ends with a slightly swelled stroke, then a release of pressure that creates the point.

208

■
A celebratory drawing for the Fifth Annual International Diseño Conferencia. The logo combines a figure and letters to create a wordmark.
Top—*Pencil drawing on vellum.*
Bottom—*Original same-size rough.*

■
Opposite—*Script and italic fonts are sloped differently. Five of the examples employ a top, pointed, calligraphic finishing stroke, and three examples, 6, 7, and 8, use a reverse curve in the manner of a swung dash, though 6 is more consistently weighted to its tip. Note the different strokes of the Bodoni roman and the italic (2 and 6).*

I finished the looped **o** with a wider repeat of the **5**'s flourish. Traditional formal script lowercase **cs** usually have circular or teardrop terminals; this one is an open loop, slightly weighted on the right-hand side. The logo's stem weights are light—difficult to find among commercial formal script fonts. Formal script fonts are not always drawn at the same angle. A script **5**, example 1, written by Emanuel Austin, from *The Universal Penman*, has an extreme slope; more than his traditional script letters. Note that the Bodoni **5** angle, example 2, is less acute, following the general 11– 17-degree slope of the italics. Like the Austin script, its top curved stroke is created by extreme pen pressure, which is released at its tip to form a point. This shape appears in many font styles—scripts, italics, and romans—though the Bodoni roman five, example 6, is drawn with a reverse curve and a bowed, vertical thin that joins the lower bowl. Young Baroque, example 7, has a 36-degree angle.

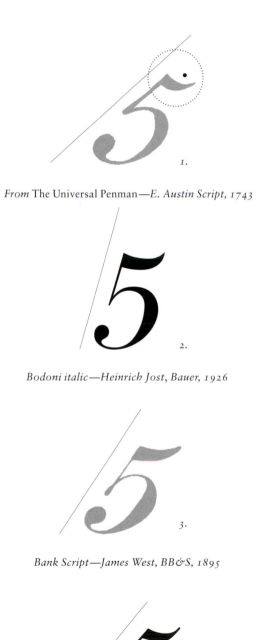

1.

From The Universal Penman—*E. Austin Script, 1743*

2.

Bodoni italic—Heinrich Jost, Bauer, 1926

3.

Bank Script—James West, BB&S, 1895

4.

Hogarth Script—URW, 1993

5.

Palace Script—Stephenson Blake, 1923

6.

Bodoni roman—Heinrich Jost, Bauer, 1926

7.

Young Baroque—Doyald Young, ITC, 1992

8.

Künstler Script—Hans Bohn, Stempel, 1957

SCRIPT LOGOS

Cire Perdue
Burbank, California
Doyald Young, Designer/Artist
Artists & Sculptors Foundry
Burbank, California

Ancient civilizations in Mesopotamia, Egypt, Greece, and Africa are known to have used *cire perdue*, the "lost wax" process for casting sculpture. The process involves a wax mold formed around a clay or plaster sculpture, that is coated with a perforated clay covering. When heated, the wax drips out leaving a shell cavity—an ideal process for casting intricately shaped objects. Donatello, the fifteenth-century Italian sculptor, cast his famous bronze figure of David in this manner.

This logo was designed for the cover of a facilities brochure for an artist's casting foundry. It is a narrow, traditional, classic English roundhand that gains uniqueness with the use of extravagant capitals. There is some organization within the logotype. The caps align at the top; the large left loop of the **C** generally aligns with the beginning

210

■

*A logo with extravagant capitals
for a facilities brochure for an
artist's foundry. The logo jogs to
permit tighter word spacing.*

FONTS & LOGOS

loop of the *P* and the top-right curl of the *P*'s ogee downstroke. *Cire* is raised to allow the bottom loop to act as an underscore. I like to draw formal script caps that drop below the baseline. I do not completely tuck a lowercase under a cap *P*, because the bowl seems too large a shape to suspend over the word. The space between the cap and lowercase helps to optically support the bowl. There is no set relationship of cap-to-lowercase height in a formal script logo. What is needed is an identifiable image, and opulent caps are often an asset. The lowercase is drawn simply, with no tricks, as legible as possible, and takes a backseat to the overscale **C** and **P**. The tail of the *P*'s lower loop has no required length—it may be longer, or even wrap upward around *Perdu*, for a more showy statement. Below are some *P*s from *The Universal Penman* that illustrate the inventiveness of seventeenth-century writing masters. Number 5 is a ligature that begins: I Promise . . . .

1.

2.

3.

4.

5.

Some voluptuous cap **P**s drawn from the 1743 edition of The Universal Penman. In example 1 each swelled portion of the curves is a different thickness. The letter widens in eleven different areas. It graces the front binding of the 1941 Dover reprint from which it is reproduced. Number 5 is enlarged.

SCRIPT LOGOS

Pierre Cossette Productions
Los Angeles, California
Robert Keene,
Production Design
Doyald Young, Designer / Artist
The Harry Connick, Jr.
TV Christmas Special

When Harry Connick was told that the main title graphic for his Christmas Special was to be custom designed, he requested that it not look like an MTV title but instead like a "Perry Como Special."

Mr. Connick is reminiscent of a youthful Frank Sinatra. His voice and singing style echo Sinatra's early years. Connick is multi-talented: singer, band leader, pianist, a good hoofer, and now a movie star.

This style of script is useful when maximum legibility is wanted. It is a flowing, evenly spaced, slightly two-weight letter, drawn as legibly as the semi-bold weight dictates. There are brush traces, and some of the letters are built up. The style is populist—a term not intended derogatorily, but to describe a friendly, accessible script with no pretensions—a "heartland" title designed to be eminently legible. The title's greatest asset

212

By permission Conn-X Productions, Inc. & Wilkens Management

ABCDEFGHIJKLMNOPQRSTUVWXYZ

Arrighi swash capitals—Frederic Warde, Monotype, 1929
Additional characters by Robin Nicholas and Patricia Saunders

ABCDEFGHI JKLM NOPQRSTUV WXYZ

Centaur—Bruce Rogers, 1914; Monotype, 1929

■

*Connick's "signature" is the most important element of the TV title. The use of the swash caps is restrained, with only flanking swashes for **Christmas**, and a swash **R** for relief. **The** is a commonplace word that is often part of a title, yet its importance is more grammatical than visual. It's position is often tenuous—I'm never quite happy with its placement on logotypes. It works here; between the **H** and **C** because it seems to be a natural position, affording a visual center lineup of the **S** in **Special**, which is centered under Christmas.*

is its lucky combinations of letters: luck plays an important part in the success of any logo-type. Admittedly, some invention must be used to choose the particular capital shapes, and the looped descenders that are its distinguishing feature. The *H* and *J* loops frame and con-tain the name. There is great movement in the *H*'s generous loop, which leads the eye quick-ly into the word. The overscale caps suggest an autograph, though Connick's signature was not used for reference. There is a change of pace; the *r*s in Harry are cursive, while the *r* of *Jr.* is "printed," as the style is commonly known (a misno-mer—sheets of paper are printed, and lettering is drawn or writ-ten). **The** and **Christmas Special** are a bold version of Frederic Warde's Arrighi italic designed in 1929 and paired with Bruce Rogers's Centaur, one of the great twentieth-century fonts. Arrighi's generous complement of swash characters lends a special, festive air to the title. (*See* Arrighi on pages 296–97).

Caps are generous and drop below baseline; their weight can be bolder

Spacing varies, yet for maximum legibility there should be an equal optical division of space within and between the letters

Angle closely parallels normal handwriting; ascenders may be looped

Connick,

Single-weight stroke indicates a round-nibbed pen or a blunted brush loaded with paint or ink. A pronounced thinning around the turns reveals that the writing instrument is held at an angle from the vertical and perpendicular to the picture plane

Upstrokes taper and, like handwriting, are thinner than downstrokes

Stem's centerline does not lean as much as centerline of negative letterspace and angles may vary

Freestyle, or casual, scripts are characterized by letters that bounce above and below a common baseline. Letter heights vary

There may be brushy beginning or ending blobs, which recall the amount of paint or ink that the brush or pen carries

Above—*Casual scripts are drawn in many different ways; there are no set rules. The call-outs suggest general ways to treat a script logo.*

Right—*Art Deco caps and single-weight script applied to Connick's musician bandstand shell, designed by Robert Keene. Its repetitive form is an important visual element of a large orchestra.*

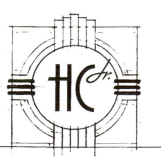

SCRIPT LOGOS

International Design Associates
Tokyo, Japan
Mari Makinami, Executive
Creative Director
Hideo Hosaka, Art Director
Doyald Young, Designer / Artist
Palace Hotel, Tokyo, Japan
Crown, Main Dining Room

214

From atop the Palace Hotel, the Crown restaurant affords a spectacular view of downtown Tokyo, and more important, the Imperial Palace, where Akihito, the 125th emperor, resides, continuing the blood line from Emperor Jinmu, enthroned in 660 B.C. This logo attempts to capture regal qualities. I drew some condensed versions first, because narrow serif letters can be formal and stately and, depending on their boldness, suggest elegance. (An all-cap word is more formal than cap and lowercase; some consider cap and small caps the most formal typographic arrangement of all. Tests have shown caps and lowercase to be 15 percent more legible than all caps.) Conveying the concept of gourmet dining is the prime focus.

Comp 1 is a Bodoni with influences of Cochin, evidenced by the terminal of the *r* and the cap C's beaks. Comp 2 is a mix of italic

A logo designed for the Palace Hotel's prestigious restaurant, located across the boulevard from the Emperor's Palace in downtown Tokyo. The word gains distinction from an ornate capital, and restrained, classically drawn, English roundhand forms.

and script with an Optima terminal for the *r*, and a *w* terminal reminiscent of Benguiat's Korinna. Comp 3 references the 1930s: it resembles Eden, designed by R. H. Middleton, with influences of Imré Reiner's Corvinus, a flat-sided form derived from the Moderns. Comp 4 is based on Century condensed, and comp 5 is a classic side-shadowed, outline roman style, used sometimes by the British monarchy on coins, that resembles Trajan. The script comps, 6 through 10, use the same lowercase with different capitals, which are average size to prevent them from overpowering the lowercase—an exercise in restraint. The only liberty taken with the letters are the *n*'s slightly descending stem and the unfilled loops of the *r* and *w*.

Crown

Bodoni (Bauer)

Crown

Optima

CROWN

Eden light

CROWN

ITC Century light condensed

CROWN

Trajan

Crown

1.

Crown

2.

CROWN

3.

CROWN

4.

CROWN

5.

Crown

6.

Crown

7.

Crown

8.

Crown

9.

Crown

10.

■

Pencil comprehensive designs, half of them favoring a formal script direction. The condensed serif romans are stately and formal—many of these were popular in the 1930s.

SCRIPT LOGOS

Maddocks & Company
New York, New York
Julia Precht, Art Director
Martin Ledyard, Designer
Doyald Young, Artist
Cutex, for Coty

216

Cutex is an old product. Coty, a French cosmetic firm, has manufactured it since the early 1920s, when women took to painting their nails with a passion.

Coty has used the same Cutex logo since it was first introduced. Maddocks & Company were asked to redesign the product line of over a hundred separate items, many of them sold in drugstores and supermarkets in blister-package card hangers.

Two things were important: to keep the logotype related to the original, and legibility, for a busy marketplace. The art director showed numerous versions to the client and from these a slightly two-weight version was chosen instead of the original monotone script.

My approach was cautious, and designs 2 through 6 contain only minor variations on comp 1. First, I drew an almost mono-

Original 1920s logotype

Final art

tone style comp with a **C** that the client liked, comp 1; then one with thinner thins with a longer *t* crossbar, comp 2; then a version that carries a generous amount of weight around the bottom turns, comp 3. Comps 4, 5, and 6 are the ink comprehensives with only minor changes in thicks and thins. The final art is a thinner version of comp 6.

Its weight distribution is calligraphic, reflecting a chisel-shaped tool held at a rather steep angle. The top stems of the *u* and *t* and both top and bottom of the *x* are blunted, which suggests a brush laden with paint instead of the crisp corners of a broad-pen. Similar to the original, the cap descends below the baseline slightly while the *ute* aligns, and the *x* descends with a wide, rounded, sweeping curve.

1.

4.

2.

5.

3.

6.

Only minor changes from the original logo (opposite, top) were allowed. The first drawings show how closely the design approach stayed to the original.

Gradually, though, the two-weight version with bold calligraphic turns around the bottom curves emerged (opposite, bottom). It is a bit lighter, with a longer, and pronounced reverse curve *t* crossbar.

Number 3 above is the preliminary outline drawing used to ink comp 6.

SCRIPT LOGOS

Max Factor & Co.

Hollywood, California
James Engleman,
Creative Director
Doyald Young, Designer / Artist
Maxi, Fragrance Promotion

Before the advent of photo- and digital typesetting, type designers struggled to produce truly casual style scripts. The early Civilités (page 178) were designed to hood-wink an unsuspecting public into believing that the types were handwriting. These civil hands with expressive caps, ascenders, and descenders still clung to a rigid horizontal baseline, and did so until the birth of photolettering, when multiple letterforms were offered. Judiciously selected and spaced, these hand-lettered shapes were among the first connected, spontaneous-appearing script types.

In the 1950s two metal types were designed to attack the problem: Murray Hill and Mistral. The former aligns evenly on the baseline, but varies the height of some letters. Mistral looks like different size strung beads, because there is a strong lateral centerline. The letters change size

218

Don't you love being a woman!

A hybrid script, with traces of brush and formal script, that suggests fashionable handwriting. The line was first written quickly at this size with a soft HB pencil, then traced more carefully to correct the spacing, the size of the letters, and the breaks within the words.

and height and stagger at the baseline equally.

The phrase shown was used on collateral to promote the Maxi fragrance—Max Factor's response to Charlie, Revlon's wildly successful fragrance for the liberated woman in the 1980s. Its style attempts to mir-

ror fashionable handwriting. The script is studied and hybrid; not even the most chic debutante could duplicate the hand for casual correspondence.

The script's bowls and round forms are larger than the *n*s and *m*s. Breaks keep the words open. The *on* join is repeated on the

*om; a*s vary, and the bowl of the *g* is almost identical to the first *a*. Ascenders are short, and the two descending loops are similar. Often in freestyle scripts the first and last letter of a word are a bit larger; here the cap is expansive.

Murray Hill—Emil Klumpp, ATF, c. 1956

Mistral—Roger Excoffon, Olive, 1953

Freestyle Script—Martin Wait, Fontek, 1987

Elli—Jean Harris, Font Bureau, 1993

■

Script fonts that illustrate the problems of casual letters. Many letters do not join (e.g., Murray Hill), and it has the appearance of unconnected script letters. Elli is a beautiful, spontaneous example of forms based on a casual chancery hand, though in my opinion, it

is more italic than script. For a font to truly simulate handwriting, there must be alternate characters. Two or three for each round form is a good beginning, but this calls for a separate expert font, and judicious selections by the user (neither Murray Hill nor Mistral

has alternate characters). The connections are always a problem, because it is difficult to draw individual letters that appear to be part of a continuous line. If there's a budget for it, hand-lettering is still the most interesting answer.

SCRIPT LOGOS

International Design Associates
Tokyo, Japan
Mari Makinami, Executive Creative Director
Hideo Hosaka, Art Director
Doyald Young, Designer / Artist
Hotel East 21, Tokyo
Restaurant & Lounge Logotypes

Restaurant and amenity logos for a first-class hotel should be varied, each tailored to carefully chosen names. Dining logos invariably suggest elegance or the contemporary; lounges are frequently named for adventure or urban luxury. The ink comprehensive designs below were the front-runners in the final selection process for East 21 Hotel. Script forms predominate.

The East, comps 1 and 6, are designed to suggest urban flair for the predominantly businessman clientele.

Lobby Lounge, comp 2, suggests traditional elegance. The large inline script *L* was intended to be a second color or hot foil stamped. Comp 7, the alternate design, is a traditional italic that borrows a **g** from Bulmer, and a **y** from Zapf's Civilité (*see* page 178).

To conjure up safari adventure, the men's bar is named *Elephant*; the illustrative treatment of the

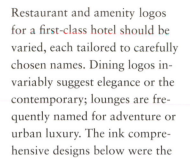

1.

6.

2.

7.

3.

8.

4.

9.

5.

10.

■ *Ink comprehensives reproduced in color for design presentation. These were selected from a wide group of designs and presented to three different management teams and the board of directors for final approval.*

p 's descender and the brute force of the extra-black biform of comp 8 reflect the concept. The choice of the cap *E* scaled to x-height creates a biform style.

Harmony, the main dining room logo, is a slightly extended Optima, though top stems of the *m* and *n* are squared off. An ogee crossbar shared by the *H* and *a* is a simple and restrained device that acts as a graceful introduction to epicure. The formal script of comp 9 with its elaborate cap *H*, was chosen.

Un is the hotel's bakery shop. The Didot-style lowercase, with unbracketed hairline serifs and a swelled underscore swash, lost to the more expressive brush script.

Shown below are comps of the logos all in script, done at the request of the hotel management.

Elephant

Panorama

Un

Corporate logo

■

A design study of the hotel amenity logos using the script style of the hotel's logo.

SCRIPT LOGOS

Woody Fraser Productions
Los Angeles, California
Robert Keene,
Production Design
Doyald Young, Designer/Artist

This daytime TV show granted wishes to special, selected participants—within reason.

The style is reminiscent of fashionable backhand writing. Left-handed persons like me find the angle more comfortable than a gentle right-hand slope. The client wanted script and the upright style was a bit different than the usual leaning scripts. I didn't refer to a specific style when I drew it, though it references Murray Hill, a semi-brush/pen script and the calligraphic qualities of Rondine and Trafton. I do refer to type styles when a specific font is requested by a client if I am not familiar with its structure. Rarely do I attempt a spontaneous write-out with a brush, for to be proficient at brush script requires frequent practice and a gifted hand.

The logo is contrived from its very beginning, for it was carefully drawn, not written.

A brush held at a slight angle from the horizontal, similar to the broad-pen angle of Oldstyle fonts, will produce a thin upstroke and a heavy downstroke. In drawing casual scripts, avoid patterns of alignment, either at the baseline or at x-height. This may be accomplished by changing the letter size, and/or the letters may bounce in an up-down pattern, relieved occasionally. Round-form letters look good enlarged; **h**, **i**, **m**, and **n** can sometimes be drawn smaller. The combination of letters of a specific word often dictates the bounce.

But as always, the trick is to make the drawing appear spontaneous. The main stem of the cap is rather rigid, though it does have a slight reverse curve to it. This is repeated on the **t**. Both the crossbar of the **t** and **F** curve slightly also, ending obliquely to reveal a calligraphic heritage. The top cross-stroke of the **F** begins with the lightest weight of the logo; its thinness suggests a hurried write-out. The thick-and-thin strokes of the title suggests that it is based on the action of a rigger brush, a chisel-shaped brush used by sign painters and showcard artists to paint sizing on plate glass preparatory to laying gold leaf. (In England a rigger is a pointed sable brush once used by ship's painters to identify the "rigging" or cordage of a sailing ship).

There is great carriage of weight around the top curves of the **as** and the **s**, but less at the bottom turns. The top turns of the **n** and the bottom curve of the **y**'s tail are calligraphic, and suggest that more pressure was applied to produce an almost constant thickness. The **n** and main body of the **y** are smaller, which produces a bounced, casual appearance.

ABCDEFGHIJKLMNOPQRS
TUVWXYZ
abcdefghijklmnopqrstuvwxyz
1234567890

Murray Hill—Emil Klumpp, ATF, c. 1956

ABCDEFGHIJKLMNOPQuRS
TUVWXYZÇÆŒ
abcdefghijklmnopqrstuvwxyzçœœ
1234567890

Rondine—A. Butti, Nebiolo, 1948

ABCDEFGHIJKLMNOPQu2RS
TJUVWXYZ
abcdefghijklmnopqrstuvwxyz 12345678

Trafton Script—Howard Allen Trafton, Bauer, 1933

■

Casual font styles that are gently referenced in the logo opposite. Murray Hill appears as a combination brush and pen script, while Rondine and Trafton seem to be written with a broad-pen. Rondine references the Trafton, an earlier font, with great style and precise calligraphic structure. It is one of my favorite scripts.

SCRIPT LOGOS

Mari Makinami,
Design Resource
Tokyo, Japan
Mari Makinami, Executive
Creative Director
Doyald Young, Designer/Artist
Royal Park Hotel Sendai
Sendai, Japan
Fontaine Lounge

These logotype designs explore classical, formal, and decorative motifs. The designs allude to the type style more than being a derivative design. Comp 1 is a light face based on Garamond with exaggerated beaks on the cap **F** and **E**, and irregular vertical and diagonal beaks on the **T**.

Comp 2 is a Didoni characterized by the **a**'s teardrop terminal and the cupped Bodoni *t*. In this narrow bold form it has qualities of R. H. Middleton's Bodoni black condensed. It is the capital that gives the word shape and image. The capital is a hybrid with a script flourish at the top and an italic descender fitted with a teardrop common to many italic forms.

Comp 3, the script, again relies on an exaggerated cap with an unusual crossbar that repeats the shape of the main loop and ends parallel to the word's diagonal. The weight is

224

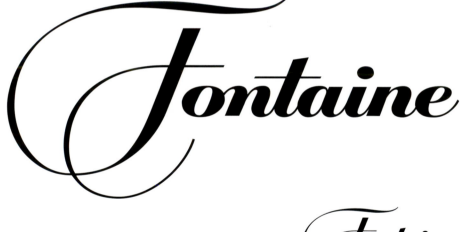

■

Above—*A bold, formal script for a hotel lounge that references Commercial Script .*

■

Opposite—*A series of pencil comprehensives that rely on classical styles of type; each modified and styled to suggest a gracious and elegant atmosphere.*

similar to Commercial Script, a bold formal script face. The first *n* connects to the *o* with a pothook. Its cap-to-lowercase height parallels traditional social printing fonts.

Comp 4 belongs to the late nineteenth century, loosely drawn with an almost cartoon **a**.

It employs an italic form of the *n* and *e*. There are traces of Oldstyle, evidenced by the carriage of weight across the **n**'s branch and the wide, heavily bracketed serifs.

Comp 5 is a modified Bernhard Tango with a tall swash *T* with a diagonal crossbar.

Comp 6 is a classic, late eighteenth-century all-cap Didot, drawn primly with only an expansive hairline swash letter **A** to relieve its classic, austere image.

FONTAINE

1.

ABCDEFGHIJKLMNOPQRSTUVWXYZ
abcdefghijklmnopqrstuvwxyz

Adobe Garamond—Robert Slimbach, Adobe, 1989

Fontaine

2.

**ABCDEFGHIJKLMNOPQRSTUVWXYZ&
abcdefghijklmnopqrstuvwxyz 1234567890 $**

Bodoni black condensed—R. Hunter Middleton, Ludlow, 1930

Fontaine

3.

*ABCDEFGHIJKLMN
OPQRSTUVWXYZ &
abcdefghijklmnopqrstuvwxyz*

Commercial Script—Morris Fuller Benton, ATF, 1906

Fontaine

4.

ABCDEFGHIJKLMNOPQRSTUVWXYZ&
abcdefghijklmnopqrstuvwxyz 1234567890
ABDMNOPRThr y ctstthooff fiflffiffl.,-:;'?

Artcraft—Robert Wiebking, Advance Typefoundry, 1912

FONTAINE

5.

ABCDEFGHIJKLMNOPQRSTUVWXYZ

Bernhard Tango—Lucian Bernhard, ATF, 1931

FONTAINE

6.

ABCDEFGHIJKLMNOPQRSTUVWXYZ
abcdefghijklmnopqrstuvwxyz

Didot—Adrian Frutiger, Linotype-Hell, 1996

SCRIPT LOGOS

Warner Bros. Records
Burbank, California
Jeri Heiden, Chief Art Director
Gregory Ross,
Art Director/Designer
Doyald Young, Artist
Courtesy of Hal Gaba,
HG Associates, Los Angeles

What's in a name? *Plenty!* Dear Mr. Gable, Mickey Rooney, Liza, Vincent Minnelli, MGM, The Harvey Girls, Meet Me in St. Louis, A Star is Born, Somewhere Over the Rainbow, The Yellow Brick Road, The Tin Man, The Cowardly Lion, Kansas—and don't forget Toto!

The album, cassette, and CD are part of a series that Warner Bros. Records reissued from 1950s and 1960s TV shows. General Electric sponsored the 1963 weekly Judy Garland show that boasted duets with her soon-to-be-famous daughter, Liza Minnelli, and the guest

appearance of an extraordinarily gifted, young 21-year-old nightclub singer named Barbra Streisand.

The decision to personalize the album posed problems of legibility, because the signature is so prominently displayed and Garland's original signature is hard to read. It was important

226

■
Top—*A photocopy of the original Judy Garland signature.*

Bottom—*Final signature version for use on albums, cassettes, and CDs. Redrawn to improve legibility yet held to the signature's original and essential qualities.*

Opposite—*Warner Bros. Records video cover (reduced).*

to retain the signature's distinctive image while making it more readable, so changes to the signature were minimal.

Judy works because the commonplace name is read as a shape. Judy must have been ebullient that day because the over-scale *J* begins, and the *y* and *d* end on optimistic shapes. The original *J*'s loop appears pointed, and the curve at two o'clock too sharp; both were softened with smoother, more gentle curves, and the exuberant finishing upstroke of the looped descender was retained. I drew a larger *d* in *Judy* and opened up its ascender; tightened the wordspace and drew the letters more legibly and a bit bolder. I doubled the size of the *G* to balance with the *J* and retained the slight reverse curve of its longish descender. The original *an* seems to read *in* or *ai*; the correct *an* is hard to come by, so I made them more legible. The original *d* in *Garland* is a hurried scrawl that surprisingly begins as a downstroke, then loops upward and downward to form a descender. I deleted the descender, but kept the basic shape and drew it smaller.

Smith + Bartels

Berkeley, California
Don Bartels, Designer
Doyald Young, Designer/Artist
GE Logo Font

A font of a company logo can be an enormous timesaver. When preparing any of the thousands of documents created every day in a global corporation, anyone from a graphic designer to an administrative assistant can simply type a font logo in place, choose its size, and color it.

General Electric Company's identity program features two versions of its famous mark. Shown at the left below is the company's primary trademark, the full Monogram, in positive and reverse forms (**g** and **e**). The other version is the Dynamic Monogram, any of the five cropped forms used as graphic support, usually large and bled, to suggest the company is too dynamic to be contained. They also are available both positive (*top row, below*) **2, 0, 3, q,** and **4** and reverse (*second row, below*).

GE's identity consultant, Don Bartels, asked me to trans-

228

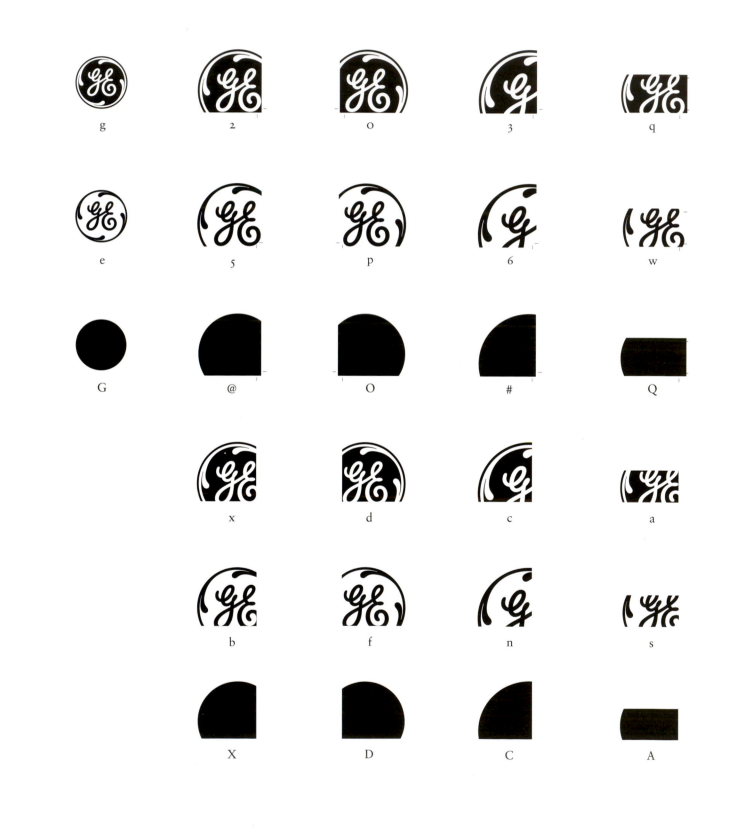

form this multitude of Mono-grams into a computer font. A few years before, I had worked with him on the final refinement drawing of the one-hundred-year-old symbol.

The challenge in developing this font was to translate those final drawings of the Monogram into digital form without loss of detail, each within the font character matrix. Despite repeated attempts, the TrueType format proved incapable of faithfully reproducing the Monogram; invariably, the subtle curves were distorted. However, thePostScript format is excellent and is used extensively in electronic artwork. The final font consists of 54 separate images, including silhouettes, masks and crop marks, plus linear patterns used for special applications such as packaging.

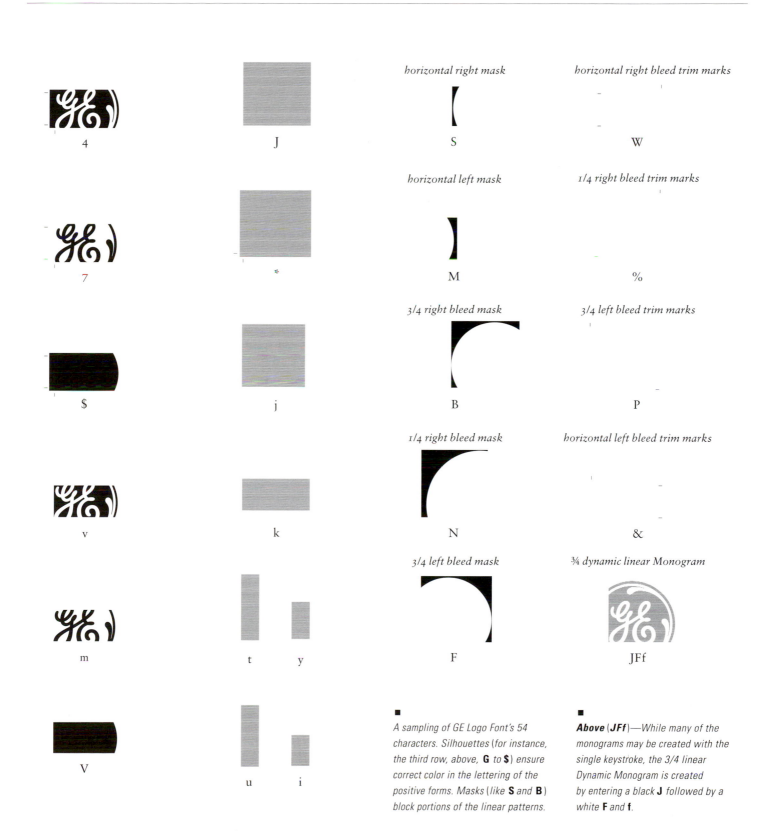

horizontal right mask

S

horizontal right bleed trim marks

W

4

J

horizontal left mask

M

1/4 right bleed trim marks

%

7

3/4 right bleed mask

B

3/4 left bleed trim marks

P

$

j

1/4 right bleed mask

N

horizontal left bleed trim marks

&

v

k

3/4 left bleed mask

F

3/4 dynamic linear Monogram

JFf

m

t   y

V

u   i

A sampling of GE Logo Font's 54 characters. Silhouettes (for instance, the third row, above, **G** to **$**) ensure correct color in the lettering of the positive forms. Masks (like **S** and **B**) block portions of the linear patterns.

Above (**JFf**)—While many of the monograms may be created with the single keystroke, the 3/4 linear Dynamic Monogram is created by entering a black **J** followed by a white **F** and **f**.

The National Academy of Recording Arts and Sciences, Inc.
Santa Monica, California
Pierre Cossette Productions
Robert Keene,
Production Design
Doyald Young, Designer/Artist

Rock, rap, jazz, country, and classical music are feted in the Grammy event. Award shows—the Tonys, the Oscars, and the Kennedy Honors, are filled with glitter and pomp; music awards shows are produced with a lighter touch; and the title design may reflect this.

The name of a TV special's main title often originates with the producer, and is then submitted for network approval. When the name is approved, the production designer commissions a graphic designer or a firm that specializes in title design to prepare a series of comprehensives.

In this design the cap *G* and the *A* are generous. With the *A*'s long, slim up-stroke, its stem almost becomes the focal point of the title. The letters are kept simple because the descender of the *G*, the loops of the restrained cap *L*, the dot of the *i*, the cross-bar of the *t*, and the ascender/

For economy, many titles for TV specials are designed to superimpose over live action, or are conceived as title cards with different backgrounds that are photographed, with color later applied by computer, known in the entertainment industry as a "paint box."

Freely drawn, the title script has strong references to handwriting. The Caflisch Script and Freestyle Script echo some characteristics of the title.

FONTS & LOGOS

descender of the *f* all create a nest of complex shapes. To achieve any freedom at all, the crossbar of a *t* needs to be longish, and that poses problems with the following dot of an *i*. It is usually necessary to place the dot above the crossbar, and a little to the right of the stem.

(Observe how far away the dot is from the *i* in handwriting.)

The style is a casual, slight two-weight brush script with some thinning around the baseline curves. Few fonts resemble the style.

Robert Slimbach created Caflisch Script to honor the Swiss calligrapher Max Caflisch and based it on his handwriting. The script is almost monotone, its x-height large, its fit open, but its turns are more pointed than the title script and reflect Chancery hands that are usually written with a broad-pen. The Freestyle script is monotone as though it had been written with a round-tipped point. Its style is more condensed than the example, and its caps resemble so-called "printed" caps, instead of the example's free-flowing script caps.

abcdefghijklmnopqrstuvwxyz

ABCDEFGHIJKLMNOPQRSTUVWXYZ

1234567890 !@#$%^&*()_+

Caflisch Script—Robert Slimbach, Adobe, 1993

abcdefghijklmnopqrstuvwxyz

ABCDEFGHIJKLMNOPQRSTUVWXYZ

1234567890 ! $%&*()_

Freestyle Script—Martin Wait, Fontek, 1987

International Design Associates
Tokyo, Japan
Tohru Uraoka, President
Mari Makinami, Executive
Creative Director
Doyald Young, Designer/Artist
Japan Air Terminal (Haneda)
Tokyo, Japan

Named after the respective wings of the building, **The L** and **The R** logos are for two first-class Art Deco–style restaurants in Tokyo's reconstructed Haneda Airport Terminal. The initial request called for a logo to match the Art Deco interiors. Even though most of the comps are sans serif, script dominates in the selected designs shown below.

Comp 1 is a stylized Trafton Script, a truly calligraphic script that is locked securely in the 1930s. Its shape is produced by a constant angle of a flat pen. *The* is subordinate to the initials and the lowercase e connects tangently to the large caps. Comp 2 is a generic Art Deco face that relies on a pumped-up bowl for the **R**. Script typefaces rarely use the same looped scheme for the *L* and the *R*. I drew these to match in comp 3. The tops of the caps are related, and the *L*'s closed loop is re-

232

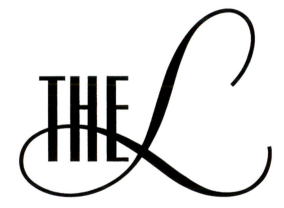

■
Above—Art Deco–style restaurant logos for the left and right wings of the Tokyo Haneda airport.

■
Opposite—The comps are mostly sans serif forms from the '30s, yet they are included here because the selected design is predominantly script. The logos reference in some manner the fonts shown at the right.

F O N T S & L O G O S

peated on the bottom stem of the *R*. The script cap weight distribution is similar to Trafton but it is closer in shape to Tempo light italic, a charming, single-weight sans serif with cap letters that are more script than italic. While there is much to admire in the font, the top cross-strokes of the *F* and *T* are stiff and clumsy, and the initial strokes at the top of the *M*, *N*, *V*, and *W* are stingy. The design parallels many 1920s sans serifs that sought to breathe some grace into the austere German-style sans serifs of the day. Comp 4 is derived from Pump, with its rounded right-angle turns.

Broadway, a sans serif face designed by Morris Benton in 1928, is almost a typographic cliche for the 1920s and '30s. Benton designed it as a titling face, caps only, and Sol Hess at Monotype duplicated the design, adding a lowercase that was virtually descenderless. After seventy years its use is unabated. In comp 5, the Broadway style is extended and beefed up, and combined with a typical narrow skyscraper sans serif of the 1930s.

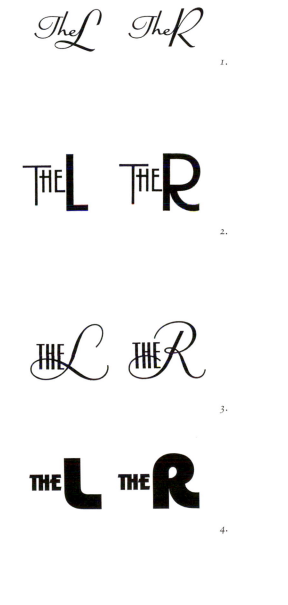

1.

Trafton Script—Howard Allen Trafton, Bauer, 1933

2.

Premier Lightline—Letraset, 1969

3.

Tempo light italic—R. Hunter Middleton, Ludlow 1930

4.

Pump demi bold—Letraset, 1980

5.

Broadway—Morris Fuller Benton, ATF, 1927

Dr. and Mrs. Gerald Labiner
Bel Air, California
Doyald Young, Designer/Artist
Collector's Mark for
Hogarth Print Collection

Suzanne and Gerald Labiner asked me to design a collector's mark for their extensive collection of William Hogarth prints. The mark would be a small rubber stamp, about ⅜ inch wide, to be used with a special Library of Congress indelible ink that will not chemically harm the paper.

The collector's mark can only be used on the back of a print, preferably behind a dark area on a print's front side, yet within the confines of the illustration so that the mark cannot be cut off.

The Labiners wanted the design to reflect eighteenth-century typography, so I chose a roman and combined it with formal script, an arrangement common to many of Hogarth's title blocks. Often these were filled with lines of meticulous formal script with elaborate flourishes in the style of the day. Hogarth's roman style is indefinite with unbracketed serifs

234

MORNING

The
LOTTERY

■
Above—*A collector's mark to be used as a 3/8 inch rubber stamp.*

■
Left—*An elaborate engraved script title from a series of Hogarth prints,* Morning, Noon, *and* Evening. *From a separate print,* The Lottery *has strong influences of Bodoni.*

that suggest a style closer to Bodoni's refined Italian forms, which are too delicate for the rubber stamp mark.

Hogarth's letters were engraved in copper with a burin, which with slight pressure produced the thins and with heavy pressure gouged the metal to produce a wide stem, a technique quite different from a letter drawn with a square-tipped broad-pen.

The first rough sketches strive to reflect the baroque style of eighteenth-century script. The letter *L* is one of the most beautiful letters in all of formal script, possessing two ogee curves (of which Hogarth was so enamored that he called the curve "The Line of Beauty").

I drew the *L* large for first reading and kept the first name initials small and drawn in a style that borrows from Caslon and Baskerville, two popular fonts of the day. Surrounding them is a linear cartouche, a fashionable device of the period. To integrate the elements, I joined the bottom reverse curve of the *L* to the border to create a strong visual element, which is prominent even in its small size.

1.

2.

3.

4.

5.

6.

7.

8.

9.

10.

11.

12.

13.

14.

15.

■ **Above**—A series of quick pencil studies designed to give equal importance to both first-name initials. Comps 1, 2, and 14 explored same-size letters for all three initials.

■ **Right**—In "The Analysis of Beauty," Hogarth drew a series of illustrations that displayed the reverse, or ogee curve in natural elements and in man-made objects. The "Line of Beauty" stands as the keystone of his esthetic theory.

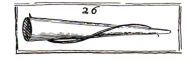

SCRIPT LOGOS

Warner Bros. Records
Burbank, California
Jeri Heiden, Chief Art Director
Greg Ross, Art Director
Doyald Young, Designer / Artist
CD Title Design
The New York Rock and Soul

Built in 1929, Manhattan's fabled Beacon Hotel leases its theater to music promoters for concerts. This is a title for a CD recording of a concert at the Beacon. Greg Ross, the art director, wanted a script, so there was no need to explore different styles. Only the three comprehensives (*below*)

were shown—pencil comps that simulate brush script.

As usual, I lightly wrote them out at about this size with a pointed pencil, then used the write-out as an underlay to create a built-up version. I refined the letters with an HB pencil and retouched with black ink and

white gouache. The first version shows great variation in the size of the letters: note the first *a* and *c*. The upstroke join of the *l* into the *i* is thin and the downstrokes of the *l*, *B*, and *t* in *the* and the left side of the *c* are heavy. The letters of the first and second comps have the same skeletal form; only the

236

■
Three styles of script for a Warner Bros. Records CD that imitates brush script, though written first with a pointed pencil. The logo was drawn as a positive image (opposite) but is shown here in reverse as it appears on the album cover.

FONTS & LOGOS

angle and weight are different, except that the *ac* in the first comp is separated. The second design, which was selected, has the most freedom. It is the most widely spaced and appears hurriedly written, aided by an exaggerated beginning stroke for the *B*'s bowl. The third comp imitates a style made popular in GM ads for the Pontiac. Only a few of the letters join; the rest are isolated script forms, extremely condensed and tightly spaced, with abrupt turns as ending strokes that taper quickly to points. The script is textured and leans more than the other comps—it is also the most difficult to read.

A few words of freestyle script are welcome in many layouts of rigid types. Scripts are friendly and accessible. Their particular structure changes only slightly every few years. Many are used on supermarket food products and their casual qualities suggest ease of preparation. Extremely bold and simplified examples are often seen for auto accessories and aggressive headline ads. Used in this context, they command attention.

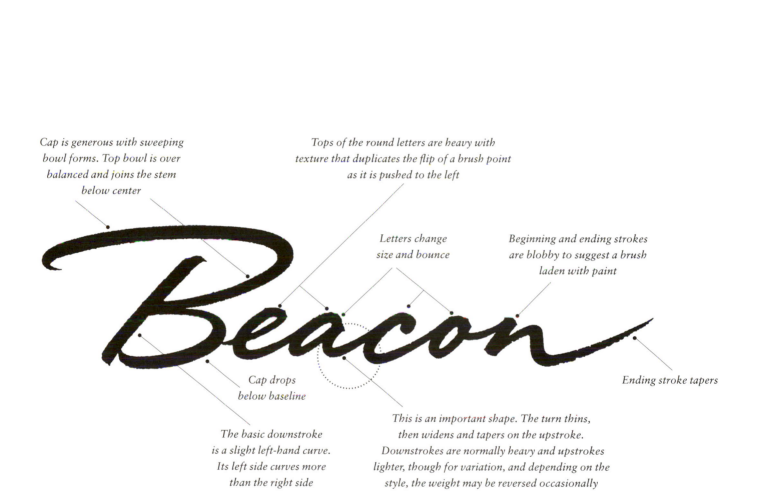

Cap is generous with sweeping bowl forms. Top bowl is over balanced and joins the stem below center

Tops of the round letters are heavy with texture that duplicates the flip of a brush point as it is pushed to the left

Letters change size and bounce

Beginning and ending strokes are blobby to suggest a brush laden with paint

Cap drops below baseline

Ending stroke tapers

The basic downstroke is a slight left-hand curve. Its left side curves more than the right side

This is an important shape. The turn thins, then widens and tapers on the upstroke. Downstrokes are normally heavy and upstrokes lighter, though for variation, and depending on the style, the weight may be reversed occasionally

Above—There are a multitude of valuable script styles. This basic one simulates the action of a pointed brush generously loaded with paint, held in a normal writing position and done rather quickly with arm motions rather than the fingers.

SCRIPT LOGOS

Nestlé, U.S.A.
Glendale, California
Quito Trujillo,
Creative Director
Doyald Young, Artist
Point-of-Purchase
Supermarket Easel

America has long had a love affair with coffee mugs—they are everywhere, at work stations, on dashboards, and at desks. On weekends they are found in rec rooms and garage workshops. They proliferate in tourist gift shops, and are prized by collectors. This logo was designed for a point-of-purchase easel that offered coffee mugs for a Coffee-Mate non-dairy creamer proof-of-purchase receipt.

The general size, curve, and weight of the lettering was established by the art director, Mr. Trujillo, who roughly indicated some hairline flourishes to sweeten the layout. The style looks like an upright script with each letter perpendicular to the arc of the curve, but closer reading reveals a few italic forms. Here the **o** is pure Bodoni, while the top of the **s** is a Bodoni italic form in an upright position and the bottom half is script.

238

A semi-upright, script/italic form that is casual and romantic. It contains swash letters and has hairlines that are extension of the letters. An additional hairline around the cap **L** is used to create a cartouche-like shape.

A secondary weight is used for the top loops of the *L* and the *C*.

I was taught that a leaning script should never wrap around a curve because the angles of the stems fan and will never appear to lean in a consistent manner. They are also difficult to space. The logo's letters give the illusion of being at right angles to the curve. They are casual shapes; they change size and do not always follow the tight, prescribed curve. With the exception of the **o**, they are italic swash shapes: the **n** and **u** have generous ogee stems, and the **s** ends as an overscale letter. The stems are concave with flared tips, and the dot of the **i**, in the manner of handwriting, is casually off-center. The letters' general style is a relaxed Modern, and the absence of serifs lends the quasiscript quality to the two words. An additional hairline is used to frame the *L* and suggests a normal loop. With looped extensions of the caps, **g**, and **p**, the overall effect is a romantic curving cartouche border.

ABCDEFGHIJKL
MNOPQRSTUVWXYZ
abcdefghijklmnopqrstuvwxyz
.,;?!/" " ' 1234567890
@#$%^&*() []_+=

Modern No. 216 bold italic—Ed Benguiat, ITC, 1982

ABCDEFGHIJKL
MNOPQRSTUVWXYZ
abcdefghijklmnopqrstuvwxyz
.,;?!/" " ' 1234567890
@#$% ^&*()[]_+=

Bodoni bold italic—Heinrich Jost, Bauer, 1926

■
The Loving Cups logo is based on these Modern style italic shapes in upright position and drawn with an absence of serifs.

dick clark productions, inc.
Jack Seifert, producer
Robert Keene,
Production Designer
Burbank, California
Doyald Young, Designer/Artist
Daytime TV Show

Script written at an uphill angle intrigues me. As a graphic device, the angle sets the words apart, which attracts attention within a rectilinear layout. The custom of signing a greeting card or writing a brief message at an angle reveals that the sender is saying that the sentiment is special, and proves it by writing it in an uncommon orientation.

This television title is middle-of-the-road—there is nothing unique in its letterforms, and nothing sets it apart except the generous caps. The script is drawn, not written. It is contrived—in the sense of fabrication. It is impossible to directly produce such shapes with the simple action of either a pointed or a rigger brush. The forms are premeditated; nothing is left to chance. Many casual brush scripts are successful because of the spontaneous "accidents" that happen with an intentionally hurried

240

execution. **Moments** is conceived as a continuously moving line with no interruption. All of the turns at the baseline carry slightly greater weight than the thinner upstrokes. I drew it to approximate a carefully modeled thick-and-thin script that is written with a narrow, square-tipped

brush, held at an almost constant angle. There is variation in the cap *M*s; the second one begins with a more generous upstroke. The baseline of both words is optically straight; the x-height finds variation. Endings of the *c*, *t*'s cross-stroke, and the *s* are related; the cross-stroke curves less.

Tails of *g*s may be simple curved strokes or looped—the choice is personal. Here the descender is a variation of the *M*'s beginning strokes. A loop with another ending would complicate the area near the *t*'s crossbar by adding another ending point.

The crossbar of the t is an ogee curve. Its placement is off-center to prevent it from appearing static

There are three ways to make a t: (1) an overlapped up-and-downstroke that appears to be a single stroke; (2) a tightly filled loop; and (3) an open loop, as here. The choice depends on the particular combination of letters within the design

The ending stroke, sometimes called a finishing stroke, widens slightly before it turns quickly

Weight is carried around top and bottom curves

Counters are drawn as teardrops, symmetrical on the major axis. Note e and t counters

■

The letters in this logo retain the effects of normal handwriting pressure: heavy on the downstrokes, less pressure on the upstrokes. I drew them as individual joined letters (not written with a brush, and the best ones selected). Each letter is based on the

assumption that it begins its shape at the top. The style is a combined pen/brush style with cleaned-up edges. The spacing is average, with occasional variation to prevent the words from becoming static and to lend a touch of spontaneity.

SCRIPT LOGOS

Pasadena Concours d'Elegance
James Hull, President
Pasadena, California
Richard Pietruska, Designer
Doyald Young, Designer

242

Strother McMinn taught automotive design to thousands of students at Art Center College of Design in Pasadena, and was considered an authority in the international automotive design community. The Pasadena Concours d'Elegance committee asked Art Center to sponsor an award for their annual competition to honor McMinn. Richard Pietruska, designer and professor of illustration, designed the 2-inch-thick irregular pentagram plexiglass award and asked me to create the graphics. I used two fonts: Palatino capitals and Young Baroque, my elaborate formal script, designed expressly for use where a limited number of words requires special treatment. Palatino caps suggest formality and their sturdy humanist forms are ideal for this size. Center dots between words are normally placed at the lowercase x-height, but here I centered them on cap

PHOTO: RICHARD PIETRUSKA

An award designed with an elaborate script that honors one of the great designers and teachers of automotive design.

FONTS & LOGOS

height. Young Baroque's capitals do not connect to the lowercase, but instead drop below the baseline, lending more importance to the words than normal aligning caps. I used three of the 26 alternate lowercase letters that accompany the font: *g, l*, and the looped ascender *d*. The gener-ously looped *g* is useful to finish a word, or when a decorative flourish is needed. A pair of looped *l*s sometimes creates too much space for the balance of the word, so I used two straight, eighteenth-century-style ones. The typographic design is based on coin and medal inscriptions with the Palatino capitals right-reading, instead of upside down at the circle's bottom edge.

The graphics were lightly laser etched on the backside of the plexiglass.

Young Baroque—Doyald Young, ITC, 1992

International Design Associates

Tokyo, Japan
Tohru Uraoka, President
Ken Nakata, Art Director
Doyald Young, Designer/Artist
Japan Railways,
Hotel Granvia Nihon, Okayama
Prix d'Or, French Restaurant

Primer, meaning in French to excel, surpass, or lead, was the name first considered for Hotel Granvia's elegant French restaurant. In English the word has quite different meanings (an elementary book; a small charge to detonate an explosive; or a like amount of liquid to prime a pump or a carburetor). Thus the name was changed to *Prix d'Or* which means gold prize in both languages. The comps were designed to complement the hotel's Art Deco interiors (see the hotel's other amenity logos, Lumìere, and Olivier, pages 116 and 170). Comp 1 echoes the style of Broadway, Chic, Chicago, and Parisian, typified by partially weighted bowl forms that are only one-third of the stem's thickness, plus high-waisted **R**s. The style was popular in the 1920s and '30s and was often used for fashion statements. Comp 2 has similar proportions

244

Prix d'Or

Prix d'Or

■
Hotel Granvia's French restaurant logotype. Instead of the requested Art Deco style, a formal script was chosen.

but is drawn with linear **R**s that are a reminder of Rudolf Koch's Cable initials and Parisian. Comp 3, the selected design, is a wide, semi-bold formal script drawn with tall, extravagantly wide caps that create its memorable image. The x-height is small and the *r* begins below the baseline; the caps are a different size. The style cannot be pigeonholed in any period. It is based on a wide, bold, hand-lettered style with a slight lean that has been used since the dawn of advertising.

The ligature **R** and **D** of comp 4 create a saddle that spans two letters and the word space, a somewhat excessive statement, characteristic of many exaggerations of letterforms in the Art Deco period.

Comp 5 has more graceful shapes: the *P*, *R*s, and *D* are swash forms. The *X* and *D* create a ligature and a strong identifying diagonal shape. Comp 9 is monotone, with an **R**'s tail that points to the **M**'s center; the **E** is a script form. Comp 10 borrows from Typo Script, but uses a much larger cap.

PRIX D'OR

1.

PRIX D'OR

2.

Prix d'Or

3.

PRIX D'OR

4.

PRIX D'OR

5.

PRIMER

6.

PRIMER

7.

Primer

8.

PRIMER

9.

Primer

10.

IMPORTED

Parisian

LOPQRS

Cable Initials

Prix d'Or

Commercial Script

PRIX D'OR

Newport

Primer

Typo Upright

The Raymond Company

Raymond D. Swarens, CEO
Robert Wilcomb, President
Doyald Young, Designer/Artist
Manufacturers of Ceramic Lamps and Giftware

The Raymond Company, which began as a small ceramic lamp factory that sold to low-end surplus stores and then to all of the major department stores in America, with showrooms in major U.S. cities, wished to upgrade its company image and commisssioned a new logo.

I chose a formal script to convey the concept of quality home furnishings. The logo, in a burnished gold, was to be applied to sample books, stationery, business cards, and special brochures. The shape and style of the lowercase is restrained. It is only in the dramatic forms of the caps and

the *y*'s descender that the logotype assumes its positive shape and image. I avoided tight volutes and used the two long horizontal curves of the *T* and *y* to frame the three words and produce an overall triangular shape. The straight stems of the *h, y, d,* and *p* contrast with the repetitive curved

*Extravagant caps are paired with conservative lowercase forms. To nest the three lines, the caps change size. Two types of descender are used for the **y**s, a simple straight form, and a final loop that serves as an ending flourish.*

FONTS & LOGOS

forms. Most daring of all is the volute of the *R*'s downstroke; its ellipse retains its dramatic shape even in the smallest applications. Sizes of the capitals are varied to employ minus leading, including the *y*'s descender in **Raymond**. The top of the last *y*'s loop is weighted with a strong ogee swelling stroke. Instead of the normal hairline beginning, a weighted, straight stem is used for the *m* in **Raymond**. An eighteenth-century-style *p* repeats the ogee curves of the *h*, *m*, and *n*.

A B C D E F G H I J K L M N O P Q R S T U V W X Y Z

abcdefghijklmnopqrstuvwxyz

1234567890

Künstler Script medium—Hans Bohn, Stempel, 1957

A B C D E F G H I J K L M N O P Q R S T U V W X Y Z

abcdefghijklmnopqrstuvwxyz

lɔçaff 8t~hrœgz4¨öh"åß∫∫sm˙l...la

kçl~dcb 1234567890

Young Baroque—Doyald Young, ITC, 1992

■

The Raymond Company logo is derived from these roundhand forms. The Künstler font was originally cut in metal; Young Baroque was designed as a dry-transfer face, with 26 separate alternate lowercase letters, and later digitized as a Type 1 PostScript font.

SCRIPT LOGOS

Mari Makinami, Design Resource
Tokyo, Japan
Mari Makinami, Executive
Creative Director
Doyald Young Designer / Artist
Rose illustration drawn by
David Solon
Royal Park Hotels logo

Royal Park Hotels is a wholly owned subsidiary of the Mitsubishi Corporation, whose original hotel is located near the downtown Tokyo airport terminal. All of their hotels are designed with classic, traditional decor. The restaurants and bars have English and French names (*see* Fontaine, Tiara, and Vincennes, pages 224, 126, and 128.)

The hotel chain expressed interest in a monogram design that would incorporate a rose, a symbol for English monarchy. Ms. Makinami requested a series of script monograms that narrowed the design direction considerably. Four-star hotels the world over have long used formal script logotypes as the expression of quality and professional hospitality (*see* page 107). I drew preliminary monogram sketches, then David Solon (who drew the roses) and I decided where the roses could be incor-

248

■
Above—Final art.
Left—These two versions are a more straightforward approach and designed for one of the many presentations to the various RPH executives. Only the name Royal Park Hotels accompanies the monogram; no symbol is used. The left version is a condensed Century with weighted hairlines and serifs, and swash extensions. Radiant, Trafton, and generic script forms make up the shapes that interconnect with each other in the right version.

F O N T S & L O G O S

porated into the designs. The styles of script are mostly traditional English roundhand forms: comps 1, 2, 3, 5, and 6. Comp 2 follows the orientation of Typo Upright. Comp 4 is Middleton's Radiant transformed into script. In each case I attempted to join the letters so that they form a cohesive unit yet remain legible and do not become abstract shapes. Some letter combinations make a happy marriage. Other dissimilar shapes require great modification, effort, and exploration to achieve a harmonious unity. Comps 2, 4, 5, and 6 have the same beginning *R* loop. In many script alphabets the weighted ogee swelling downstroke is the same on all three letters, but here only the *P* and *R* are ogival. In comp 5, the *H* bar is an extension of the *P*'s bowl.

1.

4.

2.

5.

3.

6.

■

Pencil comprehensives that explored the placement of the rose, a symbol of English monarchy.

SCRIPT LOGOS

International Design Associates
Tokyo, Japan
Tohru Uraoka, President
Mari Makinami, Executive
Creative Director
Doyald Young, Designer/Artist
Singapore Country Club,
Singapore, Malaysia

Formal scripts, or copperplates as the British prefer to call them, have been used for country club logotypes for generations. The conservative styles typified by Palace Script, Bank Script, Künstler Script, and Royal Script can sometimes look straight-laced and commonplace. This example, designed for the main dining room, is less formal, but still has an elegant pose achieved by combining the freedom of hurried handwriting with the weight distribution of the classic formals. The traditional heavy pressure for a downstroke and lighter pressure for an upstroke is maintained. Many examples in George Bickham's *Universal Penman* show forms that do not carry weight around the bottom and the curved connecting loops. This structure can be adhered to, or a slight calligraphic carriage of weight can be used with discretion. Scripts that are

A freestyle script logo for Singapore Country Club's dining room. It is best to avoid patterns in freestyle scripts, i.e., groups of same-sized letters or a pattern of angles produced by either the tops or bottoms of the stair-stepped letters. Break words at syllables, or where congestion occurs. Breaks create lighter, more open words. Open up groups of straight stems (*i, u, n, m*). A break relieves the monotony and helps readability.

written with a nibbed pen held at a rather steep angle have a completely different nature (see Grayda). There are no set rules for the amount of weight that is carried, nor for the amount of exuberance that the script can have. The normally straight strokes can arc slightly: *m*, *n*, and *u*. Descenders of the *p*s and *q*s should be more rigid so as not to appear bent. Forms may be extravagant. Ending strokes of letters that do not connect can be generous in length, especially with the final loop of the last letter. Generally, these will parallel the other up-strokes, sometimes reaching higher than the letters. For a more positive statement, they can be almost horizontal, tapering to a point.

The art director requested only four comp designs, so I presented a slightly condensed Bodoni with a generous swash P, comp 1; a restrained formal script, comp 2; and a highly stylized condensed sans serif, comp 3, with a lowercase **n** and a **G** with a descender (*see* page 120 for the Singapore Country Club logotype).

1.

2.

3.

The two top comps are conservative approaches based on traditional designs; the bottom one takes a more adventuresome stance with a biform concept.

Smith + **Bartels**

Berkeley, California
Doyald Young, Designer/Artist
Nancy Smith and
Donald H. Bartels
S+B Personal Monogram

Monograms are often highly stylized letters, but seldom do clients prefer an abstract shape, because to unquestionably identify, the letters must read.

The shape's complexity depends on client preference and the method of reproduction. A two-dimensional black and white design is transformed into a completely different image if it is blind embossed on paper, or engraved with a v-cut on silver flatware or on crystal goblets. Light and shadow are introduced and the contrast of black and white is considerably lessened. I began this design with no restrictions. I showed some completely different styles, from joined roman serif letters to simplified linear shapes. All have scriptorial qualities. The client favored the traditional leaning formal script capitals. Formal script *S*s can sometimes be confused with cap *L*s, so I made

■
Top—*Final art.*
Left—*Separate consecutive keystrokes typed to produce the 42-point composite monogram.*
Opposite—*Personal monogram designs with different orientation, weights, and letter styles, which explored S+B and S&B. The finished art for the monogram was drawn as a font since it was to be used primarily for stationery.*

FONTS & LOGOS

several drawings using the more traditional **S** shape. I tried the plus sign on a few designs, but some look more like crosses than plus signs. Comps 1 and 6 suggest a heart shape, and comp 5 has an intimate quality. Comp 3 is the simplest statement (and my preference), comp 10 is the most organized, but Nancy and Don preferred the elaborate formality of comp 12.

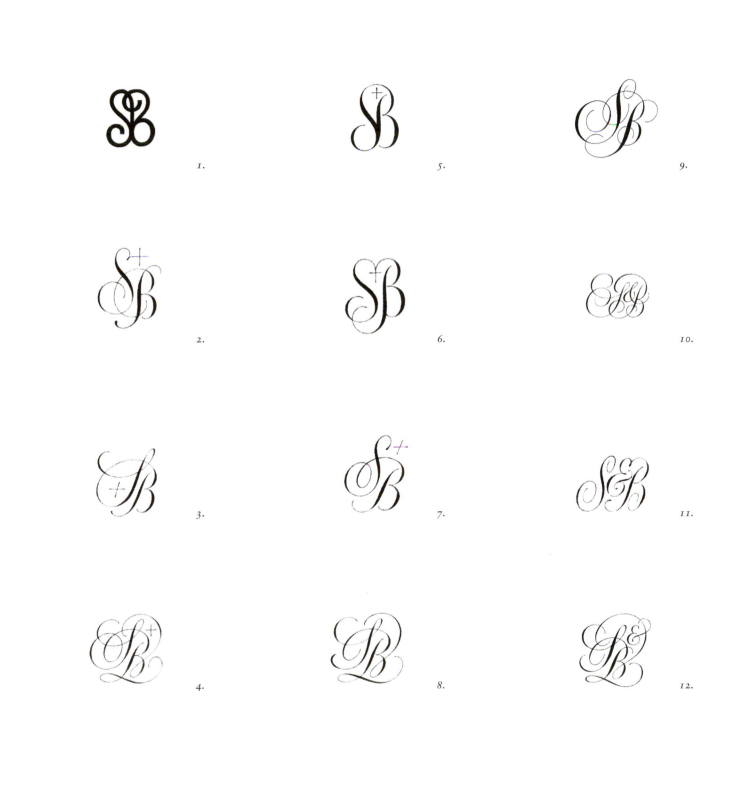

1.

2.

3.

4.

5.

6.

7.

8.

9.

10.

11.

12.

Mari Makinami, Design Resource
Tokyo, Japan
Mari Makinami, Executive
Creative Director
Doyald Young/Mari Makinami,
Designer/Artists
Advertising agency:
Intervision, Incorporated

254

Sony Corporation's corporate identity manual states that only the Craw Clarendon cap logo may be used on products; all other applications are required to use lowercase letters. Their corporate logo is set in Helvetica bold cap and lowercase. This assignment was for the design of a logotype for the Hawaiian Golf Open. It was also the first assignment from an advertising agency newly formed by Sony and Dentsu and created as an umbrella agency to monitor and direct all of Sony's advertising worldwide. Sports logos have used scripts for many years: note the number of bold script logos for baseball clubs such as the Los Angeles Dodgers.

The creative director requested that one of the presentation comprehensives should be set in cap and lowercase Helvetica bold to reference Sony's corporate logo; comp 1 resulted.

Casual scripts combine easily with sans serifs, and are an effective choice for black and white newspaper advertising. The problem is to find the proper emphasis for each word, and I experimented to determine which was most effective. I carefully drew the comps and then Ms. Makinami applied various golf symbols to the logo—golf clubs, tees, and golf balls. The art director and Ms. Makinami ultimately settled instead on the leaves that transform the cap **O** into a pineapple, one of the more easily recognized symbols for Hawaii and hospitality. Reproduced in black and white, *Open* is screened to 40 percent. When the logo is reproduced in color, **Sony** is dark blue, the script golden, and the leaves dark green.

1.

2.

3.

4.

5.

6.

■

Casual scripts and sans serifs combine easily. The arrangement is one of the basic tenets of design—contrast: contrast of cap and lowercase sans, of cap and lowercase script, and of vertical and leaning letters.

SCRIPT LOGOS

Display figure: Fino. Text: 30/50 Prudential roman

Readers of failing eyesight
rightfully ask for types that are
plain and unequivocal, that reveal
the entire character at a glance and are
not discerned with difficulty by body
marks joined to hairlines and
serifs that are but half seen
or not seen at all.

THEODORE DE VINNE

Publisher, Printer, Typographer, and Editor,

Century Magazine

Prudential

The Prudential Insurance
Company of America
John R. March
Director, Corporate Identity
and Art Director
Doyald Young, Designer / Artist

Prudential, the largest insurance company in the United States, sought a friendlier image than the bold Helvetica corporate signature that had identified the company for over 12 years. **The** was to be omitted and **Prudential** would be used, in cap and lowercase in a highly legible font or one created especially for the new corporate identity program. The signature must appear clearly on the thousands of documents published annually by the company and its many subsidiaries: policies, contracts, and brochures.

Trial settings of Prudential and a few subsidiary names were typeset at the start of the design program: two versions of Century, Garamond, Sabon, and Times Roman bold; all were considered to be "friendly," yet March, the corporate identity director, thought that the often-used styles would not create strong brand identification.

Note: *The Rock of Gibraltar trademark was updated in 1989 by Prudential and was not modified for this study.*

■
Corporate signature style long used by Prudential. The name change offered a chance to look at some type styles to reflect management's wish for a friendly stance.

FONTS & LOGOS

42-point ITC Century bold

42-point Century 725 bold

42-point Adobe Garamond bold

42-point Sabon bold

42-point Times Roman bold

Of the many type styles set, the Times Roman bold and Century 725 were strong contenders. Here each font is set at the same point size with zero tracking. Not satisfied, the corporate crea-tive director requested some hand-drawn versions closely following type forms, though not necessarily in the same weight or proportion of the original font style. The pencil-drawn versions are shown together on the fol-lowing pages with an approximate type setting. Management planned to set subsidiary names in a font created in the same style as the logotype design.

Many elements make a logotype distinctive: its length, short or long; its particular combination or repetition of letters; its case, caps or lowercase; its orientation, roman or italic; and its proportion, normal, condensed, or extended. All of these affect the look of the name even before

the family, historical style, and/or design direction is chosen. Then letterspacing, normal, tight, or open, comes into play.

If marketing requirements demand that the logo design should be conservative, only subtle variations in the letters are needed. A change of weight and/or propor-

tion can readily affect the word's appearance. For the logo to achieve a degree of uniqueness, the weight should be either lighter or bolder, and bolder is preferred. *Avoid the ordinary* is the basic rule of logotype design.

The two large hand-drawn versions of Century shown below are

Prudential

Tight, hand-lettered pencil comprehensive on tracing paper

Prudential

Century bold—Tony Stan, ITC, 1975–80

abcdefghijklmnopqrstuvwxyz

Monotype's version of ATF's 36-point Century Schoolbook, the original hand-set metal font (foundry type) designed by Morris Fuller Benton in 1917–19

abcdefghijklmnopqrstuvwxyz

Monotype's PostScript version of 36-point Century Schoolbook

Monotype metal font

Pru

Monotype digital font

Hand-drawn or computer-modified logotypes are often distinguished by a change of proportion, weight, or orientation. Logos for conservative companies often rely on subtlety and nuance of design, where only minor changes are

made to the letterforms, either in weight distribution, serif structure, or variation in cap-to-height ratio. These two drawings are modifications of Morris Benton's Century Schoolbook, a font designed for textbook publishing in

the early part of the twentieth century. The sturdy thins of the original font have been retained, forms are slightly condensed, the bracketed serifs are more crisp, serifs are shorter for a tighter fit, and more weight is added

F O N T S   &   L O G O S

based on Morris Benton's pellucid, 80-year-old Century Schoolbook for ATF (American Type Founders). My letters are a bit condensed, and at the client's request, rather snugly fitted.

Both drawings show a more condensed **P** than normal to reduce the hole at the word's beginning. The **rs** are kerned more tightly, and the **u**'s left serif is shortened for the same reason. A more obvious change is the **a**'s tail, shortened so that **al** doesn't create a misspacing within the word's tight confines.

On the opposite page, the pencil drawing x-height serifs are angled and the **t**'s ascender simplified. The top of its ascending stem is angled, not cupped; many font **t** stems are chopped horizontally. Note that the wide tail of the **t** of the typeset word creates a misspacing and creates a visual **ti** ligature. The ball terminals are not bracketed. On this page, the pencil drawing retains the original Century's cupped, pointed **t** ascender. The letters are more narrow than the type, are not as bold, and are more openly spaced than the type. The tail of the **a** is yet more restrained.

Prudential

Tight, hand-lettered pencil comprehensive on tracing paper

Prudential

Century 725

abcdefghijklmnopqrstuvwxyz
ABCDEFGHIJKLMNOP
QRSTUVWXYZ

Century 725 bold, Bitstream, 1990;
Madison—Heinrich Hoffmeister, Stempel, 1965

to the shoulders of the curved forms, **P**, **a**, **d**, and **e**. The **a**'s terminal tail is restrained to allow for tight spacing. For variation of design (opposite, top), serifs are slightly angled, including the **d**'s ascender. The top version above, aligns the x-height horizontal serifs with the **t**'s crossbar—a less active design approach. In both hand-lettered versions the **e**'s crossbar is well above center of the x-height to prevent the **e** from appearing top heavy. Compare with Century 725.

A C A S E S T U D Y

Times Roman is everywhere. It is the resident text font for the majority of the world's laser printers. Times Roman can be found in most foundry libraries, licensed or as a redrawn version. Because it is so commonplace, it is almost invisible; it is not noticed. A corporate signature set in Times Roman lacks the uniqueness that most logotypes require for assertive, memorable advertising. If Times is to succeed as a distinguished logo, then its basic characteristics need to be adjusted. Turned upside down, a traditional **n** becomes a **u**, but in the regular weight of Times, the horizontal serifs of the upside-down **u** have been retained and conflict with the x-height **m** and **n**'s triangular serifs. In the bold-face font (*opposite*) both **u** and **n** serifs are horizontal (flat-head). Purity of form and design is exhibited, but using the bold with the regular weight in large sizes is jarring.

Prudential

Tight, hand-lettered pencil comprehensive on tracing paper

Prudential

Times New Roman, Monotype

abcdefghijklmnopqrstuvwxyz
ABCDEFGHIJKLMNOP
QRSTUVWXYZ

36-point Times New Roman—Stanley Morison & Victor Lardent, Monotype, 1932

Times New Roman · · · · · · · Times Roman Bold

Left—*Times Roman bold has a vertical stress for its round forms, while the regular weight is tilted, mirroring the angle of a broad-pen.*

Monotype called the font The Times New Roman *up until 1950, when the name was changed to* Times New Roman, *the boldface was named* Times bold. *Linotype called it* Times Roman *as do many founders.*

FONTS & LOGOS

(Many fonts are designed with the same conceit.) I have used the original font **u** and **n** serifs on the pencil drawing (*opposite, top*). The bold sketch (*below*) breaks with this tradition and is drawn with triangular serifs, though the **r**'s serif should slant more. For my taste, Times's bowl forms are too narrow for the branch forms, (note the **ud**) and I have adjusted them in my pencil version (*below*). Thins of the sketch are heavier and the **a**'s bowl has less slope than the type. True to the Oldstyle concept of the original Times Roman, the **t**'s crossbar is calligraphically weighted.

In contrast, the Times Roman bold characters are dissimilar shapes. The **e**'s top right curve ignores its calligraphic heritage and is thinner than the left side; a broad-pen produces the widest part of a curve above center right, and below center left. When flanked with verticals, the **r**'s ball terminal creates spacing problems, and at large sizes looks better when shortened. Times bold is shorter than many font **rs**.

Prudential

Tight, hand-lettered pencil comprehensive on tracing paper

Prudential

Times Roman bold, Adobe Systems, Inc.

abcdefghijklmnopqrstuvwxyz
ABCDEFGHIJKLMNOP
QRSTUVWXYZ

36-point Times Roman bold, Adobe Systems, Inc.

■

Right—Walter Tracy pointed out in his Letters of Credit *that the bold-face design of Times Roman departed from the regular version with vertical stress and flat-head serifs, instead of the triangular ones found at x-height and at the baseline on the* **u***.*

flathead serifs

Times New Roman   *Times Roman bold*

A CASE STUDY

Francesco da Bologna (Griffo) designed the first italic type, which closely paralleled the angle of writing hands. There were limitations of angle; the greater the slope, the more widely spaced the italic type would be. Most contemporary text italics range from 12 to 17 degrees from the vertical to match the general color and size of the upright roman. Logos with increased slope have a dynamic quality that distinguishes the name from ordinary italics. There is a drawback: it is difficult to create visual alignment between an italic and a second line of justified roman type. The hand-drawn Times italic below leans only a few degrees more than the font. It is wider, bolder, and tightly spaced. The **t** has an angled top echoed on the **u**'s right-hand stem. Because the set is tight, a **ti** ligature is used. The forms closely follow the type.

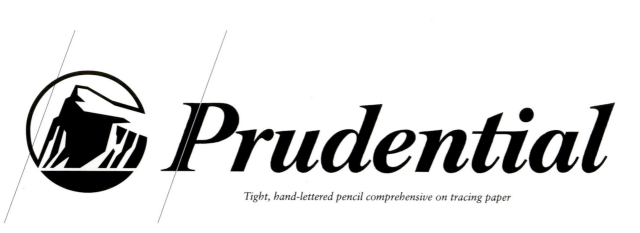

Tight, hand-lettered pencil comprehensive on tracing paper

Prudential

Times bold italic

abcdefghijklmnopqrstuvwxyz
ABCDEFGHIJKLMNOP
QRSTUVWXYZ

Times Bold italic—Stanley Morison & Victor Lardent, Monotype, 1932

Top—*The client wanted to see an italic version of the logo drawn with the same angle as the left side of the Rock of Gibraltar (not in scale).*

Bodoni is a modern face, simple in structure, with a formal no-nonsense quality that has made it popular for financial community logos. Its shapes are less fussy than the Venetians and Oldstyles. It is easy to use in display and text sizes because its symmetrical distribution of mass is easily scaled in weight and proportion. I have used the ATF Bodoni as a springboard. Its forms are not as round as the Bauer version and lack the spirited points of the stem's serifs, which at large sizes are too prominent. The bowl counters of the pencil sketch are oval and less taut than ATF's version. The spacing is tight, letters are of average proportion, and its weight is somewhere between the normal and bold settings. Hairlines are beefed up and serif's lengths adjusted to improve color spacing. The swing of the r's ball terminal is more restrained than the type and the ball is not bracketed to the hairline, a design trait found in some of Bodoni's thousands of metal sorts. Note the short ascender of the ATF Bodoni **t**.

Prudential

Tight, hand-lettered pencil comprehensive on tracing paper

Prudential

Bodoni—Morris Fuller Benton, ATF, 1910—11

abcdefghijklmnopqrstuvwxyz
ABCDEFGHIJKLMNOP
QRSTUVWXYZ

Bauer Bodoni—Heinrich Jost, Bauer, 1926

Right—*Bracketed terminal, medium weight of Giambattista Bodoni's Ducale, Manuale Tipographia, Parma, 1818. Foundries use different serif treatments. ATF's are flat and the Bauer has a pronounced point.*

1818 Bodoni (enlarged)

ATF Bodoni (enlarged)

Bauer Bodoni

A C A S E S T U D Y

The hand-lettered Bodoni (*below*), is a bolder and wider version than the preceding design, on page 265. It is slightly more open, but its chief characteristic is the small cap **P**, which is not as tall as the ascenders to minimize the importance of the caps in five- and six-word subsid-iary names (*see* pages 284–85). I've drawn the **t** to the same height as the **d** and **l**, and angled its top, which is traditionally shorter in serif fonts.

Bodoni is characterized by thin hairlines and an absence of weight carried around the tops and bottom portions of the bowls and round forms. This makes the **c** and **e** create holes. I weighted the lower right hairline portion of the **e** and blunted its ending to compensate. I favored the **a**'s tail by shortening the lower left serif of the **l** to prevent them from touching. Compare the two letters in the Bodoni bold typeset version.

Prudential

Tight, hand-lettered pencil comprehensive on tracing paper

Shortened ascender and narrow crossbar

Prudential

Bodoni bold—Morris Fuller Benton, ATF, 1910–11 (Adobe)

ABCDEFGHIJKLMNOPQRSTU
abcdefghijklmnopqrstuvwxyz

Bodoni bold—Morris Fuller Benton, ATF, 1910–11

ATF's bold versions of Bodoni have a pronounced corner on the **a**'s stem that doesn't relate to the other branch forms. To avoid clogging, the branches are angular, and both **S**s have strong horizontal spines. The straight counter bowls are more rigid than Bodoni's original shapes. My sketch is almost an extended ultra-bold weight with a diminished cap **P** and snug letterspacing. The **t** is the same height as the **d** and **l**.

Garamond is an old type, as age-less as the Rock. It belongs in any serious presentation of classical font drawings. Present-day foundries have cleaned up Claude Garamond's elegant forms, but what remains of the 450-year-old style is inimitable. The caps are beautifully proportioned, and printers have loved the type for its sturdy hairlines but are wary of the small counters of the **a** and **e**. Robert Slimbach has drawn a superb family for Adobe Systems, and R. H. Middleton's 1929 italic for Ludlow is as elegant today as was Garamond's in the court of Francis I. Garamond's types were later included in the Imprimerie Nationale de France and were used by Richelieu and Louis III.

My semi-bold drawing has a pronounced cup in the triangular serifs, and the horizontal serifs have less cup than Slimbach's version. Its forms are relaxed. Characteristic of all Garamond fonts is an absence of points. Branches and bowls are bracketed at the stems, which softens the letters. Goudy, Middleton, and Benton's versions, plus Tschichold's Sabon, have been the most popular, but Slimbach's version is equal to them, with masterful forms not seen since Tschichold's Sabon.

The ascender and x-height triangular serifs are drawn with a pronounced cup

Prudential

Hand-lettered Garamond

Prudential

Adobe Garamond bold

abcdefghijklmnopqrstuvwxyz
ABCDEFGHIJKLMNOP
QRSTUVWXYZ

Adobe Garamond bold—Robert Slimbach, Adobe Systems, 1989

*Except for Nicholas Jenson's roman, Garamond has reigned for four centuries as the classic roman face. The caps are beautifully proportioned, and the lowercase colors well. The forms are drawn with ultra-sensitive curved lines. My hand-drawn version has exaggerated, cupped triangular serifs, and is between bold and extra bold. **P**'s bowl is closed. The **d**'s baseline serif drops slightly.*

A C A S E   S T U D Y

The client wanted to see a design in classic roman caps. Friz Quadrata, with its generously bracketed serifs, was a good place to start. The shapes are less formal than Carol Twombly's Trajan, and seemed better suited for the logo. My drawing does not reference the Friz Quadrata shapes exactly, but is classic in the basic structure, which is based on a square (*see* page 44). I used a large cap and simplified the downward point of the E's middle arm; the top and bottom arms are nearly equal in length. The **R**'s tail is more restrained than that in Friz, whose tip does not appear to rest on the baseline. Instead of the **A**'s top half-serif, I used a diagonal beginning stroke that recalls the font's calligraphic origins.

An early **U** form, with two weighted vertical stems, appears in both the sketch and the font; it colors better than the traditional thinner right-hand upstroke.

PRUDENTIAL

Tight, hand-lettered pencil comprehensive on tracing paper

PRUDENTIAL

Friz Quadrata

abcdefghijklmnopqrstuvwxyz
ABCDEFGHIJKLMNOP
QRSTUVWXYZ

Friz Quadrata—Ernst Friz, VGC; ITC, 1974

ABCDEFGHI

Trajan—Carol Twombly, Adobe Systems, 1989

.

Using a classic roman lends a substantial look to the word instead of a friendly quality. The pencil drawing has reduced serifs and is a marriage of Optima and Friz Quadrata. The drawing and the font are almost monotone.

FONTS & LOGOS

Baskerville is an old friend. I like its almost symmetrical distribution of weight and generous open forms. In the Fry hand-set version (not drawn by Baskerville), serifs are heavily bracketed well into the stem so that a vertical stem has the illusion of tapering, which adds grace to its forms. Baskerville's plump lobes are friendly to the eye. It is more intellectual than the humanist faces because its structure is a result of drawing, instead of broad-pen writing, which magically produces a letter. The letter's symmetry allows it to be extended, weighted, or narrowed without great distortion. When set openly, the caps are stately and in the fashion of their day, designed to color more darkly than the lowercase (like the Scotch Romans). My letters are bolder and wider, the thins refined. I have not joined the **d**'s bowl as deeply as the font. With its reverse curve and tangent join to the stem, the **a**'s bowl is closer to the Fry Baskerville than to John Baskerville's early shapes. I have finessed the serifs into finer, tapered shapes.

Prudential

Tight, hand-lettered pencil comprehensive on tracing paper

Prudential

ITC New Baskerville Bold

abcdefghijklmnopqrstuvwxyz
ABCDEFGHIJKLMNOP
QRSTUVWXYZ

ITC New Baskerville bold—George W. Jones, Linotype, 1926

■

Baskerville's forms are open, wide, and friendly. It is one of the rare fonts that function beautifully either as a text or display face. My drawing references some of the Fry Baskerville qualities. The forms are extended, weighted up, tightly spaced, and the serifs are thinned a bit, though its hairlines are rather thin to do the tough work of a logotype, which must work in a wide range of sizes, positive and negative.

Fry Baskerville—Isaac Moore, Fry Foundry, c. 1795

Perpetua is Eric Gill's monument. Monotype's Perpetua Book and Perpetua titling are rarefied specimens of type design; there are some unusual letters. The **d** has a high distribution of weight, which is normally below center, reflecting the broad-pen's angle, which is in strong evidence in many of the letters. As a design, Perpetua has features that reference Times Roman and Baskerville, with a lowercase Jenson **a** tossed in for good measure. Its italic is named Felicity. Typophiles are fond of its "inscriptional qualities." Like Victor Lardent's sketches for Times Roman, judging from Gill's drawings, the type has been greatly finessed by Monotype's designers. The extra bold has great carriage of weight across the top of the **a**, and the **g**'s tail is a long diagonal with a diagonal stressed counter.

270

Prudential

Tight, hand-lettered pencil comprehensive on tracing paper

Prudential

Perpetua bold—Eric Gill, Monotype, 1925–30

abcdefghijklmnopqrstuvwxyz
ABCDEFGHIJKLMNOP
QRSTUVWXYZ

Perpetua bold—Eric Gill, Monotype, 1925–1930

agqdbp

Perpetua bold

Left—*Perpetua's* **q** *is a modified upside down* **d***, which is a modified and flopped* **b***, and the* **p** *relates to neither. The counter of the* **g***'s loop has an angled repose.*

Below, the twelve comprehensives discussed on the preceding pages present a conservative approach to the logotype design. Recall the original request: design the word **Prudential** closely following a font in a highly legible, individual manner, easily identified, without straying too far from accepted type forms. The client favored Century and requested a taller x-height, which condenses the letters. The version at bottom right was chosen and used as a model for a corporate font for subsidiary names. Many of these names are long, and the narrower proportion permits them to be set in one line. The design was scanned from a pencil comprehensive and drawn in a font drawing program.

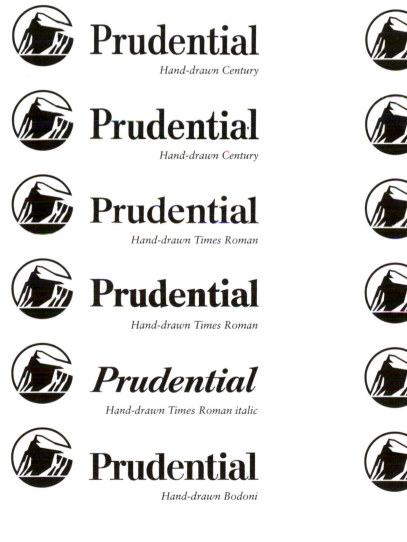

Hand-drawn Century

Hand-drawn Century

Hand-drawn Times Roman

Hand-drawn Times Roman

Hand-drawn Times Roman italic

Hand-drawn Bodoni

Hand-drawn Bodoni

Hand-drawn Garamond

Hand-drawn classic roman

Hand-drawn Baskerville

Hand-drawn Perpetua

Hand-drawn Century condensed

Beta version, PostScript outline

For comparison, the twelve comprehensive hand-lettered versions based on type forms.

A C A S E S T U D Y

Shown below is a 72-point setting of the version shown at the bottom right on the previous page, with a slight amount of letterspacing added. **Prudential** is a difficult word to space in lowercase letters. When set in caps the general color is more even because each letter fits an approximate rectangle (except for the **P**, which is an asymmetric shape). For more even color, I narrowed the **P** slightly and shortened the **r**'s ball terminal to decrease the space between the **ru**, reduced the **t**'s crossbar width, drew a more narrow looped tail, and chopped the **i**'s left serifs. Alternatively, the **t**'s tail may be drawn higher to fill the space created by the crossbar, but that makes the letter appear more condensed. The following letters, **ial**, color well because of the **a**'s footed stem.

The setting on the opposite page was tested with the Rock on stationery and collateral. The creative director thought that the letters were too condensed and not in sympathy with the Rock's circular shape. The wider proportion and spacing shown below was finally chosen from various tests shown on the following pages.

The split word test shown below was created to demonstrate that words are read at x-height. Spacing is therefore more critical at x-height than at the baseline. The top half of **Prudential** is legible, the lower half is not.

■

The top portion of words and lines of type is more legible than the bottom half. The top spacing is more even than the lower half, but the overall spacing must be a compromise of the two.

A CASE STUDY

Logo testing is time consuming. Numerous tests were made using the Prudential logo to determine ideal spacing and proportion for the logo and the font: 5-percent increase in letter width; 10-percent additional letter width; and 10-percent letter width, plus 10 percent more weight. Letterspacing was then added, in 5-, 10-, and 15-unit increments, each measuring a thousandth of an em. The third example, 10 percent extended, was chosen. It determined the corporate font's proportion. Then tests were made on different printers, in various page layout programs, in positive and negative, in a range of sizes, on different paper stock (coated and uncoated), on a 600- and 1,000-dpi laser printer, and at 2,540 dpi Linotronic resolution. Business card engraving tests were done, and—one of the most important tests of all—small-scale building sign mockups.

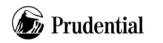

Keystroke logotype, regular proportion

10% extended + 10% weight, 5 units letterspaced

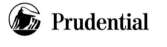

5% extended

10% extended + 10% weight, 10 units letterspaced

10% extended

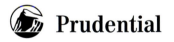

10% extended + 10% weight, 15 units letterspaced

10% extended + 10% weight

18-point Prudential roman

Keystroke logotype, regular proportion

10% extended + 10% weight, 5 units letterspaced

5% extended

10% extended + 10% weight, 10 units letterspaced

10% extended

10% extended + 10% weight, 15 units letterspaced

10% extended + 10% weight

When tested on collateral, the logo proved a bit too narrow in relation to the Rock. Different versions of weight, width, and spacing were explored. The straightforward 10-percent extended version, left column, was chosen.

36-point Prudential roman

A C A S E S T U D Y

When the slightly condensed logo was first approved, I drew this font (*below*) to match. After the stationery tests proved the logo and font were too narrow, I drew the wider font shown on the opposite page, which is the authorized corporate font. Because the logo had been digitally drawn, only one-half of the lowercase alphabet remained to complete. These I drew in a font program without first making preliminary pencil drawings of each letter. Not much time was saved by skipping the drawings, because the system does not give an accurate representation of the letters at each step: the screen is curved, which distorts the picture's outer edges; bitmaps are deceptive; and a 1,000 dpi printer doesn't render the shapes accurately at small sizes. A higher resolution, at least 1,540 dpi, is helpful in assessing the letters, and 2,540 is even better. Because **Prudential** was snugly spaced, the font serifs needed to be short to ensure a tight set. The **al** combination established the fit. Some subsidiary names contain six capitals and normal-sized caps were overpowering, so I drew them a bit more narrow. (There are fonts designed with smaller caps for

abcdefghijklm

nopqrstuvwxyz

ABCDEFGHIJKLMNOPQ

RSTUVWXYZ

. , : ; - / | & y g &

48-point beta version Prudential roman—Doyald Young, 1996

This setting of the Prudential font is set with zero tracking and flat letterspacing. The left and right sidebearings create its basic letterspacing. There is generally more weight on the top and lower portions of curved forms. This characteristic, together with the proportion and snug fit, help to create even color and a semi-bold weight.

use in languages with a lot of capitalized nouns.) Both March and I rejected the K's curved stem that begins the lower diagonal (*opposite*); instead, the traditional straight diagonal won out. The ear of the **g** creates spacing problems if drawn at x-height, so to preserve the tight fit I positioned it near the bowl's centerline. The creative director liked the half-serifed **h**, **m**, **n**, and **u**, a feature found on many slab serif fonts and on some Oldstyle fonts. Benton used it on his 1904 Century bold, and it appears throughout Tony Stan's ITC Century family. For more even color, I used the Oldstyle **C** with an upper and lower beak. I explored cap-high, x-height, and medium-height ampersands; the medium one was favored.

The alphabet was made into a Type 1 font. The **Rock** is in keystroke 1, and **Prudential** is in number 2. The logotype may be keystroked individually, then letterspaced to accommodate reverses or setting of small point sizes. The caesura, or vertical bar, is offered as a dividing device between two names instead of the traditional diagonal slash (virgule).

277

abcdefghijklm nopqrstuvwxyz ABCDEFGHIJKLMNOPQ RSTUVWXYZ . , : ; - / | fi fl &

48-point Prudential roman—Doyald Young, 1996

Approved corporate font. A straightforward 10 percent extended letter was chosen for the final font. To test proportion, a host of divisions were set in 16-point, the minimum size for the font.

A CASE STUDY

In some manner all fonts are derivative. Type designers borrow from the past, sometimes carefully; others tip their hats to geniuses and gently mold their forms to suit a new interpretation. Morris Benton took the Scotch Romans and Moderns (derived from Bodoni), beefed up the thins, touched up some shapes here and there, bracketed the serifs, and named it Century. Fair enough. He changed the forms sufficiently to deserve credit for a new font.

I've taken inspiration from Bulmer (designed by William Martin, in 1790, who bowed to Baskerville) and used his **Q** because I think its simplicity is more in keeping with the Prudential font. I ignored the small ball at the tail's lower left for the same reason; its origin, I think, is a pointed, slotted, and flexible pen pressure. I could not draw as sweeping an ogee curve as the Bulmer because

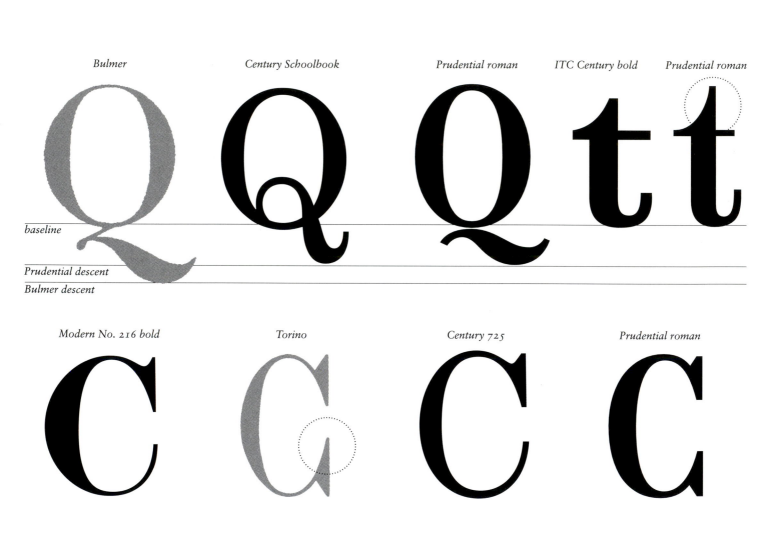

Bulmer — Century Schoolbook — Prudential roman — ITC Century bold — Prudential roman

baseline

Prudential descent

Bulmer descent

Modern No. 216 bold — Torino — Century 725 — Prudential roman

■

The Prudential font is a slightly modified Century, with only a few characters that change their basic shape. Caps are a bit more narrow than the lowercase, so as not to overpower names that contain numerous caps. The font's slightly condensed form and tight fit give it its distinctive, even color.

the descent of **Prudential** is considerably less. The **t**'s ascender is taller than the type versions. A Modern **C** has a single beak at the top, but Torino, an elegant, narrow Modern, borrowed from the nineteenth century, comes adorned with two. Ears of **gs** were once quite simple: Jenson's type for *Eusebius* shows a short, thin horizontal stroke, similar to Times Roman. The arched thin stroke here is typical of the Moderns and Centurys and I retained it despite its troublesome, upward thrust. I tried a wide tailed **y** but it runs into trouble with the **g**. The branched letters, **h, m, n,** half-serif, right-hand stems prevent congestion. Narrow or bold, double-sided serifs are troublesome in small sizes because if too long, they run together, if too short, they barely count visually.

Type design is a time-consuming and demanding discipline, filled with many compromises. Because logotype design is concerned with a few letters that must relate only to each other, and therefore has fewer limitations, a more cohesive design can be achieved.

Times New Roman

Prudential roman

Prudential roman

Wide-tailed *y*

Narrow-tailed *y*

Palatino
Angular effect of broad-pen

ITC Century bold
Accelerating curve branch

Prudential roman
Symmetrical curve branch

■

*The **gy** demonstrates the need to draw a restrained and cramped **y** that will not kern on top of another letter. Even so a wider tailed **y** character is offered. The half serifs of the **h**, **m**, and **n** appear in several fonts, and the ploy is designed to visually open up these letters. The form can be found in early French and Italian calligraphic writing hands, and numerous twentieth-century revival fonts.*

A C A S E   S T U D Y

Bowls are one of the most distinguishing characteristics of a font, in either the caps or the lowercase. When two bowls converge as they do in the **B**, there is the recurring problem of fill-in, visually and physically with ink when the type is printed on soft, absorbent paper. The Prudential roman B stays very close to Century 725 with a narrow waist, whereas the ITC Century bold condensed is wider and bolder. Both the 725 and ITC Century bold bracket the horizontal thins to the top vertical stem. This produces a softer and darker design than the crisp right-angle join of the Prudential version. Es are usually divided in the same manner as the **B**, and both type versions repeat the bracket at the top and bottom of the letter; their beaks are mostly vertical, and all three serifs attempt to repeat the general color of the stems. Prudential's bracket is more flat, and the tran-

Century 725 bold condensed

ITC Century bold condensed

Prudential roman

Century 725 bold condensed

ITC Century bold condensed

Prudential roman

sitions (including the serifs) into the stems are abrupt.

The straight weighted diagonal stem that connects to the thin upper diagonal is the traditionally narrow-waisted serif K. This produces a large triangular negative area that seldom colors well, particularly when the letter is flanked by a group of vertical stems, or a cap **A**. This is the preferred version, though the curved branch join into the vertical stem allows for a steep diagonal, which fills the negative space more comfortably. Straight diagonal-tailed **R**s are the most often seen form in the history of type up until the nineteenth century. Some classic forms bowed the shape. Bodoni drew his forms more steeply and flipped the curved tail upward with a thin hairline. A vertical or near vertical stroke fills the right side of an **R** more comfortably, and its tip can be controlled more easily than the straight Baskerville tail, though the diagonal is a more distinctive shape. Morris Benton followed the Modern style in his Century. Bulmer has a handsome **R**. Prudential's **R** is steeper and it curves gently to join the bowl.

Prudential Roman *Prudential Roman* *Prudential Roman*

K K k

Monotype Century Schoolbook bold *ITC Century bold condensed* *Prudential Roman*

R R R

■

*Curved-tail **R**s are troublesome to space; the terminal hook is an extravagant shape and almost invariably creates a slight misspacing. A straight diagonal stem may be angled more steeply for better fit. Depending on letter combinations, its serif may be shortened and joined to a following serif. Note Baskerville's ungainly RA combination.*

R RAI RA RA

Bulmer *ITC New Baskerville* *Bauer Bodoni* *Prudential Roman*

A C A S E S T U D Y

A ball terminal is one of a font's defining characteristics because the shape is found on almost one fourth of the lowercase: **a, c, f, g, j, r,** and **y.** Type designers choose different shapes. ITC Century and Prudential's terminals are not bracketed, but Century 725 has a minute fillet.

The four **as** (*below*) are classified as Century, yet their bowls are distinctly different. Century 725's bowl is angular and its thins refined when compared to the ITC version. Prudential's bowl is arched, and the space-saving footed stem lends a distinctive quality to the letter.

The bowl letters **b, d, p,** and **q** occur frequently, which sets up a strong pattern in text (there are eighteen bowl letters in the column at the left). Text-font bowls are designed to join deeply top and bottom to prevent clogging at small sizes. A display face, one that is 14-point or larger, need

ITC Century bold

Century 725 bold condensed

ITC Century bold condensed

Prudential roman

ITC Century bold

Century 725 bold condensed

ITC Century bold condensed

Prudential roman

Bowl joins are deep to prevent clogging in small sizes

■

Prudential's thicks and thins have greater contrast than the Centurys shown, which makes for a crisp and sparkling font. Even its round terminals are considerably thinner to avoid massing.

Bowl shapes differ from font to font. Note that ITC's are elliptical with pronounced angular shoulders; the Century 725 bold condensed is quite pointed with a decidedly left, flat counter; Prudential's are more full.

FONTS & LOGOS

not make as extreme an adjustment. The amount of weight carried on the bowl's shoulders both top and bottom also greatly influences a font's overall color.

In these showings, the width ratio of the **as** and **ss** varies. With the exception of the ITC Century bold, the spine angles of the **s** are almost equal. What is different and apparent, is the amount of weight carried around the top and bottom curves. The top and bottom spurs of the Prudential **s** are more crisp with less weight than the other fonts, and join more deeply. All diagonal letters are troublesome: **k, v, w, x, y,** and **z**. Their shapes usually create too much negative space, and either their proportion must be compromised or their serifs brutally shortened to space easily. The Prudential **k**'s thin diagonal weight nearly duplicates the 725, but because the letter widths are different, the angles change.

Even the bracketed serifs are not the same length or thickness, and the x-heights vary considerably.

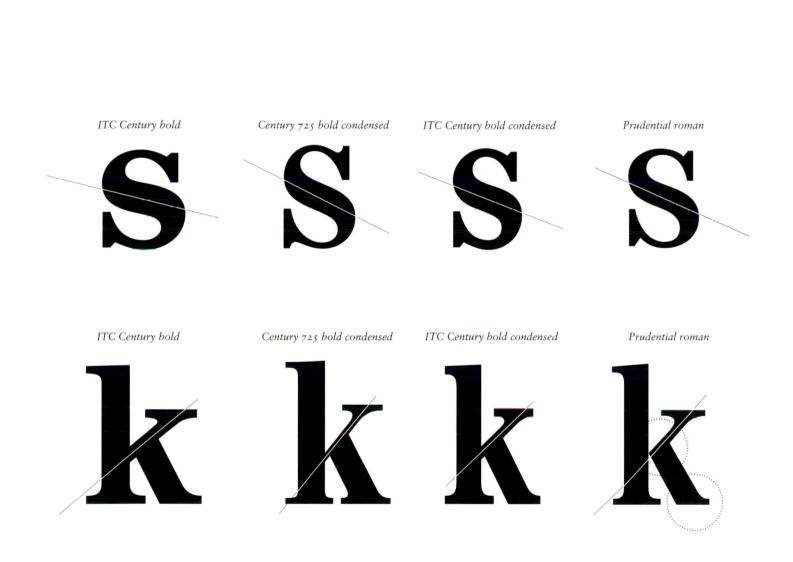

ITC Century bold   *Century 725 bold condensed*   *ITC Century bold condensed*   *Prudential roman*

ITC Century bold   *Century 725 bold condensed*   *ITC Century bold condensed*   *Prudential roman*

■

*Beaks of the **s** are often bracketed to pick up more mass to counteract the top and bottom holes and the thin strokes. How much to bracket is debatable, and depends on the designer's intentions— to create a monotone look or a font with contrast. Depending on proportion and weight, a narrow or wide waist, the **k**'s diagonal angles vary considerably.*

A C A S E S T U D Y

A partial list of Prudential's subsidiaries demonstrates the use of the font. The showings below are set in the original design shown on page 272, which is slightly condensed in an effort to minimize the length of the five- and six-word subsidiary names. The opposite page shows the approved corporate font shown on page 277. On the following double spread is management's ultimate decision on the brand name and subgroups treatment.

Prudential Asset Management Group

Prudential Capital Corporation Insurance Company

Prudential HealthCare

Prudential Home Mortgage

Prudential Homeowners Insurance

Prudential Information Systems Office

Prudential Insurance Company & Financial Services

Prudential Investment Corporation

Prudential Mutual Fund Management

Prudential Northeastern Group Operations

Prudential Property and Casualty Insurance Company

Prudential Property Company

Prudential roman test font

Prudential Asset Management Group

Prudential Capital Corporation Insurance Company

Prudential HealthCare

Prudential Home Mortgage

Prudential Homeowners Insurance

Prudential Information Systems Office

Prudential Insurance Company & Financial Services

Prudential Investment Corporation

Prudential Mutual Fund Management

Prudential Northeastern Group Operations

Prudential Property and Casualty Insurance Company

Prudential Property Company

The approved corporate Prudential roman font

The Prudential roman font was originally designed to unify the image of the company's many subsidiaries and to be used in collateral and for advertising. Management instead chose to divide the large group of subsidiaries into seven brands: Bank, Foundation, HealthCare, Insurance, Investments, Real Estate, and Securities.

Blue is the corporate color for the Rock and Prudential; the brand names are gray.

Prudential roman is compared with Tony Stan's ITC Century book and Century bold. Prudential's narrow forms and snug fit is apparent. Its weight falls between Century Book and Century bold. The ITC Century is set with default word-and letterspacing, and the Prudential Roman's letterspacing is increased to 4 percent. The fit is happy and there is an absence of rivers.

The image of Prudential and our highly recognizable rock symbol are among our most valued assets. Public opinion surveys show time and again that millions of people regard our signature and service mark as symbols of financial strength and dependability. The image of Prudential and our highly recognizable rock symbol are among our most valued assets. Public opinion surveys show time and again that millions of people regard our signature and service mark as symbols of financial strength and dependability.

ITC Century book—Tony Stan, 1975–80

The image of Prudential and our highly recognizable rock symbol are among our most valued assets. Public opinion surveys show time and again that millions of people regard our signature and service mark as symbols of financial strength and dependability. The image of Prudential and our highly recognizable rock symbol are among our most valued assets. Public opinion surveys show time and again that millions of people regard our signature and service mark as symbols of financial strength and dependability.

Prudential roman—Doyald Young,
Prudential Insurance Company of America, 1996

The image of Prudential and our highly recognizable rock symbol are among our most valued assets. Public opinion surveys show time and again that millions of people regard our signature and service mark as symbols of financial strength and dependability. The image of Prudential and our highly recognizable rock symbol are among our most valued assets. Public opinion surveys show time and again that millions of people regard our signature and service mark as symbols of financial strength and dependability.

ITC Century bold—Tony Stan, 1975–80

Insurance

Bank

Investments

Foundation

Real Estate

HealthCare

Securities

Display figure: Fino. Text: 36/64 Diotima

Letterforms
that honor and elucidate
what humans see and say
deserve to be honored
in their turn.

ROBERT BRINGHURST

Poet, Designer, Typographer, Author,

The Elements of Typographic Style

ARRIGHI	*ABCDEFGHIJKLMNOPQRSTUVWXYZ abcdefghijklmnopqrstuvwxyz*
BASKERVILLE	ABCDEFGHIJKLMNOPQRSTUVWXYZ abcdefghijklmnopqrstuvwxyz
BODONI	ABCDEFGHIJKLMNOPQRSTUVWXYZ abcdefghijklmnopqrstuvwxyz
CENTAUR	ABCDEFGHIJKLMNOPQRSTUVWXYZ abcdefghijklmnopqrstuvwxyz
CENTURY SCHOOLBOOK	ABCDEFGHIJKLMNOPQRSTUVWXYZ abcdefghijklmnopqrstuvwxyz
COPPERPLATE GOTHIC	ABCDEFGHIJKLMNOPQRSTUVWXYZ
DIOTIMA	ABCDEFGHIJKLMNOPQRSTUVWXYZ abcdefghijklmnopqrstuvwxyz
FRANKLIN GOTHIC	**ABCDEFGHIJKLMNOPQRSTUVWXYZ abcdefghijklmnopqrstuvwxyz**
FRUTIGER	ABCDEFGHIJKLMNOPQRSTUVWXYZ abcdefghijklmnopqrstuvwxyz
FUTURA	ABCDEFGHIJKLMNOPQRSTUVWXYZ abcdefghijklmnopqrstuvwxyz
ADOBE GARAMOND	ABCDEFGHIJKLMNOPQRSTUVWXYZ abcdefghijklmnopqrstuvwxyz
HAARLEMMER	ABCDEFGHIJKLMNOPQRSTUVWXYZ abcdefghijklmnopqrstuvwxyz
ADOBE JENSON	ABCDEFGHIJKLMNOPQRSTUVWXYZ abcdefghijklmnopqrstuvwxyz
MICHELANGELO TITLING	ABCDEFGHIJKLMNOPQRSTUVWXYZ
OPTIMA	ABCDEFGHIJKLMNOPQRSTUVWXYZ abcdefghijklmnopqrstuvwxyz
PALACE SCRIPT	*ABCDEFGHIJKLMNOPQRSTUVWXYZ abcdefghijklmnopqrstuvwxyz*
ROMANÉE	ABCDEFGHIJKLMNOPQ_RSTUVWXYZ abcdefghijklmnopqrstuvwxyz
SERIFA	ABCDEFGHIJKLMNOPQRSTUVWXYZ abcdefghijklmnopqrstuvwxyz
TIMES NEW ROMAN	ABCDEFGHIJKLMNOPQRSTUVWXYZ abcdefghijklmnopqrstuvwxyz
TRAJAN	ABCDEFGHIJKLMNOPQRSTUVWXYZ
UNIVERS	ABCDEFGHIJKLMNOPQRSTUVWXYZ abcdefghijklmnopqrstuvwxyz
OPEN ROMAN CAPITALS	ABCDEFGHIJKLMNOPQRSTUVWXYZ
ZAPF RENAISSANCE	ABCDEFGHIJKLMNOPQRSTUVWXYZ abcdefghijklmnopqrstuvwxyz

This font sampler is not a historical outline, or a collection of today's most popular fonts, or favorite fonts, or classic fonts. Nor are type families as such considered; the bold and/or italics of the roman are not always shown. Instead, I have included some individual workhorses, a few classic fonts, and some obscure fonts that I admire very much. It is a personal sampler without a theme. For economy of space, one third of the collection is shown at a generous size and the rest are approximately half the size of the first group.

There are enlargements of metal types to clearly show some detail. Purists will object, because metal types were designed for a specific size (or range of sizes) and were never intended to be either reduced or enlarged, a subtlety that the digital world is only beginning to confront with MultipleMaster Fonts. The images are rough because when pressed into soft paper the metal image spreads slightly, and enlargements reveal the texture of the paper fibers. This texture is unimportant; it is the *form* that matters.

I have pointed out some features that a newly interested devotee of typography might find helpful. Some of the comments wish for better and more resolved drawings, but as I have stated earlier, there is no one way to draw a letter or a group of letters. My evaluations are concerned with the designer's premise and the consistency of design, which again is based on an individual esthetic. As stated repeatedly throughout these pages, type designers are forced into many compromises if a font is to space and color evenly.

Several of Herman Zapf's faces are here; he is a twentieth-century living treasure. Gudrun Zapf von Hesse's Diotima is included, a wondrous and unique concept.

Robert Slimbach's Adobe Garamond is shown, and his recently drawn Jenson revival, a five-hundred-year-old face that keeps recurring.

Morris Benton made an enormous contribution, and several of his efforts are discussed. Jan van Krimpen, who for many years was the type designer at Holland's Enschedé Type foundry, is a hero who is undergoing a revival, and four of his fonts are shown. Monotype Typography and Frank E. Blokland of the Dutch Type Library have formed a partnership and are producing some digital versions of Van Krimpen's designs. Haarlemmer, designed in 1938, for the Vereeniging voor Duken Boekkunst (Society for the Art of Printing & Books), is their first release.[1]

Like any other lover of type, I could fill a whole book with types I admire, but for space considerations, I have restricted the chapter to 73 fonts, with regrets to the many fine designers who are not included.

1. *The Monotype Recorder*, New Series /Volume 9, "The Dutch Connection," page 40.

Ludovico degli Arrighi (c. 1493–1527) published his writing manual *La Operina* in 1522, and in 1523, *Il Modo de Temperare le Penne,* which showed his first italic type based on a popular round-hand of the day, *cancelleresca cursivia.* The type became the model for many of the chancery types that followed: Arrighi, Bembo, Blado, Cancelleresca Bastarda, Cloister, Dante, Haarlemmer, Lutetia, Palatino, Minion, Poetica, Poliphilus, Zapf Renaissance, Romanée, Spectrum, and Zapf Chancery. All are indebted to Arrighi's broad-pens. In England, Edward Johnston, the calligrapher, and Stanley Morison, consultant to Monotype Corporation, are credited with the twentieth-century revival of the style. Hermann Zapf has suggested that no true understanding of a roman or italic letter can be fully attained without knowledge of the broad-pen.

The plates shown here and on page 297 are reproduced by permission of David Zeidberg, Special Collections Department, University of California at Los Angeles Research Library, from the sixteenth-century volume of Arrighi's writing book La Operina.

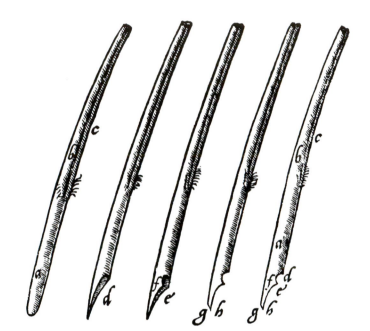

a – *Tondo dela penna* .
b – *Canaletto* .
c – *Curuita* .
d – *Primo taglio* .
e – *Secondi tagli* .
f – *Vomero* .
g – *Sguinzo* .
h – *Punta temperata* .

Ludovico degli Arrighi—Rome 1522–23
La Operina

■
***Above and opposite**—*
Pages from Ludovico degli Arrighi's manual of writing.

These two pages are from *La Operina da Imparare di scriure littera Cancelerescha*, which was printed from wood plates, miraculously incised at *this size*. The illustration (*opposite*) describes the parts of a quill and the steps required to fashion the shaft into a writing instrument.

a–Tondo dela penna
    (round of the pen)
b–Canaletto (little channel)
c–Curuita (little curve)
d–Primo taglio (first cut)
e–Secondi tagli (second cuts)
f–Vomero (curved cut)
g–Sguinzo (clipped or slotted)
h–Punta temperara (sharpened point)

LITERA DA BREVI

A a b c d e e'f g g h i k l m n o p q r s ſt u x y z

~: Marcus Antonius ſasanoua :~
Pierÿ vates, laudem ſi opera iſta merentur,
Praxiteli noſtro carmina pauca date'.
Non placet hoc; noſtri pietas laudanda ſoryti eſt;
Qui dicat hæc; niſi vos forſan uterqȝ mouet ;
Debetis ſaltem Dÿs carmina, ni quoqȝ, et iſtis
Illa datis. iam nos mollia ſaxa ſumus .

A A B B ſC c D D E E F F G G H H Jl
K Ll M M N N O P P Q Q R R S
S T T U V V X X Y Z & & & & &

Ludouicus Vicentinus ſcribebat Roma' anno
ſalutis M DXXIII

*Dilecto filio **Ludouico de Henricis** laico*
Vicencio familiari noſtro ♦

Frederic Warde designed Arrighi first as a private face embellished with sixteenth-century calligraphic flourishes and later as a restrained italic modified to match Bruce Rogers's Centaur, a roman based on Nicolas Jenson's types (*see* page 306). Of all the attempts to translate the Renaissance forms into twentieth-century technology, Warde's Arrighi has been one of the most applauded. Warde, a New York typographer and book designer, designed the font for a book on Ludovico Arrighi. The narrow, slightly leaning letterforms are produced by the action of a broad-pen held *mostly* at a consistent angle, approximately 30 degrees from the vertical. Ascenders and descenders are generous and, in Oldstyle fashion, ascenders are taller than the caps. The caps' curved shapes do not follow the weight distribution of most calligraphic letters: Warde placed the

ABCDEFGHI
JKLMNOPQR
STUVWXYZ
abcdefghijklmnopqrstuvwxyz
!$%&*()[];:" ""?/
1234567890

Arrighi—Frederic Warde, Monotype, 1929
(Font Club)

widest part of the curved stroke at center or, in the case of the *D*, below center. Cap widths are average; *M* is narrow; *G*'s beard points up; and some horizontal serifs stretch to fill unwanted space: *F*, *I*, *M*, *P*, *T*, and *Y*. Branches depart at severe angles and match the pothook, which

reflects the pen's angle. Without an ear, the *g* appears unfinished; *w* and *x* are wide and *k*'s bowl is squeezed. Warde designed a few swash letters: *M, L, z, g, v, sp, Qu, è, e, ö, û,* and *ct.* The rest were designed at Monotype (*see* following pages).

11-degree angle

Teardrop terminals are typical; *f*'s descender is wide

Bowl is narrow and cramped

Ascenders and descenders are generous and there is only a slight angle to the letters

Bowls and pothooks are angular; terminals parallel

M is narrow

Stress is centered or below center, instead of the usual weight distribution of the Oldstyle, i.e., Palatino

Beard of *G* points upward

Arrighi   Palatino   Arrighi

F's right-hand serif is not bracketed

Serifs are extended on the right-hand side as flourishes to fill unwanted space

Proportions of the *w* and *x* are wide, and the *y*'s tail takes a wide arc, changing the angle of the triangular shape

■ Frederic Warde designed the Arrighi font for the introduction to a special edition The Calligraphic Models of Ludovico degli Arrighi, *a facsimile*

book printed by Hans Mardersteig at the Oficina Bodoni in Switzerland, one of the twentieth century's great printer/typographers. Later, when Monotype

cut Bruce Rogers's Centaur type, the Arrighi was modified and paired with the roman. The pairing was classical: an open roman against a narrow italic.

Present day italics tend to match the proportions of the roman. Compare Bodoni, page 300 and Haarlemmer, page 322.

FONT SAMPLER

Swash characters play an important role in typography. They are the jewelry, the embellishments used to enliven gray, lifeless pages, either as initials to mark an important beginning, or for words that require special emphasis—awards, congratulations, or for special celebratory occasions. This set of caps, special swash lowercase characters and tied letters, are some of the most beautiful letters available today—though restraint should be exercised in their use.

Frederic Warde designed only a few swashes for the 1929 Arrighi font; the rest are from the talented hands of Patricia Saunders and Robin Nicholas at Monotype Corporation and were created especially for the Post-Script version shown below.

Compared to Arrighi's original writing books, many of the forms have not intrinsically changed. The change is often in

Arrighi Swash Italic—Frederic Warde, Monotype, 1929
Additional characters by Patricia Saunders and Robin Nicholas
Monotype Typography Ltd., Salfords, England, 1993

■
Swash letters to accompany the Arrighi italic font. These are used for pure decoration—to delight the eye.

size relationship, or a sweeping arc that has been restrained. The most common swash is an extension of the cap lobe forms: **B, D, P,** and **R.** The same shape occurs in different places in different fonts, and it may be applied to the top serifs of the **E, F, H, I, J, K, L, M, N, U, V, W, X,** and **Y.**

Diagonal extensions are common: note the **A, K, V, W, X,** and **Y.** Small loops and long elegant teardrop terminals show up. There are no set rules for the design of swashes, yet many of the original sixteenth-century forms are still drawn today because the original idea is too

good to pass up. Compare the following letters of the Monotype font to Arrighi's forms: **A, B, C, D, E, e, G, L, M, N, P, Q, R, T, Z,** and **&** (*see* pages 57 and 90 for Robert Slimbach's Poetica).

Ludovico Arrighi—Rome, 1522
LA OPERINA

Beyond personal preference, a text font may be judged by four important criteria. First, even color: no one letter or group of letters stands out. Second, fit: the extraordinary placement within an imaginary box that allows each letter to space comfortably next to any letter or character within the font. Third, clarity of form: the letter can be easily recognized when combined into words in a range of sizes. Fourth, design relationship: the basic groups of letters are drawn so that they appear closely related to each other. There is an indefinable magic in a great font design. After all the forms are analyzed, the basic reason for its greatness is ineffable, and I consider Baskerville a great font design. I particularly like the roundness of its letters. They are full and wide. Classified as Transitional, they are more Modern than Oldstyle because of their mostly symme-

ABCDEFGHIJKLM
NOPQRSTUVWXYZ
abcdefghijklmnopqrstuvwxyz
!@#$%^&*()+[]{};:""''?/
1234567890 1234567890

ABCDEFGHIJKLM
NOPQRSTUVWXYZ
abcdefghijklmnopqrstuvwxyz
*!@#$%^& *( )+[ ]{ };:""''?/*
1234567890 1234567890

ITC New Baskerville—George W. Jones (First issued by Linotype in 1926)

■

Color, fit, clarity of form, and close family design relationships mark a great typeface. Baskerville's wide curved letters, generous lobes, and beautiful proportions make it eminently legible. The heavily bracketed serifs are distinctive, and were an aid to keep the fine serif tips from breaking in the original metal type. Terminals are elegant tear-drop shapes lighter than the basic stems. There are many foundry versions, each slightly different. Fry Baskerville

trical stress. The bowl forms are beautiful; widest at mid x-height, the outer shape is a plump 60-degree ellipse without a trace of a corner or flat area as it tapers to its thinnest hairline before joining the stem. The counter gives the illusion that it is a symmetrical ellipse because the hairlines flow deeply and gradually into the stems. Minimum weight is carried past a vertical centerline, which gives the baseline and x-height a graceful horizontal lightness. In some versions, branches of the **h**, **m**, **n**, and **u** are a tad flat for my taste, but they too join smoothly and deeply into the stems. Serif tips of this font are chopped, but in the original 1754 version they were sharp. Each serif brackets generously into the stems, and is minutely cupped at the baseline. Except for a narrow **s** and bowl of the lowercase **g**, the lowercase is evenly proportioned; even the caps abandon the roman quadrata and are voluptous forms, though the wide arms of the **E**, **L**, and **T** are troublesome to space.

Round, voluptuous curves diminish smoothly to hairlines

cupped

Lower bowl of the **B** and the **D**'s rounded stems are weighted more below lateral center and are narrow at the top

cupped

Brackets are generous and blend deeply into the stem

Arms are wide and sometimes create misspacings in all-cap settings. E's lower arm is long

Serif tips of Baskerville's original 1754 font are sharply rounded. Serifs are gently cupped on the straight stems

cupped

Bowls are full and generous with widest point mid-x-height. There is minimum carriage of weight past a vertical centerline

Triangular serifs are thinner than Oldstyles, and the angle is less acute

Branches are almost symmetrical with minimum carriage of weight past the centerline

g and **s** are narrow

The **r**'s stem and branch angle away from each other to avoid a visual fill-in

Lowercase pothooks are thin

Fry's Baskerville (below) attributed to Isaac Moore, 1795, is more heavily bracketed, the hairlines finer, serifs longer, and branches of the **a**, **h**, **m**, **n**, and **u** flatter. This is the model for ATF hand-set Baskerville

was used as a metal, handset display font. It is a more elegant drawing than the original Baskerville's great thick and thin contrast; serifs are heavily bracketed.

From Baskerville's Preface to Milton, Birmingham, 1758 (200%)

Note lack of top bracket and extreme bracket at baseline

Bowl shape is different; joins tangent to stem with an ogee curve

Bodoni

Scholars suggest that Philippe Grandjean's *Roman du Roi*, designed expressly for the Sun King Louis XIV, was the seminal modern type; its fine, straight, horizontal serifs were an abrupt departure from the traditional, triangular, Oldstyle serifs (*see* page 73). Generally, Bodoni and Didot are considered the first Moderns. Updike says that they were designed to appear classical; to emulate Rome, "the unique Emporium of the Beautiful and the Temple of Taste."[1] The two styles are similar. Their major design characteristics are thin hairlines and vertical symmetry. Didot's serifs are not bracketed, but teardrop terminals of the **a**, **c**, and **r** are generously bracketed and the branches are more angular than Bodoni's.

Giambattista Bodoni, court printer to the Duke of Parma, was prolific: when a special type size was called for, he would cut

ABCDEFGHIJKLM
NOPQRSTUVWXYZ
abcdefghijklmnopqrstuvwxyz
!@#$%^&*()+[]{};:""''?/
1234567890 1234567890

ABCDEFGHIJKLM
NOPQRSTUVWXYZ
abcdefghijklmnopqrstuvwxyz
!@#$%^&()+[]{};:""''?/*
1234567890 1234567890

ITC Bodoni—Janice Fishman, Holly Goldsmith, Jim Parkinson. Sumner Stone, art director, ITC, 1994

ABCDEFGHIJKLMNOPQRSTUVWXYZ
abcdefghijklmnopqrstuvwxyz
!@#$%^&*()+[]{};:""''?/1234567890 1234567890

Didot—Firmin Didot (c. 1784); Deberny & Peignot, 1910–11; Adrian Frutiger, Linotype-Hell, 1991

only the characters needed. All told, he cut into metal more than 25,000 separate letters.

ITC, using Adobe's Multiple-Master technology, has created a family with three master formats: 6, 12, and 72, all drawn from the original *Manuale Tipografico* published in 1818.

Bodoni's proportions are generally even, and depart from the classic Trajan capital widths of wide bowl forms and narrow **B, E, F, K, L, P, R,** and **S.** The diagonal of the **R**'s tail is finished with a fussy droplet. Lowercase proportions are even and the italic is extremely sloped.

Today, neither Didot nor Bodoni is thought of as "Classical." Instead their use is often associated with elegance, refinement, and fashion. The logo of Giorgio Armani, the ultra-laid-back Italian fashion designer, is set in Bauer Bodoni caps. In this faithful ITC version there is a softness

and slightly hand-drawn quality to the letters that previous versions lack. (*See* ATF Bodoni and Bauer Bodoni.)

1. D. B. Updike, *Printing Types: Their History, Forms and Use, A Study in Survivals,* vol. 1, page 241.

301

DIDOT

Branches suggest symmetry

Serifs are fine and minutely bracketed. Some are cupped with small rounded tips

na acfmnu

Weight is distributed generously around bowls

Straight stem is low

Arm beaks are only slightly bracketed. Note different angles

M *is narrow and* **W** *is a double* **V**

BRGELMW

R's *tail ends with fussy ball kern*

Round stems diminish gradually and gracefully into hairlines

Spine of the **S** *is sinuous. Top and bottom beaks are cupped*

SCOU

Counter is almost symmetrical

Bowl of **g** *is off-center and the enclosed loop thrusts upward. The ear is low and slides downward. The finishing stroke of the loop is generously weighted*

y *is narrow*

Bowls have the appearance of symmetry, though stress of the **b** *is high. None joins deeply into the stem*

gybdpq

ITC Bodoni 72—Janice Fishman, Holly Goldsmith, Jim Parkinson, Sumner Stone, art director, ITC, 1994

■

Bodoni and Didot are the first of the Modern fonts, Bodoni in Italy and Didot in France. Didot sought to reflect the pomp of Napoleon's Empire regime.

FONT SAMPLER

Romulus was one of the first metal type families conceived expressly for book work. It comprises a roman, a sloping roman (known also as oblique), a bold roman, condensed bold, four weights of sans serif, a set of Greek characters, and a script font, Cancelleresca Bastarda.

Van Krimpen agreed with Stanley Morison that only a cap and last letter of a word are needed to suggest a script.[1] In efforts to draw a generous, free shape, he increased the point size but used the same size letters to match the roman, which he leaded to align with the script. It was a cumbersome and difficult solution that today's computer technology could easily accommodate. Later, in his book *Designing and Devising Type*, he wrote that he thought "the whole thing about as serious an error as Robert Granjon's *Civilité* whatever its merits may be."[2]

Despite Van Krimpen's confession, I consider it one of the twentieth century's most beautiful fonts. Because of its graceful caps and alternate lowercase letters, it is ideal for setting

302

ABCDEFGHIJKLMNOPQRSTUVWXYZÆŒÇ

The Gospel According to Saint John

THE GOSPEL ACCORDING TO SAINT JOHN

In the beginning was the Word, and the Word was with God, and the Word was God. The same was in the beginning with God. All things were made by him; and without him was not any thing made that was made. In him was life; and the life was the light of men. And the light shineth in darkness; and the darkness comprehended it not.

There was a man sent from God, whose name was John. The same came for a witness, to bear witness of the Light, that all men through him might believe. He was not that Light, but was sent to bear witness of that Light. That was the true Light, which lighteth every man that cometh into the world. He was in the world, and the world was made by him, and the world knew him not. He came unto his own, and his own received him not. But as many as received him, to them gave he power to become the sons of God, even to them that believe on his name: Which were born, not of blood, nor of the will of the flesh, nor of the will of man, but of God. And the Word was made flesh, and dwelt among us, (and we beheld his glory, the glory as of the only begotten of the Father,) full of grace and truth.

abcdeffghhijklmnopqrstuvwxyyzijæœçctcffbffffiflfhfifkflggigjgyllspsp st sf sL tt

1234567890.,''„":;!?-[]()&ßß$£₤

Cancelleresca Bastarda—Jan van Krimpen, Enschedé, 1934
Reproduced by kind permission from
The Work of Jan van Krimpen by John Dreyfus
Joh. Enschedé en Zonen, Haarlem, 1952

■

These sloping forms—Stanley Morison called them script—are based on six-teenth-century chancery hands; compare Monotype Bembo (page 81), Slimbach's Adobe Minion (page 357), and Poetica (pages 57 and 90). Jan van Krimpen's forms compose beautifully, the proportions are exceptional, and the shapes of the letters, while adhering to the chancery style, are inventive and beautiful.

The forms are special, and special fonts require special tasks and extreme care in setting. As yet no digital version has been released.

■

***Opposite**—Van Krimpen's beautiful ink drawings that P. H. Rädisch, Enschedé's punchcutter, used as a guide to cut the steel punches to produce the handset type.*

poetry. Its ascenders and descenders are long, and it has multiple caps. The *B*'s swash stroke is the size of the cap itself; serifs are calligraphic and curve softly. The cap *L*s, always a beautiful form—are unequaled. The *g*'s tail is opulent, and the script ampersand is a creative tour de force, with its lowercase *e* and high-flying cap *T*. The *f*'s cursive form, combined with the other descenders, presents an unusually distinctive pattern for special texts. The parentheses are beautiful, dynamic calligraphic strokes. Many of the 49 swash capitals descend.

In addition, there are 36 initial or terminal characters and 21 ligatures, making a total of 210 characters for the font. But as with all fonts where the designer offers a cornucopia, extreme care is required for successful setting.

1. John Dreyfus, *The Work of Jan van Krimpen*. See also *J. van Krimpen on Designing and Devising Type*, page 39.

2. John Dreyfus, *Jan van Krimpen, A Letter to Philip Hofer on Certain Problems connected with the Mechanical Cutting of Punches* (Cambridge: Harvard College Library and Boston: David Godine, 1972), page 67.

303

Some swashes are as large as the letter: *B*, *D*, *P*, and *R*. Loops are a favorite ploy and bow to Arrighi's La Operina

Serifs are asymmetric, long, and strongly calligraphic. Swashes often descend, and there is an abundance of teardrop kerns

The ampersand in classic dress, with both letters of *et* inventively defined

Looped *g* is full and the negative counter space is beautifully drawn

Descenders are extravagantly long and graceful and set up a decided pattern in mass

Parentheses are pure calligraphic penstrokes, and the alternate *Q*'s tail is a sweeping ogee flourish

There are multiple beautiful ligatures with loops formed by ogee curves

Swashes are bountiful, as terminal letters or as descending flourishes

Van Krimpen's original drawings are from the collection of the University Library of Amsterdam and are reproduced by the kind permission of Dr Jos A.A.M Bieman, Curator of Manuscripts

Caslon was my first assignment in lettering—it made a lasting impression. To the discomfort of many of my students, it is also the beginning assignment that I have given for 25 years at the Art Center College of Design.

I have never been fond of its individual forms, and type critics have leveled barbs at its stodginess. Despite this, Caslon has been recognized for almost three hundred years as one of the world's most important text faces. Its merits have been endlessly written about, and whatever its individual shortcomings, the font is greater than its parts.

Only a general discussion of Caslon is possible because there have been so many permutations of the original face; McGrew lists 58 separate metal font cuttings. This does not include ITC's version, the photolettering drawings, nor present digital versions.

Carol Twombly worked from several sources: a broadside published by Caslon in 1734, and some showings found in the British Museum. Caslon's forms

304

ABCDEFGHIJKLM
NOPQRSTUVWXYZ
abcdefghijklmnopqrstuvwxyz
!@#$%^&*()+[]{};:""''?/
1234567890

*ABCDEFGHIJKLM
NOPQRSTUVWXYZ
abcdefghijklmnopqrstuvwxyz
!@#$%^&*()+[]{};:""''?/
1234567890*

Adobe Caslon—Carol Twombly, Adobe Systems, 1990

■

William Caslon translated the roman letters that he engraved on gunstocks into one of the world's most enduring text and display faces. Historians say that he borrowed his forms from the imported Dutch Elzevirs. Caslon is a straightforward roman letter without affectation—its forms are simple. The italic is drawn in condensed proportion to the day's fashion and later, twentieth-century machine versions widened their forms to fit a duplex character cell. Most typefounders have versions, and several avow that theirs are from Caslon's original types.

are as generic as Times Roman: plain, simple, straightforward, clear, open, without pretense. Only the cap Q's tail is fussy (the italic ampersand is a different matter). It is a true text face.

The original thins were fine, and when pressed into paper, they weighted up, a point not considered by some metal type foundries whose fonts, when printed by offset lithography, reproduced fine lines exactly. An Oldstyle letter with diagonal stress sets up a vibration if the thins are too fine; fine lines need the vertical thrust of Moderns—Carol Twombly's version for Adobe of 22 separate fonts has sturdy thins that pay homage to Caslon's original concept.

Caslon's types were immensely popular—they were imported to the Colonies, and the Declaration of Independence was first set in Caslon. Benjamin Franklin admired the types and used them in his printing shop.[1] Two versions have been popular in the U.S.: Caslon 471 and 540, the latter with short descenders.

1. Mac McGrew, *American Metal Typefaces of the Twentieth Century*, pages 76–81.

Below left—ATF Caslon 540 (metal). S *is overbalanced and lists to the right; there is great carriage of weight around its side curves; Beak tips have a radius; arms of the* T *are extremely wide and the bracket is a gentle curve*

ST ST ST

Above right—Carol Twombly's PostScript Caslon, S *and* T *are narrowed; there is less weight on the side curves, and* T*'s arm brackets are more abrupt; serifs are shorter, chopped, and thins are heavier*

Serifs of the original ATF are generously bracketed, the a*'s bowl has an extreme slope, the* s *is narrow, over balanced and the beaks are long*

Bowl is small, the ear tight and mashed; the enclosed tail is wide, compressed and short

The American Type Founders 1923 Specimen Book states that the 471 Oldstyle was cast from original matrices left by Caslon in 1766

asneg

ATF Caslon 540, 1901

asneg

Mortimer Leach's hand-lettered Caslon c. 1950

*Mortimer Leach was my teacher at Art Center.
The beautiful, hand-lettered narrow proportions of Leach's Caslon were never meant for side-by-side type comparison, but their comparative design is relevant.
Leach's forms are more crisp, the* n*'s branch is angular and repeated on the* a *whose tail corresponds to a calligraphic turn; Leach's bowl counter is a vertical shape;
Top and bottom curves of the* s *have less arc; the* e *is more upright where the type* e *rolls to the left. The bowl of the* g *is more nearly the same size as the enclosed loop*

There are strong similarities between Caslon and Baskerville. Baskerville's individual letters are more polished and resolved than the earlier Caslon, a trait that some type experts consider a detriment to a good text face. The broad-pen is evident in his forms, though Caslon ignored its diagonal stress when he drew the cap and lowercase os. *All of the caps have a Modern stress, and the actions of a broad-pen on the lowercase have been greatly modified. The* T*'s wide arms are troublesome, for example, in* **Th**.

FONT SAMPLER

William Morris, father of the late-nineteenth-century back-to-nature Arts and Crafts movement, drew his Golden Type in 1890 and based it on Nicolas Jenson's 1470 Roman.[1] ATF issued Jenson Oldstyle 1893, and in 1913, Morris Benton began Cloister, another copy,

completing the family in 1922.[2] Bruce Rogers, artist and book designer, tried his hand at the Jenson-based Montaigne, which he later named Centaur. Redrawing Jenson was a popular pastime; Ernst Detterer designed Eusebius, yet another copy, for Ludlow in 1929.

Lanston Monotype issued Centaur in 1929 and paired it with Frederic Warde's Arrighi, and Adobe released Robert Slimbach's superb Jenson in 1996.

Rogers traced over enlargements of the Jenson and complained later that he had tidied up the letters too much.

ABCDEFGHI JKLMNOPQR STUVWXYZ abcdefghijklmnop qrstuvwxyz !@#$%^&*( )+[ ]{};:""'?/ 1234567890 1234567890

Centaur—Bruce Rogers, Monotype, 1929

Centaur is a Venetian based on Jenson, though its thins are not as beefy as Slimbach's version. Its serifs are chopped off, unlike the Monotype metal version that had more pointed tips, though rounded. Its drawing is rustic and eccentric.

F O N T S   &   L O G O S

Centaur's serifs are wide and cupped, and their tips are fine. Despite Rogers's complaint, the letters are, so to speak, rustic. Straight stems taper and serifs are bracketed well into the stems. The curves are uneven, a sign of an unsteady hand; there are flat spots; the S's weight is uneven, it appears to bend instead of curve. Rogers considered the loose technique to be vital, unlike the machine-like edges of text faces. Rogers followed Jenson's wide E and F. Centaur is surprisingly evenly proportioned; note that the cap N is visually wider than the O. The G has a beard; the R, a pointed tail, and the C's beaks are parallel; the vertical serifs of T fall in step. Counters of a, g, e, p, and u are uneven; m's branches are staggered at x-height, and the zs are wide. (*See* Arrighi, Frederic Warde's companion italic, page 294.)

1. Jaspert, Berry & Johnson, *Encyclopaedia of Typefaces*, page 123.

2. Mac McGrew, *American Metal Typefaces of the Twentieth Century*, pages 76–81.

72-point foundry type with rounded beak tips. Serifs and beaks are long; both Ss list to the right

Arms are wide: center arm is almost full width. Serifs are square-cornered

Though wider, the O appears more narrow than the N

G has a bracketed beard

Tail of R is tapered similar to Bembo; stem serif is greatly cupped

Counter of C is smoothed out; note corners of the original metal type (left)

T's straight serifs, like C's beaks, are angled

Counters are often pointed

Serif angles change; m's stem height and branches are different heights, and middle and outer stems are bowed

Zs are wide, their beaks change angle, and the bottom beaks of the lowercase z is slightly bowed

Centaur (left) and Slimbach's Jenson (right)

■
Note that the left **S** and the left **C** are the original metal Monotype version.

FONT SAMPLER

Chances are most readers of this book will have first learned to read with words set in 24-point Century Schoolbook. For years primers and grade school text books have been set in Morris Benton's perennial face, which he designed for Ginn & Company, textbook publishers.

Released in 1918–21, the roman and the bold were the last of the large Century family that comprised 18 different designs, including the italic. Sixty years after Century's introduction, ATF released Charles Hughes' Century Nova and italic that recalled Century's original narrow pro-

portions,[1] and in 1980 ITC released Tony Stan's large and successful Century family.

Useful whenever utmost legibility is desired, Schoolbook reverses easily because of its sturdy thins. It is a relatively open face with generous serifs. The thins are its distinguishing feature—

308

ABCDEFGHIJKLM
NOPQRSTUVWXYZ
abcdefghijklmnopqrstuvwxyz
!@#$%^&*()+[]{};:""''?/
1234567890

ABCDEFGHIJKLM
NOPQRSTUVWXYZ
abcdefghijklmnopqrstuvwxyz
!@#$%^&*()+[]{};:""''?/
1234567890

Century Schoolbook—Morris Fuller Benton, ATF, 1917–19
(Monotype)

almost half the thickness of its stems. The x-height is generous, and its stress is Modern. Shapes of the letters are simple and straightforward, with only the enclosed loop of the cap **Q** to call attention to itself. The **R**'s bowl is top heavy; the **M** too narrow; and the **C** minutely too wide. Vertical serifs of the **E**, **F**, **L**, **T**, and **Z**, and the beaks of the **C**, **G**, and **S**, are gently angled. Both the vertical serifs and beaks are amply bracketed. The branch joins are deep, the **r**'s deeper still. The **b** and **q** are tipped with a slender pointed spear and on some versions the descenders are short. Counters of the **b**, **d**, **p**, and **q** appear to be symmetrical ellipses and carry a slight bit of weight around their centerlines. The **a**'s bowl is one-half of the x-height, as is the **e**'s crossbar that forms its eye. The **t** ascender is pointed and tall, and its crossbar and tail are generous. Because of its chunky thins, the face is more monotone than the Oldstyle Caslon or the Transitional Baskerville.

1. Mac McGrew, *American Metal Typefaces of the Twentieth Century*, pages 76–81.

Thin strokes are strong, giving the font a monotone quality. Stress is Modern with minimum weight carriage past the centerline

CETR

Beaks are angled and vertical serifs long; their brackets match the stem's general color

Bowl is top heavy, and the tail is a swelled ogee curve heavy at the baseline

*Branch joins are low and the **r** join is lowest*

mnr bqt

*Bowl divides the **a** x-height and extends past the top kern. Crossbar of **e** is slightly lower, and bracketed*

*Bowls and serifs are generous; descenders are short. Spurs are thin and sharp; **t** is tall, crossbar and tail are wide*

ae

*Century Expanded (1900) preceded Schoolbook. Its thins are lighter, and pothooks of the **n**, **m**, **u**, **v**, **w**, **x**, and **y** lend a rhythmic quality to the font*

*Italic serifs are long, slightly angled, bracketed, and thinner than Oldstyles. The right stems of the **n**, **m**, **u** are straight*

n bmn

Century Expanded

Century Schoolbook

Century Schoolbook is a member of the large Century family. Some of these are: Expanded, Oldstyle, Bold, Bold Condensed, and Century Nova. Schoolbook was designed as a textbook face, and has been used extensively for grade school texts. Its structure is Modern, yet its thins relate to Oldstyles. The x-height is generous and its overall texture is almost monotone. Century Expanded is lighter-weight and its italic borrows pothooks from Baskerville.

Frederic Goudy, dean of American type designers, is noted for his trove of serif faces. He also designed an eponymous sans serif, Goudy Sans (*see* page 325), with romantic scriptlike caps. In 1903 he introduced Copperplate Gothic Heavy, which evolved into one of the most widely used type families in America.

Once "Gothic" meant a sans serif letter, generally referred to as block letters. More precisely, Gothic describes a *flat-sided* letter: Goudy Text, Old English, Fraktur, or Textura. Goudy's Copperplate is finished with minute serifs, imitating an engraver's finishing strokes that square a corner. The family was successful because of its neutral design, and its range of eight small sizes that aligned: four each for the 6- and 12-point, plus two sizes each for the 18- and 24-point. This meant that

MENDING

Copperplate Gothic heavy extended (enlarged)—Frederic Goudy, ATF 1903

ENSURED

Copperplate Gothic light extended (enlarged)—Clarence C. Marder, ATF 1903

A B C D E F G
H I J K L M N O
P Q R S T U V
W X Y Z & $ 1 2
3 4 5 6 7 8 9 0

6 Point No. 4
PREPARED ELEMENTARY COURSE
SCHOOL TEACHERS DIRECT BOYS

6 Point No. 3
INTERNATIONAL IMPROVEMENT SOCIETY
FOREIGN BRANCH OFFICES CONSIDERED

6 Point No. 2
AMERICAN RAILROADS CHANGE TIME SCHEDULE
COMMUTERS REJOICED WHEN THEY HEARD NEWS

6 Point No. 1
FURNISHED APARTMENT HOUSE NOW BEING REMODELED
WORK TO BE DONE BEFORE THE COLD WEATHER ARRIVES

ABCDEFGHIJKLMNOPQRSTUVWXYZ
ABCDEFGHIJKLMNOPQRSTUVWXYZ
ABCDEFGHIJKLMNOPQRSTUVWXYZ
ABCDEFGHIJKLMNOPQRSTUVWXYZ
ABCDEFGHIJKLMNOPQRSTUVWXYZ
ABCDEFGHIJKLMNOPQRSTUVWXYZ
ABCDEFGHIJKLMNOPQRSTUVWXYZ

Copperplate Gothic—Linotype, 1989

■
Top—*The heavy and light extended metal Copperplates were handset only.*

all sizes aligned at the baseline. The sizes were ideally suited
for business cards and stationery, and almost every business
form was set in Copperplate
Gothic. Notes of credit and
business and personal checks
used the multiple sizes and different weights.

The light extended version
is one of my favorites. Gently
spaced, the 6/1, the smallest size,
at only two-and-a-half points
tall, is one of the most legible of
all small-size types (*opposite*).
The proportions are good. Perhaps arms of the **E**, **F**, and **L**
could be shortened for better

color. With the exception of the
S, the letters are well drawn. The
S appears to rock because the
curves are too small top and bottom, and the turns that form the
spine are abrupt and so distort
the letter.

Arms are long: the **E**'s *center arm is
short; compare the* **F**, **L**, *and* **T**;
*the stubby serifs are bracketed
with rounded tips*

*Round forms are wide;
there is a smooth transition from
straight to curve*

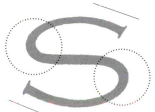

The bottom of the **U** *is flat. The curve
transition into the straight stems is too
abrupt, which creates optical corners*

The **S**-curves are arched top and bottom
and do not relate to the font's other curves*

*Double serifs are used at top and bottom
of the joined stems*

Bowl divides the cap **R** *height
happily; its shape is good and the diagonal
tail is well placed*

From American Type Founders 1923 Specimen Book (enlarged)

■

*In daily parlance, sans serifs may be
be called Gothics. Copperplate gothic
is an anomaly, it is not a sans serif,
nor is it a true Gothic with flat sides.
It may be called more precisely a
monotone serif letter.*

6/4   6/3   6/2 6/1

*Schematic:
6-point nos. 4, 3, 2, and 1,
Copperplate Gothic regular*

FONT SAMPLER

In their quest for attention, designers often overlook the light and delicate fonts, forgetting that when used at a large size or surrounded by generous space, the fonts may be as effective as a smaller, bold statement. Diotima (named after Socrates' teacher), designed by Gudrun Zapf von Hesse, was introduced into the United States in the late 1950s. Its use has been limited but, now that it is available in PostScript form, it is receiving the attention that it deserves.

Diotima possesses style, that wonderful quality of distinctive excellence. It is unique. No other font matches its light and graceful forms. The letters are strongly calligraphic, with stems that taper to a pronounced waist. There is great carriage of weight across the branches; hairlines are fine and the serifs unbracketed. Return strokes, hairline stems, and arms widen for color and are

ABCDEFGHIJKLM
NOPQRSTUVWXYZ
abcdefghijklmnopqrstuvwxyz
!@#$%^&*()+[]{};:""'?/
1234567890

ABCDEFGHIJKLM
NOPQRSTUVWXYZ
abcdefghijklmnopqrstuvwxyz
!@#$%^&*()+II{};:""'?/
1234567890

Diotima—Gudrun Zapf von Hesse, Stempel, 1952

■

Diotima, a light, beautiful, calligraphic roman, is ideal for settings of elegant typography, social printing, and for initials and titles for fine book work. The roman's proportions are more classical than the italic, which tends to be even. The lowercase is wide and the fit is open. The italic has a greater diagonal stress.

not bracketed. The bowls are plump and opulent with weight distributed in an almost Modern style. In the fashion of italic forms, the **b**'s bowl is rounded at the baseline. Ascenders are taller than caps and the x-height is generous. The italic caps are evenly proportioned, while the roman shows more classic influences, with wide round forms, a narrow **B** and **S**, and an absence of serifs atop the **N** and **M**. The **a** is footed, and the top beginning stroke is narrow, one of the font's most distinctive characteristics. The **l** has a tail instead of a horizontal serif. Right-hand stems of the **h**, **m**, and **n** and the **u**'s left stem are serifed on one side only. The loop of the **g** is open and attached to the bowl with a slim, vertical hairline.

I am extraordinarily fond of the italic. Its proportions and fit are beautiful and color evenly. Bowl weight is strongly placed near the baseline for left-hand curves and high near x-height for right-hand curves.

Proportions of the roman tend to follow classical widths: M, N, U, V, and W are wide; B and S are narrow; the italic is more evenly proportioned

MBO

Top curve is narrow, a distinguishing feature, and the stem is footed

Branches are strongly calligraphic with great carriage of weight across the curves

Open loop of g is distinctive, particularly its vertical attachment to the bowl

abhmug

Bowl follows italic forms

Outside stems are serifed on one side only. Lower serifs are bracketed, u is not

Italic M and N have serifs, the R is well balanced, and the S, a difficult letter to draw, is high-spirited

MRS

Instead of the usual two-story form, the g is drawn with a bowl to match the other bowl letters

Diagonal tail of the k elegantly drops below the baseline

gabdpqk

Unlike the roman, bowls have pronounced weights above center on a right-hand curve and below center on left-hand curve

Franklin Gothic is ubiquitous. For many years the face has been used for headings for *Time*, and it can be found in dramatic sizes in *Interview*, first published in the 1960s as an underground, tabloid rag for self-aggrandizement by Andy Warhol. Morris Benton drew it in three propor-

tions: regular in 1902; condensed and extra condensed in 1906. It was named for Benjamin Franklin, and it was Benton's first modernization of nineteenth-century Gothics inherited from ATF's buying sweep of 23 foundries. The design is the basis for the News

Gothic family and Lightline Gothic.[1] While the family's fortunes have ebbed, Franklin has never disappeared, and Lightline has been used for years as unobtrusive type for the mandatory copy for packaging, particularly in the cosmetics industry. The proportions are Modern.

ABCDEFGHI
JKLMNOPQRST
UVWXY&Z
1234567890
abcdefghijklmno
pqrstuvwxyz
.';?!/()$*

Franklin Gothic—Morris Fuller Benton, American Type Founders, 1902

■

Based on evenly proportioned nineteenth-century sans serifs, Franklin Gothic spawned News Gothic, News Gothic Bold, Lightline Gothic, Monotone Gothic (a handsome and slightly ex-

tended version of News Gothic), Franklin Gothic condensed, extra condensed, wide, and the italic.

Note the angular ascender of the **t**, square points (periods), short cross

arms, bulky diagonal join of the M, and angled endings to the lowercase **a**, **c**, **e**, and **s**. The slight thick and thin qualities make it more legible than the monotone Gothics typified by Helvetica. Curved

form endings are angular, a particularly useful open design trait for small sizes of the lowercase. Branches of the lowercase are angular, a device that allows more air between the stem and the con-

The caps color well, except for the **A**, which is narrow, and too bold; **E** and **F** seem wide, and I wish that their center arms were longer, instead of stubby.

McGrew mentions the bold, heavy top-ending stroke of the **C**. I am more perplexed by the vertical stroke of the **G**, which is cleft at its baseline. The small spur-like stroke is light; its design relates to nothing else in the font. When compared to the **N**, the **M** seems to belong to another, bolder font. The **N** is more resolved, with a pronounced overlap of diagonal and vertical stems. Its structure relates to the **V** and **W**. The **X** is visually almost single-weight. The figure **1** is serifed at the baseline—the only figure treated thus, but designed to help fill the en space to tabulate. The figures are apple pie. They are seen everywhere—Franklin and Helvetica are the generic figures in American print. From stick-on letters to mail-order versions cut out of brass, they are the ones we have grown up with and know as "real numbers."

1. Mac McGrew, *American Metal Typefaces of the Twentieth Century*, pages 142–43.

Top terminal stroke is wider. Franklin is a thick and thin letter that mostly follows weight distribution of a two-weight serif face

Narrow spur

Arms are short

CGEF

Branches are strongly angled to prevent clogging at stem juncture. (Compare the almost symmetrical Helvetica)

Compared to the N, M is narrow and heavy

hMN

Terminals are angled; c follows cap shape; top of t tapers

Bowl and loop of g are thinner than basic stems to prevent massing

acestg

ABCDEFGHIJKLMNOPQRSTUVWXYZ
abcdefghijklmnopqrstuvwxyz 1234567890

Franklin Gothic extra condensed—Morris Fuller Benton, ATF, 1906
(See Franklin Gothic Wide, page 157)

necting curved strokes, which prevents a congestion of weight where the two meet (see *Branches, page 78*). The **k** is wide and heavy, and the ascender of the **t** is taller than most sans serifs. Considerable thinning has been employed in the **g** in order to draw a bowl and tail of a conventional serifed face **g** design. Franklin extra condensed fits my idea of a near-perfect condensed sans. The thick-and-thin proportion prevents the style from setting as black as some drawings of Helvetica, but the taut oval shapes and the two-weight form make for an eminently legible and condensed font—if you must narrow a letter so much. In all versions, the punctuation is horsey.

FONT SAMPLER

Much of type preference is personal and you will find devotees for Helvetica or Univers; Futura is based on classical proportions and should be assessed with different criteria. Type preference depends, too, on usage. If a good type is used excessively, it becomes cloying.

Adrian Frutiger designed Univers in the late 1950s as a family of 22 fonts. He has recently digitally recreated the family, bringing the total to 58. In the 1970s Frutiger was asked to design a font of great clarity for use at the DeGaulle airport outside of Paris. The design was

so well received that he drew it as a type family.[1] His drawing is clearly identifiable—he is a master artist with great style. The proportions are different from those of Frutiger's popular font Univers, suggesting classical influence. Note that the **B, E, F, L,** and **S** are narrow, while the

ABCDEFGHIJKLM NOPQRSTUVWXYZ abcdefghijklmnopqrstuvwxyz !@#$%^&*()+[]{};:""''?/ 1234567890

Frutiger 55—Adrian Frutiger, Stempel / Linotype, 1976

ABCDEFGHIJKLM NOPQRSTUVWXYZ abcdefghijklmnopqrstuvwxyz !@#$%^&*()+[]{};:""''?/ 1234567890

Frutiger 56—Adrian Frutiger, Stempel / Linotype, 1976

Frutiger's proportions lean toward the classical, instead of the more evenly proportioned Univers, with more open curved letters. It is very legible at small sizes. The round forms are not as square as Univers. The **a** and **s** are beautifully drawn, a true test of a designer's skills.

C, D, G, M, O, and **W** are generous. The distinguishing characteristics of Frutiger are the curved form endings, which resemble Futura. These letters have endings that are almost vertical: **C, G, S, a, c, e, f, g, s,** and **y;** the **S** is more angled. The **R**'s tail is curved in the manner of Gill Sans. Capitals and figures are reduced, and the ascenders are tall. While Univers was drawn with a pronounced shoulder on all curved forms to make up for the loss of serifs, Frutiger is a rounded face. In the light and regular weights the letters are monotone, with minute horizontal and diagonal adjustments to color evenly. In the bolder weights, the letters are distinctly thick and thin to prevent congestion. Numbering is the same as Univers (*see* page 348).

1. Adrian Frutiger, *Type, Sign, Symbol* (Zurich, Switzerland: ABC Edition, 1980), pages 80–88.

Round forms have less shoulder than Univers

Frutiger

Terminals are slightly canted, particularly the S

Round terminals are nearly vertical; the c has more angle. The hand of the designer is revealed in the shape of the a's bowl. Frutiger's simplified shapes are more open than Univers at small sizes

Univers

Branches are quite rounded and curve well into the stem

Univers   *Frutiger*

Arms are short; R is narrow, and the diagonal tail departs with a radius. W is open; its diagonals barely overlap at the join

The top right stem is shifted

Erbar (*opposite bottom*) was the first of the new sans serifs that departed from the evenly proportioned sans of the nineteenth century. Designed in 1922 by Jakob Erbar, it was widely received, yet over the years it has been eclipsed by Paul Renner's Futura. The design of Futura is based partly on minimalist concepts that originated with the Bauhaus. Letterforms that are stripped to their bones are difficult to draw—everything counts; there are no serifs to lean on, no gradual diminishing of weights that hide drawing limitations, only pure form that must be manipulated, thinned, extended, adjusted, shaded and nuanced to appear deceptively simple, optical, single-weight letters.

Futura follows general proportions set up by the romans, all based on a square (*see* page 44). Roughly speaking, the A, G, O, and N fit a square; the B,

ABCDEFGHIJKLM
NOPQRSTUVWXYZ
abcdefghijklmnopqrstuvwxyz
!@#$%^&*()+[]{};:""'?/
1234567890

ABCDEFGHIJKLM
NOPQRSTUVWXYZ
abcdefghijklmnopqrstuvwxyz
!@#$%^&*()+[]{};:""'?/
1234567890

Futura—Paul Renner, Bauer, 1927 (Adobe)

■

Futura is based on classical proportions. It is referred to as the "German Sans," a departure from the evenly proportioned nineteenth-century sans. The style is notable for its taller-than-caps ascenders and one-story a. Other fonts of the same period that followed the style include: Erbar, Atlantis, Bernhard Gothic, Kabel, Kristal, and Metro. Futura is a large family now, from its light book weight to Twentieth Century ultrabold extended, Monotype's copy of Futura, designed by Sol Hess.

E, F, P, R, and S are half as wide. Renner's original lowercase a, b, d, g, p, and q drawing shows a bowl that thins gradually as it rolls and joins tangent to a stem without a trace of a corner. There is a mix of curved form endings; some are vertical chops and some terminate on the diag-

onal. Ascenders are slightly taller than the caps, and in some new digital versions these have been shortened for a larger x-height. Straight and curved horizontals are thinned imperceptibly to appear equal to vertical stems. There is no italic, only an oblique —that is, a leaning version of the

roman with no change of character shapes. The a is one-story and its simplicity hampers its legibility. The u is unusual in that its right stem is not a complete straight line; compare Helvetica (page 132). Designed in 1929, Futura has been used extensively for almost seventy years—before

Helvetica was introduced, excessively. Monotype's Twentieth Century ultra bold extended is a permutation of Renner's design (*see* page 145).

Some letters fit a square; others are half as wide

Ascenders are taller than caps, an Oldstyle design trait

Fonts vary. Adobe (left) and Mergenthaler Linotype (right) **R:** *note weight difference and waists*

vertical stem thickness

Horizontal arms are thinned to optically match vertical stems, and horizontal curves are thinner to match vertical stems

Bowls and branches taper as they join tangent to stems. There are different round-form endings: vertical, diagonal, and horizontal

U *is a horseshoe in contrast to sans* **u** *s with a rectangular vertical stem*

Futura's bowls are the ultimate family characteristic

ABCDEFGHIJKLMNOPQRSTUVWXYZ&
abcdefghijklmnopqrstuvwxyzæœfiflffffiffl

Erbar—Jakob Erbar, Ludwig & Meyer 1922–30

Garamond is as comfortable as an old shoe. Classified as Old-style and Garalde, the type has been used for almost 500 years. Printers like it because of its sturdy hairlines.

Claude Garamond cut his types around 1544; though influenced by hands of the day, he drew them as types, and not as slavish manuscript copies.[1]

There are many Garamonds: ATF's version by Morris Benton, is a mainstay (Linotype copied it and named it Garamond No. 3). Goudy's 1921 Garamont version for Monotype enjoyed great success, though critics said that both designs were based on the types of Jannon, and not Garamond.[2] Linotype's version came out in 1929, and R. H. Middleton's more elegant drawing, said to be drawn from authentic sources, was introduced that year also.

A close examination of the forms reveals that all joins are

ABCDEFGHIJKLM
NOPQRSTUVWXYZ
abcdefghijklmnopqrstuvwxyz
!@#$%^&*()+[]{};:""''?/
1234567890 1234567890

ABCDEFGHIJKLM
NOPQRSTUVWXYZ
abcdefghijklmnopqrstuvwxyz
!@#$%^&()+[]{};:""''?/*
1234567890 1234567890

Adobe Garamond—Robert Slimbach, Abobe Systems, 1989

■
There are probably as many versions of Garamond as there are Caslon. Note that this version leans the cap **O**, *but orients the lowercase* **o** *in a vertical posture. The* **G** *has a beard;* *the* **W** *is made up of two* **V**s. *The figures are beautiful, and the italic* **5** *is distinctive. The roman cipher is a single, light-weight line, but the italic is two-weight. Jan Tschichold's Sabon* *(opposite, bottom) is based on Garamond's forms, but is drawn with a larger x-height than Slimbach's Garamond, which does not fill the vertical height of the character cell.*

bracketed, some minutely, but a radius nevertheless. The cap **T** is distinctive, its right-hand arm tipped with a vertical serif, and the left one finished with a slightly canted serif. Slimbach uses a beard on the **G**'s straight stroke; **U** is rounded; the **A**'s weighted stem is cupped at the top. All serifs are blunted and subtly cupped. The **a** and **f** kerns differ—the **a** reveals traces of a broad-pen and the **f** is a tear-drop; the **g**'s tail departs from the bowl with a straight stroke.

Faces designed as text fonts often lack finesse when used at large display sizes, unless the font has been specifically redrawn at a display size. Slimbach's Garamond Titling solves that handily; the elegant letter is lighter and more condensed than the regular font.

1. D. B. Updike, *Printing Types: Their History, Forms, and Use, A Study in Survivals*, vol. 1, page 234.

2. Mac McGrew, *American Metal Typefaces of the Twentieth Century*, page 149.

Terminal of the **a** is calligraphic. Garamond is noted for the small counters of its **a** and **e**

There are no points in Garamond. Each join is bracketed, and tips of all serifs are blunted

Crossbar of the **f** begins with diagonal calligraphic stroke

Tail of the **g** departs with a straight stroke, and the ear is a straight line with blunted tip

Waist of the **k** is drawn with a horizontal. Serifs on all letters are subtly cupped

Thin strokes are sturdy, and branches of the **h**, **m**, **n**, and **u** are gracefully curved

Pothooks bend abruptly at top and bottom ending stem

Bowls of the italic, unlike many Oldstyles, carry only a minimum amount of weight around turns. The **p** is a swash form

regular caps   titling caps

Regular caps often are too bold at large sizes. Titling caps are offered, drawn with thinner stems and hairlines

Sabon   Garamond

FONT SAMPLER

In 1938, the Society for the Art of Printing & Books invited Jan van Krimpen to design a new typeface for a special edition of the Dutch Authorized version of the Bible (*Staten Bijbel*).

Van Krimpen had to design the font to fit the keyboard of an existing Monotype font layout. He was unhappy with Monotype's trial proofs and the project was abandoned.[1] Now after 50 years, Frank Blokland has created a digital family that addresses the problems of the un-

finished version. Blokland has added special characters, italic small caps, and additional weights. Troublesome proportions were adjusted, and the contrast, or sparkle, was lessened. Haarlemmer's italic clearly reveals its chancery beginnings, though it is wide, unlike other

Van Krimpen italics. Italic proportions have always posed problems for type designers: how to differentiate their design from the roman for emphasis, and still maintain a compatible design relationship. Machine composition created additional problems because the italic must be equal

ABCDEFGHIJKLM
NOPQRSTUVWXYZ
abcdefghijklmnopqrstuvwxyz
ABCDEFGHIJKLMNOPQRSTUVWXYZ
!@#$%^&*( ) + [ ] {}; : " ""?/
1234567890
1234567890

ABCDEFGHIJKLM
NOPQRSTUVWXYZ
abcdefghijklmnopqrstuvwxyz
!@#$%^&( ) + [ ]{};:" "'?/*
1234567890
1234567890

Haarlemmer—Jan van Krimpen, Monotype, 1938
Frank Blokland, Dutch Type Library, 1998

to the roman width, otherwise the italic will have different spacing or fit. (If the italic is narrow it will be more openly spaced than the roman.) Typical Van Krimpen, roman **C** and **G**'s top curves are taut; the **E**, **F**, and **Z** wide; the bowls of the **B** beautifully balanced; the tail of the **R** strong and angular (which requires an open set in metal; compare the angle of the Sabon **R** tail); the beaks sharp and deftly bracketed; and there is a gentle, diagonal thrust to the round forms. The large bowl **g** appears, a favorite ploy; and the arched **a** bowl references Lutetia and Spectrum.

Van Krimpen's penchant for squarish Us is lessened, and the accents are longish and light. The quirky italic **k** bowl and the bent stem of the **g** bow to the past, and the long, taut ogee curve of the **f** and its ligatures are beautiful. The small caps are robust and handsomely proportioned.

1. *The Monotype Recorder*, The Dutch Connection, New Series/Volume 9. Frank E. Blokland, Robin Nicolas, and Steve Matteson, Editors. ('s Hertogenbosch: Monotype and the Dutch Type Library), page 30.

323

B, **P**, and **R** *bowls have a slight diagonal stress, yet the* **B**'s *lower bowl borders on the Modern*

The **R** *is wide with a generous tail that widens to show the effect of pressure at its tip*

D's bowl is weighted more at the top

Thins are sturdy, and serifs taper to refined endings that produce sparkle. The **C** *and* **D** *have a Modern stress*

The **O** *has a slight diagonal stress and its counter is almost plumb*

Van Krimpen favored Ss with a slightly rigid spine; compare Baskerville. The lower portion admits a generous amount of space. There is a vestige of a spur on the **C**, **G**, *and* **S** *beaks*

T's arm serifs are canted and gently cupped

Kerns of the **c** *and* **f** *have an unusual spoon shape; the* **f** *kerns generously*

Bowls depart from the stems with a flattened curve, which repeats the **c** *and* **e** *endings and the italic's bowls and branches*

s *repeats the cap shape though in a wider proportion*

A rarity in italic design, the **y**'s *upper portion is parallel to the type's slant. Its stem curves opposite to the* **v** *and* **w** *stems*

The x-height is generous. The **g**'s *tail is based on 16th-century shapes*

Haarlemmer

z *has a true calligraphic distribution of weights*

Haarlemmer Sans

Haarlemmer Sans is an unusual sans serif. Its proportion is similar to Erbar and Futura, the German sans of the 1920s. It is a two-weight letter, though with only slight contrast between its thicks and thins. There is a gentle calligraphic quality to the round forms as though first conceived with a broad-pen held in the same manner that produced the Humanistic forms of the Renaissance. The slight widening of the lowercase stems below x-height on left-hand curves and above center on right-hand curves is the clue. Although the straight stems are perfectly rigid, there is a softness to the font lacking in the geometric German sans.

The right-hand side of the **A** is weighted. **B, E, F, P, R,** and **S** proportions are not as narrow as Futura. The tail of the **R** references the serif Haarlemmer with a slight widening at its tip. The curved and tapered tail of the Q

ABCDEFGHIJKLM
NOPQRSTUVWXYZ
ABCDEFGHIJKLMNOPQRSTUVWXYZ
abcdefghijklmnopqrstuvwxyz
!@#$%^&*()+[]{};:""''?/
1234567890
1234567890

ABCDEFGHIJKLM
NOPQRSTUVWXYZ
ABCDEFGHIJKLMNOPQRSTUVWXYZ
abcdefghijklmnopqrstuvwxyz
!@#$%^&()+[]{};:""''?/*
1234567890
1234567890

Haarlemmer Sans—Frank Blokland, Dutch Type Library, 1998

is handsome. Endings of the **C**, **G**, and **S** have a vertical chop, though there is the slightest angle to their endings. In the manner of Optima, the **a** and **t** have curved stem endings, which helps soften the font's appearance. There are roman and italic small caps. The italic is unusual be-cause it departs from the ro-man structure, and its skeleton is reminiscent of the chancery hands, with branches and bowls that deeply depart from the stems. Even the stem base turns of the *a, d, h, m, n,* and *u* reveal its heritage. Compare it with Goudy Sans Serif and Poetica.

AABCDEFGHIJKLMMNN
OPQRSTUVWXYZ&
abcdefghijklmnopqrstuvwxyz
$1234567890

Goudy Sans Serif Light—Frederic Goudy, Lanston Monotype, 1929

325

The round forms **C, D, G, O,** *and* **Q** *are wide, following Oldstyle proportions*

Diagonal letters **K, M, N, V, W, X, Y,** *and* **Z** *generally follow Oldstyle weight distribution*

Convergence of the **A**'s *diagonal is narrow and the crossbar is high*

Bottoms of **P** *and* **R** *bowl counters are rounded instead of horizontal*

Both the **O** *and* **Q** *are broad-shouldered and offer a slightly squarish appearance.* **Q**'s *tail is beautifully drawn*

Top and bottom curves of the **S** *are restrained, matching the* **C** *and* **G**. *The bottom curve extends generously to the left and imparts a subtle forward thrust to the letter*

Curved stem endings are diagonal, opposed to some vertically chopped capital endings

Beginning **a** *stem and branches* **h, m, n,** *and* **u** *are angular*

In the manner of Franklin Gothic, the left side of the **t**'s *ascender is angled*

Bowls reveal a diagonal stress

Baseline stem turns reference chancery forms like Arrighi, Palatino, Poetica, and Sabon italic. The **g** *shows its chancery heritage also. Compare its reverse curve descender to the Poetica* **g**

Haarlemmer Sans

The curved diagonals of the **k, v, w, y, x,** *and* **z** *lend a graceful touch to the italic—a rarity among sans serifs*

Poetica Chancery I—Robert Slimbach, Adobe Systems, 1992

Type designers using the same source material may sometimes produce completely different concepts. Bruce Rogers's Centaur and Robert Slimbach's Jenson are remarkable examples and both are highly acclaimed.

Robert Slimbach researched his Jenson from Eusebius's *De Evangelica Præparatione* in the Bancroft Library in Berkeley. This famous book is considered to be the best resource for Jenson's types, since none of the original punches or types remain.

Using photo enlargements from the book's printed pages of the printed type, Slimbach cross-referenced key letters to determine which irregularities should be ruled out. From an enlarged drawing, he drew additional master drawings to complete the optical size and weight ranges required for the MultipleMaster font. For the italic he followed the same procedure and then add-

ABCDEFGHI JKLMNOPQRS TUVWXYZ

abcdefghijklmn opqrstuvwxyz

!@#$%^&*()+[]{};:""''?/

1234567890

1234567890

Adobe Jenson, MultipleMaster—Robert Slimbach, Adobe Systems, Inc., 1995

Of all the Jenson versions, Robert Slimbach's drawing of the 500-year-old face is my favorite. Slimbach is a master calligrapher, which is evident throughout his work.

FONTS & LOGOS

ed swash italics and expert fonts. Jenson cut only a 16-point roman size—italics did not appear until 1500, thirty years later.[1]

All designers of fonts based on Jenson have faced the dilemma of what style italics to use—the narrow pointed chancery forms of the sixteenth century, or softer shapes that relate to the roundness of the roman. Slimbach's roman and italic Jenson are sturdy, though in comparison, his version has greater contrast of thicks and thins.

1. *Font & Function:* Adobe Jenson, The Revival of a Renaissance Classic. (San Jose, California: Adobe Systems, Inc. Spring 1996).

Photo enlargement of Jenson's face from De Evangelica Præparatione *by Eusebius, 1470–76*

Center arm is almost as wide as the top and bottom arms
Jenson   Times Roman

R's bowl is overbalanced and the tail is curved

Arm serifs are almost parallel and angle in the manner of Garamond. The right arm is shortened for better fit with **h**

The **a** is a vigorous shape, with its calligraphic structure clearly revealed. Note the **e**'s crossbar, which reveals the broad-pen's angle

The **g** is seminal; its basic shape is reflected in Times Roman and Sabon
Jenson   Times Roman   Sabon

Walbaum repeats the diagonal stem joined to the horizontal
Jenson   Walbaum

Bowls are generous, and the departing top curve repeats the broad-pen's angle

s is small and divided noticeably above center

The **y** leans and the thin stroke widens at its tip

z is wide and calligraphic

FONT SAMPLER

Michelangelo

Michelangelo is one of the great titling faces. It is majestic, heroic, perfect for when typography must reflect dignity and lofty aspirations. There are no descenders to worry about; each letter fills the space of the character cell. Hermann Zapf says Michelangelo was "designed in 1949 as a special display face to be used within the Palatino type family." The Greek letters named Phidias were added in 1953. The design is based on Roman inscriptions but with a strong broad-edged pen influence."[1] Michelangelo, Sistina (its bolder counterpart), and Palatino constitute a family.

Zapf relates that these handsome caps were a result of his studies of fifteenth- and sixteenth-century letterforms one summer in Florence, Pisa, and at the Vatican and Laurentian Libraries in Rome. The caps are pure Renaissance forms, including their sturdy thins. The broad-edged pen is in evidence throughout the alphabet, and only slight modeling shows. Left-hand curved strokes are widest below center and right-hand curves, widest above center.

328

Bowls are open, and their convergence reveals the flat pen's angle

Stress is diagonal and wider below center on left-hand curves and above center on right-hand curves

In the classic roman fashion the crossbar is high, near center

Arms are short; center ones lack serifs

Straight stem is short

Serifs are short, blunted, bracketed, and cupped

*Cap **M** is of heroic proportion, splayed, with thin strokes weighted at the serifs*

U is an early form, and shaped like the lowercase; the right stem has a double serif

S is rounded and tipped with canted serifs

*Bowls are open; **B**, **P**, and **R** are narrow*

(*Note: alphabet enlarged from* Manuale Typographicum)
Michelangelo Titling—Hermann Zapf, Stempel, 1949–50

An angled ending of the convergence of the **B**'s bowls reveals the diagonal broad-pen: tips of the **C** and **G**'s beak; mid-arms of the **E** and **F**; the tail of the **K**, and **R**; and the left-hand stroke of the **Y**. The **U** is a later form, since the Romans did not have it and used a **V** instead.

Michelangelo is a light face; its stem-to-cap-height ratio is 1:12, while Palatino is 1:9. In true calligraphic fashion, the vertical stems flare at both ends of the stems. Serifs are squarish with rounded corners, and cupped. There are a brace of Ks, and Ss, the latter with a pro-

nounced reverse curve, and an alternate **R** with a generous tail that may be used at the end of a word or line where it is not troublesome. In a normal setting, the tail may be gently tucked beneath the left arm of a **T** or **Y**. Titling caps are most handsome when amply spaced.

1. *Hermann Zapf and His Design Philosophy* (Chicago: Society of Typographic Arts Chicago, 1987), page 22.

See Hermann Zapf's use of the caps in his monumental *Manuale Typographicum* (Frankfurt: Stempel, 1954, vol. 1, and vol. 11, Frankfurt: Z Press, 1968), two excellent examples of type design, book design, letterpress printing, and book binding.

*Instead of a point, **V** and **W** terminate with a pronounced broad-pen ending*

*The broad-pen edge is revealed at the stem's beginning, a shape that repeats on the ends of **K**, **R**, and **X***

WXYZ&

*Alternate letters with generous tails to end a word or line, or to tuck beneath a **T** or **Y***

[⁑RKS✳]

123456

The ampersand (above) and figures are not as tall as the caps, and the diagonal stem of the 7 bows slightly

7890

Zapf's Phidias, named for a great artist of ancient Athens, is a sister face to Michelangelo, consummate homage to the noble Greek letter. In his keynote speech at a Symposium on the Greek Letter sponsored by the Greek Font Society in Athens, Zapf outlined the history of Greek fonts from Nicolas Jenson's fifteenth-century seminal font to Kris Holmes and Chuck Bigelow's 1985 Lucida Greek font for *Scientific American* magazine.[1] In efforts to create a Greek alphabet compatible with the roman letter, European type designers first added serifs to the capital letters, and later to the lowercase, a more difficult task because the forms are cursive and scriptlike. In the late fifteenth century, Francesco Griffo of Bologna cut a Greek font for the Venetian printer, Aldus Manutius, that emulated Greek handwriting. Similar to the Aldine italic, the

330

(Note: *alphabet enlarged from* Manuale Typographicum)
Phidias Greek—Hermann Zapf, Stempel, 1952

letters are narrow, the capitals upright, and the lowercase slanted. In 1544 Claude Garamond cut a font for King Francis I, for exclusive use in the Imprimerie Royale in Paris, named Grec du Roi. Robert Granjon followed with a Greek type cut for the Antwerp printer, Christophe Plantin, circa 1560. In the late eighteenth century Bodoni cut 28 Greek faces that appeared in his 1788 *Manuale Tipografico*. While in France, the Didots, publishers, punchcutters, and typefounders, produced a highly popular Greek font whose form is the basis for today's Didot Greek.

1. "The Development of Greek Typefaces" by Hermann Zapf, in *Greek Letters From Tablets to Pixels*, Greek Font Society. Edited by Michael S. Macrakis, with essays by Hermann Zapf, Matthew Carter, Stephen V. Tracy, Nicolas Barker, and others (New Castle, Delaware: Oak Knoll Press, 1996), pages 1–29.

Greek type by Nicolas Jenson—Venice, 1472

Greek type by Francesco Griffo for Aldus Manutius—Venice, 1501

Top—*Nicolas Jenson's 1472 Greek type, remarkably, after 500 years, is still the prototype for classic Greek fonts. Reproduced from* Greek Letters, from Tablets to Pixels.
Bottom—*Greek type used in* Philostratus: *Aldus, Venice, 1501. Cut by the punchcutter Francesco Griffo. Reproduced by permission of Harvard University Press, from* Printing Types, Their History, Forms, and Use, a Study in Survivals *by D. B. Updike.*

In the late summer of 1956 Jan van Krimpen granted me an interview in a richly paneled eighteenth-century conference room at the Enschedé type foundry and patiently answered my questions about the rules of proportion, drawing, engraving, smoke proofs, typographic directions, etc. Many of his answers can be found in his later writings. In John Dreyfus's superb *The Work of Jan van Krimpen* there is a fascinating account of the modifications of his Lutetia font for Porter Garnett, of the Frick Museum. Dreyfus writes about Van Krimpen's open capitals: "For use with Antigone Greek, a series of open capitals was originally cast on 24-point, to serve as two-line initials with text set in 12-point. Later they were recut in a heavier weight for the Nonesuch Press editions of *The Iliad* and *The Odyssey,* in which enlarged and retouched line-block reproductions of them were used on the title pages."[1]

Besides their beauty of proportion, their line quality is im-

ABCDEFGHIJK LMNOPQR STUVWXYZ

(24-point enlarged)

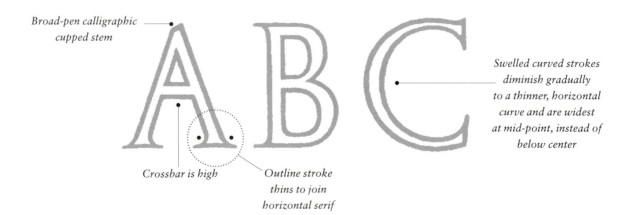

Broad-pen calligraphic cupped stem

Crossbar is high

Outline stroke thins to join horizontal serif

Swelled curved strokes diminish gradually to a thinner, horizontal curve and are widest at mid-point, instead of below center

Open Roman Capitals—Jan van Krimpen, Enschedé, 1929

Designed at the 300-year-old Enschedé Type Foundry, Haarlem, Holland, Van Krimpen's superb classic outline caps were conceived to complement his Antigone font (opposite). Slightly more condensed than the Trajan column capitals, the Open Capitals are distinguished by a beautifully executed calligraphic stroke that creates the outline, which thins at joins and around the hori-

pressive. This is not a simple outline: the lines are thinned on the horizontal curves, widening gradually and beautifully to their fullest width at half the capital's height. The vertical outlines gracefully taper and curve to meet the serifs, which creates the font's magical sparkle.

Van Krimpen was a calligrapher, type designer, typographer, and great book designer. His types were handcut by his engraver, Paul Helmuth Rädisch, a genius who translated Van Krimpen's pencil drawings into full-fledged works of art—at the actual size of the font. With John

Dreyfus as a technical advisor, Monotype produced Van Krimpen's Spectrum typeface. Van Krimpen designed Holland's currency and postage stamps, and an admirable cover for a special edition of the *Fleuron*, plus numerous engraved plaques. His Antigone, Cancelleresca

Bastarda, Lutetia, Romanée, Romulus, Open Caps, and Spectrum are fonts of exceptional beauty.

1. John Dreyfus, *The Work of Jan van Krimpen* (Haarlem: Joh. Enschedé en Zonen, 1952). *See also: J. van Krimpen on Designing and Devising Type* (New York: The Typophiles, 1957).

ΑΒΓΔΕΖΗΘΙΚΛΜΝΞΟΠΡ
ΣΤΥΦΧΨΩ

ΕΥΑΓΓΕΛΙΟΝ ΚΑΤΑ
ΙΩΑΝΗΝ

ΑΒΓΔΕΖΗΘΙΚΛΜΝΞΟΠΡΣΤΥΦΧΨΩ

ΕΥΑΓΓΕΛΙΟΝ ΚΑΤΑ ΙΩΑΝΗΝ
Ἐν ἀρχῇ ἦν ὁ λόγος, καὶ ὁ λόγος ἦν πρὸς τὸν θεόν, καὶ θεὸς ἦν ὁ λόγος. Οὗτος ἦν ἐν ἀρχῇ πρὸς τὸν θεόν. πάντα δι' αὐτοῦ ἐγένετο, καὶ χωρὶς αὐτοῦ ἐγένετο οὐδὲ ἓν ὃ γέγονεν. ἐν αὐτῷ ζωὴ ἦν, καὶ ἡ ζωὴ ἦν τὸ φῶς τῶν ἀνθρώπων. καὶ τὸ φῶς ἐν τῇ σκοτίᾳ φαίνει, καὶ ἡ σκοτία αὐτὸ οὐ κατέλαβεν.

α β γ δ ε ζ η θ ι κ λ μ ν ξ ο π ρ σ ς τ υ φ χ ψ ω

Antigone—Jan van Krimpen, Enschedé, 1927

zontal curves, and adds sparkle to the gray shapes. **B**, **P**, and **R** are narrow, and the **P** bowl is open. The **A**'s top beginning downstroke shows its broad-pen heritage, and its crossbar is correctly high

for this style; the straight stem of the **G** is also held high and creates a beautifully balanced letter. Only one pointed join is found on the **N**; the troublesome tail of the **R** is restrained in width; the

M is not splayed; arms of the **E**, and **F** are generous, and the **L** is minimum width. An early form of the **Y** is used, and a wide **Z**. An overlapped brace of **V**s create a narrow, congested **W**, and

the bottom curve of the **U** turns quickly as it joins the vertical stems to create a somewhat flat curve. The tail of **Q** is inventive: a scimitar-shaped tail that hugs the baseline.

Zapf's Optima design is unique, for it falls between serif and sans serifs with broad-pen influences. But above all, it is a *beautiful* drawing. Upon its introduction, Optima was an immediate success and everyone used it repeatedly. The world of advertising seized it because it was new, as did architects and industrial designers, who saw it as a minimal statement without design affectation. As in many other text faces, the capital proportions are more varied in width than the lowercase. Zapf has a penchant for As that list gently to the right (Optima's apex is to the right of center) with crossbars that are slightly below center. The M is splayed; there is the slightest, most subtle reverse curve as a thin stroke departs from the vertical stem to form the bowls of the B, D, P, and R. Curved forms maintain a generous weight before they diminish into thin

¶åbcdèfghijklmnö
pqrstúvwxyz&ß
»[(.,:;?!£$¢¥ƒ*§#†)]«
ABCDEFG
HIJKLMNOPQRST
UVWXYZÆŒØ
@1234567890%

Optima—Hermann Zapf
Neu-Antiqua (New Roman)
Linotype Library GmbH, Eschborn/Frankfurt, Germany
(Produced originally by Stempel Typefoundry, 1954)

strokes, and because of Zapf's skillful drawing, this gives an even color to the font without producing a square-shouldered letter. Bowl counters are near-symmetrical ovals without a trace of corner as they join to the vertical stems. Instead of the teardrop terminals of classic forms, Zapf employs calligraphic stroke endings that begin thin and then widen immediately, terminating with a diagonal, adding more life to the forms. Both the **a** and the **t**, unlike most nineteenth-century grotesques that end with ungainly stumps, have graceful, meaningful tails. Perhaps the most subtle nuance of the original metal type is the fit, that magical relationship between the weight of the font, its natural proportion, and the amount of space that envelops each character. The fit is designed to balance the counters and the space between them—down to the smallest legible size.

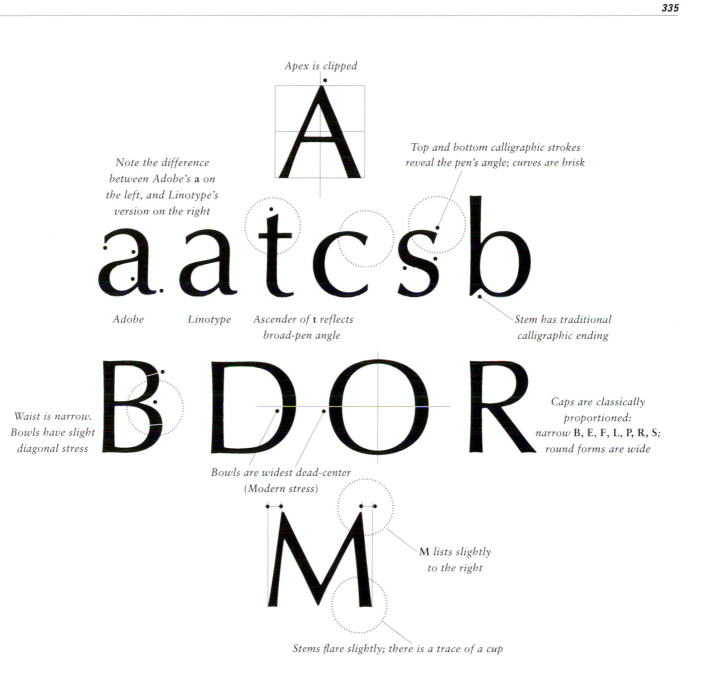

Apex is clipped

Note the difference between Adobe's **a** on the left, and Linotype's version on the right

Top and bottom calligraphic strokes reveal the pen's angle; curves are brisk

Adobe   Linotype   Ascender of **t** reflects broad-pen angle

Stem has traditional calligraphic ending

Waist is narrow. Bowls have slight diagonal stress

Caps are classically proportioned: narrow B, E, F, L, P, R, S; round forms are wide

Bowls are widest dead-center (Modern stress)

M lists slightly to the right

Stems flare slightly; there is a trace of a cup

Optima, a font of two-weight contrast, is drawn with subtleties. The premise is a seriless roman, or, as Zapf describes it as "alternating weights of stroke." Designed to accompany the Palatino, and Melior group, Optima was inspired by incised lettering on the arch of Constantine (A.D. 315), gravestones in Santa Croce in Florence, and examples in the Laurentian and Vatican Libraries. The font was designed to avoid the problem of small, sans serif metal types in long print-runs in which the corners erode and become rounded. Optima's stems were widened top and bottom to offset this. Above 14-point, the ratio of x-height-to-ascender/descender length is based on the Golden Section.

Stephenson Blake's Palace Script is a generic face based on late nineteenth-century scripts. Many of its letters are almost identical to other fonts: Bank Script, Royal Script, and Typo Script. The font has a small x-height, tall ascenders, and even taller caps.

As noted in Script Letters, formal scripts are often used for announcements and invitations, and in smaller sizes for calling cards. Fine jewelers offer a wide range of scripts for social stationery, which are traditionally (correctly) steel-die-engraved and embossed on fine papers.

Palace Script has a ratio of 3:1 cap-to-x-height and the letters have simplified shapes. Though small enclosed loops tend to fill in with letterpress printing, the *F* in both versions ends with a minute loop to the crossbar, and the lowercase *f* is equally fussy; hairlines of the

336

Note the D's different loops

ABCDEFGHIJKLMNOP
QRSTUVWXYZ
abcdefghijklmnopqrstuvwxyz

Palace Script—Stephenson Blake, 1923

ABCDEFGHIJKLMNOPQRST
UVWXYZ abcdefghijklmnopqrstuvwxyz 12345

Palace Script—Monotype, 1923

Lowercase scripts usually have a wide fit for ease of reading in small sizes. The f, g, and y are looped. Some turns at the baseline are rather pointed

Palace Script (digital)—Monotype / Adobe, 1992

O, P, and Q skirt dangerously close to the downstroke stems. The congested style of the *M* dates back to Bickham's *Universal Penman*.

The initial ogee swelling strokes of the *B*, *D*, *P*, and *R* begin at different heights and curve differently.

Only three basic swash shapes are used: a hanging loop found on the *B*, *D*, *P*, *Q*, *R*, *T*, *X*, and *Y*; a second group of generous sweeping loops: *C*, *G*, *L*, and *S*; and a third group of reverse curve swashes used on the *H*, *V*, *W*, and *Z*. A round terminal is used on the *A*, *B*, *F*, *G*, *I*, *K*, *M*,

N, *S*, *T*, and *Y*. The *s* is excessively wide and the *t*'s crossbar is too stingy. The *h*, *n*, and *p* are drawn with the same ogee swelling stem. Monotype's version of Palace is similar to Stephenson Blake's, but compare the former's simplified *D* hanging loop and the capital *Q* .

HANGING LOOPS

Hanging loops are recurring elements modified to fit individual letters. H, K, V, W, and Z share a common design trait. But note that only the D has a weighted loop

Sweeping loops are commonly found on many formal scripts and their widths may vary

SWEEPING LOOPS

Caps are more than three times the x-height

Ball terminals occur in many formal scripts, and may be traced back to Bickham

REVERSE CURVE SWASHES

Reverse curve, the third group of swashes used to create the cap's secondary strokes

■

Palace Script is one of the faces based on formal script styles popular in the late nineteenth century, known as

English roundhands. They are typified by small x-heights, tall ascenders with a minimum number of loops, and even

taller caps. Some fonts came with different size lowercase. The design style is simple, only a few letters show fussy loops.

FONT SAMPLER

Palatino is named after a six-teenth-century Italian writing master, Giovambattista Palatino; one of the famous trio of Renaissance scribes that included Arrighi and Tagliente—each of whom wrote a writing book.[1]

Hermann Zapf designed the font first as a display face, and later for the type-setting machine with a wider italic to match the width of the roman. A lighter version of Palatino, called Aldus Buchschrift, was designed a few years later, as a book face. Originally, the thins and open counters were designed to meet high-speed printing requirements.

Michelangelo, a light classic titling roman, and Sistina, its bolder sister face, make up the Palatino display family.[2] All four faces clearly show the influence of broad-pen writing. This is evident in Palatino's lowercase italic, with its angular beginning stems and endings that flick upwards and

ABCDEFGHIJKLM
NOPQRSTUVWXYZ
abcdefghijklmnopqrstuvwxyz
1234567890 1234567890

ABCDEFGHIJKLM
NOPQRSTUVWXYZ
abcdefghijklmnopqrstuvwxyz
1234567890 1234567890

ABCDEFGHIJKLMN
OPQRSTUVWXYZ&

Palatino—Hermann Zapf, Stempel, 1948
Linotype Library GmbH, Eschborn / Frankfurt, Germany

point to the next letter. The italic bowls angle away from the stems: *a*, *b*, *d*, *p*, and *q*. Return strokes are clearly defined at the top of the *a* and *b*, and at the bottoms of the *d* and *p*. Bowls of the lowercase roman recall the broad-pen as it departs from a stem with a straight line that quickly turns to enclose a counter. Instead of a teardrop terminal, a return stroke repeats on the top stroke of *f* and *r*; the stem of the *t* is high, and its short crossbar is pointed and angular on the left side, again revealing the pen's angle. The *E* and *F* are narrow, and only the top of the *C* wears a serif; the *Y*'s right diagonal is unadorned; and the hand-set version *A*'s crossbar is high. The bowls of *R* and *P* are open. As in many calligraphic faces, the flicks and master turns of the pen add crispness to a page of text and lend it vitality.

1. A. F. Johnson and Oscar Ogg. *Three Classics of Italian Calligraphy* (New York: Dover Publications, 1953).

2. Hermann Zapf, *About Alphabets* (Cambridge, Massachusetts: The M.I.T. Press, 1960), pages 27–35.

Bowls reflect the approximate 30-degree angle of the broad-pen as they join the straight stems. Stem is footed

Beginning stroke of the t and the left-side of the crossbar strongly reflect the broad-pen's shape

Upper parts of the f and r have calligraphic endings

C's left curved stroke is widest below center; beak is bracketed, and terminal stroke is angled

Y's beginning stroke has a diagonal serif and the right thin stroke is bare. Left side of A gently widens near the baseline

Vertical serifs have minimum brackets, though the arm widens to create mass

Bowls of P and R are open and curved stems are widest above center

■
Palatino was designed first as a display face. The Linotype Aldus version required matching the width of the italic to the wider roman. Shown is the Adobe digital version based on Aldus. A beautiful set of swash caps accompanies the handset italic (opposite, bottom).

FONT SAMPLER

John Dreyfus relates that in 1928 Van Krimpen designed Romanée to match a 1768 Enschedé italic, Kleine Text Roman No. 2, attributed to Christoffel van Dijck (1601–1672). Unhappy with the italic, Van Krimpen had P. H. Rädisch recut it twenty years later, following an entirely new design.[1] Romanée's italic is similar to the narrowly proportioned Aldine with its minimal slant. The roman is wide and full, an artistic trait of many of Van Krimpen's designs. (Critics have haggled over the wide/narrow roman/italic concept.)

At Stanley Morison's suggestion, Van Krimpen drew the Romulus oblique with the same proportion as the roman (*see page 92*). In the Aldine fashion, caps for the italic are roman upright, with a set of roman swash caps, which Van Krimpen seemed to favor in much of his

ABCDEFGHIJKLMNOPQRST
UVWXYZÆŒQUQV&Q
ÄÇÉÈÊËÖÜQu

abcdefghijklmnopqrstuvwxyz
æctfbffffiffifflfhfifkflijßœ

*†‡§-'""[(áàâäçéèêëíìîïóòôöúùûü)]"'—,.;:!?

1234567890

ABCDEFGHIJKLLMNQR
STUVWXY&Z

abcdefghijklmnopqrstuvwxy&z
æfbffffiffifflfhfifjfkflijßœ

,;:[(áàâäçéèêëíìîïóòôöúùûü)]!?

1234567890

ABCDEFGHIJKLMNOPQRSTUVWXYZ
ÆŒÂÄÇÉÈÊËÖÜQUQV

Romanée—Jan van Krimpen, Enschedé, 1928;
the italic was redrawn in 1949
(enlarged)

work—he was greatly influenced by early Italian writing masters. When the swashes are used sparingly with the roman, the effect is special, elegant and stately. The roman has many qualities of the Venetians: the **a** is particularly beautiful, and the **g**, with its large bowl and tight, connecting turn that begins the loop, is successful. The poorly balanced **g** can be a repetitive cripple in a page of text. The tall **A** follows the original italic; there is an exuberant long-tailed **Q**; the **R** seems perfectly balanced; the **E** and **F** are are narrower than Van Krimpen's usual style. Accents are long and lightly drawn. Ascenders and descenders are classically generous, and the italic *f* is memorably beautiful, though the repose of the italic **Z** is precarious. The fit is remarkable.

Van Krimpen had a fondness for swash caps; he drew some for Lutetia, some unpublished ones for Spectrum, and a cornucopia of them for Cancelleresca Bastarda, a member of the Romulus family designed expressly to set poetry, consisting of 210 characters (*see* pages 302–03).

1. John Dreyfus, *The Work of Jan van Krimpen*, pages 31–33.

341

---

*The tall **A** mimics the original italic that served as a model for the roman*

*Top curve of **a** is drawn in the manner of Jenson and the Venetians. Tail has a strong calligraphic ending stroke. Bowl of the **g** is generous and the tail more so*

ag ABC

*Alternate **Q**'s tail sweeps under the **u**; the two are cut on one piece of metal*

QURST

*Balance of **R** is good. The **S** refers to Garamond, and the vertical serifs of the **T** are pronounced*

EF

*E and **F** are narrow with heavily weighted arms*

Accents are unusually tall, though light and elegant

áàâäçéèêëíìîïóòô

*f is an oblique form instead of the usual Aldine or chancery form that curves to the left at bottom and often is tipped with a teardrop kern. Ascenders and descenders are long, and the **g**'s tail is closed*

fgh f Y & Z

Haarlemmer italic chancery form

Romanée has no italic caps, only a regular set of roman and an elaborate set of swash caps. This setting is from a beautiful Romanee type specimen sheet, hand-composed and printed by Charles Whitehouse, Zurich, Switzerland.

(greatly enlarged)

FONT SAMPLER

Square serif is another name for the Egyptians, a type style popular in the early eighteenth century, so named after the interest generated by Napolean's forays into Egypt.[1] Bolder versions are known as slab serifs. The style was available in a wide number of weights and proportions, *e.g.*, Hellenic wide and Antique Expanded (Egyptian Expanded). Serifs of early versions were unbracketed; by mid-century the bracketed Clarendons arrived. Most foundries have a version: Consort, Cairo, Memphis, Stymie, Karnak, Beton, and Graph. Slab serifs were prompted by advertising demands, and accomplished by merely adding weight to generic serif letters. Proportions are usually even. Instead of an italic, an oblique was paired with the roman. The weight distribution in the lighter weights is monotone. As the family expanded with other weights, the letters

ABCDEFGHIJKLM
NOPQRSTUVWXYZ
abcdefghijklmnopqrstuvwxyz
!@#$%^&*()+[]{};:" "'?/
1234567890

ABCDEFGHIJKLM
NOPQRSTUVWXYZ
abcdefghijklmnopqrstuvwxyz
!@#$%^&()+[]{};:" "'?/*
1234567890

Serifa 55 and 56—Adrian Frutiger, Bauersche Gießerei, Fundición Tipográfica Neufville S. A., 1968

assumed a two-weight structure. Adrian Frutiger's Serifa is numbered in the same manner as his Univers and Frutiger, except here the light weight begins with a pencil-thin number 35, progresses 36, 45, 46, 55, 56, 65, 75, and then skips to the 67 bold condensed. Frutiger's beautiful style of drawing is apparent in the well-constructed footed lowercase **a**. The *t* has a tail (Stymie and Karnak use a foot); branches roll into a straight stem without a trace of a corner or flat spot. Instead of the usual bowl and ear for the **g**, the typical **b, d, p,** and **q** bowl is used. The cap **K** has a narrow waist, the lowercase a supporting diagonal. Serifa's x-height is generous, which produces small proportioned caps. In the 72-point size the ratio is almost 3:4. The tail of the **R** is similar to Frutiger, and departs from the stem and bowl with a radius. The round forms are squarish, almost like Univers. Diagonal letters are troublesome: Serifa's are a generous width so that the counter's white space may be forced between the stems for even color.

1. Alexander Lawson: *Anatomy of a Typeface*, pages 310–11.

The **a** is footed, **t** is not

Serifa

*Stymie
(foundry type)*

A large bowl is used
for the **g**, instead of the
usual small bowl and loop
of traditional serif faces

x-height is large

K's waist is v-shaped in
the cap version;
bottom diagonal of
lowercase supports
top diagonal

Diagonal tail
departs with a curve,
as in Universe
and Frutiger

Universe   Frutiger   Serifa

Round forms are
square-shouldered.
There is careful thinning of
the curves as they roll to
join straight strokes

Diagonal letters are
wide with counter points
that almost divide the
converged diagonals

Punctuation
and dots of the **i** and **j**
are square

Square serifs or Egyptians are mono-tone in their light and regular weights. Bolder, extended, or condensed forms by necessity are drawn with two weights. By mid-nineteenth century, the fashion was to bracket the serifs, and the Clarendons were born.

Hellenic Wide, Bauer (nineteenth century)

Expanded Antique, Stevens & Shanks, c. 1880

Walter Tracy relates in detail Times Roman's genesis in his excellent book *Letters of Credit.*[1] In 1932 Stanley Morison wanted to design a legible font for The *Times* newspaper of London. He did not foresee that the font would one day be *the* generic serif face and a resident printer font for the majority of the world's computer printers. Tracy suggests that Plantin, designed by F. H. Pierpont in 1910 for Monotype, was perhaps the basis for the design; then the trail gets murky. At Monotype, Victor Lardent, working from Plantin, did some drawings that reduced the thins and sharpened the serifs. (A reproduction of a font used by Plantin in 1582, while crude, is similar to Caslon.[2]) Tracy says, "To my eye Times Roman lacks the insignia of true creation; it is too much the re-working of some thing else, the Plantin type." What Morison, Lardent, and Monotype

344

ABCDEFGHIJKLM
NOPQRSTUVWXYZ
abcdefghijklmnopqrstuvwxyz
!@#$%^&*()+[]{};:""''?/
1234567890

ABCDEFGHIJKLM
NOPQRSTUVWXYZ
abcdefghijklmnopqrstuvwxyz
!@#$%^&( )+[ ]{};:""''?/*
1234567890

Times New Roman—Stanley Morison and Victor Lardent, 1932
(Monotype/Adobe, 1988)

did produce was a middle-of-the-road design, with a few distinctive characters and an overriding trait: a three-weight letter with distinctly different stems, thins, serifs, and a large x-height. The sharpened serifs were an attempt to overcome problems in stereotyping, where asbestos molds made from locked-up type forms were used to cast cylindrical printing plates.

There are countless types with character shapes that relate to Times. Carefully spaced, the caps are handsome, their proportions are good, and the brilliant sharpened serifs add sparkle.

The **g** is distinctive with its abruptly turning tail, and its straight ear and bowl with Oldstyle stress; the cap **O** has vertical stress; and **b** is spurless. Serifs of the digital version are chopped also, and thins have been weighted.

1. Walter Tracy, *Letters of Credit*, (Boston, Massachusetts: David R. Godine, 1986), pages 194–210.

2. D.B. Updike, *Printing Types: Their History, Forms, and Use*, vol. 11, page 15.

*Original Monotype version of **a** has tail and serif ending with a slender tail; teardrop terminal is smaller and elongated.*

a m

Branch joins deeply

Serifs are crisply bracketed; (72-point enlarged)

*Digital **a** version's tail is chopped; thins are heavier. Proportion of digital font version is wider*

a m

(100-point)

Serif tips are chopped

*Top serifs of **u** are horizontal, **b, d, i, j, m, n, p,** and **r** are triangular*

*Stress of lowercase **o** is diagonal (Oldstyle); cap **O** is vertical (Modern)*

*Lowercase **o** diagonal*

x-height is large

bcdunoOg

*Ear of **g** is horizontal; tail turns abruptly twice*

ABCDEFGHIJKLMNOPQRSTUVWXYZ
abcdefghijklmnopqrstuvwxyz

Plantin—F. H. Pierpont, Monotype, 1910

Times New Roman was cut by Monotype for exclusive use by The Times *newspaper in 1931 (whence* Times *"New" Roman). The face has been the most widely used font in the world, and there are thousands of special characters designed for it. Some type foundries have drawn their own versions, which differ slightly from Monotype's original drawing. The font is three-weight: stem, thins and even finer tipped serifs; its x-height is large, and the caps when carefully spaced are superb. Italic **z** retains calligraphic distribution of weight: the horizontal is weighted, diagonal is thin, and bottom stroke is a swash, tipped with a kern terminal.*

With Trajan, this font sampler comes full circle from Arrighi; both were drawn in homage to the roman letter.

The incised letters that appear in a nine-foot-long inscription at the base of the Trajan Column in the heart of Rome commemorate the Emperor Trajan's deeds. The letters continue to fascinate typophiles, and numerous treatises have been written about it. Edward Catich, a scholar and highly acclaimed sculptor of letters, showed that a cast in the Albert and Victoria Museum made from the plaque (which had served as the basis for many scholarly writings) was flawed and distorted. Earlier, Frederic Goudy, impressed with the forms, drew his version of the letters in a handsome volume of his design.[1]

The letters and plaque of the column are rendered with exquisite subtlety and nuance, rarely ob-

ABCDEFGHIJKLM

Trajan—Carol Twombly, Adobe Systems, 1989

■

A detail from the Trajan Column in Rome (c.A.D.113) that commemorates the Emperor's deeds, and is one of the most exalted examples of the incised roman letter. Numerous fonts are based on its forms and a famous cast is in the Victoria and Albert Museum in London.

Photo by James Mosley. An Atlas of Typeforms, by James Sutton and Alan Bartram, London: from Percy Lund, Humphries & Co Ltd. London: 1968.

served in our present fast-food world. There are four lines of caps, and because the plaque is 15 feet above the viewer, the artist compensated for perspective by drawing each line, and the three spaces between the lines progressively larger to the top line to offset the normal perspective reduction, making all of the lines appear to be the same height, and the line spacing equal.

Carol Twombly's drawing of Trajan is beautiful. The eternal qualities are still there: pure calligraphic distribution of weights; elegant cupped, tapering serifs; and wide, opulent round forms with diagonal stress. The **E** and **F** are decidedly narrow; the diagonal stroke joins are pointed; **P** and **R**'s bowls are open, and the **Q**'s tail is drawn in a bravura sweep.

1. Frederic Goudy, *The Capitals from the Trajan Column at Rome.*

NOPQRSTVWXYZ

Photo: James Mosley

Adrian Frutiger said that letters stripped of serifs are difficult to space properly. To make up for this loss, he drew the round letters of Univers with more shoulder to help fill the space vacated by serifs of the flanked letters. He also gave Univers an open fit, that is, a generous space around each letter called sidebearings. A font is made legible by its interior space and letter weight that is carefully balanced with its surrounding space. This ratio is not fixed, and varies in sizes from 6- to 14-point and larger. Generally, as letters become smaller, their proportion and letterspacing needs to be increased for the sake of legibility and to properly balance with larger sizes so that they will appear to be the same visual weight and proportion— no easy task. (MultipleMaster fonts have made this refinement possible, a task that previously required endless hours to

348

ABCDEFGHIJKLM NOPQRSTUVWXYZ abcdefghijklmnopqrstuvwxyz !@#$%^&*()+[]{};:""''?/ 1234567890

Univers 65—Adrian Frutiger, Deberny Peignot, 1957

ABCDEFGHIJKLM NOPQRSTUVWXYZ abcdefghijklmnopqrstuvwxyz !@#$%^&()+[]{};:""''?/ 1234567890*

Univers 66—Adrian Frutiger, Deberny Peignot, 1957

achieve in the design of metal typeface families.)

Univers was one of the first well-ordered families. The 22 different weights and proportions are carefully organized from light to extra bold, condensed to expanded. In the original metal fonts, Frutiger bowed the vertical and diagonal connecting stems in efforts to reduce mass (*top right below*). This forced white space between the stems, which he blunted to prevent filling. The solution was superb at small sizes, but ungainly when enlarged to generous display sizes. Univers' proportions are mostly even; the **M**, **N**, **V**, and **W** are wide, and there is a slight two-weight quality in the medium to bold weights. The **G** and **R** are distinguished, and I have always admired the **a** and **s** drawings. The branches, **h**, **m**, **n**, and **u**, are drawn with a curve that is almost symmetrical.

For a more even
distribution of weight,
letters with diagonal
stems are wide

Diagonal stems of the
metal fonts curve to
let more air between the
strokes' convergence

*48-point Univers 75
(foundry type, enlarged)*

G's bottom curve
is shallow, and the
R's tail has a
gentle ogee curve

With its right-angle
top join, the **a**'s bowl
is distinctively Frutiger,
and the **s** is balanced
and well drawn.
Curved stem endings
are horizontal

Diagonal joins
barely overlap

Bowls are drawn with
generous shoulders to
compensate for the loss
of serifs, so that
the type colors evenly

Stem curves away from
bowl join to avoid massing

Branch counter of the original
metal type is almost symmetrical;
wider and less bold than
the digital version

Vertical stems
are thinned at branch
joinings to avoid
congestion

*48-point Univers 65
metal type* **h**
(enlarged)

■

Opposite—The normal bold proportion of Univers, Adrian Frutiger's monument that originally included 22 separate weights and proportions. A new family designed by Frutiger contains a staggering array of 58 weights and proportions. Originally conceived with a wider fit than Helvetica, the font is notable for its squarish round forms, which Frutiger says makes up for the loss of serifs.

FONT SAMPLER

Scangraphic used the original metal Palatino as a model to create a digital version. Zapf persuaded the company to discard the effort and create a new interpretation of Palatino with hairline weights and descender proportions not based on metal technology. Zapf named the new family Renaissance Antiqua, though the family is marketed under the name Zapf Renaissance.

The swash italic version is unusually spirited and expressive. The roman caps are more evenly proportioned than Palatino, and there is more modeling, that is, the shapes are smoother. It is a slightly lighter weight created by finer thin strokes. The bowls are more rounded, with fewer flat planes created by the broad-pen. The **a** has a much wider bowl, and beaks of the **C, G, S,** and **T** are sharper and bolder. The caps are not as tall as Palatino, and the **S** has a smaller top counter;

ABCDEFGHIJKLMNOPQRSTUVWXYZ

abcdefghijklmnopqrstuvwx yz.,;:'""!?/1234567890 @ # $ % & * ( ) [ ]

abcdefghijklmnopqrstuvwxyz .,;:'""!?/1234567890

¡™ £ ¢ § ¶ • ªº – œ ´ ® † ¥ ¨ ø '' å ß ƒ © ˙ °¬ … æ ç ˜µ ÷ ` « »

/ ¤ ◊ fi fl ‡ ° · , — ± Œ „ ´ ‰ ˇÁ '"ÅÍÎ Ï ˝ÓÔÒÚÆÇ ˜Â˘¿

ABCDEFGHIJKLMNOPQRSTUVWXYZ

abcdefghijklmnopqrstuvwxyz.,;:'""!?/1234567890 @#$% & *( ) [ ]

abcdefghijklmnopqrstuvwxyz.,;:'""!?/1234567890

¡™ £ ¢ §¶• ªº – œ ´® † ¥ ¨ ø '' å ß ƒ © ˙ °¬…æ ç ˜µ ÷ `«»

/ ¤ ◊ fi fl ‡ ° · , — ± Œ „ ´ ‰ ˇÁ '"ÅÍÎ Ï ˝ÓÔÒÚÆÇ ˜Â˘¿

Zapf Renaissance book—Hermann Zapf, Scangraphic, Dr Böger GmbH (roman 1984, italic 1984)

AABCDEEFGGHIJKLLMNOPQRSTThUVWXYZ&

a bcde e e f f ff ffiffigh ijkl ll mm n oppqur's sps t t t u v v wxyz

1234567890 [ ] # ❦ ❧ ✿ ❀ ❦ ¶ ¶ ¶ ¶ ¶

∂ µ ª º ™ ® © @ ¥

¬ … ÷ # ^ _ + { } " < > ~ |

Zapf Renaissance Swash book—Hermann Zapf
Scangraphic, Dr. Böger GmbH, 1985

Palatino's **S** top and bottom curves are almost equal. In the swash font, only the caps **C**, **I**, and **L** are without swashes. Some are exuberant: **G**, **K**, and **R**. In the manner of Jan van Krimpen's Cancelleresca Bastarda, there are lowercase terminal letters with generous, sweeping tails **a**, **e**, **m**, **n**, **st**, **r**, and **t**; the loop of the **g** is open. In most English spellings, the **q** is followed by the **u**. Here they are joined and thus are a ligature, shapes designed to overcome misspacings within a font. The **ff** ligature has a truly original shape that joins the two troublesome letters with great flair. And to make the skilled typographer happy, Zapf has drawn a few swash-beginning letters, **u**, **v**, and **w**, all with ample curves to introduce a hand-drawn look to the font. To dress up some text, or to separate lines of text, there are four distinctive fleurons; the fleur-de-lis is beautiful.

Zapf Renaissance is a tour de force by the master calligrapher and type designer of our time.

*Hairlines are lighter than Palatino. Top curve of **a** is more narrow*

Renaissance   Palatino

Smoother shapes and less evidence of the broad-pen's edge; serifs are more pointed

Renaissance

Palatino

Renaissance

Many of Renaissance's proportions are more narrow than Palatino

Palatino

Swash strokes are beautiful, and the beginning and terminal swash letters are inventive shapes

Zapf Renaissance Book and Swash Book

There isn't room to display the following fonts as double spreads, yet to show as many different styles as possible, I've set these at a smaller size with brief comments about each font. Only the caps, lowercase, figures, and punctuation, are shown.

Aachen is quintessentially an Egyptian display font, its stubby serifs, and narrow proportions are ideal for snug spacing when space is a premium. **Albertus** is a sturdy roman with classic proportions, distinguished by an airy **M. Banco** is one of many distinctive designs from Excoffon,

a master of style; Calypso and Olive Antique are from his hand. **Bernhard Tango**, a favorite, is a social printing face with elaborate swash caps. **Berkeley** is based on Frederic Goudy's 1938 University of California Oldstyle, which is also known as Californian. Heinrich Jost

was type director at Bauer for many years and was responsible for the popular Bauer Bodoni. His **Beton** is a bold Egyptian that comes in a range of weights; the y descender has an unusual serif. **Bodoni black condensed** is ideal for tight settings. William Martin apprenticed to John Baskerville

---

Aachen Bold—Colin Brignall, Letraset, 1969

ABCDEFGHIJKLMNOPQRSTVWXYZ abcdefghijklmop qrstuvwxyz.,:'""!?/1234567890$%&*() [ ]

Albertus—Berthold Wolpe, Monotype, 1932–40

ABCDEFGHIJKLMNOPQRSTUVWXYZ abcdefghijklmo pqrstuvwxyz.,;:' ""!?/1234567890@ #$% ^ &*() []

Banco—Roger Excoffon, Olive, 1951

ABCDEFGHIJKLMNOPQRSTUVWXYZ .,;:'""!?/1234567890$%&*() [ ]

Bernhard Tango—Lucian Bernhard, ATF, 1931

ABCDEFGHIJKLMNOPQRSTUVWXYZ abcdefghijkl mnopqrstuvwxyz.,;:'""!?/1234567890 @#$% ^ &*() [ ]

ITC Berkeley Oldstyle (Californian—Frederic Goudy, University of California, 1938)—Tony Stan, ITC, 1983

ABCDEFGHIJKLMNOPQRSTUVWXYZabcdefghijklmnop qrstuvwxyz.,;:'""!?/1234567890 @#$% &*() []
ABCDEFGHIJKLMNOPQRSTUVWXYZ abcdefghijklmnopqrs tuvwxyz.,;:'""!?/1234567890 @#$% &*() []

Beton extra bold—Heinrich Jost, Bauer, 1931–36

ABCDEFGHIJKLMNOPQRSTUVWXYZabcdefghijk lmnopqrstuvwxyz.,;:'""!?/1234567890 @#$%&*() []

and his **Bulmer** types reveal Baskerville's influence; Martin's Transitional forms are more narrow and lighter weight. The italic caps are drawn with three beautiful swashes: *K, N,* and *T.* Of special note is the beautiful Q with a secondary weight and an opulent tail. The italic am-persand is one of the most beautiful in all of typography. The font's hairlines are lighter than the serifs, and the italic is almost an exact copy of Baskerville's forms. In addition to designing **Cheltenham**, Bertram Goodhue was the architect of the Caltech campus. Cheltenham has been one of the most widely used fonts of the twentieth century. The *New York Times Magazine* uses a redrawn version for its headings. Slab serif is a generic name for the **Clarendons** and Egyptians first designed for dictionaries. Serifs of the Clarendons are usually bracketed. Nicolas **Cochin** was court engraver to Louis XV, and Mme. Pompador was his patron.[1] The Oldstyle font is based on his engraving titles. The italic is semi-script.

1. Ron Eason and Sarah Rookledge, *Rookledge's International Directory of Type Designers,* additions by Boyd Hill (New York: The Sarabande Press. 1994).

Bodoni black condensed—Heinrich Jost, Bauer, 1926

ABCDEFGHIJKLMNOPQRSTUVWXYZ abcdefghijklmnopqr stuvwxyz.,;:'""!?/1234567890 @#$% &*( ) [ ]

Bulmer—William Martin c. 1790; Morris Fuller Benton, ATF, 1925–26

ABCDEFGHIJKLMNOPQRSTUVWXYZ abcdefghijklmn opqrstuvwxyz.,;:'""!?/1234567890@#$%&*()[] *ABCDEF GHIJKLMNOPQRSTUVWXYZ abcdefghijklmnopqrstuvwxyz.,;:' ""!?/1234567890@#$%&*()[]*

ITC Cheltenham—Tony Stan, 1975; Cheltenham bold—Bertram Goodhue & Ingalls Kimball, ATF, 1896

ABCDEFGHIJKLMNOPQRSTUVWXYZ abcdefghijklmnopqrstu vwxyz . , ; : ' " " ! ?/ 1234567890 @ #$ & *( ) [ ]

Clarendon bold (Craw Clarendon)—Freeman Craw, ATF, 1955; Besley & Co., 1845

ABCDEFGHIJKLMNOPQRSTUVWXYZ abcdefghijklm nopqrstuvwxyz . , ; : ' " " ! ?/ 1234567890 @ #$ & *( ) [ ]

Cochin—Nicolas Cochin (Moreau-le-jeune) c. 1760; Deberny & Peignot, 1915

ABCDEFGHIJKLMNOPQRSTUVWXYZ abcdefghijklm nopqrstuvwxyz . , ; : ' " " !?/ 1234567890 @ #$ % & *( ) [ ] *ABCDEFGHIJKLMNOPQRSTUVWXYZ abcdefghijklmnopqrstu vwxyz . , ; : ' " " !?/ 1234567890 @ #$% &*( ) [ ]*

Corvinus Skyline, a flat-sided Modern, is also available in wider proportions, and notable for its fine vertical serifs on both the caps and the lowercase. It is named for a fifteenth-century Hungarian king; the word is also Latin for "crow." **Dorchester** is a Modern italic/script. The lowercase is not connected in the manner of scripts, though its forms are distinctly script-like, evidenced by the looped ascenders and descenders. It references one of Bodoni's fanciful cap fonts with its romantic ringlets; a pure social printer's font. The figures are small to complement the lower-case. Named after the great jazz band leader/composer, (Duke) **Ellington**, is more narrow than Melior, but is more calligraphic, with greater thick and thin stem contrast. The vertical stems flare in the manner of Diotima. **Empire** emulates 1930s skyscrapers, and was originally a titling face. This digital version has a lowercase. **Eras** is a highly successful French sans contribution that uses the classical proportions of the 1920s German sans, though its round forms are squarish. The **M** is splayed; the **P**, **R**, and **a** are open, a distraction. Aldo Novarese was one of the twentieth century's

Corvinus Skyline—Imre Reiner, Bauer, 1929–34

ABCDEFGHIJKLMNOPQRSTUVWXYZ abcdefghijklmnopqrstuvwxyz
.,;:'""!?/ 1234567890 @#$ &*() [ ]

Dorchester Script—Monotype, 1938

ABCDEFGHIJKLMNOPQRSTUVWXYZ
abcdefghijklmnopqrstuvwxyz .,;:'""!?/ 1234567890 #$% &*() [ ]

Ellington—Michael Harvey, Monotype, 1990

ABCDEFGHIJKLMNOPQRSTUVWXYZ abcdefghijklmnopqrstu
vwxyz .,;:'""!?/1234567890 @#$% &*() [ ]

Empire—Morris Fuller Benton, ATF, 1937; Digital version by David Berlow/Roger Black, The Font Bureau 1989–90

ABCDEFGHIJKLMNOPQRSTUVWXYZ abcdefghijklmnopqrstuvwxyz
.,;:'""!?/ 1234567890 @#$% &*() [ ]

ITC Eras medium—Albert Boton/Albert Hollenstein, ITC, 1976

ABCDEFGHIJKLMNOPQRSTUVWXYZ abcdefghijklmnopqrstuv
wxyz .,;:'""!?/1234567890 @#$% &*() []

ITC Eras bold—Albert Boton / Albert Hollenstein, ITC, 1976

ABCDEFGHIJKLMNOPQRSTUVWXYZ abcdefghijklmno
pqrstuvwxyz .,;:'""!?/1234567890 @#$% &*() [ ]

great font designers, and his drawing of **Fenice**, a Modern, references beaks of Cochin and Perpetua. Its x-height is generous at the expense of both the ascenders and descenders. Arms of the **T** have been shortened to color more evenly; the **H** is narrow, the **S** wide, and tips of the **V** and **W** are clipped. The **g** is ungainly with its crouching, aggressive, forward thrust. **Franklin Gothic extra condensed** remains one of the most legible of all condensed sans fonts primarily because the bowls and round forms have retained their roundness, unlike the narrow, flat sides of the condensed Helveticas. Its figure **1** has serifs to fill its en-width. **Frutiger**, one of my favorite sans serifs, a face designed expressly for Paris's DeGaulle airport signage, is numbered like the designer's Univers: 45, 55, 65 are normal proportions, but are progressively heavier. Numbers 46, 56, and 66 are italics, and 47, 57, and 67 are the corresponding condensed versions. The terminal endings are vertical and admit generous white space that keeps the letter legible. The fonts displayed below show the consistent clarity of Frutiger's design.

ITC Fenice—Aldo Novarese, ITC, 1980

ABCDEFGHIJKLMNOPQRSTUVWXYZ abcdefghijklmnopqrstuvwxyz
.,;:'""!?/1234567890 @#$% &*() []

*ABCDEFGHIJKLMNOPQRSTUVWXYZ abcdefghijklmnopqrstuvwxyz
.,;:'""!?/1234567890 @#$% &*() []*

Franklin Gothic extra condensed—Morris Benton, ATF, 1906

**ABCDEFGHIJKLMNOPQRSTUVWXYZ abcdefghijklmnopqrstuvwxyz
., ; : ' "" !?/1234567890 @#$% &*() [ ]**

Frutiger 45 & 46—Adrian Frutiger, Stempel, 1976

ABCDEFGHIJKLMNOPQRSTUVWXYZ abcdefghijklmnopqrst
uvwxyz .,;:'" "!?/ 1234567890 @#$% &*() []

*ABCDEFGHIJKLMNOPQRSTUVWXYZ abcdefghijklmnopqrst
uvwxyz .,;:'""!?/ 1234567890@#$% &*() []*

Frutiger 65 & 66—Adrian Frutiger, Stempel, 1976

**ABCDEFGHIJKLMNOPQRSTUVWXYZ abcdefghijklmnopqrst
tuvwxyz .,;:'""!?/1234567890 @#$% &*() []**

***ABCDEFGHIJKLMNOPQRSTUVWXYZ abcdefghijklmnopqrst
uvwxyz .,;:'""!?/1234567890 @#$% &*( ) []***

Frutiger 95—Adrian Frutiger, Stempel, 1976

**ABCDEFGHIJKLMNOPQRSTUVWXYZ
abcdefghijklmnopqrstuvwxyz .,;:'""!?/
1234567890 @#$% &*() []**

The ITC Baskerville that appears thoughout the Serif Letter chapter differs from the **Fry** version below, which was produced by Morris Benton for ATF as hand-set type. It was not drawn by John Baskerville, but by Isaac Moore, his shop foreman.[1] The font is far more delicate than the machine versions that have been the model for many of the digital showings. **Galliard** is a popular text face—Granjon re-examined. **Handel Gothic** has some of the squarish qualities of Eurostile (*see* page 132); in its day it was considered a statement of the ultra-new. **Haarlemmer** is a clasically proportioned sans designed to accompany its serif text face. It is graced with both roman and italic small caps. **Hobo**, despite its bizarre, bowed stems that make the letters appear puffed-up, is a display sans without descenders that has been used continually since its introduction.

De Roos was a prolific Dutch designer; his **Libra**, a semi-uncial, is often used for liturgical works. **Medici Script**, a chancery, was designed for Mergenthaler's 18-unit Linofilmsetter, and its forms have Zapf's hallmark. **Minion's** italic is designed in the tradition of the great fifteenth-century

356

Fry Baskerville—Isaac Moore, 1795; Morris Fuller Benton—ATF, 1915

ABCDEFGHIJKLMNOPQRSTUVWXYZ abcdefghijklmopqrstu vwxyz .,;:'""!?/1234567890 @#$% &*( ) [ ]

ITC Galliard—Matthew Carter, Mergenthaler Linotype, 1978

ABCDEFGHIJKLMNOPQRSVWXYZ abcdefghijklmnopqrstuvwxyz .,;:'""!?/1234567890 @#$% &*( ) [ ]

ABCDEFGHIJKLMNOPQRSVWXYZ abcdefghijklmnopqrstuvwxyz .,;:'""!?/1234567890 @#$% &( )[ ]*

Handel Gothic—Don Handel, VGC, 1965

ABCDEFGHIJKLMNOPQRSVWXYZ abcdefghijklmnopqrstu vwxyz.,;:'""!?/1234567890 @#$% &*( ) [ ]

DTL Haarlemmer Sans regular & regular small caps—Frank Blokland, Dutch Type Library, 1998

ABCDEFGHIJKLMNOPQRSVWXYZ abcdefghijklmnopqrstuvwxyz .,;:'""!?/1234567890 @#$% &*() [ ]ABCDEFGHIJKLMNOPQRSTUVWXYZ

ABCDEFGHIJKLMNOPQRSTVWXYZ *abcdefghijklmnopqrstuvwxyz* .,;:'""!?/1234567890 @#$% &*() [ ]ABCDEFGHIJKLMNOPQRSTUVWXYZ

Hobo—Morris Fuller Benton, ATF, 1910

ABCDEFGHIJKLMNOPQRSTUVWXYZ abcdefghijklmnopqrstu vwxyz .,;:'""!? 1234567890 $% &*( ) [ ]

Libra—S. H. DeRoos, Amsterdam, 1938

abcdefghijklmnopqrstuvwxyz .,;:'""!?/1234567890 #$% &*( ) [ ]

types; compare Arrighi and Bembo. It has found great popularity as a book face. Its caps are restrained and faintly echo Slimbach's Adobe Garamond. In 1908 Morris Benton designed **News Gothic** and McGrew says it was an attempt to update ATF's collection of nineteenth-century gothics. It is considered to be part of the Franklin Gothic family and has been a mainstay in American advertising for many years. Adrian Frutiger has done a recent drawing of it. With its narrow skyscraper forms, **Onyx** is a pure statement of 1930s elegance. It should never be used in great quantity because its proportions hamper legibility. The round forms have been held, except for the bowl of the lowercase **a**. The font is a compressed Modern, derived from Bodoni. **Photina**, designed to harmonize with the Univers series, is a hybrid. It lies between the Oldstyles and Transitional fonts, yet its thins relate to Oldstyles. Instead of teardrops, the terminals are a mixture; some relate to Melior. The beaks are similar to Cochin. It is a highly legible, popular book face.

1. Mac McGrew, *American Metal Typefaces of the Twentieth Century*, page 27.

Medici Script—Hermann Zapf, Mergenthaler Linofilm, 1969

ABCDEFGHIJKLMNOPQRSTUVWXYZ abcdef ghijklmnopqrstuvwxyz.,;:'""!?/1234567890 @#$% &*( ) [ ]

Minion—Robert Slimbach, Adobe Systems, 1990

ABCDEFGHIJKLMNOPQRSTUVWXYZ abcdefghijklmnopqrstuvwxyz .,;:'""!?/1234567890 @#$% &*( ) [ ]

ABCDEFGHIJKLMNOPQRSTUVWXYZ abcdefghijklmnopqrstuvwxyz .,;:'""!?/1234567890 @#$% &( ) [ ]*

News Gothic—Morris Fuller Benton, ATF, 1908

ABCDEFGHIJKLMNOPQRSTUVWXYZ abcdefghijklmnopqrstu vwxyz .,;:'""!?/234567890 @#$% &*( ) [ ]

News Gothic condensed—Morris Fuller Benton, ATF, 1908

ABCDEFGHIJKLMNOPQRSTUVWXYZ abcdefghijklmnopqrstuvwxyz .,;:'""!?/1234567890 @#$% &*( ) [ ]

Onyx—Gerry Powell, ATF, 1937

ABCDEFGHIJKLMNOPQRSTUVWXYZ abcdefghijklmnopqrstuvwxyz .,;:'""!?/1234567890 $ % &* ( ) [ ]

Photina—Jose Mendosa y Almedia, Monotype, 1971

ABCDEFGHIJKLMNOPQRSTUVWXYZ abcdefghijklmnopqrstuvwxyz .,;:'""!?/1234567890 @#$% &*( ) [ ]

ABCDEFGHIJKLMNOPQRSTUVWXYZ abcdefghijklmnopqrstuvwxyz .,;:'""!?/1234567890 @#$% &( ) [ ]*

FONT SAMPLER

Pietra is based on the 5-foot-tall mosaic lettering surrounding the clerestory architrave in St Peter's in Rome. Slimbach's **Poetica** Chancery is a tour de force, a family of twenty-one fonts, one of which has multiple ampersands to satisfy any degree of opulence. A hand-lettered version of **Radiant** is used for the *Vanity Fair* masthead; the font has been associated with fashion. The metal versions were offered in several weights and proportions. **Stone Sans** leans to the classically proportioned German sans of the 1920s, though the italic does not follow their oblique scheme. The diagonal stems end with right angles, the bowls are round, and graceful. The **s** is narrow, the **t** has a tail, the **a** does not. **Tekton** references draftsmen's lettering. It bounces slightly, the round forms are a bit warped, and it has a distinctive hand-drawn quality. Without Monotype's original 18-unit restraints, the ubiquitous **Times Roman's condensed** series is well drawn with even proportions; the bold is an improvement over the original. The family enjoys a wider use than any other font. Hermann Zapf admires the work of Georg Trump; **Trump Mediaeval** is his

358

Pietra—Garrett Boge in collaboration with Paul Shaw, LetterPerfect Design, 1996

ABCDEFGHIJKLMNOPQRSVWXYZ ABCDEFGHIJKLMNOPQRSTU VWXYZ .,;:'""!?/1234567890 @# $%^&*( ) [ ]

Poetica Chancery I—Robert Slimbach, Adobe Systems, 1992

ABCDEFGHIJKLMNOPQRSVWXYZ abcdefghijklmnopqrstuvwxyz .,;:'""!?/1234567890 @#$% ^ & *( ) [ ]

Poetica Chancery II—Robert Slimbach, Adobe Systems, 1992

ABCDEFGHIJKLMNOPQRSVWXYZ abcdefghijklmnopqrstuvwxyz .,;:'""!?/1234567890 @#$% ^ & *( ) [ ]

Radiant—R. H. Middleton, Ludlow, 1938

ABCDEFGHIJKLMNOPQRSTUVWXYZ abcdefghijklmnopqrstuvwxyz .,;:'""!?/1234567890 @#$% &*( ) [ ]

Stone Sans semi bold—Sumner Stone, Adobe Systems, 1980

ABCDEFGHIJKLMNOPQRSTUVWXYZ abcdefghijklmnopqrstuvwx yz.,;:'""!?/1234567890 @#$% &*( ) [ ]

ABCDEFGHIJKLMNOPQRSTUVWXYZ abcdefghijklmnopqrstuvwxyz .,;:'""!?/1234567890 @#$% &*( ) [ ]

Tekton regular—David Siegel, Adobe Systems, 1989–90

ABCDEFGHIJKLMNOPQRSTUVWXYZ abcdefghijklmnopqrstuvwxyz .,;:'""!?/1234567890 @#$% &*( ) [ ]

most famous face. It is a text face, strongly calligraphic though it has a slight mechanical look. Printers like its sturdy thins and crisp sloping serifs. The **M** is splayed, the **K** references Walbaum, the **G** has a minute beard, the figures are wide and clear, particularly in the italics. Its italic ampersand is lively and inventive, and reveals the Latin *et*. **Typo Upright** is calligraphic, though based on a flexible pointed pen instead of the broad-pen. It is beautifully conceived, though the **M** is narrow and doesn't fit the round flowing scheme of the other caps. The **V** and **W** endings seem unnecessarily fussy. The right-hand swashes of the **v** and **w** are beautiful and lively. **Weiss Antiqua**, is a book face designed by Emil Weiss, a book designer, poet, and calligrapher.[1] Antiqua is the German term that distinguishes the roman letter from textura, or blackletter. Its proportions border on the classic; thins are sturdy and serifs are short, **E** and **F** arms are long; the **U** has two weighted stems. There are no serifs on the top of the **M**, nor on the top left and bottom right stems of the **N**.

1. Ron Eason and Sarah Rookledge, *Rookledge's International Directory of Type Designers*, pages 220–21.

Times New Roman condensed—Type Drawing Office staff, Monotype, 1969

ABCDEFGHIJKLMNOPQRSTUVWXYZ abcdefghijklmnopqrstuvwxyz .,;:'""!?/1234567890 @#$%&*()[]

ABCDEFGHIJKLMNOPQRSTUVWXYZ abcdefghijklmnopqrstuvwxyz .,;:'""!?/1234567890 @#$%&()[]*

Times New Roman bold condensed—Type Drawing Office staff, Monotype, 1969

ABCDEFGHIJKLMNOPQRSTUVWXYZ abcdefghijklmnopqrstuvwxyz .,;:'""!?/1234567890 @#$%&*()[]

Trump Mediaeval—Georg Trump, Weber, 1954–60

ABCDEFGHIJKLMNOPQRSTUVWXYZ abcdefghijklmnopqrstuvwxyz .,;:'""!?/1234567890 @#$%&*()[]

ABCDEFGHIJKLMNOPQRSTUVWXYZ abcdefghijklmnopqrstuvwxyz .,;:'""!?/1234567890 @#$%&()[]*

Typo Upright—Morris Fuller Benton, ATF, 1905

ABCDEFGHIJKLMNOPQRSTUVWXYZ abcdefghijklmnopqrstuvwxyz .,;:'""!?/1234567890 @#$%&()[]*

Weiss Antiqua—Emil Rudolf Weiss, Bauer, 1926–31

ABCDEFGHIJKLMNOPQRSTUVWXYZ
abcdefghijklmnopqrstuvwxyz .,;:'""!?/1234567890 @#$%&*()[]
ABCDEFGHIJKLMNOPQRSTUVWXYZ
abcdefghijklmnopqrstuvwxyz .,;:'""!?/1234567890 @#$%&()[]*

A book that talks about type would not be complete if it did not include fleurons, originally small pieces of metal that, when combined and rotated, create magical shapes in the hands of artists. Printers often call them flowers. Depending on their shape, they may be used singly as a finishing touch or to separate blocks of text. Some are used for title-page borders, or hot-foil-stamped in gold or silver on fine bindings. They may be used next to a folio, or as a piece of jewelry on a title page, or for chapter headings. The leaf fleuron was first used to indicate a paragraph beginning in running text. Shown below are different Renaissance fleurons; the pilcrow, familiar as a paragraph mark, is used in the last paragraph.

In the history of printing, fleurons are a carryover from hand-illumination, decorative objects used to embellish text and delight the eye. Some of the earliest fleurons are, to my eye, the most beautiful. Stanley Morison, in the *Fleuron*, observes, "Moreover, these flowers were developed, not merely by the greatest of the type designers themselves, but by those very type designers whose types we even now use or

Vine leaf,
Jean de Tournes
Lyon, 1556
(Monotype 224)

Granjon's acorn,
Robert Granjon
Antwerp, 1570
(Monotype 267)

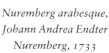

Nuremberg arabesque,
Johann Andrea Endter
Nuremberg, 1733
(Monotype 240)

Louis Luce's sunray,
Imprimerie Royale
Paris, c. 1740
(Monotype 224)

Trattner's angels,
Johann Thomas Trattner
Vienna, 1760
(Monotype 1029)

Fleurons from
Zapf Renaissance
swash, 1985
(Scangraphic)

Two typographical jewels
created by Saul and Lillian Marks for a tribute by
Norman Katkov for Rudi Baumfeld's 70th birthday,
Los Angeles, 1974

Ah, fill the Cup:—what boots it
to repeat
How Time is slipping underneath
our Feet:
Unborn To-morrow and dead
Yesterday,
Why fret about them if To-day
be sweet!

Rubáiyát, XXXVII.

■
Top—*Classic fleurons.*
Above Left—*Elaborate borders composed of multiple pieces of metal.*

Above Right —*Typographical whimsy from the Plantin Press by Saul and Lillian Marks, the great West Coast* typographers/ printers. Ephemera for Ronce & Coffin Club honoring Huib van Krimpen, Los Angeles, 1968.

reproduce in our best daily work. Thus they provide to the present-day printer that precise harmony of colour between type and ornament which is the essential of good typography."[1] Morison further explains that many of the early arabesque designs were introduced to Venetian printers by Moorish traders in the fifteenth century. The Nuremberg arabesque is a floral design (*opposite*) and Luce's sun is composed of a single sort rotated. Many are charming. Trattnor's angel, while small, reads clearly. Saul and Lillian Marks's borders for Rudi Baumfeld's 70th birthday celebration are magical, and the decanter and goblet, whimsical.

¶ Fournier le jeune's decorative, and complex ornaments (*below*) are reminders of the elegance of eighteenth-century France.

1. Stanley Morison, *The Fleuron* (London: At the Office of the Fleuron, 1923), number 1, page 4).

Typographical ornaments from Fournier le jeune's
Modèles des Caractères, Paris 1742
(reproduced from *Printing Types, their History Forms, and Use*, page 252)

IF THERE IS TIME, I like to think about a new job a day or so before I put pencil to paper. I begin the design process in the same way that I first learned how to draw letters: with an HB pencil on tracing paper at a small size.

I first fold a letter-size sheet of bond paper from top to bottom to use as an underlay for my hand so that the graphite doesn't smudge.

Depending on how long the logo is, I usually make a rough sketch at about 1½ to 2 inches wide, sometimes smaller if it is a short word. Additional letterspacing will lengthen the word and often give it more importance. I also explore extended letters and try to make the word a distinctive shape. If there is a troublesome spacing combination, I try to minimize it by joining two letters with a ligature. I explore the standard possibilities: caps and lowercase; all caps; caps and small caps; italic. If the name or product suggests elegance and quality, I might draw one or more letters with restrained swashes.

When the logo is for a large corporation, I draw conservative shapes. Many of the world's great corporations often have logos that appear to be plain and familiar fonts, but close observation often reveals subtle modifications.

After a few roughs, when the word begins to take shape, I trace the letters with more detail and add stem thickness and serifs, or I weight up the skeleton letters and make a sans serif letter. I continue roughs in this manner until I am satisfied that I have some workable solutions, including roughs for client requests for a particular style or direction (though clients often request a direction and then chose a different concept).

There are days when ideas are elusive, and then I go to type reference books for inspiration. Jaspert, Berry and Johnson's *The Encyclopaedia of Typefaces* is a favorite because over 3,000 fonts are shown in the major categories: serifs, scripts, sans serifs, and decorative faces. I also have a "morgue" of examples that I have clipped from various sources over a long time.

From twenty or thirty small rough idea sketches, I select from three to ten designs to draw in a tighter fashion. If I am unhappy with my efforts, I do more sketches. The number of designs I submit varies and greatly depends on the client's budget and schedule.

Usually, I make laser copies of equal size for proper evaluation, and trace these, adjusting the weights, spacing, and proportions, and draw the letters more carefully. I then make a final, tight pencil tracing at this size on white vellum. Using a finely pointed 2H pencil, I draw barely perceptible horizontal guide lines. If the design is an italic or a script, diagonal guide lines are drawn too (a request that many students balk at). These are faint but still useful—yet I think enhance the sketch quality. Whether I use an HB, F, or 2H pencil greatly depends on the humidity. In California, where I work, the humidity varies from damp mornings to dry afternoons. When there is moisture in the paper a softer pencil is required to produce a dark, filled-in letter. Later in the day a 2H produces a density equal to the early morning HB.

The great trick, though, in producing a beautiful, tight comp is to keep the pencil constantly pointed, because vellum is toothy and quickly wears down the lead point; I use an electric draftsman's lead pointer. A sand pad works equally well, though the graphite dust is messy. I like the standard size leads, not the .05 leads that maliciously break—but surely this is personal preference. The points can't be sharpened, and are not pointed enough for my habits. As I draw, I rotate the pencil from time to time to find new points; this minimizes sharpening time. Depending on the letter style's complexity, I spend from thirty minutes to one hour at most on each comp.

Original same-size rough

Tight, same-size
pencil comprehensive

63-point TJRM font

I use short overlapping strokes and light pressure to get the shape just right. When satisfied, I darken the thick parts of a stem by filling in the paper's loose fibers with graphite by repeatedly going over the letter without too much pressure (dark, shiny, buckled logos don't give a true picture). I keep the thin portions and serifs as light gray pencil lines, and draw the serif tips first with a bit more pressure so that the ends are darker in the manner of a draftsman's snapped dimension lines. Excess graphite dust from around the word or between the letters can be blown off, or lifted with a pliable, well-worked kneaded eraser. Fussy areas can be cleaned up by squeezing the eraser to create a thin edge. If a letter is too heavy, I place tracing paper over it, exposing only the amount to be removed, which can be done cleanly and expertly with the kneaded eraser, or a white or pink Pearl eraser. This works fine for straight stems, but larger portions of curves must be removed and then re-drawn. When satisfied, I spray-fix each comp with three or four light coats and back it with 28-pound ledger paper so that the vellum appears opaque. This can be accomplished with a small amount of rubber cement along the top edge, or the vellum can be affixed with half-inch-wide white drafting tape. In the lower

right-hand corner I draw a discrete 12-point Bodoni figure for easy reference.

Clients seem always impressed with a carefully drawn comp, more so than with a bloodless computer rendering.

Often a client will select two or three versions for evaluation, and these are used to prepare a letterhead and business card design where color can be applied. To create these I make a 300-percent enlargement and trace it carefully on tracing paper to make adjustments in the shapes and spacing. Then I make another tracing (using guide lines too); this time I ink it with a fine felt-tipped pen. I rarely use retouch white; if the consistency is too wet it buckles the thin tracing paper, which distorts the image when it is scanned. Without too much trouble, some areas of the scanned image may be smoothed out, trimmed, or added to in Photoshop using the eraser, the pencil, or brush tool.

The tight ink-comp laser image is often shown to the client for final approval.

I prepare camera-ready art by importing the image into the template layer of a font drawing program. I don't use the outlining command, because it creates excessive points that must be removed. If "remove points" is done automatically, the shape becomes distorted, so I draw the

outlines from scratch. When the word or image is excessively long, or if there is an abundance of points and it will not print, I divide the logo into two or more character cells.

There are various rules to follow when using Bézier curves, but the most important to remember are: (1) use a minimum number of points so that the logo will print quickly; (2) make the Bézier point's arms of equal length to avoid corners when possible; (3) don't cross another arm's path or place the points in close proximity except at corners; (4) keep the arms parallel to the curve; (5) examine laser printouts frequently and adjust the position of the points so that corners or interruptions of a curve's flow are smoothed out; and (6) remember that there must be points placed on the outermost limits of curve, *i.e.*, top, bottom, left, and right. Be sure also, to read the manufacturer's users manual.

The completed logo is a font and can be mixed easily with other fonts. Its great advantage is that it may be scaled from 4 points to large sizes for signage without any loss of detail.

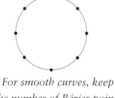

For smooth curves, keep the number of Bézier points to a minimum. The ones at 2, 4, 8, and 10 o'clock are not needed

Make the Bézier point's arms equal length when possible

Don't cross the arm path of a Bézier point with the arm of another Bézier point

Use two Bézier points at juncture if angle is less than 30 degrees

Accents (*caps*)—In the U.S. capitals are rarely accented. Lines of type must be leaded to accommodate them.

Accents (*floating*)—Floating accents are extremely difficult to place with small type size. Better, specify a font complete with accents.

Alignment—See Centered, Flush left, Flush right, and Justified.

Alignment (*optical*)—Type should align visually, not mechanically. If type is set flush left, punctuation such as quotation marks may hang in the margins. Ts, As, Vs, Ws; and any letters with large amounts of negative space should hang to the left. In right-justified settings, periods, commas, and quotation marks should hang to the right. Align figures on the decimal points.

Asymmetrical (*contemporary*) **format**—A layout in which the type relates more closely to the edge of the page than normal margins. Negative space between words or paragraphs becomes an integral part of the design. Shifting the margins of the page has significant impact on the design.

Body text—Avoid setting body text in all caps, or italics, or reversed out type. It is difficult to read. Do not use headline faces for body copy: they were not designed for this purpose. There are many examples of good text settings in books and magazines on typography.

Bullets—Unless you are selling used auto parts, or dumpsters, avoid using bullets heavier than the text; they are distracting. If a stop is needed between disparate bits of copy, a center dot of the same point size will do the trick in a more subdued manner. Use half-word spacing around it.

Brackets—Brackets can embrace an otherwise lonely folio. Centaur's is an elegant thin line; other versions are two-weighted.

Caps (*hung*)—To optically align, hang the diagonals of **A, W, V,** and **Y** and the arms of the **T** when using justified lines of caps.

Caps (*regular*)—Five to ten percent additional spacing often improves the color of a line of caps. Kern the troublesome combinations if required: **LT, LY, AT,** etc. Most Type 1 fonts are well fitted and kerned.

Caps (*small*)—Small caps are usually a bit taller than the x-height. Use them spaced half again as much normal spacing (or a bit more) following an initial letter or following a regular sized cap.

The opening sentence of an article, essay, or book can be set flush left with letterspaced small caps optional; subsequent paragraphs are indented.

Centering (*caps*)—To center a second line of capitals ending with an **L**, set an en space in front of the second line; this will optically center the line.

Centering (*type*)—Set an en space in front of the second line if it ends with a period.

Color—Type should have an overall evenness of value: when you squint your eyes at a paragraph, it should be consistent in its overall value of gray or light areas and have no dark areas. The gray value of a bold type will be darker than that of a light face.

Communication—The ultimate purpose of typographic design is to communicate. Therefore, the more quickly and easily the viewer receives the communication, the more successful the design is. It is common to see personal taste, likes and dislikes, interfere with the communication. A design that is too unconventional or bizarre can become an obstacle to communicating clearly, quickly, and effectively.

Condensed type—Long columns of condensed type are tiresome and hard to read. Avoid them if possible.

Decks—A deck is a contrasting type set within runaround or surrounding text. Decks can be placed in the margin and/or extend into a column. Often deck type is larger than text size; the font may be the same style as the text or may be of contrasting weight, angle, or style.

Distortion—As a general rule, types are not designed to be significantly distorted—condensed, extended, or stretched. Noticeable distortions destroy the integrity of the font. Instead use a font that comes with condensed and extended versions (for example, Univers, Helvetica, Bodoni).

MultipleMaster font families allow the letters to change weight and proportion without distortion. Use these fonts when you need to extend or condense a type face exactly.

Duplicate words—Avoid repetitive words at the beginning or end of consecutive lines.

Ellipses—The space before and within an ellipsis should be the same. A period set before an ellipsis is set closed up to the sentence....

En/em dash—Use the en dash to indicate a range of pages: 15–20 or 1940–45. It is now fashionable to use an en dash surrounded with a full word space instead of an em dash for an aside, or separate thought, though the em dash is correct. Divide the space on either side of the dash to prevent an optical hole. If you do not use the space around the dash and it is followed or preceded by a round form, add one or two points to prevent touching.

Figures—Oldstyle figures (typographers like to call them that instead of numbers or numerals) are best used with text. Cap-high figures tend to dominate. But for copy with many figures, like balance sheets, cap high figures work better.

Oldstyle figures visually align with the x-height of the font. Some of the characters have ascenders and descenders. Use these when they are available and you want a classic, refined look to your typography.

Filling a line—In justified settings, word processing programs will automatically fill a line. The results can sometimes be unhappy. Hyphenation zones may be changed for better fill. Or increase word spacing in the offending line, or increase tracking minimally; the line, or lines should not appear openly spaced. In dire circumstances the type width may be expanded 1 percent, but never more than 2.

Fleurons—Explore the use of fleurons, sometimes called flowers or ornaments. Some, over 400 years old, have yet to be excelled in design. Caslon's are inimitable, Bodoni's contemporary, and Fournier's exquisite. They have a rightful home in fine typography.

Flush right—Flush right text looks "arty," or pretentious, and is uncomfortable to read except in small amounts of text because the eye wants to return to the origin of the first line.

Folio—Folio is from the Latin *folium*, leaf, and is a page number.

Folios are generally the same size as the text, and Oldstyle figures are recommended. Even-numbered pages are referred to as verso, odd-numbered pages as recto (left and right). Depending on format style, folios may be a contrasting font, size, and style (italic), as in this book.

Font mixing—Be judicious in the choice of types. Use no more than three different fonts in a layout and restrict the number of sizes. Successful layouts can be made with a single font, cap-and-lowercase and different sizes. In advertising, package design, and special uses, capitals are used for emphasis; so are italics, though not in the text of proper bookwork.

For more prominence, use a bold face (*e.g.*, for important information). Or use a hierarchy of weights: ultra bold, bold, or medium coupled with a light weight for text. Mix bold sans serif with light or regular weight sans serif, or with a serif face. Don't combine an Oldstyle serif face with a Modern face. If you must, make certain they are contrasting weights. Change weight or size if you change type style.

Footnotes—Depending on the font, set notes two points smaller than text size, and no less than 8-point if set solid, 7-point if leaded.

Fonts—Familiarize yourself with as many fonts as possible. It will save valuable time when you must choose an appropriate type style. As a general rule, use traditional, classic type faces for body text. It is hard to go wrong with Garamond, Times Roman, Baskerville, and Bodoni.

Fractions—Proper fractions generally do not exceed cap height. Use the fractions that come with the font instead of making them yourself. Word processing programs reduce the font's figures and the resulting fraction is a lighter weight than the font.

Hairline rule justification—Hairline (¼-point) rules that separate copy, or underscores, will optically align with type if set one-half to one-point wider.

Hierarchy—Remember that most layouts contain information in degrees of importance. Let the sizes of type or weights reflect these levels. Greater contrast creates a dynamic layout.

Hyphenation—There are purists who hold that hyphenation is forbidden in flush-left layouts. Rarely is a text so sacrosanct that words cannot be broken to avoid extreme ragged lines.

Hyphenation restraints—Use a dictionary for correct hyphenation. There must be two letters before the hyphen and three after it.

Hyphens—Avoid more than two consecutive hyphens at the end of a line. Rewrite if necessary. Some style manuals permit three hyphens.

Initial caps—Initial capitals perk up masses of gray text. Stand-up initials use the same baseline as the opening line, and stand up as much as you dare; drop initials can be 2, 3, 4, or more lines deep. Initials may be placed to the left of the text. The initial may be the same font, or a contrasting one, *i.e.*, sans serif initial with serif text, or a script cap with serif text.

Italic—For small sizes of text, choose a font with a wide italic for greater legibility, and gently letterspace.

Justification—Flush left and flush right text is commonly used in periodicals, books, and in the world of advertising, though the word spacing is not as consistent as unjustified text. With the proper measure and adequate line-spacing, "rivers" of space can be avoided. Short measures of justified text, depending on the point size and proportion, produce extreme word spacing or excessive hyphenations. Avoid.

Kerned fonts—Purchase kerned fonts only. Additional kerning may be required.

Kerning—Kerned characters invade the space of another to improve letterspacing: **AT, Yo, LT,** etc. Be cautious when kerning a lowercase r and n. If too tight, the combination will read as an **m: rn.**

Leaders—Repeated characters, usually periods, are used to fill space, often in tabular material.

Leading—Leading originally meant pieces of lead inserted between lines of metal type. Some computer programs use the term line spacing in its place. There are three types: proportional, baseline to baseline, and top of caps. If possible, avoid setting type solid (8/8, 10/10, etc.) because it is hard to read unless the type is Oldstyle with long descenders, described as "light color" by typographers. Otherwise, at least one point leading is desirable.

Ideally, line leading should exceed word spacing, so that the type reads in horizontal bands.

Consecutive lines of caps should be line-spaced sufficiently to avoid a "stacked caps" look, or word spacing that is greater than line spacing. This often produces irregular "rivers" of white space.

With flush-left copy and no paragraph indention, use more line spacing between paragraphs. A rule of thumb is 150 percent (or more) line leading.

With small heads, either in bold face or same-size text caps,

lead more than text, and more still than preceding text.

Wide measures of type are tiresome to read. If you must, increase the leading for greater readability.

Use average letterspacing, and average word spacing for text matter. Ideally there should be a slightly greater amount of space within letters than between the letters, yet the two should appear to be equal. In small sizes (7, 6, 5, and 4 points): increase the space between letters for legibility.

Depending on the font, some small point sizes of type are more legible with a slight increase of letter- and word-spacing.

Legibility—Type should be legible. Avoid tricky, complicated settings if you want the type to be read.

Letterspacing—Except for special projects, avoid trendy letterspaced lowercase letters. Romans fare better than the italics, and the legibility of sans serifs is sometimes enhanced by letterspacing, but only in a limited number of words.

If the next to last line of a paragraph is letterspaced, the last line should be spaced half as much to avoid an abrupt visual change of line color.

Ligatures—Ligatures, two or more joined letters, such as **fi** and **fl**, give words more even color. Using them assures a more professional result. Some italic fonts have many ligatures, for example, Arrighi.

Line spacing—*See* Leading.

Margin notes—The style varies, flush or centered. Traditionally, notes are set in italic, smaller than the text. They may be dramatic in size, weight, or style.

Measure—In book work, text is most readable when set from 40 to 60 characters wide, including spaces between words. Advertising copy usually runs 40 or more characters, or an alphabet and a half. Avoid short measures of justified copy, which force hyphenation and are difficult to read.

Mixing fonts—Don't mix Oldstyle fonts, nor Oldstyle and Moderns, unless there is a generous change of size and/or a change of weight.

Script and italic are not an ideal combination, either in one or two lines, because the sloping angles seldom match.

Negative space—The space around the letters essentially defines the positive space of type on the page. Learn to see negative space between and around letters, words, lines of type, and on the overall page at the same time as the positive space.

Paragraph—Avoid opening a paragraph on the last line of a column or ending a paragraph on the first line of a column.

Avoid excessive paragraph indention in general running text. It leaves unsightly slots in columns of text.

Parentheses—Whether your text is italic or roman, Robert Bringhurst[1] suggests roman parentheses. He does not consider the characters to be letters, and thus excludes the italic style. There are examples of roman parentheses mixed with italic text as far back as the sixteenth century. Some purists object.

Period—In the U.S., quote marks go outside periods at the end of a quotation, colons and semi-colons follow the close quote. Use only one space after a period.

Proofreader's marks—For more precise communication with typographers, learn the most commonly used proofreader's marks.

Punctuation (hung)—For an optical vertical alignment, when possible, hang punctuation outside the edge of a justified column.

Quotation marks—Reduce the word space before and after quotation marks.

Ragged right—Flush left copy (ragged right) will produce consistent word spacing and even color, though the method is difficult to "rag" smoothly. The avoidance of hyphenation produces extreme, and often undesirable, "rags."

Reversed type—Type below 8-point should not be reversed out of 4-color process, unless the type is sans serif of normal weight, or the line screen is 175 lines-per-inch, or finer.

Increase the letter and word-spacing if the type is reversed. Negative images visually close and weight up.

Rivers—Hold a page of type at an angle and squint your eyes. A pattern of negative or white space running between words, which looks like rivers, is undesirable, an indication of poor typography. Eliminate them by editing or respacing the copy.

Running paragraphs—Paragraphs can be separated by ornaments, bullets, or quads in special cases. Do not set large amounts of type this way.

Set width—Some programs permit fonts to change proportion, often with disastrous results. Don't use set width to squeeze type to fit. It destroys the color of the text. In dire circumstances, 1 or 2 percent wider or more narrow is virtually undetectable. With thousands of types to choose from, you can find one of the right proportion.

Script caps—Do not set a word in all script caps. There are exceptions: if the word is short and easily read, or if quick reading is not of prime importance.

Small caps—Capital letters that are approximately the same height as the body of the lowercase letter are nice to use for lead-ins to text where you want emphasis without the exaggeration of all caps.

Stacked type—Avoid setting type vertically (one letter below the next). It is difficult to read. A better solution—if you have a limited horizontal space—is to turn the word sideways.

Subheads—Typesetting often requires levels of subheads. These should be set to reflect their relative importance; for example, with small heads that are not run-in, either in bold face or caps of text size. Usually the subheads are set with more space above than below.

Symmetrical (formal) format—A layout that is generally centered on the page and flush on both sides, or type that is centered one line over the other. The margins have a minimal effect on the composition of the page. If you move the margins, the integrity of the type basically remains the same.

Tangent spacing—If you must space letters tangently, or touching, do so only with alternating straight-to-curve, curve-to-curve letters, and rarely more than one or two words (bunches of vertical stems become hard-to-read black blobs). However, some layouts demand dramatic statements, possible only with letterspacing that breaks the rules.

Textured backgrounds—Despite technology that permits you to do so, do not radically change values in the background

of type. The type becomes illegible and no longer serves to communicate.

Type size—Pity your grandmother. Unless the copy is strictly for legal purposes, or on a CD album, don't use 4-point type.

Type weight—If you change type styles, change either the size or the weight of the type.

Typography—There are many styles of typography: literary, advertising, packaging, product, billboard advertising, and web type. While these may be considered applications, each style seems almost a different discipline, because of their special restraints and needs.

Value—There should be enough difference in value between the background and the type to facilitate legibility. Value problems may occur when colored type is used against a colored background and there is not enough differentiation in value for the type to be legible. Counter close values by using type large enough to read.

Wordbreaks—Ungainly wordbreaks may be avoided by letterspacing previous lines.

Word spacing—Normal word spacing is one third of an em.

1. Robert Bringhurst, *The Elements of Typographic Style* (Vancouver, B.C.: Hartley & Marks, 1992), page 82.

Note—Depending on the source, the usage may vary for terms given here, which are the ones used in this book.

Agate—1. Originally, an English typeface whose body size was 5.5 points. 2. A 5.5-point type used primarily in newspaper advertising. 3. A unit of the same measure used to measure depth in newspaper advertising.

Alphabet—A set of letters in which a language is written.

Ampersand (&)—The symbol for "and." A contraction of "and per se and." It derives its form or shape from the Latin word *et*, meaning "and."

Arm—A horizontal extension from the vertical stem of an E, F, L, and T.

Antiqua—A German type classification. Font styles other than the blackletter.

Ascender—The portion of a letter that extends above the body or x-height of a lowercase letter, as in b, d, f, k, l, and t.

Ballot box (□)—An outline square. For use primarily as a device in which to indicate a preference. Also used in place of a center dot or square dot.

Bar—The horizontal stroke on the A, H, and lowercase e.

Baseline—Horizontal base alignment of capital letters and non-descending lowercase letters.

Beard—1. The bottom sloping edge of hand-set type between the face baseline and the shoulder. 2. A projection on the bottom right stem of the capital G.

Beak—The triangular shape usually found on the s, z, C, E, F, L, T, and Z.

Biform—Same-height caps and lowercase without ascenders or descenders.

Blackletter—A flat-sided and pointed letter used in the medieval period. Sometimes called *lettre de forme, textura,* or *fraktur.* Type used in the Gutenberg Bible.

Bodoni dash—A horizontal swelled stroke tapering to hairlines at both ends. Used to denote an ending and sometimes to separate different items of copy.

Body matter—The text of an ad or other copy, also known as body copy, body text, or reading matter.

Boldface—1. A heavy-weight typeface. 2. In machine type some fonts contain the regular letter and either the boldface or italic companion on the same matrix, called *duplex.*

Bowl—An enclosed projection of a letter, either rounded or flat, as in B, D, P, R, a, b, d, g, p, and q.

Brackets—1. The filled-in area that connects the serif to a stroke on capital and lowercase letters. Also called *fillet.* 2. ([ ])Brackets are used to enclose a phrase within a parenthesis.

Branch—The curved stroke that connects to the stem on lowercase letters such as h,m,n, and u.

Brass—A one-point-wide spacing unit in hand-set (metal) type.

Calligraphic type—Type that derives its form from letters written with a brush, quill, flat pen, or a chisel instrument held at a slight angle from the horizontal. Examples are Palatino and Trump.

Cap height—Exclusive of accent marks, the vertical measurement of caps. In many Oldstyle fonts, the caps are not as tall as the ascenders. The caps and ascenders of most Modern fonts are the same height.

Caps and small caps—1. Originally, two different sizes of capitals cast on the same-size type body. 2. Caps set with small caps that are same size as the lowercase body.

Center dot (·)—Also called a *bullet* (but bullets are usually larger), and usually round, a dot that centers vertically on the x-height of the lowercase. Primarily used to set apart phrases or listings. The weight used is usually balanced to the weight of the type.

Chancery script—A style of writing developed by papal scribes in the fifteenth century, and the model for many early italic types.

Character—Any letter, figure, punctuation, mark, symbol, or space.

Cipher—The figure o (zero).

Civilité—A French Gothic cursive type of the sixteenth century, based on the handwriting of Robert Granjon. Zapf Civilité is an example.

Color spacing—The addition of space to congested areas of words or word spacing to achieve a more pleasing appearance after a line has been set normally. Color also refers to the length of the ascenders and descenders. If they are long, the color of a page will be lighter than if they are short.

Column gutter—The space between two columns of type.

Condensed type—Type that is compressed horizontally— Empire, Onyx, Tower, Helvetica Condensed, Franklin Gothic Condensed, etc. Called *elongated* in England.

Copper—Hand-set typespacing unit that is .5 point wide.

Counter—1. The enclosed lobe or interior spaces of letters: a, b, d, g, o, p, q, A, B, D, O, P, Q, R. 2. The area, including the shoulder, surrounding a letter, figure, punctuation mark, or symbol in metal type below the face or printing surface.

Crossbar—The horizontal stroke on the f and t. Also *cross stroke.*

Cupped—1. Refers to slightly arched serifs, to the top of the lowercase *t,* and sometimes to the top of the cap A. 2. A design feature in some sans serif stems; Optima is typical.

Cursive—Literally, running: possessing a flowing quality.

Formal scripts are cursive. The fifteenth-century chancery hand is described as cursive.

Curved stem—The heavy portion of curved letters, either serif or sans serif.

Dagger (†)—1. A mark used for a reference. Also called *diesis*. 2. Symbol meaning "deceased."

Descender—The portion of a lowercase letter that descends below the baseline, as in **g,j,p,q,** and **y**. In some Oldstyle fonts, the cap **J** descends.

Diagonal hairline—The thin portions of the **A,K,M,V,W,X, Y,k,v,w,x,** and **y**.

Didoni—A hand-lettered style that combines Didot and Bodoni. See *Didone* in "Type Classification," page 17.

Diphthong ligature—Two vowels joined together; for example, **æ**.

Display faces—Type used for headings and titles and generally larger than 14 point, as opposed to text faces, and often spaced tightly for visual impact.

Ear—The projection from the right-hand side of the bowl of the lowercase **g**.

Egyptian types—Originally, from 1815 on, bold faces with heavy slab or square serifs (though Caslon drew a sans serif in the eighteenth century that he named Egyptian). Lighter versions are Beton, Cairo, Clarendon, Egyptian expanded, Fortune, Graph, Stymie, Memphis, and Rockwell.

Elite—A typewriter face that contains twelve characters to the linear inch, and six to the vertical inch; compare Pica.

Em—The square of any point size of type. Three-em and four-em spaces or ⅓ and ¼ of an em are commonly used as word spacing. Sometimes called *mutton* or *mutt*.

En—Half the width of any point size of type. Also called *nut*.

Extended type—Typefaces whose proportions are wide horizontally, such as Egyptian expanded, Hellenic, Latin wide, Microgramma extended, Standard extended, Univers 53 and 63.

Eye—Enclosed portion of an *e*.

Extrema points—Points placed at outermost edges of curved shapes in font drawing programs that enable printers to render fonts accurately.

Face—1. Any style of type. 2. In letterpress, that portion of type that creates the printed impression.

Fat faces—An extremely bold and often extended type style from the late nineteenth century, based on the modern forms of Bodoni and Didot. Normandia and Thorowgood are examples.

Figures—Numbers or numerals.

Fleurons—Ornaments often resembling flowers or leaves. Also called *flowers*.

Flush left—Copy that is aligned vertically on the left-hand side.

Flush right—Copy that aligns vertically on the right-hand side.

Folio—A page number. Left-hand pages are even numbered, right-hand pages are odd numbered.

Font—The complete set of characters, figures, punctuation marks, and symbols of a typeface.

Foot—1. In some faces, the horizontal serif or stroke that appears at the bottom of the lowercase **a** and **t**. 2. The bottom of metal type. (The expression "off its feet" means the type is not standing square and only part of the letter or letters will print.)

Foundry type—A bas-relief letter cast in reverse on a block of metal. Block height to paper is .918 inch. Set by hand and justified in a composing stick; usually 6- to 72-point. Also called *hand type*.

Grotesque—From *grottesca*, or grotto, and the primitive drawings found there. European for sans serif (often round faces, *i.e.*, Helvetica normal).

Gothic—1. A widely accepted name for sans serif faces—Helvetica, Futura, News Gothic, etc. 2. More traditionally, the German blackletter and Old English, such as Goudy Text, Engraver's Old English, American Text, etc.

Glyph—The font style of any symbol or character. For example, the letter **g** is the character, and a Garamond **g** is a glyph shape.

Hairline—1. The thin portion of a two-weight roman letter. 2. A ¼-point or thinner rule. 3. Small pieces of metal (sometimes called *fins*) that appear between letters when matrices on metal line-casting machines become worn.

Head—A line or lines of copy set in a larger face than body copy. Short for headline or heading.

Leader—Line of dots or dashes to connect copy.

Leading—The vertical space between lines of type. Also called line spacing.

Ligature—Two or more connected letters: **ff, fi, fl, ffl**. Formerly, in metal type, the same letters cast on one piece of metal (*see also* Logotype).

Logotype—1. An identifying name. 2. A symbol or mark. 3. Separate letters cast on one piece of metal to avoid open letter-spacing—**TA, TO, VA, WE,** and **QU**.

Loop—The lower portion of the lowercase **g** in most serifed faces and in some sans serif faces.

Majuscule—Capital letter.

Masthead—The name of a periodical; also staff credits of the publication.

Minuscule—Lowercase letter.

Modern—Type that originated in the late eighteenth century, characterized by vertical stress and extreme contrast between the thick-and- thin strokes. Serifs are usually horizontal and mostly unbracketed. Examples are Bodoni, Corvinus, De Vinne, Didot, Scotch Roman, Torino.

Modern-style figures—Figures that are the same size as the caps (in many faces) and align at the top as well as with the baseline: 1234567890. Also called *lining*.

Oblique—A slanted letter of the same form as the roman version, for example, Bookman, Cairo, and often sans serifs such as Futura and Helvetica.

Ogee curve—A reverse curve. Found on the tail or loop of the g, and the spine of the s, S, and sometimes on the tail of the cap R and some swash caps, and in many italic forms.

Oldstyle—Letters with slight differentiation between the thick and thin strokes. The rounded forms possess a diagonal axis. Examples are Berkeley, Caslon, Centaur, Garamond, Janson, Kennerly. Generally, based on sixteenth-century Italian forms.

Oldstyle figures—Forms derived from the Hindi and Arabic alphabets: 1234567890. The 1, 2, and 0 are the same height as the lowercase body. The 3, 4, 5, 7, and 9 align with the x-height and descend below the baseline. The 6 and 8 align with the baseline and ascend above the x-height. (Bodoni Oldstyle does not follow this pattern exactly.)

Pica—1. A measuring unit of type equal to 12 points. Approximately one-sixth of an inch. 2. A typewriter face size

with ten characters to the inch. 3. A 12-point English typeface.

Point—A measurement used for type sizes and letterspacing and line leading. There are twelve points to a pica, and six picas to the inch, or seventy-two points to the inch.

Pothook—Initial curved hooks on some lowercase italic faces, such as Baskerville, Torino, Century expanded.

Proportion—The width-to-height ratio of any given typeface.

Return stroke—Left-hand side of the g's loop.

Rivers—Word spaces that create irregular vertical lines of white space in body type. These occur when lines of type have been set with excessive word spacing, with little or no hyphenation in justified copy.

Roman—1. A letter modeled after the letterforms of classic Rome. 2. An upright letter, as opposed to a slanted one.

Rule—Lines in varying point-size thicknesses. Used for borders and also to separate copy blocks or columns.

Run-in—Heads ususlly set in a different style from the text, which follows on the same line. Also called *lead-in*.

Sans serif—Letters without serifs. Commonly called *sans* or *Gothics*.

Script—Connected letters, resembling pen handwriting, that may be upright or slanted to the left or right. Some classifications include separated letters.

Serif—A short line stemming from and at an angle to upper and lower ends of the strokes of a letter.

Set—The width of all characters or individual letters of a given font. Used to determine alphabet length for copyfitting.

Shoulder—1. The top left or right side of a round letterform. 2. In metal type, the counter beneath a descender that prevents the descenders of a line of type from touching the ascenders of the following line when the lines have been set solid (that is, with no leading).

Single-story—Describes the *a* in most italics, opposed to a two-story *a*. Many sans serifs have both a one-story roman and italic *a*. See Erbar, Futura, Kabel, Metro, and Tempo.

Small caps—Capitals, usually the same height as the x-height of the lowercase and drawn in a wider proportion and a weight to match the lowercase. Most PostScript fonts include small caps as well as fractions, fleurons, and odd characters in "expert" sets.

Solid—Lines of type set with no line leading. Also called *unleaded*.

Sort—1. An individual piece of type, whence the expression "out

of sorts." 2. A special character or symbol not usually included in a font.

Specimen sheet—A sheet or brochure from a type maker, usually showing the complete font and reading matter set in the same face in available sizes.

Spine—Reverse curve of the *S*.

Spur—The triangular extension at the top of the beaks of some serif letters, as in *s,C,G,S*, and sometimes T and Z.

Square spot—A solid square, used in place of a center dot as an accent or lead-in to paragraphs or listings, usually drawn to align with the x-height.

Stem—A letter's vertical, diagonal, or curved weighted stroke.

Stroke (stem)—The lines of a letter, horizontal, vertical, curved, diagonal, thick, or thin.

Subhead—A secondary heading or display line(s) of lesser importance than the main headline(s).

Superscript—Small raised figures or letters in type, used for reference, such as footnotes, or mathematical and chemical symbols.

Swash letters—Capitals or lowercase letters, roman or italic, embellished with flourishes, often ending with a teardrop or circular shape based on the forms of the early sixteenth-century writing masters Arrighi, Palatino, and Tagliente. Jan van Krimpen's Cancelleresca Bastarda is an example.

Swelled stroke—The reverse curve of the righthand side of the italic *h,m,n,u*, sometimes *v*, *w*, and *y*. Also, the script versions of these letters.

Tail—The curved stroke at the bottom of the lowercase *a* and *t*. Also, the curved or horizontal stroke at the bottom of the *Q* and the diagonal stroke attached to the bowl of the cap **R**.

Terminals—In most serifed faces, the circular, teardrop, or wedge-shaped endings occurring on the lowercase letters **a, c, f, j, r,** and **y**, and on swash extensions of some capitals, mostly italic.

Thins—The thin portions of a letter, also called *hairlines*.

Titling faces—Fonts of capital letters without a corresponding lowercase, which occupy almost the full point size (minus the shoulder) of the type. Examples are Adobe Original Garamond Titling, Perpetua Titling, Michelangelo Titling, Microgramma, Trajan, Bauer Text.

Transitional—Letters with greater contrast between thick and thin strokes than in Oldstyle. Curved forms usually possess a vertical axis. In classification, the style is regarded as a transition from Garalde to Didone. Some examples are Baskerville, Bulmer, Caledonia.

Triangular serifs—Serifs found on the lowercase ascenders and tops of the straight stems of many Oldstyle fonts. Sometimes called *oblique*.

TrueType—Fonts based on a second order equation which cannot draw an ogee curve except by combining multiple segments, which can result in abrupt turns (optical corner). *See* also Type 1 fonts.

Two-story—Lowercase **a** with a small bowl, opposed to a single-story *a* whose bowl occupies the full x-height.

Type—A letter or character, originally in bas-relief, from which an inked impression is made.

Type 1 Fonts—Adobe Systems encrypted fonts with "hinting" for printing small sizes of type on low-resolution printers.

Typeface—Type of a single design, regardless of size. Also called *type*. In letterpress, its printing surface.

Type family—A group of typefaces of the same design but with different weights and proportions. Examples are Bodoni, Century, Helvetica, Futura, Univers.

Type series—A range of sizes of one typeface, usually from 6- to 72-point, in machine faces, and 4- to 650-point in computer fonts.

Uncial—Lettering style based on letters freely written with a quill or flat pen in the fourth to eighth centuries. Early uncial capitals sometimes assumed the shape of lowercase letters and served as a basis for our present lowercase alphabet.

Vertical serif—The serif found on the center arm of **E** and lower arm of **F**.

Waist—The narrow part of *K*, *X*, or *R*, or the convergence of the *Y*'s diagonals.

Weight—The thickness of a letter stroke, characterized as light, extra light, regular, medium, demi bold, bold, extra bold, and ultra bold.

Weighted diagonal—The thick strokes of the letters **A, K, M, N, R, V, W, X, Y, Z, k, v, w, x, y,** and **z**.

Widow—An undesirably short line, word, or part of a word that occurs at the top of a page or column, called an *orphan* when it occurs at the bottom of a page or column.

x-height—The height of the lowercase **x**. Sometimes called *body height*.

American Type Founders
Specimen Book and Catalogue
Jersey City, New Jersey:
American Type Founders Company, 1923

Book of American Types Standard Faces
Jersey City, New Jersey:
American Type Founders Sales Corporation, 1934

Andersch, Martin
Symbols Signs Letters
About Handwriting, Experimenting with Alphabets,
and the Interpretation of Texts
New York: Design Press, 1989

Anderson, Donald M.
The Art of Written Forms
The Theory and Practice of Calligraphy
New York: Holt, Rinehart and Winston, Inc., 1969

Berthold Fototypes E2 Body Types
Vol. 1, Layouts, 577 Typefaces
Berlin: Berthold; München: Callwey, 1980

Berthold Headlines (E3)
1400 Headlines Faces Arranged According to Similarity
Berlin: Berthold; München: Callwey, 1982

Blackletter: Type and National Identity
Peter Bain and Paul Shaw, eds.
New York: 1998
The Cooper Union / Princeton Architectural Press

Bickham, George
The Universal Penman, 1743
Reprint, New York: Dover Publications, 1941

Bigelow, Charles,
Paul Hayden Duensing, and
Linnea Gentry, eds.
Fine Print on Type
The Best of *Fine Print* Magazine on Type and Typography
San Francisco: Fine Print/Bedford Arts, 1989

Blumenthal, Joseph
Bruce Rogers: A Life in Letters 1870–1957
Austin: W. Thomas Taylor, 1989

Bringhurst, Robert
The Elements of Typographic Style
Vancouver: Hartley & Marks, Publishers, 1996

Carter, Sebastian
Twentieth Century Type Designers
New York: W.W. Norton & Company, 1995
Character Code Standard
Xerox System Integration Standard
Sunnyvale, California: Xerox Corporation, 1987

The Chicago Manual of Style
14th Edition
Chicago and London:
The University of Chicago Press, 1992

Dreyfus, John
The Work of Jan van Krimpen
A Record in Honor of His Sixtieth Birthday
Haarlem: Joh. Enschedé en Zonen, 1952

Dwiggins, William A.
WAD to RR, a letter about designing TYPE
Cambridge, Massachusetts:
Harvard College Library Department of Printing
and Graphic Arts, 1940

Fairbank, Alfred
A Book of Scripts
New York: Penguin Books, 1955

Frutiger, Adrian
Type Sign Symbol
Zurich: ABC Verlag, 1980

Gottschall, Edward M.
Typographic Communications Today
International Typeface Corporation,
Cambridge: The MIT Press, 1989

Goudy, Frederick W.
The Capitals From the Trajan Column at Rome
With Twenty-five Plates Drawn and
Engraved by the Author
New York: Oxford University Press, 1936

Haley, Allan
ABC's of Type
A Guide to Contemporary Typography
New York: Watson-Guptill, 1990

Typographic Milestones
New York: Van Nostrand Reinhold, 1992

Alphabet: The History, Evolution & Design of the Letters We Use Today
New York: Watson-Guptill, 1995

Hlavsa, Oldrich
A Book of Type and Design
Prague: SNTL,
Publishers of Technical Literature, 1960

Jaspert, W. Pincus, W. Turner Berry, and A. F. Johnson
The Encyclopaedia of Type Faces
London: Blandford Press, 1983

Johnston, Edward
Writing and Illuminating & Lettering
London: Pitman, 1906

Lawson, Alexander
Anatomy of a Typeface
Boston: David R. Godine, 1990

Leach, Mortimer
Lettering for Advertising
New York: Reinhold Publishing Corporation, 1956

Lindegren, Erik
ABC of Lettering and Printing Types (3 vols.)
Askim, Sweden: Erik Lindegren Grafisk Studio, 1964

Ludlow Typefaces
Chicago: Ludlow Typograph Company, n.d.

McGrew, Mac
American Metal Typefaces of the Twentieth Century
New Castle, Delaware: Oak Knoll Books, 1993

McLean, Ruari
Jan Tschichold: typographer
Boston: David R. Godine, 1975

Merriman, Frank
A.T.A. Type Comparison Book
New York: Advertising Typographers Association
of America, Inc., 1965

Morison, Stanley
On Type Designs, Past and Present
A Brief Introduction (New Edition)
First Published by the Fleuron, 1926
London: Ernest Benn, 1962

A Tally of Types
With Additions by Several Hands
Edited by Brooke Crutchley
Cambridge: Cambridge University Press, 1973
Selected Essays on the History of Letter-forms in Manuscript and Print (2 vols.)
Cambridge: Cambridge University Press, 1981

Pardoe, F. E.
John Baskerville of Birmingham
Letter-Founder & Printer
London: Frederick Muller Limited, 1975

Ryder, John
A Suite of Fleurons; or,
A Preliminary Enquiry into the history &
combinable natures of certain printers' flowers
conducted by John Ryder
Liverpool: Tinglings of Liverpool;
London: Phoenix House Ltd., 1956

Printing for Pleasure
Chicago: Henry Regnery Company, 1977

The Case for Legibility
London: Moretus Press, 1979

Simon, Oliver
The Fleuron
Edited by Oliver Simon (1923–25)
and Stanley Morison (1926–30)
(7 vols.) 1923–30
Reprint, Westport, Connecticut:
Greenwich Reprint Corporation, 1960

Introduction to Typography
Edited by David Bland
London: Faber and Faber, 1963

Specimen Book of Monotype Printing Types (2 vols.)
Salfords, Redhill, England:
Monotype Corporation Limited, 1970

Specimen Book of Monotype Non-Latin Faces
Salfords, Redhill, England:
Monotype Corporation Limited, 1970

Specimen Book of Monotype Filmsetter Faces
Salfords, Redhill, England:
Monotype Corporation Limited, 197

Specimen Book of Monotype Printing Types (2 vols.)
Salfords, Redhill, England:
Monotype Corporation Limited, 1970

Specimen Book of Monotype Non-Latin Faces
Salfords, Redhill, England:
Monotype Corporation Limited, 1970

Standard, Paul
Calligraphy's Flowering, Decay & Restoration
Chicago: The Society of Typographic Arts, 1947

Three Classics of Italian Calligraphy
An Unabridged Reissue of the Writing Books of
Arrighi, Tagliente and Palatino
New York: Dover Publications, Inc., 1953

Tracy, Walter
Letters of Credit: A View of Type Design
Boston: David R. Godine, 1986

Tschichold, Jan
Asymmetric Typography
New York: Reinhold Publishing Corporation;
Toronto: Cooper & Beatty, Ltd., 1967

Timperley, C. H.
William Bulmer and the Shakspeare Press
A Biography of William Bulmer from a
Dictionary of Printers and Printing, 1839
Reprint, with introductory note by Laurance B. Siegfried,
Syracuse: Syracuse University Press, 1957

The Unicode Consortium
The Unicode Standard, Version 2.0
Reading, Massachusetts:
Addison Wesley Developers Press, 1991–1996

Updike, Daniel Berkeley
Printing Types: Their History, Forms, and Use
A Study in Survivals
(2 vols.)
Cambridge, Massuchusetts: Harvard University Press, 1937

Van Krimpen, Jan
J. van Krimpen on Designing and Devising Type
New York: The Typophiles, 1957

A Letter to Philip Hofer on Certain Problems
Connected with the Mechanical Cutting of Punches
Cambridge, Massachusetts, Harvard College Library;
Boston: David R. Godine, 1972

Whalley, Joyce Irene
English Handwriting 1540–1853
An Illustrated Survey based on Material in the
National Art Library, Victoria and Albert Museum
London: Her Majesty's Stationery Office, 1969

Zapf, Hermann
Pen and Graver
Alphabets & Pages of Calligraphy by Hermann Zapf
Cut in Metal by August Rosenberger
New York: Museum Books, 1952

Manuale Typographicum
Frankfurt: Stempel AG, 1954

About Alphabets
Some Marginal Notes on Type Designs
New York: The Typophiles, 1960

Hermann Zapf
Calligrapher, Type-designer and Typographer
Cincinnati: Contemporary Arts Center, 1960–61

Typographic Variations
Designed by Hermann Zapf on Themes in
Contemporary Book Design and Typography
New York: Museum Books, 1964

Hunt Roman: The Birth of a Type
Commentary and Notes by Hermann Zapf
and Jack Werner Stauffacher
Pittsburgh: The Pittsburgh Typophiles, 1965

Manuale Typographicum
100 Typographical Arrangements with
Considerations about Types, Typography and the
Art of Printing Selected from Past and Present
New York: Museum Books, 1968

Hora Fugit, Carpe Diem
Hamburg: Maximilian-Gesellschaft, 1984

Creative Calligraphy
Instructions and Alphabets
A New Instruction Manual for Learning
the Art of Calligraphy
West Germany: Rotring·Werke Riepe KG, 1985

Hermann Zapf and His Design Philosophy
Selected Articles and Lectures on Calligraphy and Contemporary
Developments in Type Design
Chicago: Society of Typographic Arts, 1987

This is a list of type designers whose fonts are represented in this book, plus the foundry or other source of the font, and its design, or date of issue. The subject index which starts on page 379 contains references to the specific fonts.

Griffo, Francesco
Bembo, 1495; Monotype, 1929
Greek type,
Aldus Manutius, 1501
Gutenberg, Johann
Textura, 1455
types, c. 1455

Handel, Don
Handel Gothic, VGC, 1965
Harris, Jean,
Elli, Font Bureau, 1993
Harvey, Michael
Ellington, Monotype, 1990
Hess, Sol
Century bold condensed,
Monotype, 1938
Sans Serif bold (Kabel),
Monotype, 1930–33
Twentieth Century,
Lanston Monotype, 1947
Hoefer, Karlgeorg
Salto, Klingspor, 1952–53
Hoffmeister, Heinrich
Century 725 bold condensed
(Madison), Stempel, 1965
Century 725 bold
(Madison), Stempel, 1965
Hollenstein, Albert
Eras bold, ITC, 1976
Eras medium, ITC, 1976
Hughes, Charles E.
Century Nova, ATF, 1964

Irvin, Rea
Irvin, Monotype, 1925
Isbell, Richard
Americana, ATF, 1966

Jenson, Nicolas
Greek type, 1472
Types, 1470–76
Jones, George W.
Baskerville, 1926
ITC, 1978
Linotype revised, 1978
Granjon, Linotype, 1928
Jost, Heinrich
Beton extra bold,
Bauer, 1931–36
Bodoni,
Bauer, 1926
Juenger, Richard
Jana, VGC, 1966

Kimball, Ingalls
Cheltenham bold,
ATF, 1896

Kis, Nicolas
Janson
Klauss, Karl
Adagio,
Geuzsch & Heyse, 1953
Klumpp, Emil
Murray Hill,
ATF, 1956
Koch, Rudolf
Cable (Kabel),
Klingspor, 1927–29
Koch Cursive,
Klingspor, 1922
Kabel Initials,
Klingspor, 1927–29
Locarno,
Klingspor, 1922
Neuland,
Klingspor, 1923

Lange, Gunter Gerhard
Boulevard, Berthold, 1955
Lardent, Victor
Times New Roman,
Monotype, 1932; Adobe, 1988
Low, Marcus J.
Basilea,
VGC, 1965, ITC

Maile, Robert
Basilea,
Bright & Associates/
Sitmar Cruises, 1985
Marder, Clarence
Copperplate Gothic light
extended,
ATF, 1903
Martin, William
Bulmer, c. 1790
Meeks, Alan
Locarno,
Letraset, 1986
Meidinger, Max
Helvetica,
Haas, 1957
Mendosa y Almedia, José
Photina, Monotype, 1971
Middleton, R. Hunter
Bodoni black condensed, 1930
Eden Light,
Ludlow, 1934
Formal Script,
Ludlow, 1956
Garamond swash capitals,
Ludlow, 1929
Radiant, Ludlow, 1938
Stencil, Ludlow, 1937
Tempo, Ludlow, 1930–42

Moore, Isaac
Fry Baskerville,
Fry Foundry, c. 1795; ATF, 1915
Moreau, Pierre
Calligraphic Type, 1644
Script, 1644
Morison, Stanley
Times New Roman,
Monotype, 1932; Adobe, 1988

Nicholas, Robin
Arrighi swash capitals,
Monotype, 1993
Centaur Swash caps,
Monotype, 1993
Novarese, Aldo
Elite, Nebiolo, 1968
Eurostile, Nebiolo, 1962
Eurostile demi-bold, 1962
Eurostile bold extended, 1962
Fenice, Nebiolo, 1980
Juliet, Nebiolo, 1955
Stop, Nebiolo, 1970

Parkinson, Jim
Bodoni, ITC, 1994
Peignot, Charles
Touraine bold,
Deberny & Peignot, 1947
Phemister, A. C.
Bookman, Miller & Richard, 1860;
Monotype, 1909
Pierpont, F. H.
Plantin light, Monotype, 1913
Plantin, Christophe
Types, c. 1567
Powell, Gerry
Onyx, ATF, 1937

Reiner, Imré
Corvinus light oblique,
Bauer, 1929–34
Corvinus Skyline, Bauer, 1929–34
Stradivarius, Bauer, 1945
Renner, Paul
Futura, Bauer, 1927–30
Topic Bold (Steile Futura),
Bauer, 1953–55
Renshaw, John L.
Franklin Gothic wide (metal),
ATF, c. 1952
Riley, Frank H.
Grayda, ATF, 1939
Rogers, Bruce
Centaur, 1914; Monotype, 1929

A NOTE ON THE TYPE
in which this book is set

JAN TSCHICHOLD, who designed Sabon, is the
father of modern typography. The guidelines that he set
down in 1928 in *The New Typography*, and later in a slim volume,
Asymmetric Typography, are valid still. He was a meticulous
and prolific book designer, whose classical work
for Penguin Books is timeless.
His Sabon is a more restrained interpretation of Garamond
than the Frederic Goudy and Morris Benton versions. There are no
idiosyncrasies, even the curled stem of the lowercase *h* has been gently stifled.
The family was originally created for hand-set metal
composition for Stempel, and the Linotype and Monotype systems.
This digital version was adapted by Linotype
using Adobe's software tools.

Printed and bound by Toppan Printing Company (H.K. Ltd.)
Text is 128 gsm Kinmari matte Artpaper
Endpapers are printed on 157 gsm Kinmari matte Artpaper
Silver-foil stamped and blind debossed on
Excelin cloth over 3mm board
Jacket printed on 157 gsm gloss Artpaper
with gloss film lamination

DY
9/2007